THE WORD

Also by Charlton Laird

NOVELS

Thunder on the River (1949)
West of the River (1953)

STUDIES IN LANGUAGE AND PEDAGOGY

The Miracle of Language (1953)
The Tree of Language, with Helene Laird (1957)
Thinking About Language (1959)
Language in America (1970)
And Gladly Teche (1970)
You and Your Language (1973)

REFERENCE WORKS

Laird's Promptory (1948)
Webster's New World Thesaurus (1971)

TEXTBOOKS

Modern English Handbook, with Robert M. Gorrell (1953; 6th ed., 1976)
Modern English Workbook, with Gorrell (1957; 2nd ed., 1963)
A Course in Modern English, with Gorrell (1960)
English as Language, with Gorrell (1961)
A Basic Course in Modern English, with Gorrell and Raymond J. Pflug (1963)
A Writer's Handbook (1964)
Pickett at Gettysburg, editor (1965)
Casebooks for Objective Writing, general editor (1965-7)
Modern English Reader, editor with others (1970; 2nd ed., 1977)
Words, Words, Words (1970)
Reading About Language, with Gorrell (1971)
Writing Modern English, with Gorrell (1973)

CRITICISM AND LITERARY SCHOLARSHIP

"Manuscripts of the *Manuel des Pechiez*," in *Stanford Studies in Language and Literature* (1941)
"Character and Growth of the *Manuel des Pechiez*," in *Traditio* (1946)
The World through Literature, editor (1951)

THE WORD

A Look at the Vocabulary of English

BY

CHARLTON LAIRD

SIMON AND SCHUSTER
NEW YORK

For Sven Liljeblad
Friend and Unacknowledged Mentor

Contents

Foreword

Using language to expound language has been so much the fashion of late that an additional book may call for more than routine justification. Although we have had no dearth of excellent dictionaries, along with many studies of language and aspects of language, including the vocabulary of Americanisms, general discussions of the English word stock have been rare. No such volume has attracted much attention in this country since the opening of the century, when two professors at Harvard University, one in the Classics and one in Germanic studies, James Bradstreet Greenough and George Lyman Kittredge, collaborated to bring out *Words and Their Ways in English Speech*. It was an excellent survey, authoritative and readable, and deserved the esteem it enjoyed for decades.

Even so, a modern student reading the volume may find it more dated than it need have been. Greenough and Kittredge cannot be faulted for neglecting sociolinguistics and psycholinguistics, disciplines developed long after their day, but we may wonder why they made as little use of comparative philology as they did. They knew, of course, that Sir William Jones had discovered that some now-lost language (since called Proto-Indo-European) must lie back of several European and Asiatic tongues. They knew, also, that nineteenth-century philologists, mostly Continental, had been ransacking the known bodies of speech, tracing the growth and spread of the widely ramified Indo-European language family. They even expounded such tenets—they were both deeply learned scholars—but in ways that they probably did not intend or sense, they did much to perpetuate a common notion that the English language is derivative and hence inferior.

They knew about Indo-European and its relationships, but they did not allow the new insights to enter as much into their thinking as they might have. Before the philologists, the common notion among Christian peoples had been that language sprang mainly from one miracle, and whatever form it took after the days of Babel, speech in its purity was best reflected in Hebrew or Greek, perhaps in Chaldean. Many theologians believed that young children, left to their own devices, would turn their babblings into Hebrew, and some philosophers, noticing the similarities among the Classical and European vernacular tongues, postulated that Latin was a debased sort of Greek and English a debased sort of Latin.

Greenough and Kittredge knew better. If we could now call them up from whatever Elysian Fields, they would give essentially correct answers, that English descended directly from the Indo-European ancestor and thus participated as directly as any other language in the grandmother tongue. But their interests were traditional enough so that they did not do much to further such notions. Greenough was at his engaging best when he traced the ramifications of Greek and Latin terms through Romance speech and into Modern English. Kittredge ranged freely among northern languages, especially through Old Norse and Anglo-Saxon. Thus, although neither of the professors espoused such heresy—they supported both the antiquity and the adequacy of English—many a reader of *Words and Their Ways* came away with the notion that the English vocabulary, whatever its charms, was a pack rat sort of jumble that speakers of English had picked up from their linguistic betters.

Greenough and Kittredge did not invent or deliberately foster such interpretations. *Words and Their Ways* was a far better book than those it replaced, but however the notions were engendered and fostered, several have survived that we could do without. They include the following:

1. The correct meaning of a word is whatever it used to be.
2. English vocabulary is inferior because it is mainly borrowed; it had no antiquity such as Greek, Latin, and Hebrew had.
3. Ancient tongues have little practical use nowadays.

We might examine these. First: "The correct meaning of a word is whatever it used to be." The opposite is true; the "correct" use or uses of a word—if such a concept as correctness has much pertinence in a subject so fluid—are whatever the modern users of a term need from it. This is probably the best way for languages to work, but whether we like it or not, that is the way they do work, and probably the only way they can work. Most meanings of most words—we can probably say all meanings of all words—have developed or have undergone change in recent times.

Consider the word *man*. In Old English it presumably meant the human species or a member of it. The male was called *waep(n)man*, "weapon person," and the female *wifman* (Modern English *woman*), which may have meant "veiled person," a term for a bride. Since then, the word has so proliferated that it can be a noun, a verb, or a modifier, and dictionaries list a dozen or more meanings, which are only a selection from those available, along with special senses in compounds, such as *merchantman*, a ship, and *man-of-war*, another sort of ship. It has become an organic part of the language and can be freely used in new terms such as *workmanship* and *one-upmanship*. These meanings have grown by use, from within the language.

Viewed superficially, a few meanings may appear to have survived unaltered, but if we examine these uses their seeming durability declines. Presumably, *man* came from the Indo-European root *man- or *mon-, meaning "a human being." The word still has that sense, but our concepts of what makes a being human have shifted, and the working meaning of the term has changed with them. *Man- happens to be one of those roots for which we have no early meaning, and thus we do not know what in reality a speaker of Proto-Indo-European was implying when he used the idiom, but if he meant that the two-legged mammal is the creature made in the image of the Deity, he was not alone—the idea, of course, is the one we have from the Hebraic tradition. Some etymologists derive *man* from the root *men-, a term that meant "to revolve in the mind, to think." If this is the etymology, then man could be defined as the thinking animal. This etymology is currently out of favor, but even though it may be erroneous it has been entertained, and it has at times determined the use of the term.

These ancient interpretations are only the beginning. From classical sources the notion grew that man appears as he does because he is a microcosm of the earth, as the earth is a microcosm of the universe. That is, he is a divine demonstration of cosmic unity, having a system of tubes carrying life-giving blood as the earth has a system of rivers carrying life-giving water, and man has been given the ability to grow hair to parallel the fact that the earth has the power to grow vegetation. During the Middle Ages many theologians taught that men were incipient angels. They had been ordained by the Deity in order to repopulate Heaven, whose ranks were depleted when God hurled Satan and his followers to the lower depths. Believers in the Great Chain of Being—and for centuries they were many—trusted that man was one of the links in the universal chain of being that stretches from inert matter to God. Currently, many persons would define man as the creature who, by the Lord's will, rules the world and may pillage it if he wishes. Others see him as one of the primates that fill out the patterns of evolution. Today many persons assume that man can be defined as a creature uniquely endowed with certain "unalienable Rights," such as "Life, Liberty, and the pursuit of Happiness." Meanwhile, man seems to be embarking on a prolonged endeavor to inhabit portions of outer space. We can only speculate how denizens of the Moon or Venus would look upon themselves, but certainly not as exclusively earthlings. That is, vocabulary as it is used is shaped by the users, presumably everywhere and always, even those parts of it that may seem to have been impervious to change.

Second, "English is inferior because it is mainly borrowed; it had no antiquity such as Greek, Latin, and Hebrew had.'' Again, this is largely wrong in its detail and totally wrong in its implications. Even if English terms were mostly borrowed, there would be nothing wrong with that. In language, all the world are borrowers, and a borrowed term is none the worse for having come through another language. Borrowers unconsciously turn a loan word to their own purposes, just as they have adapted the native term *man* to new uses. One sort of word, a native or a loan, is not necessarily better than the other.

As for the antiquity of languages, all Indo-European bodies of speech are equally old, having all come from Proto-Indo-European. Speakers of an Indo-European dialect found their way into the Balkan Peninsula. We call their tongue *Hellenic*; from it came Classical Greek and then Modern Greek. Another body of migrants, speaking dialects of Indo-European that we call Proto-Germanic, found their way to the plains of northern Europe. Translated to offshore islands, some of these dialects became Old English, and in due time Modern English. That is, Greek, French, Russian, Sanskrit, English, and all other Indo-European languages came from the same ancestor. They are all equally old, and if there is honor in antiquity, they are all equally honorable. Furthermore, the most active parts of the vocabulary have mainly descended from Indo-European in a direct line to Modern English. The grammatical terms, words like *is, and, who*, and *of*, without which the language could not work, are almost all "native." That is, they have come directly from the ancestor language and have not been borrowed from anywhere. Similarly, many of the commonest nouns, verbs, and modifiers, words like *life, moon, father, eat*, and *breathe* were never borrowed. They descended from Proto-Indo-European to Germanic to Old English to Modern English. English is Indo-European speech as it developed in one way, whereas Latin and Greek are Indo-European speech that developed in other ways.

Third, "Ancient tongues have little practical use nowadays." This statement will take more disproving than I have room for in a foreword, but it is as fallacious as are the other two. Learning to work with Indo-European roots is not hard, and understanding enough about relationships within the Indo-European family to make use of these elements is no more so. Once the speaker of English has a nodding acquaintance with linguistic links within the Indo-European language family, he will find he has very useful tools. He can for instance, learn new words, especially the long, rare ones more easily than he can in any other way I know of. And once he can do a bit of elementary etymology, he is likely to find that he is improving his command of language in ways he never could have imagined.

This book, then, is intended to bring together the most telling observations that have been made about the English word stock. Inevitably much of the exposition must be old; fine minds have been busy with language for millennia. But some is new, partly because popularization must always lag behind research, but partly also because the study of words and their uses has not been a major concern of many of the best linguistic minds of our day. Some have gone so far as to say that meaning and vocabulary are not fit subjects for serious study. That notion is declining, but the fact remains that many brilliant scholars have preferred to examine the sound systems of languages or their structures as revealed in grammar. We need not be surprised at this preference. Serious students have been intrigued by the nature of language and by the relationships among languages. For these, both phonology and grammar tend to be more enduring, even more revealing than are words and their uses. This willingness to view vocabulary with some nonchalance has not been the popular reaction. Many lovers of language think of it as a sequence of words having meanings, which may be the ultimate justification for a book like this one.

One more matter should perhaps be mentioned. I have tried deliberately to make this book engaging. Not everyone will approve. Many prospective users will feel that an amusing book cannot be serious. I am aware, also, that most productive study of language requires work, lots of it. But I am convinced that at least for many people, the fastest and best way to learn language is to have fun with it. I confess that I have had fun writing this book, and I hope others may have fun reading it.

Inevitably, in writing a book like this one, I have incurred many debts, which I would gladly acknowledge, but the computation would scarcely be appropriate in a volume intended for popular use. The footnotes will suggest the major areas of my reliance. Perhaps more than any other I am indebted to Dr. Sven Liljeblad, who for more than forty years has helped me to see more in language than I could have otherwise, and has put before me a standard for study that I can revere but could never emulate. In preparing the volume for the press, I wish to thank Mrs. Ingalill H. Hjelm, who edited understandingly. I am grateful especially to David B. Guralnik, who during the years that this book has been in the making has been most helpful in marshaling it through the publishing process.

Charlton Laird;
University of Nevada, Reno

THE WORD

CHAPTER I

A WORD IN YOUR EAR
Shapes, Symbols, Systems

Every utterance is an event, and no two events are precisely alike.
The extreme view, therefore, is that no word ever means the same
thing twice.

—Louis B. Saloman

1. Words at Work

'Twas the night before Christmas and all through the house,
Not a creature was stirring, not even a mouse.

This is not much as a poem, but it may suggest what words do when
they go through your eye or your ear into your brain.

'Twas. Insofar as this is a word at all, it is a defiance of conventional
grammar. It combines *it*, which fills the position of the subject of a sentence, and *was*, the verb, thus becoming subject and verb in one. Some
languages do this systematically, but on the whole, English does not.
The combination of subject and verb, usually with a complement, is the
core of English grammar. But subject-verb have here become one term
by the debasing of two good old words so that they have almost no
meaning. *It* is a form of an old demonstrative, meaning "this one," but
here *it* has little meaning except to suggest that this sentence will worry
along with no meaningful subject. *Was* is a form of an old word meaning
"to live" in the sense of "have a dwelling place," but it also has little
meaning here, except to suggest something in the past. *'Twas* is seldom
used now except in bad poetry. The conventional pronunciation of
it was when run together might be spelled something like *it'uz*. Accordingly, small children and others not much addicted to reading have
trouble with *'twas*, but most native speakers do not, and it may remind

3

us of the subtlety and flexibility of the human mind that we can live unconsciously with such heterodox means of communication. See also *was* below.

the. The commonest word[1] in the language, just like so many other common terms, has been made over from something else, in this instance an old word that meant about what the ancestor of *it* meant, that is, "this one" or "that one." The shape of the term was *se* in Old English, but the *s* sound shifted to the sound written *th*, probably because other related words began that way, and now this initial consonant is about all we have left. Nobody would read this line of poetry as though the words were *thee night*. The *th* sound is attached to the name word that is to come as though it is no more than a prefixal warning that the night is a particular night, not just any old night, and pronounced *th-night*. In fact, this device for identifying a particular object in contrast to any such object is marked in some languages by a prefix; *the* has in effect become such a prefix although the fact is not recognized in spelling.

The spelling *th* is worthy of note. We have a letter *t* with its own sound or sounds, and the letter *h* with a different sound (or no sound) of its own, but when these two are written together we recognize that they may stand for either of two sounds, as in *this* and *think*, with neither sound very closely associated with *t* or *h*. This is disorderly—the world has enough signs and symbols so that we could easily have one for each sound. The explanation is historical, stemming from the day when Norman scribes tried to write English with a French alphabet. The details are numerous; some will be found in Chapter III.8 and VI.11 below, but we might note again that the human mind deals with this illogicality. Even small children do not say *t-hat* and *t-hey* for *that* and *they*.

night. This could be any of several things, and the wonder is that, as with the previous words, we have no doubts as to what it stands for. Grammatically it is a sort of subject for the sentence, *it* being only a stand-in to assure us that the idea of the subject would be along later, but *night* seems not to be the subject in the sense that it centers our attention. It seems rather to be adverbial, setting the time, as though it and the preceding words add up to "that night." And what does *night* mean here? Milton refers to "chaos and old night," seeming to refer to a

---

1. The standard work on the frequency of English words is Henry Kučera and W. Nelson Francis, *Computation Analysis of Present-Day American English* (Providence, R.I.: Brown University Press, 1967). I have not yet seen a rival volume, Dahl Hartvig, *Word Frequencies of Spoken American English* (Essex, CT: Verbatim Books, 1980).

universal lack of enlightenment, both physical and figurative. More commonly *night* refers to diurnal darkness. Both of these uses are ruled out by *the*; *night* here has to refer to a period of time, the time in any twenty-four hours that cannot properly be called *daytime*. Once more, any child—and this is a poem for children—would resolve both of these puzzles unconsciously. The *night* here is the period of time when children go to bed and most human activities except sleep are abridged, and the night is being mentioned, not for itself, but because something happened during the dark period, something worthy of note, a fact suggested in that titillating counter, *'twas*.

The spelling *gh* warrants a note. It may remind us that Old English had a sound, spelled *h*, which is about what you would make if you tried to say k-h-k-h-k-h. It is the German guttural, heard in *Nacht*, meaning *night*. We have lost the sound, although it still appears in Scottish, which has *loch* where modern English has *lake*. In some words it has become the sound of *f*, as in *enough* and of *g*, as in *burgh*. Here, as frequently, it is silent. As a symbol, *gh* represents the attempt of Anglo-Norman scribes to write the Old English *h*, which had a sound not known in the French of the period. However illogically, it has survived, for English is conservative enough to cling to old scraps of language, especially in spelling.

before. Another of those concoctions that now tie English sentences together, but that were formerly more concerned with meaning. The *be-* part, our word *by*, no longer has much to do in this word. The *-fore* part is an old root with thousands of descendants in many languages, which used to mean what *for-* does in *forward*, "going ahead." It can refer to time (B.C., meaning "before Christ"), place (*before* the judge), preference (He would die *before* he would betray his country), and many more. Here it means only relationship within a sequence, the night that comes ahead of Christmas in the eternal sequence of nights.

How do we know this? Presumably because of the company the word keeps. Here *before* has no such exalted role as it plays in the hymn, "with the cross of Jesus, going on before." It means only place in a sequence, and we infer this from *'Twas the night*, followed by *Christmas*.

Christmas. Here we have something different. *Christmas* is a "name," a linguistic handle, because it refers to a unique individual. It has only one possible referent—that is, the real thing to which it refers—December 25, which probably was not the date of Christ's birth but has become an event in its own right. Like many proper names, this also had other meanings before it designated a festival. *Christ* comes from a Greek word to "swab" or "smear," so Jesus the Christ means Jesus the Anointed One. *Mass* is the religious service of the universal church. But for most people, such remnants of meaning have long ago fallen away, leaving Christmas a much-loved label for the most popular American festival.[2]

and. A coin with little intrinsic value, except that it is handy. It used to mean something like "next," but it has lost most of what we might call meaning and is rather like a green light, or a traffic officer waving you through an intersection. It means "keep going," with little comment except to suggest that what is coming is somehow like what is past. *But* or *or* placed here would imply that something different is coming.

all. Another term that here means very little. *All* formerly meant something like "beyond," or "exceeding," a sense preserved in related words like *ultimate* and *ultra-*. It has developed many uses: it is a noun in "All is not gold that glitters"; it appears in hundreds of compounds like *All Father*, the progenitor of all things, and it is used as a modifier or intensifier, as in the phrase *all things* or *all right*. But here it is not to be taken literally, and no one would take it so; obviously the fourteen or more hours of darkness in a late December night could not pass with no creature stirring. *All through*—which might better be written *allthrough* —is here little more than a pleasant exaggeration.

through. Another linking word that formerly stood for something more meaningful. The root **ter-* meant "to push through" and then became the hole made by pushing through, a sense preserved in *nostril*, a thirl or hole through the nose. But this is obviously not the meaning here, where *through* combines with *all* to make what is in effect one word, *allthrough*, meaning "throughout." Here is another instance of that *gh* spelling, though it replaces an Old English sound. Children quickly learn to ignore it, and some sensible people spell the word *thru*.

Incidentally, in this book I shall use the asterisk to mark an unrecorded term that we have established by reconstruction; **ter-* was never written by anybody who used it as part of his native language. For more on such terms see Chapter III.2 below.

the. The same *the* noticed above, but here it has a special use; see the next entry.

house. An old word, which may come from a verb meaning "to

---

2. The word *mass* stems, presumably, from a blunder. The service, in Latin, closed with *Ite. Missa est*, which means, "Go. It [the meeting] is dismissed." People who did not know Latin, and few did, thought it meant, "Go. It's the mass," and hence the word. Mistakes such as this, sometimes called *folk etymology*, are very common. See VI.11 below.

cover," related to *hide,* or it may be a word our remote ancestors picked up on their way west. They had been nomads, and they encountered peoples who knew how to build better dwellings than they could. They may have adopted the practice along with the term for the structure. Wherever *house* came from it has developed many uses; it can be a brothel, a legislature, an audience, the management of a gambling establishment, a business, and various other things. Here it has the specialized meaning of "my home" or "our home," so that *the* here becomes a particularizing article, not only with the sense it has in *the boy* as against *a boy.* It identifies the unique structure that is the writer's home.

not. One of the English forms of a negative that has fathered thousands of terms in dozens of languages, including *negative* from Latin. Presumably it comes from one of the oldest expressions in the world, used tens of thousands of years ago; one of the first things a man or a woman had to say was *no.* We do not know how it was pronounced, but it must have begun with a sound like *n* or *m*, and was perhaps not much more than a grunt that accompanied a shaking of the head. The form *not* can be used only when it leans on another term; other words like *no, none,* and *nothing* can be used alone.[3] See also the next entry and *not*, below.

a. This is a form (along with *an*) of the indefinite article, cut down from the same ancestor that gives us *one.* In German both ideas are embodied in a single related word, *ein,* a fact that is said to have permitted the poet Goethe an apt witticism—and whether or not the story is apocryphal, it will illustrate the language use. According to the tale, Goethe was late for a banquet; the host, Emperor Frederick II, scribbled a note and put it at Goethe's place. When the poet arrived, he read the note, smiled, but said nothing. The emperor asked him to read it aloud, which Goethe did. The emperor had written, "Goethe ist ein Esel. Friedrich der Zweite." This could mean, "Goethe is a jackass. Frederick II." Goethe, however, read the note with stress on the words *ein* and *Zweite,* so that the effect became, "Goethe is *one* jackass, Frederick the *second*."

In the Santa Claus verse, *a* has a still different use. It combines with the preceding *not,* as though the two words were one, meaning "no single one," which becomes a sort of absolute negative. An even stronger negative appears below, *not even a.*

---

3. The philosopher-critic Kenneth Burke has a theory that language sprang from man's ability to say *no;* see *Language as Symbolic Action* (Berkeley and Los Angeles: University of California Press, 1966), pp. 419–489. Linguists have mostly not taken up the suggestion.

creature. The word comes from an old term meaning "to grow," or "to make grow"—*cereal* and *crescent,* as in the crescent or growing moon, come from the same source. A *creature* was the result of the growing, and when the word was borrowed into English from Latin, it meant anything that God had created, had brought into being. Richard Rolle of Hampole, a fourteenth-century divine, called the sun and the moon God's creatures; Francis Bacon said that light was God's first creature. But now the word usually implies a living being, and a relatively large one at that—presumably the statement "not a creature was stirring" would have excluded whatever the fleas and the microbes were up to that night.

We might notice that *creature* differs from previous words we have encountered in the poem. Except for *Christmas*—two words put together—it is longer than the other words. Formerly it was even longer, being pronounced as four syllables, something like *cray-ah-tur-uh.* It is a rather uncommon word, the only one thus far that might puzzle a small child. Historically it is different from the words we have looked at, being what is called a loan, or borrowed, word. That is, it is a development in English from Latin, whereas all the words discussed above, except *Christmas,* are native words, words that have descended within the English tradition. We must take more notice of this distinction later, especially in Chapters III and IV.

was. The same *was* we encountered in *'twas,* above, but used differently. In fact, we might have difficulty saying how it is used here, although no child would be confused by it. In the previous line, the *was* of *'twas* established a previous time, with the implied assumption that something happened during that time. Here *was* may be part of the verb, *was stirring,* a form called the past progressive, which indicates that action identified in the meaningful part of the verb, *to stir,* continued for some time, the extent of time left indefinite. On the other hand, *stirring* may be a modifier, telling us what the "creatures" were not doing, but might have been expected to do. If so, *was* is only a grammatical link between *stirring* and *creature,* the word it modifies. Of itself it has little meaning except that it identifies the time. Fortunately, the recipient of the poem need not make this distinction, and few would, although a reader might be vaguely aware of both the time and the lack of movement, unconsciously running them together.

stirring. The basic idea here seems to be what is now suggested by *whirl;* it gives us our word *storm,* which was formerly a whirlwind. It appears also, without the initial *s,* in the borrowed word *turbine,* an engine that whirls. Probably the common use now is to make something whirl by agitating it, to *stir* one's coffee, but anyone would know that here *stir* has nothing to do with revolving. It has a derived, almost a figurative, meaning of being "agitated" or "in motion," and in the sense used here, "starting a motion"; one *bestirs* oneself by getting up, but not by going to bed. *Stir* here carries a sense of expectancy; there is no motion now, and when motion starts it will probably be slight.

not. This is the same *not* that appears above, but now we can observe what was not apparent in one *not*—that *not . . . not* has both rhetorical and grammatical use, tying the sentence together and suggesting that what is to come is very much like what is just past, a development or extension of it.

even. The word in its basic sense means "flat," "smooth." From this use dozens of meanings have developed denoting "equal," as in *to get even (with),* but in the Santa Claus poem *even* suggests the ultimate of something or other. The word occurs in various Germanic languages, but this use has developed only in English, where it has now become perhaps the most common.[4] In the days before houses could be built so that they were tight, the fact that no mouse was stirring was the ultimate evidence of stillness.

a. One might notice that *a* here comes close to meaning *any*—particularly when linked to *not even*—implying something more than the supposed indefiniteness of the indefinite article.

mouse. An old word for a long familiar pest. Apparently neither the rodent nor the name for it has changed much in more than seven thousand years. Our remote linguistic ancestors were pestered by mice, and at least one mouse got into an Egyptian mummy case. The term has a clear referent; it designates an object and refers to it, although it does not describe the object or tell us much about it. That the little beast is furry and given to gnawing, we know, but not because the word tells us this. In versions of the poem prepared to be read aloud to children, the second line may look like the following:

Not a creature was stirring, not even a

---

4. The meaning may have started through comparison. The poem *Beowulf* has some lines about a light, "leoht inne stod / efne swa of hevene / hadre scineth / redores candel" ("the light gleamed from within, even as, out of heaven, brightly shines the candle of the sky"). Here two things are said to be equal, the light and the sunshine, and such comparisons were pushed to the improbable. Milton assures us that God's "magnetic beam . . . shoots invisible vertue (sic) even to the deep." So we have such phrases as "even unto death."

The child is supposed to see the picture and say, "Mouse!" That is, some words can be used for not much more than to point to a referent. In addition, however, this term has come to suggest several qualities, such as timidity and furtiveness, smallness and silent activity, so that the word is now a symbol. This symbolic power of words is notable in most common terms which have clear referents, especially if they involve daily living.

Obviously, words embody a deal of living. Most of the time we use them thoughtlessly. Asked to say what one of them means, we are likely to produce a definition that formulates only a small part of what the term can imply. Words incorporate so much of what man is, and what the human race has gone through, that they can do more than we may give them credit for.

2. Signs, Symbols, and Language

How can words, which, as we hear them, are only breath used to make particularized sounds, accomplish what we have just seen them doing? Perhaps a story will help explain.

I had taken some friends to a ghost town, inhabited by a sole, longtime resident, with whom I had been corresponding. Our party was delayed— a tree had fallen across the road and had to be cut away—so that we arrived long after dark. The inhabited house was easy to spot; curtained light came through the windows. I knocked on the door. A dog started barking. The door opened a crack, and a cylindrical, black object was thrust out.

Both the bark and the elongated object can be called signs. They told me something, although not much. The sound of barking told me there was a dog inside. The elongated object told me that at least one other creature was in the building, probably human, since dogs do not thrust long objects through doorways. I recognized the object. If it had been an umbrella, it would have baffled me. When I have seen an umbrella thrust through a doorway, it meant there was no porch on the building and someone inside believed heavy rain was falling. But this was not an umbrella; it was a gun barrel. The gun also was a sign, quite an eloquent one, although not very precise. It might have meant that somebody expected to shoot me; or, more likely, it meant that somebody was re-minding me that he could shoot me if he wanted to, but that he would not if I would go away or somehow make myself welcome.

Soon I heard another sound. The nature of this new sound can be indicated by the following letters: "Who is it?" I made sounds that can be suggested by "Professor Laird." Everything changed. The gun barrel disappeared, the dog was quieted, the door swung wide, a whiskered old man was smiling, apologizing, and inviting us in. Soon I was explaining about the fallen tree that had delayed us, and the old man was accounting for his seeming inhospitality—people thought he had gold hidden in his cabin, and somebody had tried to kill him, shooting through the window.

Clearly, some sounds are more powerful than others. My knock on the door had been a sign, and it revealed something, even to the dog, but not much. It did not tell who I was, why I had come, or that my visit was peaceful. Two words had done much more; they reassured the old man and told him so much that we should need chapters of this book if we were to analyze it all. Furthermore, each of us was soon informing the other about objects not there to be seen or heard, about events that were not then happening. I had only to use a few words like *tree, fallen, road*, and *ax*, to put them together in sentences, and he could visualize events he had not seen. He had only to mention the bullets that had narrowly missed him for me to know something of him as a person, why he had covered his windows with blankets, and more about life in a ghost town.

The difference stemmed from our having turned from relying on signs to using symbols. The gun barrel through the door was a sign; it was an actual gun barrel. What I saw was there; it meant what a gun barrel can mean. Put together with some other signs, like the barking of the dog and the partly opened door, it told me something, although only a little. But as soon as each of us started using words, both of us knew much more. When he spoke, *who, is*, and *it*, the sounds were there momentarily, long enough for them to register in my mind, but they also conjured up other concepts. *Who* let me know that a person inside was interested in my identity and implied that if I could establish an appropriate one, the gun barrel would disappear. That is, *who* is not only a sign, a sound that can exist. It is also a symbol; it can suggest other things than itself.

Likewise, when I said "Professor Laird," I was using a sign, words that as a proper name can exist, either as sound or a sequence of letters. But the name was also a symbol, an identification of an individual, but a symbol so complex that it generated ideas, beliefs, facts—all sorts of things. It called up for the old man, more or less consciously, an image of a trusted, longtime friend, the correspondence we had exchanged, the conviction he had developed that he and I were in a way kindred spirits, that I represented a reputable institution of learning and was certainly not the kind of person who had come to shoot him.

In short, a sign is sharply limited. It can tell something about itself; the dog bark existed as wavelengths of disturbance, and I could have measured them if I had been carrying the proper instruments and had wanted to use them. It also had some meaning; it told me that a living and apprehensive dog was inside the cabin.

But the power of a symbol to communicate, to prompt thought, to stimulate more symbols, is almost infinite. A word may start as a limited sign, but as soon as the sign becomes a symbol it permits great leaps in meaning. In the instance above, not only did a name call up a human being; it also generated all sorts of thoughts in the old man, about his guest as well as about himself. He would have been reminded, however vaguely, of what he did and did not know about professors, as well as this particular professor, and much else. As for himself, he would have been conscious of his own life as a miner in this silver camp, of his pride in his great stamp mill that he expected to show to his guests, of his own wish to have his life and the time he had known recognized and enshrined in a great museum. All this could go on to great length, depending in part on how much the old man knew about himself, his guests, and all sorts of related topics that could be called up by the linkage of symbols within symbols, nested like a sequence of Chinese boxes.

Every word is a symbol; until it becomes a symbol it is not a word. Words are symbolic on at least two levels; a sequence of letters like *g, o,* and *d*, or a sequence of sounds associated with these letters, becomes a symbol for the word *god*, and the word can become a symbol for various things associated with supernatural power, for love or cruelty, for destiny or the secrets of the universe.

Meaning, of course, is complex, but at the center of it, apparently, is symbol and the power to make symbols and use them. In fact, we now believe that the power of man to make symbols accounts for the growth of language, and as Suzanne Langer has pointed out in *Philosophy in a New Key*, "Language is, without a doubt, the most momentous and at the same time the most mysterious product of the human mind."

3. The Chimpanzees Are Teaching Us About Language

All creatures relatively high on the evolutionary scale use signs: a bird can make a few suggestive sounds, bluster with its wings and claws, and swoop; a rattlesnake can rattle, dart its tongue, and threaten to strike; a cat can meow and rub against your leg and can even combine various gestures into what seems to be an indication of disdain. Some animals—the more intelligent apes and probably some others like dolphins and whales—can make thirty or more signs discrete enough so that man can discriminate them and even identify meaning in them. But so far as we know, no nonhuman being has ever developed what we would call a language. Apparently signs are not enough, and brains limited to signs are not good enough.

For such statements as these we need some agreement as to what we mean by the word *language*. Seemingly, the crucial criterion is what is technically called "completeness," that is, the ability to fill any need of any speaker, so that anybody who knows the language can say anything he can conceive. Lately, man has become weightless in space and is exploring the ocean floors; no speaker of a natural language has had trouble talking about these events. When Christianity swept over Europe and Islam moved through Asia, millions of illiterate people were flooded with new ideas; none of these speakers of various tongues had trouble discussing these ideas, insofar as they understood them. All natural languages provide their users with the means to say anything.

But no system of signs can do this. All known oral/aural sign systems are small, forty signs or fewer, about as many as the number of sounds needed for a language—and linguistic sounds are oral signs. Probably no system of signs could be large. English has more than two million "uses," what we call "meanings," and although nobody knows them all, any intelligent person can learn, and learn to use, a considerable portion of them. They are relatively easy to master because they are tied together in symbolic, oral, alphabetical, and grammatical relationships, but probably no one, not to mention relatively stupid creatures like cows and myna birds, could command hundreds of thousands, or even tens of thousands, of discrete unrelated sounds—even if any ear were capable of distinguishing so many.

Thus, if we think of creatures in their dealings with one another, we can distinguish three categories: those, like angleworms, that do not communicate or, if they do communicate, do so little of it that they seem not to; those that communicate in limited ways with signs; and those that have developed speech and can communicate in potentially unlimited ways with language. The last group includes all human beings and, from the dawn of time, no creatures but human beings. Now, just within the last few years, we have been discovering a fourth classification, namely, creatures that have never developed a language but seem to be able to learn to use one if it is given them. Such animals can tell us something of what language is and how words work.

Chimpanzees are the most interesting, including a little female named Washoe. She was purchased from a trader when she was about a year old and was assiduously taught American Sign Language by two research psychologists, Drs. Beatrice and Allen Gardner. Within four years Washoe had learned to use at least one hundred fifty signs—probably more—and could apparently learn signs for objects and actions she knew about. She could use her signs as symbols; the bark of a dog meant a dog to her and apparently suggested to her whatever she had learned about dogs. She accepted the sound of an airplane as evidence that a plane was in the sky. She could develop signs of her own and invest them with meaning; seeing a companion gesturing that he wanted a light for his cigarette, she adopted this gesture—it is not a recognized gesture in sign language, and she had not been taught it—and used it for anything associated with fire, heating food, and the like. She had been taught little grammar, but she developed some grammatical notions; she apparently understood predication, possession, and modification. She could talk to herself in signs and seemed to expect that other chimpanzees and all people could understand her. She could become furious if she believed signs were being misused; accustomed to food coming from cans, she refused to believe that the contents of a beer can were not food. She was able to communicate moderately complicated ideas; being cold, she signed to an attendant that she wanted the key so she could unlock the cupboard door and get a blanket.

In short, Washoe seemed to be using her sign language as a normal human infant uses its native speech. Can we say that her sign language was what we have called "complete"? Obviously she could not "say" much, somewhat less than a normal five-year-old child. But she did not have much to say—neither does an infant. Presumably her brain was not so good as a human brain, and sign language is not as good a medium as is speaking. Furthermore, she had great handicaps; she did not start to learn language until she was nearly a year old, and we now know that infants learn a great deal of language in their first year. She was not taught in the best manner; the Gardners did a superb job, but nobody knew proper chimpanzee pedagogy. And we know relatively little of chimpanzee psychology and cultural heritage; we do not know how much Washoe knew but was unable to communicate. But if her use of language was not "complete," it so much implies completeness that the best guess is this: Washoe's use of language suggests human use of language, and any shortcomings she may have had are best accounted for by her poor start in life, not by inherent inability.

This estimate gains support from Washoe's younger contemporaries. Means have now been developed with chimpanzees born in captivity to start teaching newborn chimps sign language within hours after their birth. They are learning much faster than Washoe did, and the hope is that they will mate and have offspring and that the baby chimps will learn communication from their mothers and the other infants as human children do, except that they will learn sign language rather than oral speech. Meanwhile, other scientists are demonstrating that gorillas also can learn sign language.[5]

One moral of all this would seem to be that language is mainly mental, growing from the mind, but that it requires some system, also. Previous attempts to teach primates language had failed, presumably because the teachers had used oral language, and a chimp does not have the vocal equipment to make human sounds. They have brains enough to use language, but they were being given a language based on a system they could not use. But chimpanzees have expressive hands, and given a system that utilizes hand, arm, and body movements, they could converse. So can some other primates, perhaps most apes and monkeys. Dolphins are probably as smart as chimpanzees, and whales seem to be even smarter. They can apparently make music; one would guess that if we can ever devise a language that fits their bodies and their way of life as well as gestures fit chimpanzees, they, too, could learn language.

4. *Homo Sapiens* (Man Thinking) Becomes *Homo Loquens* (Man Talking)

How did man get language? One hesitates whether to call it a discovery or an invention. In one sense he got it by talking, and we can call his vocal and bodily signs speech when they grew into behavior that we can call talk. When and how did this come about? The evidence, including the recent evidence from chimpanzees, suggests he could do this partly because he was smart enough, and partly because he was lucky, having been given an unexpected inheritance, a vocal system.

We must assume that many sorts of creatures have tried to use what-

5. While this book was in press, Washoe gave birth. The offspring died, but Washoe, at this time living in a chimpanzee colony, adopted a baby chimp and started teaching it to sign. Meanwhile, other baby chimps are teaching one another to sign.

ever senses they have for communication. Most of them have had only limited success. Restricted, one-way communication is common—even stupid creatures can let you know they are angry—but extensive, two-way communication is rare. Some senses do not serve very well; most creatures can learn something of an object by tasting it, but two-way communication by tasting presents hazards. The tasted creature may find itself being devoured. Smell works within limits; dogs learn something about one another by sniffing, and ants know which ants to fight, probably by smell. Most creatures exude odor, but few of them can control odor and vary it much. Skunks do better than human beings in this, but even a skunk, although his odoriferous attack may be overpowering, cannot carry on much of a conversation. Touch works well within limits, but it suffices for only the simplest sorts of messages, and for not many of them. A gentle pat on the cheek conveys ideas unlike those implied by a blow on the skull, but not many different sorts of touch are possible, not enough to provide signs for a language.

Two sense patterns remain, gesture/sight and sound/hearing. For most creatures gesture and sight work better than sound and hearing. Biting may have more effect than snarling, and most creatures can make many distinguishable body movements, but only a few sounds. That is, they can make more signs by gesture than by voice. And these bodily movements can be more accurately recorded and more readily interpreted than can most nonhuman sounds.

But not so man; he has inherited vocal organs although seemingly not by planned intent. Everything we use to talk with had another and earlier use. Mammals breathed with lungs before they used a column of air to make words. The teeth help make consonants, but they were used for biting and chewing millions of years before any word was uttered. Even the voice box did not get started as a means of voicing; it is a gate system to send air to the lungs, food and drink to the stomach. But curiously, a column of air can be so altered that above five hundred human sounds have been distinguished.

We do not know how, when, where, or by whom language was invented. We are likely never to know, partly because it probably never was invented in the sense that the wheel was invented. The whole process must have been very long and complex. The best current guess seems to be that humanoid creatures developed from tailless monkeys that could save themselves by escaping into trees and that thrived by the dexterity they developed with their apposable thumbs. They probably developed an unusual number of signs, using their flexible bodies and their adaptable sound-making organs to create a dual sight/sound system. This sort of growth continued, probably for tens of thousands of years, with enhanced experience promoting intelligence, and mounting intelligence contributing to new experience. The more the means of communication increased, the more the system relied on sound. For sound has advantages: meaningful sound can be made at night and in the dark of a cave; it can go around corners and permit communication while the communicators are hiding; sounds can be made while the communicator is using both hands to fight or make love. Man inherited some remarkable sign-making devices such as the vocal cords and a versatile tongue.

But sound and gesture supply only what linguists call the "shape" of the word, the mechanism for suggesting whatever the word does for the hearer or reader—the term *shape* can be used also to refer to the written spelling that signals a word. Sound and gesture could supply signs, but if each sign had only one isolated use, a full communications system would need an inestimable number of signs, so many that nothing short of an electronic brain could retain them, ready for instant use. Language became possible only when two other simplifying devices were added to the sound/gesture system. One we have noticed above in the little tale about the ghost-town miner, the power to transmogrify signs into symbols. The other is the ability to generate grammar. Roughly speaking, grammar provides the means by which words work with one another, the device that shows us how they are working. We can understand how this is so if we recall the analysis of two lines of verse at the opening of this chapter. From no single word in those lines could we tell the meaning or the use until we knew how it was interacting with the other words. That interaction and the rules that govern it we call grammar. Understandably, since language is indescribably complex, grammar and the sound system, the phonology, are elaborate studies in themselves, but our business in this book is with vocabulary. The other two interact with vocabulary, and thus we shall have to consider them, but only in an ancillary way.

Roughly, we can now describe a word. We saw at the beginning of this chapter that a word is not a sharply definable thing, and in subsequent chapters we can expect more problems of this sort. But a working understanding should be possible: a language is a complete system of communication and a word is a sign that has become a symbol in a natural language. In all natural languages we know of, these linguistic signs are oral, or they utilize some other system—like writing—that has grown from an oral system. All languages also share certain other characteristics: they are arbitrary, systematic, noninstinctive, and linked to human social, intellectual, and oral behavior. These characteristics help us understand the working of words, but the essential criterion apparently is "completeness"—that is, to be a language, a set of devices must be able to serve all the needs of its users for communication. Among its instruments are likely to be what we call words—more technically, morphemes and phrases of morphemes. This distinction has its uses and will inevitably come up later in the book (see Chapter III.4), but mainly we can talk about words, which are definable enough for most purposes and are the working linguistic units most users of English recognize.

5. Words Are a System

Oliver Goldsmith, in parts of "The Deserted Village," was having fun with the homey folk he had known as a child. From the sophistication of eighteenth-century London he described the village schoolmaster in part as follows:

> . . . words of learned length and thundering sound
> Amazed the gazing rustics ranged around;
> And still they gazed, and still the wonder grew,
> That one small head could carry all he knew.

Doubtless the schoolmaster had a good head, but how can any small head carry all it knows, even if that "all" is not "much"? How can any head carry the multitudinous details of language that the wondering rustics themselves would have possessed? We do not know, but we have seen above that two devices help, symbol making and grammar. A third habit of language is of primary importance: it works by systems. Or perhaps one should say it works by a system of systems, or a system of systems of systems, for we have sound systems, spelling systems, and writing systems, as well as systems of word form, word use, and meaning.

Meaning is not simple. The word *meaning* is a term we use to imply a relationship between a speaker and his or her hearer, between a writer and reader. A speaker utters some syllables or a writer sets down some letters. He has something in mind when he does this, which we call the meaning of the word, although he may or may not be precise in the boundaries he sets for this meaning. And the word does not have his or any other meaning in any exact sense. The word serves him as a sort of counter, and for the hearer or reader it triggers what we once more call the "meaning" of the word.

But this sense that the recipient of the word conjures up will not be more than an approximation of what was in the mind of the speaker or writer. Each of them will have created his own "meaning" for the word, using his own complex self as part of that meaning and relying upon his experience with this particular word and his knowledge of the patterns of the language. For he is aware of the systems of the language, with a working awareness that he probably could not put into words— our minds are more orderly than we know. They are also better stocked and more tolerant of inconsistency. Few users of English have any conscious awareness that the word *the* has the use we notice above in "the house" as the writer's personal dwelling, but all native speakers can deal with this use, whether they emit it or receive it. Language is the result of creation, of continual creation; our ancestors created an early form of it, and we are continuing to make it. So, presumably, will our children.

CHAPTER II

NAMES
From Handles to Meaning

Naming was word-formation as soon as the primordial squall, ma-ma, became something like "Mama!"

— Charles Baker Austin

1. The Need for Naming

A railroad station in Wales is labeled as follows: LLANFAIRPWLLGWYNBYLLGOGERICHWYRNDROBLLLLSNTYSILIOGOGOGOCR. The community comprises the parishes of Sts. Mary and Tysilio, and the agglutinated result is said to mean, "Parish of Mary in a hollow of white hazels by the rapid whirlpool and Parish of Tysilio with the red cave."

Every place of consequence needs a marker for reference, a handle for the mind to get hold of it. This place name identifies the spot, although it seems a bit cumbersome, but doubtless the local folk have ways of cutting it down to something handy. Others have done so—the residents of Jacksonville, Florida, call the place *Jax*, and El Puebla de la Nuestra Señora la Reina de los Angeles de Prociuncola (The Town of Our Lady the Queen of the Angels from Prociuncola—the last word being the name of a chapel associated with St. Francis of Assisi) is commonly *L.A.*, pronounced *ellay*.

These two skills—naming by describing, and shaping names to convenient handles—are apparently primordial. Even before man had anything we would call language, he probably had found ways to apply identificatory grunts or squawks to anything important for him, and to reshape these into working names. As the Welsh named their town by the white hazels in the hollow by the whirlpool and the red cave, we are today naming the bottom of the sea by describing it. We say the *Aleutian Trench* follows along the south side of The Aleutian Islands, intersect-

21

ing the *Kurrile Trench* and the *Emperor Seamounts*—such terms can be found on a modern map of the physical world. The giving of names, because we need verbal handles for things, must be one of the oldest linguistic acts, and is still one of the liveliest, although much of this name giving is now obscured. We shall probe the obscurity a bit, because once a sound or some letters become a name, the shape may become some other sort of vocabulary too.

2. The Celts and Their Water Names

Some Ligurian or Cro-Magnon place names may yet be lurking in Europe, but we know so little of the speech of such early peoples that we have trouble guessing. The Celts, however, we know about, partly for the very reason that they scattered their names all the way from eastern Europe to Land's End, and thousands of the names have survived. Also, we have the means to study these ancient relics, for Old Irish and Old Welsh manuscripts are numerous, and several Celtic dialects are still spoken.

Beginning some thousands of years ago[1] the Celts thrust west and south from what is now Siberia. They were in the Balkans; the statue called "The Dying Gaul" represents a Celtic warrior, stopped before he got to Athens. The Celts sacked Rome but did not bother to keep what was to become the greatest city in western Europe. They swung down into the Hispanic Peninsula, and farther north they surged across what is now France and the offshore islands in two waves, even to Ireland. For a time they must have dominated much of northern and western Europe. When Rome started pushing north the Celts were everywhere. The Romans first conquered and then protected them, but when the Roman legions withdrew, Germanic peoples swept in. The Germans had worked north and then back south and west; they clashed with the Celts as Gauls in what we call France and as Britons in what is now England.[2]

Thus the Celts were there when the great natural features got enduring names. Of course, great rivers like the Rhone, the Rhine, the Don, and the Danube have been named dozens or hundreds of times, but the older names are mainly lost, except as they may be obscured in the names

---

1. We shall get more nearly precise dates in Chapter III.
2. For an excellent illustrated map of the Celts and their conquests see *National Geographic Magazine*, 151 (1977), supplement to no. 5, p. 582A.

the Celts used, terms that grew out of such Celtic terms for water as *rhin* and *don*. Celtic terms for mountains have also survived, but since mountains are dangerous, the mother of storms and the home of wild beasts, early men sought out water, which was both life-giving and a source of food. Thus many of the oldest surviving names attach to water, and in western Europe, including the British Isles, these names tend to be Celtic, with later additions.

The stock incident must have been something like the following: some people made a home in a propitious place, on the ocean, by a lake, or near a river. A stranger arrived; whether a conqueror or a peaceful migrant, he would ask about the most important phenomenon in the community, whether he did this in a badly understood language or by pointing. The native might have had nothing but hate and contempt for this stranger, or he might have considered the new arrival stupid—after all, he could not speak the language. In either situation, the new-comer was likely to get an answer equivalent to the following: "It's the lake," "Our river," "That's water, you dumb cluck." Thus the new-comer would call the phenomenon something like *Avon, Don, Esk, Stour,* or *Tyne,* assuming that these were proper names, not knowing they were all generic terms for *water*—water standing, water running, water rippling—in various Celtic bodies of speech. He accepted the term and added his own for *water* or *river* or *lake,* so that the Avon (the river that flows through Stratford) became the *River Avon*—a pair that means "river river." Such doings have continued; we are told that modern topographers, asking a native the name of a stream or hill in Africa, have received such answers as "What?" "I don't know," and "You'll have to ask the chief," and that these replies have been solemnly recorded on maps as place names.

This sort of thing must have happened thousands of times, although the resulting names have mostly been obscured by later waves of Old English, Old Norse, and Anglo-Norman names.[3] A few are preserved because the old river name was given to a dwelling, whence it survived as a place name; the *Roden* in Essex was apparently once called the *Hyle* (etymology uncertain, possibly "the trickling stream"), but the name has survived in *Ileford,* naming a ford over the river. *Esk* has survived in hundreds of names, spelled also *Esch, Esc, Ass, Hesk, Ask, Easke, Ax, Axe,*

---

3. These languages will be identified as we need to deal with them; see Chapters II.3, III.3, III.4, and IV.2.

Uisc, Exse, Eaxa, Exe, Exse, Esse, Esshe, Iska, Husk, and many more
that can no longer be identified. It has entered into countless compounds:
*Exebrigge, Exetone, Axeminster, Exancestre, Eskdale, Exan Midstream,
Exwicke, Exeter, Upper* and *Nether Exe,* and the like. Survivals from
Old Celtic **dubra,* "river," are widespread, accounting for *Dover* in
Kent, *Doferic* and *Doverdale* farther west in Worcester, *Dover Hay* still
farther west in Somersetshire, *Dover Beck* to the north in Nottingham-
shire, and *Dour, Dore,* and probably *Dove* in many communities.

Few areas in language study are so confused as the question of the
survivals from Celtic,[4] and in few is popular rumor so unreliable—even
what gets into solemn places like encyclopedias and guidebooks. The
bulk of the evidence, however, is so extensive and so consistent that
the main outlines are not in doubt. *Bally* means an occupied place in
Erse but not in the Celtic dialect that flourished in England and Wales.
There are said to be more than two thousand inhabited places in Ireland
having a form of *bally* in the place name, but none in either Wales or
England. This can scarcely be accident, and if the evidence for *dur* and
avon is not so overwhelming, it is still so extensive and so consistently
related to bodies or streams of water that the evidence as a whole becomes convincing.

Celtic water names fall into several groups. Those given above tend
to be the old ones, which include a noun for water. Later there was a second wave of names, based on adjectives that described the water, such as

---

4. Most of these attributions are to some degree guesses. The evidence is usually less
conclusive than one could wish, so that even the most careful scholar can go astray.
Ancient terms may be variously spelled—as *esk* above—and there may be plausible
explanations in various tongues. Thus *Durham* (*dur,* water, plus *ham,* inhabited place)
was for a time supposed to mean "river town." Older manuscripts showed the name to
have been *Dunholm,* which is better suited to the commanding position of the city, since
dun is Celtic for a hill fort. *Holm* is itself an enclosed place; thus *Durham* is in effect
"fort fort," first in Celtic, then in Germanic. Partly the confusion is to be traced to Isaac
Taylor, *Words and Places: Illustrations of History, Ethnology & Geography* (first published in 1864). It is at once an engaging and a monumental book, and essentially sound,
but the good Canon of York was somewhat too credulous in accepting as Celtic terms
like *Ouse,* now more plausibly attributed to Old English, and in accepting as early names
what are now believed to be late back-formations. Taylor's was a good book in its day,
but he had frequently to rely on antiquarian speculation. Even today much is uncertain,
so much so that there is scarcely an etymology that has not been seriously questioned.
I have relied mainly on an excellent study, Eilert Ekwall, *English River-Names* (Oxford: Clarendon, 1928), with side glances at Percy H. Reaney, *The Origin of English
Place-Names* (London: Routledge and Kegan Paul, 1960). Even so, I have doubtless
made mistakes.

clear, muddy, cold, or whatever. The earlier names, those based on synonyms for *stream, river,* and *lake,* sprang in part from ignorance, from the bad guesses of migrants. The later names, those that described the quality of the water, reflect the more intimate acquaintance of dwellers on the land. The Welsh word *garw,* "rough," may appear as *Garra, Garway, Gars, Gers, Garve,* and in France as *Garonne, Gers, Guer,* and *Gironde,* dozens of rough rivers and lakes. On the other hand *garre* is a word for "crane," and rivers are often named for the birds, fish, and animals found there. A term for "black," implying dark water, appears in various Celtic languages as *dubo, du,* and *dubh.* It crops up in many water names such as *Douglas, Dulas, Dolting, Deerness,* and many others, including *Duvelis* and *Dyueleis,* which were readily confused with *devil,* so that such names readily become *Devil's Water* and *Devil's Back. Ar* probably means "running water," appearing as *Ayr* in Scotland (hence Ayrshire), the *Arrow* in Wales, the *Yarrow* in England. The root idea is apparently "swift," and the word is attached to swift rivers on the Continent, to the *Orvanne* in France, and elsewhere all the way to India. A term something like *tees* probably meant "boiling" and is found in the names of dozens of turbulent streams that have been called *Thesa, Teysa, Taise, Teesia* and in compounds like *Teesdale* and *Tees Head.*

Sometimes, even though a name is clearly Celtic, there are so many candidates that the exact one cannot be surely hit upon. The *Thames* has been related both to a term meaning "broad and quiet," a name that well describes the Thames as it approaches the sea at London, and *teme-,* meaning "dark," a widespread term in European languages. The *Tamasa* is a tributary of the Ganges in India. *Cam* can mean "crooked," and may account for *Cambridgeshire, Camden,* and *Cambeck,* along with *Cham, Kam,* and *Kamp* in Germany and Switzerland, but as so frequently, one cannot be quite sure. A sedgy stream called *The Cam* flows through Cambridge; the name would thus imply "the bridge over the crooked river," and since the waterway has meanders, this name is plausible enough. But the town was formerly called *Cantabrigge,* and *canta* means "full of mud." Since meandering streams are often muddy, the name may mean, "bridge over the crooked brook" or "bridge over the muddy meanders." But the place was still earlier called *Grauntbrigge,* meaning "big bridge." *Cambridge* has apparently meant many things to many generations.

Celtic terms for creatures or objects associated with certain streams account for some names. Oaks grew widely in England and probably give us *Derwent Water,* one of the lakes in the Lake Country, from British **derua,* "oak," Welsh *derw,* and the like, along with several rivers *Derwent* that presumably flowed through oak forests. The elm, also common in England, is reflected in names like *Lymn, Lynn, Lemon,* and *Leam,* the Celtic word for an elm in Old Irish being *leamh.* Similarly, names reflect *lugg,* meaning "shining," "bright"; *cray,* meaning "pure," "clean," and various words for "stony."

3. Germanic Peoples and Their Home Names

The early Celts have left us few names of their homes. Perhaps homes were not very important for them, but the next wave of invaders were farmers and fishermen; from them we get names of inhabited places. They were, or had been, speakers of what we call Germanic languages, and each brought with them their own variety of speech. They had some connection with the Celts, but it was so distant that it did not keep them from dispossessing the Celtic natives nor the Celts from hating them for being ousted. All that will become clearer in the next chapter, but for now we may note that they came in three waves.

1) The Romans had subdued the Celts in much of what is now England (except Cornwall), but in the early Christian centuries, when Rome was tottering, the legions withdrew and peoples from northern Europe moved in. They included two main bodies, the Angles and the Saxons, and a smaller contingent known as Jutes. They overran the lands the Romans had subdued, but made little headway against the Celts in what is now Wales, Scotland, Ireland, and some of the other islands. They spoke what we call **Anglo-Saxon** or **Old English,** abbreviated OE.

2) Beginning in the ninth century, as part of a resurgence of Scandinavian peoples, Danes and Norwegians harried the islands, and after an uneasy peace was worked out, many of them stayed. We call their speech **Old Norse.**

3) In 1066 relatives of these same Scandinavians who had settled in what is now France conquered the lands that had by now become English- or Scandinavian-speaking. They spoke a dialect of French that in England we call **Anglo-Norman.**
For our present purposes, although these peoples span nearly a thoussand years in their name giving, we can consider the three together.

Place names of this sort tend to comprise two or three elements, a generic like *hill* or *meadow,* and a limiting term like *big* or *John's,* and sometimes a relationship word. Thus, the name may be *The Big Meadow,*

John's Farm, In the Valley. These names may appear in any of four languages, each broken into dialects—Celtic, OE, Old Norse, or Anglo-Norman—and any of them may have been lost, especially when they were no longer recognized by the local speakers. *York,* the modern name for what was long the principal city in northern England, will provide an example of the sort of thing that was going on everywhere all the time. In A.D. 79 the Roman legions established their northern military center there, adopting the Celtic name for the place and giving it a Latin ending, as *Eboracum* (*eburos* being Celtic for a yew tree), or a proper name taken from the tree. During the centuries, the sound here represented by *b* came closer to v^5 and later to *f,* and when the Angles controlled the place they spelled the name *Eferwic* (c. 897). This would mean something like "boar town," *efer* or *eofor* being OE for a male pig and *wic* being a village. Then the Danes took the area and spelled the name of the place *Iorvik,* Old Norse *vik* being the designation of a stream or its estuary, so that the word now meant something like *Jarl's Bay.* In Middle English the name was recorded as ʒ*eork,* which became *York* when the *yogh* (ʒ) ceased to be part of the writing system.

OE names predominated since the Angles and Saxons outnumbered all other groups, and they arrived first, except for the Celts, who had limited influence because they were mostly killed, enslaved, or driven out of the lowlands. Thus names involving *bridge (Cambridge), ford (Oxford), hill (Dunhill), port (Portsmouth),*[6] and the like can be found everywhere. Some terms came wholly or in part from Old Norse: *car, kerr, ker,* etc., meaning "brushwood," or "swampland"; *wray* or *wroe,* from Old Norse *vrar,* meaning "corner" for some remote place. *Holmes* indicated a flat land or fenn, and *slack* (from Old Norse *slakki*) a narrow valley. After the Normans came, names from Old French were fashionable, although they were not always understood by the native sons of the Angles and Saxons, so that *Rue de le Roi,* "Street of the King," became Rotten Row.[7]

Some generics, mostly OE or Old Norse—and sometimes both—gained wide currency. Consider *tun* in its various spellings. In Celtic, it was a word for a fortified place, where it appears most frequently as *din* or *dun.* It gives us *dune* from Dutch; *tun* and *dun* from OE, which were later changed through what we shall call the Great English Vowel

---

5. We shall see in the next chapter that this was a normal development.
6. *Port* is from Latin, but it had long since become an OE word.
7. Another example of what is called folk etymology; see Chapter I, footnote 2.

Shift (see Chapter VII.4, below) to *town* and *doun*. Thus it can appear in place names as *don, ton, doon, down, din, toun, toune, town, dan*, and some others. By OE times it had come to mean an enclosed place, a surrounded farm for instance, and later a walled town. Thus it appears in the names of thousands of places where people lived: *Arlington* or *Harrington* (the first syllables may mean *"he-goat," "eagle,"* or something else), *Bardstown, Burton* (since *bur* can mean "place," the name may mean "fort fort"), and on through the alphabet to *Warburton* (which can be expanded to "farm of an Anglo-Saxon lady named Faith Fortress") to *Washington* and *Yankeetown*. Often the spellings are all mixed up, and the modern form represents nothing more than accident and circumstance. For example, the patronymic of one William appears in a set of extant manuscripts as *Waddington, Wadigton, Wadigtoun, Wuldingdoune, Windindune, Waddingdon,* and many more.

Two of the most common generics that have been incorporated into place names are *ham* and *lea*. The first is roughly equivalent to *ton* or *town* and may come from either OE—modern English *home*—or Old Norse, but it more frequently stems from the latter, so that many place names in southern England end in a form of *ton*, and northern names in -*ham*, as in *Nottingham, Birmingham, Grantham, Greatham, Seaham, Hexham, Seelyham, Durham, Kirkham*, and hundreds more. Two suburbs of London are called *Ham*, and a village *Ham* in Yorkshire is surrounded by *East Ham, West Ham,* and *South Ham*. The word I have spelled *lea* appears also as *Lee, Ley, Lay, Legh, Leigh*, and the like, many of the spellings reflecting OE *leah*, which meant "an open field," and hence could mean "bright" or "sunny," as it probably does in *Leagrove*, "a sunny grove." Often one cannot be sure; *Leighton* could mean either "sunny town" or "field farm." Most frequently it appears in compounds like *Harley*, which can be something like "bright clearing," or "wood where hares live," and *Netly*, which can be a "deserted clearing," a "clearing with nettles," or a "wet place." *Risley* or *Riseley* is a brushwood clearing; *Ridley*, a cleared field, perhaps one burned over. *Riply* is presumably a field shaped like a strip; *Kingsley* or *Kinsly*, a royal field. A similar suffix is -*by*, meaning a farm, as in *Rigby*, "the farm by the ditch."

Inevitably, these names for places where people live or work can become combined. Three occur, surely in *Hampton Court* (which means "dwelling dwelling dwelling") and probably in *Byinton* (by + ing + ton), but such combination of roots is not so common in dwelling places as it is in words for mountains and bodies of water. The rivers were there before anybody spoke a language now understood, and they tend to remain; compared with bodies of water, man and his homes are ephemeral.

4. Two Continents of Nameless Places

Naming thrived in the English colonies, especially in North America. Here were millions of square miles of land, thousands of miles of coastline, vast adjacent seas and myriads of rivers, teeming with running, crawling, flying, and swimming creatures, all of the welter "undiscovered," and accordingly nameless. Of course, it was all known to the inhabitants, and had been for thousands of years, but the invaders were mainly ignorant and, even more, oblivious of any such knowledge. They proceeded to give English names, or French, Spanish, Portuguese, German, Dutch, Yiddish, and all sorts of other names, many of which were incorporated into the English word stock. They even gave some Indian names, but many of these were Indian terms that had been adopted from an Indian language—mostly mispronounced or misinterpreted or both—and given to places for which the aborigines had other names.

Exceptions are numerically many, but few relative to the whole body of naming. *Pockwockamus Pond*, Maine, apparently means "little muddy body of water" and is presumably what some Indians called it. Likewise, *Masheshattuck Hill* in New Hampshire means "big wooded mountain," a name plausible enough. Thousands of such names have survived, especially in Oregon and Washington, but mostly for minor places recognized late. More frequently, especially for prominent phenomena, a word was transferred by white men. *Massachusetts*, meaning "big hills at" in Natik Algonquian is not very descriptive when applied to an arm of the ocean as in *Massachusetts Bay*. *Mississippi*, handsomely rendered as The Father of Waters, means "big water" in some Algonquian languages; it was recorded by a Frenchman, but whether the Indian meant to say the segment of the stream passing Wisconsin was *The Big River* or whether he meant to say only that it was "a big river" is not clear. The French carried the name south, wiping out dozens of other names used for various stretches of the stream. Similarly, *Minneapolis* is based on *Minnehaha*, a term that Longfellow picked up for the fictional Hiawatha's bride. It apparently means "waterfall," or perhaps in two dialects "water water" plus "falls falls." Anyhow, we do not know whether the Indian guide meant to say, "That's *The Waterfall*," or whether he meant to say something like, "That? That, you stupid Frenchman, is where a river runs over a ledge of rock;

the word for it is *minnehaha*." But *ha-ha* was thought to imitate laughing, as it does in English, so that the name was interpreted as "Laughing Water." Then a Greek suffix, *-polis*, meaning "city" was added to it to make up *Minneapolis*. This sort of thing happened from coast to coast, except that some supposedly Indian names have been so garbled that now they are only a jumble of syllables which no longer have discoverable meaning.

Most of the place-naming practices we have observed in the Old World were continued in the New, but a few local patterns developed. Some of the names given by explorers were preserved, whereas explorations in Europe are too shrouded in antiquity to preserve much. These names mostly honor dignitaries; English explorers saluted their sovereigns in *Jamestown, Maryland*, and *Virginia* (for the Virgin Queen). Catholic explorers commemorated holy persons and the Church—*St. Lawrence River, St. Augustine, San Antonio, San Francisco, Sacramento* (the holy sacrament). The explorers named salient features for themselves, or other people awarded them the names: *Hudson River* for Henry Hudson, *Lake Champlain* for Samuel de Champlain, *Bering Strait* for Vitus Bering, *Humboldt River* for the scientist-explorer Alexander von Humboldt, *Pike's Peak* for the officer Zebulon Pike. As local heroes developed, places were named for them: *Houston, Washington, Lincoln*.

The next wave of names, much more numerous, grew from people living on the land. Settlers would name their new home for their old one, sometimes with a word like *new;* Mencken counted more than six hundred such post offices. *Nieu Amsterdam* became *New York* when the English took over. The settlers' names were attached to their homes: *Gay's Mills, Jonesville, Meek's Bay, Baxter's Corners*. Places were named for hunting or fishing—*Oyster Bay, Bear Mountain, Deer Lick*— or for other uses; *Hogg Island* was an island in a stream where hogs could be safely left to pasture through the summer. Places were named as descriptions: *Mud Slough, Old Baldy, Dry Creek, Sandy Hook;* or for activities: *Valley Forge, Park Lane, School House Hollow*.

Unusual in the New World were some generics. Some were imported from languages not English: from Dutch, *kill*, "a river," as in *Fishkill, Schuylkill;* from French, *sault*, "a waterfall," as in *Sault Ste. Marie*, and *butte, rapids, prairie, coulee;* through French from Cherokee, *bayou;* from Spanish, *arroyo, canyon, barranca, mesa, playa, ojo, sierra*, and *vega*. Most of these are limited to certain areas: Dutch to the vicinity of New York; French along the Great Lakes, in the St. Lawrence Basin, and along the Mississippi River; Spanish to the Southwest and far West, especially in California and the southern Great Basin.

Some were English words used little or not at all in the mother country, but they became regional or common in America. Mencken/McDavid observe, "With the settlement of America, such ancient English terms as *moor, heath, dell, fell, fen, weald*, and *combe* disappeared from the vocabulary, and in place of them there arose a large stock of novelties, e.g., *branch, run, fork, bluff, hollow, bottom, lick, neck, gap, notch, divide, knob* and *flat*."[8] Elsewhere Mencken/McDavid add *barrens* and *bad lands*, and they might have added *draw, hammock, hole, pocket, swale*, and others. The variations are many: a *slough* may be a backwater or unused river channel, not the mudhole it was in England; a *branch* may be a running stream in the south, a tributary farther north; a *run* may be a stream in some areas, the running water above an estuary in others; a *bluff* in Savannah, where the term was first recorded, may be only a few feet high, but farther west a bluff is more lofty, from perhaps forty feet to several hundred; *coulee* is a sharp, short valley along the upper Mississippi River, but it is a stream of fresh water in Louisiana. *Fork* is usually limited to land that has been explored from the lowlands into the mountains, since streams seem to join in terrain that is explored from the mountain tops down, not to separate. Thus we find *fork (South Fork, North Fork, Middle Fork)* on the west side of the Sierra Mountains but not on the west slope of the Appalachians. Some terms proliferated; the word *prairie* was known in England but was rare in British English. Sir Thomas Browne in 1684 mentions "The *Prerie* or large Sea-Meadow from the Coast of Provence," but the term has not generally been preserved as a generic in place names in England. It became common in the New World for any sort of flat land, perhaps because travelers accustomed to the homey plots of ground in England were overwhelmed by the seemingly endless stretches of open, flat land. And there were variations. A plateau was a *high prairie*, swampy ground a *trembling prairie*. The *chocolate prairie* was distinguished from the lighter colored *mulatto prairie*. The *door prairies* were apparently grassy places in forested areas.[9] *Prairie* could also become a descriptive term,

---

8. H. L. Mencken and Raven I. McDavid, Jr., *The American Language: An Inquiry into the Development of English in the United States* (New York: Alfred A. Knopf, 1963), p. 664.

9. Other recorded terms include the following: Bald prairie, black prairie, border prairie, bottom prairie, camass prairie, dry prairie, fire prairie, flat prairie, Grand Prairie, grass prairie, great prairie, grub prairie, high prairie, hogbed prairie, hogwallow prairie, limestone prairie, looking-glass prairie, marsh prairie, mesquite prairie, mound prairie, oak

followed by a generic, as in *prairie belt, prairie bottom, prairie bluff,* and on through the alphabet to *prairie uplands.*

The patterns of urban street naming altered terms in the New World. In England, a road in the course of passing through a community of any size is likely to have several names, each referring to a segment of the street and the area adjacent. An important thoroughfare passing through London may have dozens of names; a street in Cambridge has three names in the course of one block, one name centered at each intersection and another name in the middle. Thus in England a householder lives *in* Oxford Street, not *on* Oxford Street. This phrase does not mean, as it would in the United States, that the householder lives between the two gutters; it means he lives in a community that centers upon that segment of the thoroughfare that is called *Oxford Street*, not in one of the communities where the same thoroughfare is called *Holborn* or *Newgate* or something else. In the United States, on the contrary, householders who have property fronting on a thoroughfare live *on* the street, and this street usually keeps its single name from one side of the municipality to the other—although once the street gets out of town, if it ever does, it may acquire a name in accordance with the State or national highway system.

Patterns of planning and naming these thoroughfares have shifted in the past three centuries. Most early communities were determined by water, and the streets followed the river bank or the shore of the lake or ocean, with such names as *Front Street, Main Street, Water Street, River Street.* The communities expanded along roads leading to other communities, named for the destination of the highway, *Worcester Road, Providence Road, Portland Road.* Communities grew at intersections, at the meeting of roads, at the points where roads crossed rivers or encountered a body of water. In New England, communities tended to center on a common (*Boston Common* is still a downtown park), and farther south on a "square," which might be oblong or any other shape, a pattern that was encouraged by French and Spanish-Mexican traditions, especially in the South and Southwest.

That is, early communities grew without much plan, sites being deter-

---

prairie, open prairie, Osage prairie, piney-woods prairie, oak-post prairie, prairie-dog prairie, ridge prairie, river prairie, rolling prairie, sage prairie, salt prairie, sand prairie, shaking prairie, shell prairie, soda prairie, stake prairie, sunken prairie, swamp prairie, timber prairie, upland prairie, water prairie, weed prairie, western prairie, wet prairie, woods prairie.

mined by the terrain, the exigencies of making a living, and the tradition of some kind of central marketplace or pasture. Philadelphia was the exception—Sir William Penn planned it, and it became, however remotely, the pattern for real estate developments that flourished in the nineteenth century and on into the twentieth. These towns and cities tended to be laid out in grids, square with the world, with "streets" running one way and "avenues" the other. These thoroughfares could be named *North* and *South, East* and *West,* the designation figured from a theoretical center of the community. In some instances numbers are used for both; sometimes numbers for one and letters of the alphabet for the other. Or one sequence may use numbers—First Street, Second Street—and the other names, perhaps limited to something like trees from Ash Avenue to Walnut Avenue, colleges from Amherst Avenue to Yale Avenue, flowers, presidents, or States. Lesser thoroughfares would be called *alleys, lanes*, or something of the sort, and important or fashionable roads might be *boulevards*—a term related to *bulwark,* once used in connection with forts but subsequently demilitarized.

With recent real-estate promotion, naming has run wild. Some new terms mean something; a *circle* is usually a circle of some sort, and an *end* may be a dead end, but currently most new names of thoroughfares reflect only the ingenuity of the developer's promotion department and the assumption that houses on *Prospect Manor* command a higher price than those on *North Street, West. Bellevue Wood* may have no view and no trees; *University Terrace* may be situated near no institution of higher learning and have no elevation at all. Thus recent American street names may follow no plan and be descriptive of nothing.

5. Person Names: Germanic, Hebraic

Places and people—these are the great sources of proper names. All tribes and cultures have traditions of naming their children. Many American Indians acquired the names of local creatures: *Black Hawk, Coyote, Rattlesnake, Sitting Bull.* Speakers of OE did not pick up many Celtic personal names; little love was lost between the Celts and their conquerors, and the Celts studiously avoided converting the newcomers to Christianity, so as not to spend eternity with any of their Germanic neighbors. But the invaders brought their own traditions of name-giving with them.

All three sets of post-Celtic invaders had common roots in religion and nomenclature. The Jutes, Angles, and Saxons venerated Wotan and

Freya, Balder and Loki, Thor and his thunderbolts. Their heaven, Valhalla, was eternal fighting, the reward of heroes. Likewise, the Norwegians and Danes, when they came, were steeped in Northern religion and Germanic mores. The Normans were Norsemen, albeit now speaking a sort of French, their name being *Norseman* slightly syncopated. These Germanic folk brought with them a robust set of names: *Aethelstan*, "noble stone"; *Alfred*, "elf counsel," "magically wise"; *Baldwin*, "bold friend"; *Breme*, "famous"; *Carl*, "full grown," "a real man"; *Deorwulf*, "brave wolf"; *Eafor*, "boar"; *Harold*, "army power"; *Hengist*, "stallion"; *Hereswith*, "army mighty"; *Rolfe*, "wolf"; *Richard*, "king," "ruler"; *Robert*, "of bright fame"; *Roger*, "famous for the spear"; *Siegfried*, "victorious in battle"; *William*, "may he be protected"; *Wulfstan*, "wolf stone"; *Wulfwig*, "wolf war," etc. Of course not all names were warlike; some, especially those for women, were even counter-belligerent, containing the syllable *Frith* (which might appear *Frig* or *Freya*) meaning "peace," and there were homey names, like *Win* and *Leof*, "friend" and "dear." With Christianity came an increasing use of *God*, as in *Godwin*, "friend of God," and *Godfrey*, "the peace of God." But the whole range of Germanic names does not lead us to assume that parents brought up their children to turn the other cheek.[10]

Then came Christianity. The old names were not entirely abandoned; *Robert* and *William* are still popular, but once Englishmen were well and thoroughly converted, parents turned more and more to the Bible, the saints, and the Church Fathers for the names they bestowed. These included *John*, "God is gracious"; *James*, a Latin form of *Jacob*, which meant "he supplanted," supposedly from the biblical story; *Matthew*, "gift of God"; *Adam*, "a human being"; *George*, "farm worker"; *Andrew*, "manly"; and *Anthony*, a Latin family name of unknown origin. Even relatively rare biblical names were picked up, like *Ebenezer*, "stone of help," and *Hezekiah*, "God helps." Likewise, names for women came from the Bible or from female saints: *Dorothy*, "gift of God"; *Catherine*, "pure," "chaste"; and *Elizabeth*, "God is my oath." *Mary* appears in dozens of forms: *Maria, May, Marion, Mae, Marietta,*

---

10. We should probably add that in actual English baptisms the origin of a name may have been obscured by time. When such names as *Wulfstan* were given, the parents were probably not thinking of wolf stones, and whoever named Bede may nor may not have known that *Beada* meant "proclaim," "announce." No doubt children were named for fathers, mothers, and other relatives, but the naming tradition reflects a tough, fighting heritage.

Marya, Maurya, Maureen, Miriam, Miriamne, Molly, and Polly.[11] Women have also been named for jewels *(Margarite, Opal, Pearl, Ruby)* and for flowers *(Rose, Lily, Tulip, Pansy)*, many of them from the Orient (but not all, *Daisy* being OE *daeges ege*, "eye of the day").

Names, especially biblical names, proliferated. Consider one that appears most commonly in English as *John*. The Hebrew *Yohanan* was composed of two elements. The first, *Yo-*, a suggestion of the holy word, not to be spoken, that is now written out as *Yahweh*, or *Jehovah*. This syllable is seen in many names from Hebrew—*Joseph, Josiah, Joab*, etc. The second element, *hanan*, means "he was gracious," the *he* referring to *Yo-*, as though one were to say "Yahweh, He was gracious."[12]

The name got into Greek through the Septuagint, representing both John the Baptist and the Apostle John, spelled *Iohannes*, into Latin as *Johannis, Iohannes, Ioannes, Joanis*, etc., and into Middle English with more spellings, *Ihos, Ywes, Iohs, Ihoes, Jehan, Jehanne, Iahs*. This may have blended with *Jacobus* to provide the pet name *Jack*, spelled also *Jacks, Jax, Jaques, Jaqueeze*, etc.

From Greek and Latin the name has spread into dozens of languages in hundreds of shapes, including diminutives like *Janson, Johnny*, and *Jenkins*, and feminine equivalents such as *Jeanne, Joan, Joanna, Juanita*, and *Hannah*. Many spellings are not readily recognizable to a speaker of English: *Jean*, French; *Jão*, Portuguese; *Jan*, Dutch; *Johan, Jon*, Scandinavian; *Hans*, German; *Juan*, Spanish; *Giovanni*, Italian; *Ivan*, Russian; *Sean* and *Shane*, Irish; *Ian, Iain*, and *Eoin*, Gaelic; *Ieuan, Ifor, Evan*, and *Evans*, Welsh. Any of these names can crop up anywhere brought by a migrant or given to his offspring, or they may make their way inexplicably; *Ivan* has become a moderately popular name in American families that have no Russian connections.

But once a shape is established, especially if it is the form for a popular word, many things happen to it, as they did to *John* and its alter ego *Jack*. The names became patronymics, *John* and *Johns*, *Jack* and *Jacks*, *Jones* and *Johannes*, to which *-son* was added, with various spellings, *Johnson, Johnston* (which may also come from John's Town), *Jonson, Jensen, Jansen* (with possible influence from other languages),

---

11. Curiously, the word seems to mean "in revolt," but doubtless pious parents did not know this; to them, *Mary* in any variety of sound or spelling was the Mother of God.

12. Until we have had a look at phonetics or phonemics, explaining what happened to these two sounds would become onerous. Suffice it to say that they had several pronunciations in Hebrew and acquired more as they found their way into various languages.

Jackson, Jaxson, Johansson, and the like. The word became derivative names, or parts of them: *Hans* can be any German or Dutchman, *Ivan* any Russian, *John Doe* any unknown person. *John Bull* is the cartoon of England and *Johnny Reb* was the Union name for a Confederate soldier. A *Johnny* was a Chinese, a Navaho, or a Portuguese coin. These half-proper names gave way to common nouns, such as *johnnycake*, which is corn bread. The currently popular term for a toilet in the United States is a *john*, a curious recurrence, since to the Elizabethans an outdoor toilet was a *jakes*, another spelling and pronunciation of *jacks*.

Jack has been fruitful in slang and other homey terms, partly because it inherited derivatives from Jacob and James as well as John. A workman can address any fellow worker whose name he does not know as *Jack*—"Hey, Jack, toss me the pliers, will you?" The term is used variously for men, as a general term, for groups as in *lumber jack* and *jack tar*, in phrases and compounds as in *Jack of all trades, Jackanapes, jack gentleman, every man jack of them*, and for almost anything that does the job of a man, especially a hoist, which has led to verbs like *jack up*, which can mean "to raise" or "to rebuke." It can be any kind of helper—*bootjack, jack leg, jack rafter*. Either a four-footed or a foolish two-footed creature can be a *jackass* and can be guilty of *jackassism*. *Jacks* are the bowers in playing cards, or six-pointed pieces of metal in children's games. The *Century Dictionary* distinguishes more than twenty uses of *jack* and more than a hundred compounds, from *Buffalo-jack*, a fish, to *Jackweight*, a fat man. *Jack rabbits, jack oak, Union jack, jack plane, jack-pot* (leading to *hit the jack-pot*), *jackknife, jack lantern, jack-in-the-pulpit*, and many more are enduring parts of the language. And, unfortunately, at this writing *hijacking* would seem to be on the increase.

6. "Ekenames," Including Surnames

Ekename, a Middle English word that means an "also-name," became Modern English *nickname*, but these added epithets include more than what are now called nicknames (surname had the same origin through French). People in the European tradition and many others formerly had only one name. Within a family that was enough to keep the various members identified.

As people multiplied, one name was not enough. In Rome, Virgil was *Publius Vergilius Maro*, but throughout most of the first Christian millennium few persons in northern Europe had more than one name, although the practice of more than one name was beginning for very important individuals—*Charlemagne* is the equivalent of *Carlus Magnus*, Charles the Great. Various rulers were called *the Bald, the Fat, the Stupid*, and one female ruler was named *Bertha Bigfoot*. The practice grew slowly during the Middle Ages; for centuries ordinary folk had only one name, and even as late as 1600, as anyone who examines Shakespeare's First Folio may notice, few of the characters need a second name to identify them.[13]

In England, as in most countries, no deliberate policy was set up to provide more names, but there were at least four ready ways to acquire an also-name in English: (1) names from a given first name, (2) nicknames, from a characteristic, (3) names from an occupation or station in life, and (4) names from places and things.

1) *Names from a given name.* Such names suggest the classical definition, in which an object is put in a class and identified in that class: a square is a plane figure (generic term) having four equal sides (specification). In proper names of this sort, the individual is put into a class, his family, and identified in that class. A man named John has a son named George, who accordingly becomes *George, John's Son*. Eventually *John's Son* becomes fixed as *Johnson*—however one spells it. Or he can be referred to as *George* [one of the] *Johns*, and becomes *George Johns*.

The system is infinitely expandable, and most of the resulting surnames

---

13. Following is the cast of characters for *The Tempest:*

Alonso, King of Naples
Sebastian, his brother
Prospero, the right Duke of Millaine
Antonio, his brother, the usurping Duke
Ferdinand, Son to the King of Naples
Gonzalo, an honest old Councellor
Adrian, and Francisco, Lords
Caliban, a saluage and deformed slaue
Trincolo, a Iester
Stephano, a drunken Butler
Master of a Ship
Boate-Swaine
Marriners
Miranda, daughter to Prospero
Ariell, an ayrie spirit

An ordinary person such as the "Master of a Ship" has no name at all; important people like lords and the "honest old Councellor" have only one name apiece, although men of such station would have had second names that could be used in official documents like deeds and wills.

are obvious enough. We have already noticed *Johnson* and *Jackson*, however spelled. Others include: *Wilson* (Will's Son); *Jamison* (James' Son); *Richardson* (or *Dickson, Dixon*); *Larson,* Lars' Son (with *Larsen* for Danes and Norwegians); *Carlson, Fredrikson.* There are variations; in Gaelic *mac* (often reduced to *mc*) means "son," producing *MacMillan, McMillan,* or *Macmillan.* Similarly, in Welsh *ap-* means "son of," which before a voiced sound could become *ab. Applethwaite* is made up of *ap,* "son of," plus *le,* "the," plus *thwaite,* meaning "farm" or "village," which could have various spellings as pronunciations reflected in *Applewhite, Ablewhite,* or *Applewaite.* The initial vowel may be lost, leaving only the consonant /p/ or /b/, so that *ap Rhys* becomes *Price, ab Evan* becomes *Bevan, ab Owen* becomes *Bowen,* and since vowels can vary, too, *ap John* becomes *Upjohn.* In Norman French and Anglo-Norman "son of" could be *Fitz* (Modern French *fils*), producing *Fitzwilliam, Fitzjohn, Fitzwalter* or *Fitzwater,* or *Fitzmaurice. Fitzroy* ("son of the king," *le Roi*) could identify a bastard, but need not, since a father could become *Roy* in all sorts of ways, including working in the royal household or acquiring what has been called a "pageant name," playing the part of the king in local theatricals.

Most surnames descended in the male line, but not all of them. *Matilda,* the name of William the Conqueror's queen, was widely adopted as a given name, and as a surname became *Maude, Mald, Malt, Mold* or *Mould(s), Molt, Moulton, Mawson, Mawhood,* and a dozen more, with pet names *Till(e), Tills, Tilson, Tillett, Tillotson,* and the like. *Alice* has provided *Aalis, Aliz, Allies, Hallis, Alison, Hallison,* etc. *Mable,* a shortening of *Amable* (Latin *amabilis,* "lovable") survives in *Anabel, Hannibal, Honneybell, Mably, Mobley, Mabs, Madbutt,* and *Mabson,* although the spellings vary. No doubt some of these names derive from bastards—fatherless children were not uncommon in the Middle Ages— but others were the children of widows, or even of dominant wives. Not all husbands were good providers, a fact testified by such names as *Geoffrey Liggebibefyre* (Lie by the fire) and *Henry Lenealday* (Lean all day).

Of course names could change, as all words do, notably by being cut down. *Andrew* became *Drew, Alexander* became *Sanders.* Principles of language change worked here as elsewhere; Hebraic *mikha'el,* "Who is like God," three syllables; in English *Michael,* two syllables, or even one syllable, *Mike.* The *k*-sound was voiced in some language, giving *Miguel;* it became a continued sound in French, *Michel.*

2) *Nicknames.* Children still call one another *Red, Skinny, Fatso,* and

Curly. The practice gives us *Brown* or *Brun, Black, White, Gray* or *Grey, Red* along with *Read* and *Reid* at least in many names (though probably not *Green* which is more likely to name a place), *Frost, Snow, Bright,* and the like. Other characteristics appear in *Lange, Long, Longfellow, Longmans (Tall* is rare); *Short, Bones* or *Baines, Strong, Strang,* or *Armstrong; Smalle* or *Petty* (French *petite); Sharp(e), Keen* or *Keane, Wise* or *Sage, Hardy* or *Harding, Wild(e)* or *Savage, Turnpenny, Scattergood, Doolittle,* or *Drinkall.* Some nicknames may involve comparisons; "strong as an ox" becomes *Ochs,* and *Fox, Bird* or *Byrd, Crane,* and *Wolf* may reflect old metaphors. Many sources are not immediately recognizable: *Cruikshank(s)* in Scottish is "lame," *Fairfax* is "fair-haired," *Ballard* is "baldheaded," *Skeat* is Old Norse "swift," *Storey* from Old Norse "strong," *Cory* is probably Old Norse "curly," and *Lloyd* is "grey" in Welsh. Names like *Firebrace* and *Farbrace* are presumably Anglo-Norman *Bras de Fer,* meaning "arm of iron." *Maine, Mayne,* and the like, from French *main,* "hand," or *main* meaning "strength," appear in various combinations. *Harfoot* is presumably from *Harefoot,* a Norseman who could run like a rabbit. Even the town bum might acquire the surname *Baron* if he was thought to be "proud as a baron," and men apparently got the name *Nun* or *Nonne,* from "demure as a nun."

3) *Names by Occupation.* If two tradesmen have shops on the same street, how better to keep them apart than by calling one John the Tailor and the other John the Baker? They may then become *John Taylor* and *John Baker* or *Baxster.* Many such names have obvious origins: *Smith* or *Smythe* (also *Goldsmith, Silversmith, Blacksmith,* named for the color of the metal he worked with, along with *Whitesmith* for a worker in silver, *Redsmith* for a worker in gold); *Miller, Wright, Wheelwright; Dyer, Brewer* or *Brewster; Weaver, Web, Webber,* or *Webster; Forrester* or *Forster; Butcher, Sawyer, Cook, Clerk, Merchant, Potter, Spicer,* and dozens more. Agriculture supplied names like *Farmer* and *Herder,* with variants like *Coward,* "cow herd," *Goddard,* "goat herd," *Calvert,* "calf herd," *Gozzett,* "goose herd," *Hoggard,* "keeper of hogs," *Lambert,* "lamb herd," and so on.

Some names are obscure because they represent unfamiliar occupations; society no longer supports *Chandlers,* "maker of candles," nor *Fletchers,* "arrowmakers." A *Fuller* softened cloth by pounding it, a *Walker* by tramping it. A *Wader, Wademan,* or *Wodeman* used the popular blue dye called *wad* and a *Corker* worked with purple dye. Obsolete terms for cobblers have given us *Cordewainer, Corwin, Cordon,* along with *Souter, Suiter, Sewter,* etc. for a blacksmith. Some names for familiar trades are strange because they appeared in French: *Offer* and *Officer* from *orfevre*, "goldsmith"; *Flann* and *Flawn* from a baker of custards; *Whittier* and *Whitehaird*, for a dresser of white leather; *Habbishaw* from a maker of hauberks; *Harbisher*, an innkeeper, from Old French *herbergeor; Maskery*, a butcher, related to Modern English *massacre*. Old French *ferreor* (Latin *ferrum*, "iron") could be applied to a blacksmith or to any other worker in iron. Thus arose *Ferrer, Ferrier, Farrar, Farrah*, and *Farrey*. After French ceased to be widely known in England, these names were occasionally changed by folk etymology to something that would seem to make sense, such as *Faro, Farrow, Furrier*, and even *Pharaoh*, however improbable it may have been that Egyptian potentates had descendants in England.[14]

4) *Names from places and things.* The largest body of linguistic shapes among surnames come from the terms for places, places where people lived or places they had come from. Any place name can become a surname. Names like *Hill, Field, Lane, Bank, Street, House, Meadow(s), Forest, Wood(s)*, and dozens more are what remain of geographically descriptive phrases, "on the hill," "from the river bank," or "in the meadows." Such terms with or without the preposition could be in French: *Duville*, "from town"; *Duffield*, "from the country"; *Duchemin*, "from" or "living on the highway." Or they could be wholly or in part from Old Norse; *by*, a Scandinavian term for an inhabited place, enters into dozens of names, as in *Ashby*, "place where ash trees grow," *Willoughby*, "village among the willows." Names from flora and fauna may or may not be remnants; *Bear* could suggest "strong as a bear" or be all that remains of *Bear Mountain*. Names including *ham* may be Norse: *Hamm, Hampton, Hammond, Hamilton*, although such names may also have come from Old French or OE.[15]

---

14. Names reflecting an exalted station in life need not always be taken at face value. Alexander Pope need not have had a bastard eponymous ancestor just because popes could not marry; his forebear need only have represented a pope or suggested one. Some laymen acquired the sobriquet *Pope* or *Cardinal* by acting the part of an ecclesiastic in a pageant or a Corpus Christi play. Obviously not everybody who bears the name *King* has descended from royalty. One whose name is *Lord* may come from one of the nobility, or the name may derive from a forebear who was thought of as "the Lord's man." Similarly, *Earl, Duke, Baron, Barnet* or *Baronet, Knight*, and even *Squire* may represent a humble as well as a socially distinguished origin. Theoretically, a clerk *(Clerk, Clark, Clarke)* was a learned man, about the equivalent of the modern holder of a Ph.D. degree, but popularly men were called *clerk* if they could read.

15. We have seen above that the Celts gave names to many places, which could, of course, become surnames: *Dun* or *Donne, Ben, Penn, Esk, Inverness, Abernathy*, and

Some confusions are natural. *John English* or *England* is likely *not* to be living in England when he gets his surname. If he lives there with thousands of other Englishmen, why call him that? He is likely to have been living in Wales or Ireland, or some such place, if he is called *John the English(man)* or *John from England.* Likewise, *Dane, French, France, Irish, Scot, Lombard, Portugal*—which could become *Portergill, Puttergill, Pettingill, Pettingale,* etc.—are likely to identify persons thought of as "foreign." And there can be other connections; *York* may stem from a Duke of York who never had lived there. Place names may be indistinguishable from occupational names; *Bridge, Bridger,* and *Dupont* (French for "from the bridge" or "of the bridge") may stem from either somebody who took tolls at a bridge or a family that lived near a bridge.

In passing we should note that in place names we are dealing with at least three bodies of vocabulary. Epithets for places have become names of persons, and we have noted also (see *John* above) that once a linguistic shape becomes attached to a human being almost anything can happen to it. Furthermore, place names are proper nouns in their own right. They readily become more than names and they attract emotions; Americans have died for *America* and Japanese for *Nippon,* and the name stands in part for the homeland. A place name can become other than a proper noun: to *Londonize* gets into dictionaries as a word for turning provincials to city ways, and *London,* with or without the capital, can be a modifier. A *London plane* can be a tree as well as an airplane; *London pride* or a *London tuft* can be any of several sorts of flowers, and *London ivy* was smog long before the blend *smog* was contrived. *Londonese* is a term for Cockney. Every American knows such terms as *Boston baked beans, Philadelphia lawyer,* and *Hollywood star.*

7. Names from Other Peoples

The four different sorts of personal names can be brought by immigrants, whose names may or may not be readily interpreted by English-speaking people. The commonest is no doubt *Schmidt,* the German equivalent of *Smith,* with various combinations, especially through Yiddish, *Goldschmidt, Silberschmidt.* The number is endless: *Stark,* from

---

many more. Celtic syllables are estimated to occur in some eighty percent of all place names in Ireland, Cornwall, Scotland, and the outlying islands, and most western England counties preserve a good smattering of Celtic in the water and mountain names.

German "strong," *Weiss* from German "white," *Roosevelt* from Dutch "rose field," *Romano* from either Italian or Spanish, *Blanc, Blanco, Blanche,* from various Romance terms for "white." The name of the explorer *Champlain* is roughly the equivalent of *Field.* Many names from other tongues were perverted into something that looked or sounded like English: German *Bauer,* a farm worker or a builder, became English *Bower,* a maker of bows. Many were translated by their bearers; the psychologist *Seashore* bore a name translated from Swedish *Sjöstrand;* many a *Schneider* became English *Taylor.* Words for common occupations appear in many forms: *Miller* is paralleled by *Moeller, Moller, Muller, Müller, Möller,* by Romance *Molinari, Moulin, Molino,* etc.; *Belinni, Bilini,* etc. from Russian and Polish; along with variations from English dialects producing *Milne* and *Milner.*

8. Common Nouns: Naming by Compounding

The commonest words in the language are names for things—common nouns. Run down a page of any dictionary of English and you will find that the nouns exceed all other parts of speech. English vocabulary is growing very rapidly in our time, and as will become apparent, we are not only making new nouns but finding new uses for old nouns. Students of language used to believe that nouns were the earliest words, but that theory no longer looks plausible. At any rate, the ability to give names to things is so old that many common objects were named long before any speech existed that we can call English. One body of naming, having occurred within recent centuries, is so notable that it cannot be ignored, namely the dialects that sprang up in the English colonies, notably in Australia and North America.

The explorers and early settlers of these lands found a world vastly different from what they or their ancestors had known. North America was a whole continent full of running, flying, swimming, crawling, and creeping creatures who lived in a geographical terrain that often showed little resemblance to the tight little island the colonists had left. The very grass and weeds were strange enough to produce a veritable binge of naming.

Some terms were picked up more or less intact from the aborigines; *moose* is not much changed from an Indian word meaning "he strips off," referring to the animal's practice of pulling off moss and bark for food; *quahog* is a relatively accurate reproduction of Pequot *p'quaughhaug,* meaning "hard clam." Other terms fared worse; *wood-*

chuck comes by folk etymology from Algonquian *wejak,* which probably meant "the fisher." Similarly, *chipmunk,* from *atchitamon,* means "head first," a description of the way the squirrel-like animal descends tree trunks.

Most of the new terms, however, were new compounds made of English words, most notably a noun preceded by one or more adjectives, or by nouns used as modifiers. The reason is obvious. The newcomers saw a creature that resembled a relative of the same species they had known in the old country; they used the same generic term, but added some qualifier to describe the creature's appearance or habits. The practice was begun as early as Captain John Smith, who wrote, "There are Beares . . . Musk[r]ats and wild beasts vnknowne." The latter term was amplified by another writer in the same century, "Musk-rats in all things shaped like our Water-rats, only something larger, and is an absolute species of Water-rats, only having a curious musky Scent." Likewise a *grizzly bear* was obviously a bear, a creature well known in Europe, where bears were white, black, or brown. The new American brute was called *mountain bear, cinnamon bear, silver-tipped bear,* or most commonly *grizzly bear* and eventually just *grizzly,* no doubt from the meaning "gray-haired" (Old French *gris,* "gray"), probably augmented by *grisly,* meaning "horrible," since the *grizzly* was known for its ferocity.

As the population expanded, so did the compounds. When President Jefferson dispatched Lewis and Clark to explore the newly acquired Louisiana Territory, he urged them to keep records of all new phenomena; and they did, zealously describing the plants and wild life, trying to learn their native names and giving names of their own. The result was hundreds of compounds added to the language. Meanwhile compounds developed as settlers lived with these evidences of a strange world, and eventually names were given to newly identified species.[16]

16. Following is the list of flies given in the *Dictionary of Americanisms:* bar fly, bee fly, black fly, blowing fly, bluetail fly, buck fly, buffalo fly, burning fly, caribou fly, carpet fly, cattle fly, chin fly, cow fly, deer fly, dog day harvest fly, drove fly, dry weather fly, ear fly, Englishman's fly, fair fly, foul fly, green fly, harvest fly, heel fly, Hessian fly, horn fly, horse fly, human fly, jar fly, Mexican fruit fly, May fly, moose fly, Mormon fly, mountain fly, mow fly, pea fly, plantation fly, pop fly, potato fly, prairie fly, salt marsh fly, screw fly, screw worm fly, shad fly, shoo fly, spittle fly, stable fly, swamp fly, sweat fly, tail fly, tobacco fly, Webster fly, wheat fly, white man's fly.

CHAPTER III

THE ROOTS OF ENGLISH
Proto-Indo-European

What is artificial in Indo-European linguistics is the conception of the root . . . . It is not asserted that the root existed as such, but only that it is the meeting point of all the inferences that can be made from a family of words.

— William J. Entwistle

1. Triangulation in Language

Here are various words referring to a female parent: *mother, modor, Mutter, mater, meter, mathir, matar, mote, muti, mathi, tamesu, dama.* The first ten have much in common. They have two syllables, the first beginning with a sound here spelled *m*, the second with a consonant associated with spellings like *t*, *d*, or *f*, and closing with a vowel or a semivowel like *r*. This is too much consistency to be accident. The geographical spread of these terms is suggestive; all come from European languages. The last two come from Africa, and if you recognize that the sounds for *t* and *d* are related phonetically, and that *-su* is probably only an ending, *tamesu* and *dama* are similar. It is then possible to construct a diagram like the following—

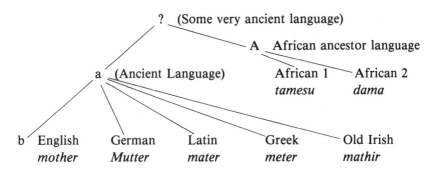

45

Thousands of other words show patterns similar to that for *mother* and its relatives, and we have evidence of this from historic times. We know that soldiers and traders carried Latin east, north, and west, and we can trace the resulting change of Vulgar Latin into modern French, Spanish, Portuguese, Italian, and Romanian. Similarly, we know that the descendants of peoples who spoke Old Norse now speak Danish, Swedish, Norwegian, and Icelandic. Russian and Polish grew from an earlier language known as Old Slavic. Modern Indic can be traced from ancient Sanskrit. We can in part prove and in part logically infer that descent accounts for much in the shape and spread of languages, as it accounts for much in the forms and distribution of plants and animals.

The notion of evolution is old—in language as well as in plants and animals. So far as language was concerned, there was evidence of descent rather comparable to that apparent in children, parents, and grand-parents. All educated west Europeans knew Latin and knew, or knew of, at least one language that had descended from it. Englishmen knew that their language had developed in an orderly way from Old English, to Middle English, to Modern English. Manuscripts established all this beyond doubt. That is, there was a strong suggestion that just as all men were supposed to have descended from Adam and Eve, all languages had descended from the language Adam and Eve talked. But there was a problem; any German could recognize a modern Greek as a human being, but no German could recognize the modern Greek tongue as anything but gibberish until he had learned it.

The key came from Sir William Jones as much as from anyone. He was a civil servant in India, having gone there in 1783, where he studied Sanskrit. He already knew Latin, Greek, and a number of other tongues. He noticed such similarities as the following:

Modern English	Classical Latin	Classical Greek	Sanskrit
two	duo	duo	dva
three	tres	treis	trayas
nine	novem	ennea	nava
ten	decem	deka	dasa

This did not look like accident, particularly since any student of language knows that the sounds here suggested by *t, th,* and *d* are closely related. The more Jones compared the older forms of language, along with scattered modern survivals, the more he became convinced that such similarities could be accounted for only by a common ancestor. He surmised that if a scholar went back to the state of languages a couple of thousand years ago, he would find likenesses that had been obscured in the multitude of modern forms, forms that had changed enough to blur the common pattern.

We might put this in another way. We have several Romance languages, such as French and Spanish. We could reconstruct their ancestor; we need only recognize that if a word or sound or anything else appears in all or most Romance languages, it must have been in the parent tongue, Latin. If it occurs in few or none of the Romance languages, it probably was not in the parent. Each of these Romance languages has grown in its own way; as soon as we have a moderate number of examples of descent, we can begin to describe how Latin changed in certain ways to become French and in other ways to become Spanish. Then, if we work back and forth, from modern to ancient, and from ancient back to modern, we can describe the parent language in detail. For example, we know that the modern French word for horse is *cheval*, the Italian, *cavallo*, and the Spanish *caball*. These are very similar, since we know that French regularly has *ch* where *c* occurs in other Romance languages, and the *b* of Spanish is here pronounced about like *v* in many tongues. If you know Classical Latin, you may object, saying that these words do not look like the word for horse, *equus*, found in such writers as Caesar and Pliny. This is true, but there was another Latin word for a horse, *caballus*, a term not common in classical writing, but the regular term used by the people, by the soldiers and traders who carried Latin to other parts of Europe. Obviously, *caballus* is the ancestor of the Romance terms for a horse. That is, by triangulation we can reconstruct Latin; we can even in this instance identify the dialect of the Latin word from which the Romance words sprang. And, of course, we have Vulgar Latin manuscripts to prove that our reconstruction and our method of working are correct.

2. The Great-Grandmother Language: Proto-Indo-European (PIE)

This reconstruction was more complicated than I am making it seem, but the method was so obvious and the first steps so successful that the hunt was taken up by hundreds of scholars in many lands. The result was the great triumph of the nineteenth century in language study. The linguistic students of the day—*philologists*, "lovers of language"—were able to reconstruct a parent speech, used somewhere in central or south-eastern Europe as early as about 3500 B.C.[1] This language is the ancestor of most languages now spoken in Europe and of some other tongues in Asia. This great-grandmother language is called Proto-Indo-European (referred to as PIE) and tongues descended from it are called Indo-European languages (IE). No word of PIE has survived in writing for the natural reason that script was not known at the time and in the area where PIE flourished.

History and archeology have revealed little about these people until very recently, although we have been able to identify their linguistic descendants all the way from Ireland to India. Because we have been able to reconstruct their vocabulary by the same methods as the Romance words for *horse*, we can infer the kind of life the Proto-Indo-Europeans lived. If their word stock included several words for grains and domestic animals, we can assume that some of them were farmers. The vocabulary they did not have is also revealing. The lack of a word or two might be only an accident, but if among hundreds of terms there is not one that refers to tropical fauna and flora we can assume that the users of the language did not live in the torrid zone. Accordingly, using the basic ideas involved in what are called PIE "roots" we can develop a consistent and tolerably detailed description.

The Proto-Indo-Europeans were hunters and fishers, learning simple agriculture in a temperate climate. They hunted bears, wolves, hares, badgers, and beavers, and their domesticated animals were hairy or woolly—sheep, cows, goats, pigs, horses—and accustomed to cold. They knew snow and ice, but they also knew forests, grasslands, even swamps, although not deserts. They ate grains, sowing rye, barley, and a seed that gives us the word *corn*, but no tropical fruits or vegetables, only the apple. They could weave cloth and sew and apparently wore belted garments. They knew gold, silver, copper, possibly bronze, but not iron —when the Celts and Germans got iron somewhat later it was known as the holy metal, probably because it was first obtained from meteorites. They caught salmon; they knew birds like eagles, sparrows, wood-peckers, starlings, and finches, and were interested in their eggs—probably for eating—but no parrots or flamingos. They had a kind of plow, probably triangular, but not until later the wheel; they apparently milked their mares before they learned to ride them. They built houses with mud,

---

1. This date is based on recent discoveries; see III,3. 3000 B.C. was formerly the standard guess.

probably daubed wattles, and probably also with wood, at least with something that had to be fitted together. They fortified the hilltops; *burg* and *town* derive from such fortified living. They were bothered by lice, mice, moths, and probably bedbugs, but we hear of no scorpions, iguanas, or boa constrictors. They ate eels and probably snakes, and they fermented honey to make an alcoholic drink, mead, a fact which associates them with southeastern Europe, since honeybees were formerly found only in a restricted area.

They had a patriarchal, deeply religious, and somewhat organized society. They had the ancestor of our word *king*, although he may have been no more than a tribal chief. The family was a large and important unit; brothers and sisters apparently included the people we would call cousins, aunts, and uncles. Wives went to live in the husband's household; one word served for both *bride* and *daughter-in-law*. The head of the household was both ruler and priest, and their religious ceremonies apparently included both preaching and musical incantations. They used ancestors of our words *justice* and *law*, and had terms for paying obligations. *Cattle*—the word then included pigs, goats, and other livestock—were thought of as movable wealth and led to the word *chattel*.

The Indo-Europeans, then, had a simple, tribal-based society. They were less sophisticated than peoples to the south, such as the Sumers and Akkads in the Tigris-Euphrates valley, the Egyptians along the Nile, and the Semites at the eastern side of the Mediterranean. But they were advanced enough to have some technology and to be grappling with simple ideas. Thus they developed a vocabulary of considerable range, a matter of some importance considering the pervading spread of IE language habits among speakers of English, French, Spanish, Portuguese, Italian, Greek, Latin, Indic, and many others.

PIE has thrust its tentacles all over the world. Languages that have sprung from it dominate all continents except Asia and Africa, and they are widely established there. Fortunately for us, the IE tongues comprise the best-known body of languages. *Samskrit*, Anglicized to "Sanskrit," means "well regulated." A holy tongue, as opposed to the Prakrits that were working dialects, it was carefully policed and preserved with remarkable purity from long before the Christian era. *Hittite* survives on hundreds of clay tablets that were long undecipherable, but the language is now known to come from PIE and can be read. Greek is richly represented; Latin, which dates from hundreds of years B.C., blends into the Romance tongues, thus providing nearly three thousand years of evidence, attested in thousands of manuscripts. Even OE survives in many manuscripts from the first millennium A.D., and Old High German and Old Norse are not much behind. Furthermore, the best-informed community of linguistic scholars in the world, without a close competitor, has come from within the IE family of languages, so that these bodies of speech have been recorded and studied as have no others. Users of English are lucky; their speech is part of the greatest network of language the world has known.

3. The Spread of IE Languages

So much we can infer from the internal evidence of the language itself, but we could make better use of this great-grandmother language if we could link it to the people who used it. Just recently a skein of discoveries all the way from Siberia to the Atlantic Ocean provides us with a plausible explanation.[2] The speakers of PIE were apparently natives of Siberia, known to archeologists as the Kurgan peoples. By 5000 B.C. they were moving south and probably west and had arrived in the vicinity of the Black and Caspian Seas by about 3500 B.C. They had been nomads, but were learning agriculture, and during their wanderings they had encountered speakers of a tongue related to theirs, who had learned the art of smelting copper into bronze. We know about the Kurgan peoples especially from burial mounds to the north of the Black Sea; these mounds gave the dwellers there the name we know them by, *kurgan* being the Turkish name for a fort—early investigators mistook the purpose of the mounds.

For the next thousand years or so these new arrivals must have prospered in the rich lands of southern Russia, for in the third millennium B.C. they were expanding in many directions, and these migrations continued for some time. The Kurgan peoples already had horses, tamed since their nomadic days; they had the hardest weapons in the world, apparently having introduced bronze into Europe. They had learned about the wheel and had developed war chariots and military tactics,

---

2. A thesis like this is sure to be fought over by scholars and, even if it is generally accepted, will be revised and elaborated. It is too important to be ignored, and since it seems sound to some of the best students of language, I shall treat it as though it will be in the main established. The published evidence is widely scattered, but two key articles are Marija Gimbutas, "The Beginning of the Bronze Age in Europe and the Indo-Europeans; 3500-2500 B.C.," *The Journal of Indo-European Studies*, 1 (1973), 163–214; by the same author, "The Indo-Europeans: Archeological Problems," *American Anthropologist*, 65 (1963), 815–836.

but archeologists attribute part of their success to their closely knit society with its interreliance on family, politics, and religion. They included the Hittites, who before 1750 B.C. had seized what is modern Anatolia and held it until they were in turn overrun by the Assyrians. They were the invaders we know as the Iranians, taking over what was later to become Persia. They broke into India, where they established Sanskrit as a language and themselves as the rulers of a subcontinent. They passed the Himalayas, where they survived long enough in the Gobi Desert to leave behind them at least two dialects of a language known as Tocharian.

Meanwhile, speakers of IE dialects were moving in other directions. More than one wave surged into the Balkan Peninsula; of them the Hellenes reached the Mediterranean Sea, where their tongue became Classical and then Modern Greek. Other IE speakers pushed past the Etruscan and other groups in the Italic peninsula and established themselves on the Tiber River, where Rome grew and whence the Romance languages spread through much of western Europe. We have already encountered the Celts as great namers of rivers; they were also ubiquitous invaders, overrunning territories previously seized by their relatives, ravaging the lands of the more northern Greeks, sacking Rome, penetrating to the uttermost western islands and to Land's End in what is now England, to the Cape of Finnisterre—which means "Land's End" in Spanish—in the Iberian Peninsula.[3] One extensive group, known as Teutons or Germans—to whom we shall return—moved west even to the Atlantic Ocean and as far north as the Arctic. Others, whom we know as Slavs, may not have moved much; we know them now as Russians and various Baltic and Adriatic peoples, but much of this territory may have been Kurgan even before the great period of PIE migrations.

Thus well before the Christian era, the descendants of one ancient language were spread over most of Europe and into Asia. One side effect of all this—surely not the most important, but powerful in the study of language—is this: many of the widespread languages, including English, have a common core in their descent from PIE. This common basis appears in the structure of IE languages, in their phonology, but perhaps especially in their vocabularies. Here we might notice what are called **cognates**. The term is from Latin, *co-gnatus*, made up of *together* and

---

3. We might notice here that by this time PIE was so fragmented that apparently neither the pillagers nor the pillaged recognized each other as members of the same linguistic family.

born. That is, terms like *work* in English, *organ* in Latin, and *erg* in Greek are called cognates, cousins if you will, "born together" because they descend from the same term in PIE. They each have changed so much in the thousands of years that have elapsed since Kurgan times that we can relate them only if we know something of language history and linguistic change, but we have here a very useful tool for understanding vocabulary, and even for learning it and learning to use it better.[4]

4. English Takes Shape: Common Germanic and Old English

The western migrants included peoples, Teutons or Germans, who older scholars assumed were among the last to leave from a supposed IE "heartland." That guess no longer seems likely, and recent discoveries suggest that they had reached the North Sea area before 2000 B.C. Their speech is different enough from all other IE languages that students have guessed they may have been a conquered people who learned PIE imperfectly. The term *Common Germanic* refers to the tongue of these migrants before they dispersed enough to provide the dialects that have sired the ancestors of English, German, Swedish, etc. One division of them, the Visigoths or Western Goths, went adventuring, got as far as North Africa, and set up a kingdom in what is now France and Spain—

4. It will probably have been noticed that I have made no attempt to date the various hegiras of IE speakers. The omission is deliberate. Scholars formerly believed in an IE "heartland," whence all migrations spread. Presumably the differences among IE tongues sprang in part from the language of these various migrants, and students assumed that much of the difference reflected differences in time. For example, scholars accepted as plausible the idea that the emigrants who took Sanskrit to India differed from the Germanic folk who took English to the western islands, because the Sanskrit speakers took with them an early stage of the mother language and the Germanic speakers took a later version of the same language.

Within limits, no doubt something of the sort did take place, but now the belief is that PIE itself was well-fragmented into dialects, and that differences between Sanskrit and OE reflect in part the differences between the dialects of the emigrants. In fact, scholars now believe that these dialects were sufficiently diverse so that they had their origins before PIE times, and the Kurgan thesis makes such an explanation the more plausible. The Kurgan peoples were an extensive, wide-ranging folk, and Sanskrit may be in part what it is because it reflects the dialect of the mound builders who lived for a time north of the Black Sea, whereas the Teutonic dialects may have come from northern Kurgan tribes that moved roughly west. At this writing, such questions are very much under study. Fortunately, although the replies will be intriguing and will help in vocabulary study, we can do very well with the central answer, that all IE languages are linked through their growth from a common ancestor, whether that ancestor is what we now call PIE or a still more remote pre-Indo-European body of speech somewhere in Siberia.

Burgos, the name of a city in Spain, is the same word as *-burg* in *Hamburg* and *-borough* in various English place names. Their relatives, the Ostrogoths, gave their name to Austria. We know something of Gothic because Bishop Ulfilas in the fourth century A.D. translated much of the Bible into his native tongue, and a manuscript of it has survived along with some other briefer pieces. Somewhat later, close relatives of the Visigoths moved into the Scandinavian Peninsula and became the speakers of Old Norse. They are important for our purposes, not only because both Gothic and Old Norse provide comparisons with English, but because these same peoples later overran much of England and Ireland and added to English vocabulary.[5]

The remaining dialects that descended from Proto-Germanic are now divided into two groups: those included in High German (the *high* referring to the high country north of the Alps) or South Germanic, from which modern German derives, and those called West Germanic or Coastal Germanic, from which several tongues descend, notably Dutch and English. Some of these Germanic speakers, the Franks, got far enough west to give their name to France, although they and the Celts they had overrun were in turn subdued by the Romans, IE speakers whom we have observed earlier establishing themselves in the Italic peninsula. In one of their conquests, soon after the opening of the Christian era, these Romans occupied a large island off the coast, often called Breoton, from the Brythonic Celts. Roman culture thrived there; the island today is dotted with the mosaic floors of their villas, and Roman columns have been dug from beneath modern English communities. Such wealth was tempting bait, and the seacoast Germans were not averse to harrying there as pirates.

The power of Rome declined, however, and as a minor echo of that widespread disaster, the English language was born. To keep off the pirates, the Romans had built a line of forts along the east coast of what is now England. As part of the attempt to stave off the fall of Rome, the garrisons of these forts were called home. When the Germanic freebooters found little resistance they moved in, a few at first, then in larger invasions. Apparently the first to establish themselves in numbers were the Jutes, who took over the southeastern tip of the island. They may

5. Germanic was formerly divided into North, East, South, and West, Gothic being known as East Germanic and Old Norse as the descendant of North Germanic. More recent Germanists tend to combine these two and attribute their differences to the dates of our evidence rather than to any regional distinction.

have come from the Frisian area; they were not, as was long supposed, from Jutland. The traditional date of their arrival is A.D. 449, but some Germanic invaders had come before that date, and the bulk of them came later. The Angles moved straight across the North Sea, seized the east coast and worked west; part of the Saxons (some remained to become Saxony in Germany) sailed around to the south and moved northeast. By A.D. 600 the two bodies of Germanic peoples were in firm control of the less mountainous parts of the main island.[6] We call their speech *Anglo-Saxon* or *Old English*. As a matter of course it existed in various dialects, some of which were brought with them by the invaders from the Continent; differences in dialect would have been accentuated and the speech further fragmented during the long centuries of relative isolation from the Continental Germanic peoples by the North Sea and the English Channel, as well as relative isolation from one another in an island heavily wooded and as yet but sparsely inhabited.

5. English and Its Ancestry

We can now identify some five stages in the growth of the English language, and specifically the English word stock. We might characterize them as follows:

Pre-Indo-European: A body of signs used by tailless primates was developed into a language at least as early as 35,000 B.C. (probably by 100,000 B.C., or even a million years earlier) which was so much more productive than signs that had never been organized into a working linguistic system that it spread rapidly throughout the world. Some late form of this once-universal language must have preceded PIE.

Proto-Indo-European (PIE): This is the oldest form of a collection of dialects that can now be reconstructed by triangulation. It thrived in what is now southern and southeastern Russia, probably farther north as well, presumably having come there with Kurgan peoples, earlier than 3500 B.C., perhaps by 5000 B.C. In succeeding millennia it spread through much of Europe and into parts of southern and southwestern Asia.

Common Germanic: Peoples known as Teutons or Germans brought IE dialects to northern Europe, probably before 2000 B.C., and expanded

---

6. The Celts and another set of invaders known as Picts continued to hold what are now Scotland, Wales, Ireland, Cornwall, and some smaller islands. For Pictish and other early languages spoken in the British Isles see W. B. Lockwood, *Languages of the British Isles Past and Present* (London: Deutsch, 1975).

vigorously both before and after the beginning of the Christian era. Their vocabulary was mainly from PIE, but they had added to it through their own experiences on their way west and north. The reconstructed stage of this speech, Common Germanic, reflects this body of language before it was much fragmented by dialect.

Old English (OE): Germanic-speaking peoples, mainly Angles and Saxons, brought dialects stemming from West or Coastal Germanic to the British Isles. This speech grew, largely from within, during some hundreds of years, c. A.D. 500—c. 1100.

Middle English, New English (ME, NE): As speakers of English learned to participate in European culture, and eventually to build a world empire and to sire new countries on other continents, the English vocabulary grew tremendously in both size and flexibility. ME dates c. 1100—c. 1500; NE dates c. 1500—the present; Current English is also called Present-Day English (PDE), and NE is often broken into Early Modern English (EME), 1500—1650, and Modern English (ModE), 1650—the present.

With that kind of ancestry, we need not be surprised that the core of the modern English vocabulary can be traced from PIE, and that some of its qualities can be best studied as the results of the long descent from this parental body of speech. Later we shall see that PIE has entered into English in other ways as well, but for the moment we might notice what has come through the line of natural descent.[7]

6. The Native English Vocabulary

Even a glance at a list of what I am calling "native"[8] terms, in contrast to those I would call nonnative, will suggest that the native terms include many of the commonest locutions in the language. In the most reliable frequency list as yet available,[9] the following are the first twenty-nine words:

the, of, and, to, a, in, that, is, was, he, for, it, with, as, his, on, be, at, by, I, this, had, not, are, but, from, or, have, an.

7. In addition to PIE and IE, I shall henceforth use the convenient symbols above, OE for Old English; ME for Middle English; NE for New English. I shall use PDE, Present-Day English, when I wish to refer exclusively to contemporary use.

8. As will probably be apparent, by "native" I mean a term that can be reconstructed as having come from PIE to Common Germanic to OE and thence to NE.

9. Various frequency lists have been prepared for English, but the best at this writing is Henry Kučera and W. Nelson Francis, *Computational Analysis of Present-Day Ameri-*

They are all native words, changed somewhat in shape and greatly in meaning and function—we shall have to note repeatedly that English words as we employ them have taken their use from their growth or decay within the direct stream of descent to PDE—but they all got started in PIE and they have a continuing history within the English language. They are all short words, of one syllable and one to four letters. They are all strong in grammatical uses, the sort of terms the language must have if it is to function. Some, like *of*, have little meaning, or such vague meaning that they almost defy definition, but most of them have many meanings (see the analysis of the lines of verse with which this book opened) and these meanings may be very potent. Consider what a word like *not* can do, or *in* as opposed to *out*.

Even after these first twenty-nine, most of the commoner words come to us by direct descent from PIE. The most common exception is *they* (number thirty), which comes from Old Norse, a language closely related to English. If we continue down the list we can notice that many of the hundred or so most common words are native, and the bulk of them are relationship words: prepositions and conjunctions, such as *over, about, where, into;* pronouns like *she, him, who;* common modifiers or determiners like *most, first, two;* along with a few much-used nouns, *house, night, world*, and some common verbs, *said, made, been.*[10] A few common words came through Latin: *people, states, school* (ultimately from Greek), *government*, and *system*. But with such nonnative loans the frequency has dropped from 69,971 for *the* and 36,411 for *of*, to 417 for *government* and 416 for *system*. Of course, these frequencies should not be taken as exact, but the difference between seventy thousand and four hundred cannot be written off. The great majority of the most common words in English come overwhelmingly from PIE by direct descent.[11]

---

can English (Providence, R.I.: Brown University Press, 1967). It is based on a well selected corpus, comprised of 1,014,232 items recognized as words, which subdivide into 50,406 distinguishable terms. Since the calculations are made by computer, these terms are shapes only. That is, no distinction is made between *can*, a noun, and *can*, a verb, nor between *ball* meaning "sphere" and *ball* meaning "a formal dance." The corpus is edited English; accordingly it is weak in slang and colloquial usage. Even so, the list is highly revealing.

10. As we noted above (see footnote 9) this list does not distinguish between nouns and verbs; many of these words have both functions in NE but did not in OE.

11. If slang terms and colloquialisms were included in this list, the percentages would favor native words even more strongly, because slang and colloquial uses employ mainly common terms, which tend to be native.

7. Cognates: Terms from the Relatives of English

Native words are not the only debt we owe to PIE. We have also *cognates*, terms which were "born together" with the English word since they, too, go back to PIE.

If we are to use these terms to their capacity, and understand the relationships between native words and their cognates—these two great bodies of English vocabulary—we must go into the sounds of language, or *phonology*. When Sir William Jones provided the key that unlocked the mysteries of word origins, he did so by studying the sounds of various tongues, and we shall need to survey the sort of evidence that intrigued him. Here are some of the comparisons (for the present, ignore the vowels in PIE):

English	Latin	PIE	English	Latin	PIE
father	pater	*peter	brother	frater	*bhrater
fish	pisces	*peisc-	mother	mater	*mater-
first	prime	*pr-	heart	cordis	*kerd-
five	pente	*penqwto-	he	cis	*ke-
fleet	ploion	*pleud-	tame	comare	*dom-
for	per	*per-	tooth	dentis	*dent- dont-
foot	pedis	*ped- *pod-	that	to	*tod-

Notice the three columns to the left. Each English word begins with /f/, a related Latin or Greek word begins with /p/, and the PIE root begins with /p/. Admittedly, I have selected these examples, but they are so numerous that I could easily have added hundreds, and I could have found but few roots beginning with /p/ that became anything but words with /p/ in Latin, Sanskrit, and many other tongues, and anything but /f/ in English and other Germanic languages. That is, a sound that has been reconstructed as /p/ in PIE can be expected to descend into Latin without much change but to have become /f/ in Common Germanic and to appear as /f/ in English and other Germanic tongues. Similarly, the three columns to the right reveal that /t/ in a PIE root is likely to appear unchanged in Latin but to become a sound spelled *th* in English, and that a /d/ in a PIE root will be but little changed in Latin but become /t/ in English. These patterns become the more potent when we observe that all these sounds stand in special relationships to one another. The sound /f/ is what we call the corresponding fricative of /p/; sounds spelled *th* are corresponding fricatives of /t/ and /d/. The stop /t/ is linguistically related to /d/, as the sound spelled in English *h* is to /k/, spelled *c* in Latin. That is, we are dealing here with systematic patterns, and in order to understand them we need to examine their sounds. (See the section **Phonemic Symbols** on page 295).

8. Phonetics and Phonemics: the Consonants of English

Consider the sound /p/. To make it you have only to close your lips, let the column of air from your lungs build up a little pressure, and open your lips suddenly. It can be called a **stop**, because you stopped the air to make it, or a **plosive**, because the result was a small explosion. Such a plosive may seem to be instantaneous, as though it were a point of sound, but it is not. It is a spread of sound as you can readily demonstrate by saying firmly *put, up*, and *upper*. You will have pronounced /p/ in three distinct ways. You probably started *put* with an explosion forceful enough so that it disturbed the whole upper lip; the flow of air would be narrowed and the sound blended into the succeeding vowel. When you said *up*, the explosion was accompanied by less air, and the sound stopped quickly because your lower jaw dropped as part of the action of opening the lips. In *upper* the /p/ was probably a shorter, higher, and sharper sound and was accompanied by very little air. And if you will now make a /p/ as the sound of an isolated letter *p*, you will produce a further variation.

For most speakers of English there are at least four sounds associated with the spelling *p*, depending on whether the sound is initial, terminal, medial, or isolated. If we were trying to record the /p/ sound with even approximate accuracy, we should need four symbols, each of which would be a unit in phonetics. More than five hundred symbols have been officially recognized; they constitute the International Phonetic Alphabet, IPA. I shall not use this system much in this book, for it is more cumbersome than need be for our limited purposes. Instead, I shall recognize that native speakers of English think of all these utterances associated with the letter *p* as one sound. That sound I shall call a **phoneme** and distinguish it from the spelling by writing the symbol within slash lines: /p/.[12]

12. For a definition of a phoneme see John Lyons, *Introduction to Theoretical Linguistics* (Cambridge: Cambridge University Press, 1968), pp. 100–101; 112–123. As a

The phoneme /p/, then, is made by closing the lips and opening them suddenly. Our ancestors made the phoneme /t/ by stopping the air with the tongue placed against the teeth, but you probably make it by putting the tip or the blade of your tongue on the alveolar ridge, just back of the teeth. You probably make /k/ by stopping air with your contracted tongue, thrusting it against the soft palate, about halfway back in your mouth. Stops can also be made still farther back, in the area of the glottis and pharynx. Amerindian languages used glottal stops, made by closing the glottis; several African languages use glottal clicks, and PIE had a versatile collection of sounds known as *laryngeals*. Glottal stops can be heard regionally in PDE; in an area centering on Connecticut and in some parts of London and East Anglia many speakers will say *bottle* as though it were spelled *bah-ul*. But in general, stops made back of the hard palate are not characteristic of English nor of the IE languages from which English has borrowed much. Accordingly, we might think of /p/, /t/, and /k/ as the basic consonantal sounds in English, made by stopping the column of air at three of the four natural areas but doing nothing else to it.

Several things can be done, not all of them used in any one language. We might vary the amount of breath we emit in a sound. We use this device, as we have seen, in the difference between initial /p/ and medial /p/. We use it, also, to speak more or less emphatically. But we do not give it phonemic value; that is, we do not use it to distinguish one phoneme from another.[13] We do use other devices. Instead of stopping the sound completely, we can almost stop it, so that the air comes through with a buzzing or whistling sound. Such consonants are called **fricatives**. The sound made at the lips is /f/ (sometimes made with both lips, but in NE mainly the lower lip and the upper teeth). It is called the corresponding fricative of /p/, and /p/ the corresponding stop of /f/. The corresponding fricative of /t/ is the initial sound in *think*, in phonemics the Greek letter *theta*, /θ/. The fricative corresponding to /k/ has mostly

---

working definition, however, a native speaker of English can assume that the phoneme /p/ includes whatever sounds he would make for the letter *p*, the phoneme /t/ is whatever sounds he would associate with the spelling *t*, and so on. The vowel phonemes (see Chapter VII.1) are somewhat more complicated.

13. In some languages aspirated /p/, a stop followed by strong breath, which we might write /pʰ/, is a different phoneme from unaspirated /p/, but not in English. The first known form of the language that has become English did use aspiration for phonemic distinctions, and this device survived in Sanskrit, but speakers in the English line of descent have not used this device for thousands of years.

been lost in NE; it is a sort of continued k-sound, as though it were written k-h-k-h-k-h. In this book I shall write /x/; it is the sound used by some Scotsmen in *loch*, the sound of *ich* in standard German.[14] This /x/ sometimes lost its fricative quality and became merely strong aspiration, written /h/, and much the same thing could happen to /k/, which regularly became /h/ or a consonant we shall mention below as /č/ (as in English *church* which was formerly pronounced like Scottish *kirk*). Air can also be restricted by directing it at the teeth; a narrow stream of air produces /s/, a somewhat broader one the sound spelled *sh*, in phonemics /š/.

We can vary consonants by voicing them. The larynx, popularly called the voice box, is an assemblage of bone, cartilage, muscles, and fibers that serves as a gateway to direct incoming air to the lungs and food and liquids to the stomach. But outgoing air passes through it likewise, and if the membranes are only partially closed they will vibrate, imparting a thready or low, rumbling quality to any sound being made at the time. This **voicing** can be heard by putting your fingers in your ears and saying alternately /f/ and /v/. The rumbling will start with the /v/ and cut off with the /f/. All vowels are voiced, and in English some consonants are also. Following are the equivalents: voiceless /p/, voiced /b/; voiceless /t/, voiced /d/; voiceless /k/, voiced /g/; voiceless /f/, voiced /v/; voiceless /θ/, voiced /ð/ as in *this;* voiceless /s/, voiced /z/; voiceless /š/, voiced /ž/, as in *measure*. If this is new to you, you will do well to run through the sounds right now to see how they work, putting your fingers in your ears and noticing how the thready sound cuts on and off with the voicing.

We can also **nasalize** sounds. To do this, the epiglottis flips down, preventing the air from entering the mouth and allowing it to vibrate in the nose. Since the vibrating column is voiced, it produces a humming sound. A nasal consonant stopped at the lips will produce /m/. That is, /m/ is the nasal corresponding to /p/ and /b/. The nasal corresponding to /t/ and /d/ is /n/, that corresponding to /k/ and /g/ is /ŋ/, the terminal sound in *thing* and the sound immediately before /k/ in *think*. We might note in passing that the difference between /n/and /ŋ/ is not that /n/ results from "dropping a *g*." This may be true of attempts to suggest dialect in spellings, as in "I ain't goin'," but it is not true of sound. The symbols /n/ and /ŋ/ are separate phonemes, made in differ-

---

14. The Greek letter *chi* /χ/ is often used to represent this sound.

ent ways, with stoppage at different points in the mouth, each having its own legitimate use, as do all phonemes. *Thing* is not pronounced /θ/ /i/ /n/ /g/; it is pronounced /θ/ /i/ /ŋ/. The sound /ŋ/ is a nasal formed with the tongue spread out against the soft palate, whereas the nasal /n/ is made with the tongue farther forward, generally for American speakers against the alveolar ridge, just back of the teeth.

Then there are a few oddities. At least two sounds, called **affricates**, seem to start as plosives and become fricatives. The voiceless form is heard in both consonants in *church;* in phonetics this sound is often written [tʃ], but in phonemics usually /č/.[15] The voiced equivalent, heard in *judge,* is usually written /dʒ/ or /ǰ/. Two sounds, sometimes called **glides** or **liquids**, are variously made by impeding the air toward the center of the mouth; the phonemic symbols are the spelling symbols put between slant lines, /l/ and /r/. Two sounds are called **semivowels** or **semiconsonants**, depending on how you think of them. The first sound in *young,* also called a glide, is written /j/. The first sound in *were,* in effect a much rounded vowel, is written /w/. Voiceless, unrestricted air is written /h/.

Now we are ready to return to the cognates from PIE and to see why they are not so different as spelling makes them appear. The main differences between English *father* and Latin *pater* are that the PIE /p/, mostly preserved in Latin, has become the corresponding fricative in English /f/, and that the PIE /t/, reflected in *pater,* has become the corresponding voiced fricative in *father,* that is /ð/. Likewise, ignoring a few endings, English *heart* is not much different from Greek *kardiakos.* They both go back to IE **kerd-,* but in English /k/ has become the aspirate /h/, as it usually did, and /t/ is the voiceless equivalent of voiced /d/. If we were to compare thousands of cognates, we should find that most of the differences could be described very simply as phonetic variation. There has been voicing or unvoicing; stops have become fricatives or fricatives have become stops; aspiration has been increased or lost. And these differences are usually small, if we think of them as sounds made in the mouth. The main difference between /p/ and /f/ is that for /p/ the lips are closed and for /f/ they are not quite closed. The main difference between /t/ and /d/ in *foot* and *pedal* is that for /d/ the voicing is turned on, for /t/ it is not.

---

15. They are not the same; /č/ does not begin with a stop. Some speakers use one, some the other, but we need not pursue the distinction here.

9. Grimm's Law and the IE Language Family

Sound change might better be called sound variation, if by *change* we are suggesting that one integral thing replaces something else that is quite different. When PIE *ped-, somewhat altered in Latin *pedis*, becomes English *foot*, the two consonants, *p* and *d*, are not being *replaced* by the consonants *f* and *t*; rather, the same sounds are being continued in both daughter languages, although a little more altered in English than in Latin. When /p/ and /t/ descended from PIE into Latin, they changed a little—preserving a sound unaltered for a thousand years or more is probably impossible—but the shift was not enough to be respected in spelling or to be recorded in phonemics. When the same *ped-* descended into English the shift was great enough to be recorded in phonemics—the initial stop became the corresponding fricative and the terminal stop was unvoiced. That is not much difference (we can ignore vowels until Chapter VII), but it was enough, when complicated by various spelling systems, to introduce infinite confusions, which we can now turn to our advantage.

Changes in sound have been minor and for the most part systematic. We have only to understand the system. As we have seen, human beings have four natural places to make consonants: the lips, the teeth, the roof of the mouth, and the back of the mouth. Sounds made at any or all four of the natural points of stoppage or friction can be voiced, nasalized, aspirated, or shifted by the use of the tongue. Thus, the human vocal facilities being what they are, dozens of distinguishable consonants are possible, so many that no known language has ever used all of them. The consonants actually in use in a language will represent some sort of selection from within these possibilities, and the selection will be in part systematic. In English the main system can be represented as follows:

Place	Nasal	Stop		Fricative	
		voiced	voiceless	voiced	voiceless
lips	m	b	p	v	f
teeth or alveolar ridge	n	d	t	ð	θ
roof of mouth	ŋ	g	k	(lost)	(lost)
glottis	(now but little used in English)				

That there must be a system was apparent once Sir William Jones had demonstrated that several languages had a common ancestor. Some time elapsed, however, before anybody did much to reveal the patterns of what is technically called *drift*. A Dane, Rasmuss Rask, made the breakthrough in the early nineteenth century, and his hypothesis was extended and refined by a German professor, Jacob Grimm, into a statement since known as Grimm's Law. It is a "law" only in the sense that it describes in an orderly way what has happened, reducing the apparent disorder among European languages and their Asian relatives. It is too complex to summarize in its entirety here, but we shall discuss it in part.

Two shifts will help most. We have already seen that in English *foot* and Latin *pedis* from PIE **ped-*, a stop has become the corresponding fricative in English. We may now add that generally in English, especially if the sound begins a word, *a PIE voiceless stop will become the corresponding fricative;* that is, /p/ became /f/, /b/ became /v/, and /k/ became /x/. The second rule is this: in English, *voiced stops in PIE generally lost their voice.* Thus in NE /b/ became /p/, /d/ became /t/, and /g/ became /k/. Naturally, these are not the only changes that have developed in English through the centuries, but the others are few and scattered, and we can postpone them until we can fit them into other patterns.

Now we might see what these IE relationships do for our understanding of native English words; we can start with a relatively small group of words that has grown from IE **werg-*. We know that /g/ is the voiced equivalent of voiceless /k/ so that **werg-* had only to lose a little voicing to become Common Germanic *werk*, OE *werc*, NE *work*. It meant "to do," and from it we get *irk* through Old Norse, "to work adversely on somebody," and from Old High German we get *bulwark*, literally "bole work," works making use of a bole or the trunk of a tree. With a suffix, OE had *wyrhta* /wuərxta/, meaning "skilled workman," which has given us *wright* as in *wheelwright, playwright,* and proper names like Frank Lloyd *Wright*. But /g/ remained in many other languages; the Classical Greek word for "work" or "action" was *ergon*, giving us *erg*, a measure of work used by scientists. Since we know that /w/ was little more than a much rounded vowel, we need not be surprised to see it blending with the following vowel in Greek, and in effect lost. From *ergon* come several dozen NE words that involve the idea of work or action: *energy, allergy, liturgy, metallurgy, surgery,* related words like *surgical,* and compounds like *dramaturgy*. A suffixed form of *ergon* gives us *organon,* seen in a working musical instrument, the *organ*. From another variation we get a term for secret doings, formerly worship, our word *orgy* (*orgasm* is probably not related but results from a coincidence).

We may look also at a larger family, one so big we cannot do more than sketch the terms descending from PIE. The PIE root **per-* involved some adverbial notion suggesting movement, such as "forward," "through," so that derived terms readily became prepositions and parts of verbs, contributing such meanings as "before," "first," "in front of," "toward," "against," "near," "at," "chief," or "around," including secondary roots that had appeared already in PIE. Descendants in English appear as /f/ plus a vowel plus /r/, as in *for, fore*, and through derivative roots, *far, fare*, meaning "to travel," *frame, fern, ford, fear*, and *first*, along with such compounds as *wayfarer* and *farewell*. Even the common words involving *for* and *fore* are numerous: *former, foremost, forth, farther, further, before*, and *from*, with derivatives and compounds as varied as *beforehand, fordable, forearm, foreboding, forecastle, foreclosure, foregather, forget, forgotten, foregone, forgive, forgo, foreshadow. Forefather* and *ferry* come as loans from Old Norse; *Vorlage*, "a predecessor," from Old High German, and *veer, farrow, heifer*, and *frump* from Dutch. A Germanic word came into English through the Romance languages as *furnish, furnishings*, and *veneer*.

Non-Germanic cognates in Latin and Greek are even more extensive, and they, of course, mainly preserve the /p/ of PIE. There are several prefixes, *pre-, pro-, par-, para-, peri-, proto-, prem-*, and others. Tens of thousands of words utilize these syllables, many obscured in such terms as *palfry*, a horse that goes along beside the master's and others in which the basic idea of going forward is still obvious, as in *promote, report, approach*, and *probe*, along with others that preserve such ideas as "first," as in *primary, primitive, prime, pristine, primate*, and even *prince* from Latin *princeps*, "he who stands first," and both *principle* and *principal*. Some words, nouns and verbs, have grown directly from **per-* not used as a prefix; *prow* from Greek is the front part of a boat and *proof* from Latin is something put forward.

Some of these words have come a long way. *Paradise* got started in Avestan, in what is now Iranian, a compound made up of the equivalent of *peri-*, "around," and a relative of our word *dough*, meaning "mold," or "turf." A paradise was thus a walled garden, and the Greek writer Xenophon used the word to describe the gardens of Oriental potentates. The word got from Greek into Latin as a sumptuous garden and was picked up to translate such passages as Luke 23:43, "Thou shalt be with me in paradise," where it was a figure of speech for "heaven."

It passed into Old French and into ME, often as *parais*, corrected on the basis of the Latin to *paradise*, but it still retained enough of the sense of an enclosed place so that in England a *parvis* is a garden attached to a church. In fact, barring possible competition from something in Chinese, **per-* and its permutations may well be the most widely spread linguistic unit. Its descendants are almost a language in themselves.[16]

10. Some PIE Roots

Those are the offspring of only two PIE roots, as they appear in English. Thousands of other terms have developed in other IE languages. Following is a selected list of the PIE roots or bases[17] that have been uncommonly fruitful of English locutions. You may find them fun to browse among, and we shall have use for them in subsequent reference.

*ak-(sharp)—egg (on), ear of corn, acute, acumen, acrid, acrimony, vinegar, oxygen

*ar-(to fit together)—arm, art, article, articulate, armada, advice, logarithm

*bha-[1](to shine)—beckon, beacon, berry, banner, pant, fantasy, phosphorus[18]

*bha-[2](to speak)—boon, abandon, fate, preface, famous, telephone, anthem

*bhel-[1](to shine)—bowl, blue, bleak, blaze, inflame, phlox, Blitzkrieg

*bhel-[2](to swell)—bull, bowl, bollix, fool, follicle, pantoffle, influence

*bhel-[3](to bloom)—blow, bloom, flour, flower, blade, portfolio, Phyllis

*bher-(to carry)—bear, bore, burden, transfer, defer, euphoria

*bheu-(to grow)—boom, build, neighbor, future, physic, physio-, neophyte

16. At least one can easily contrive sentences from nothing but **per-* words, and complex sentences at that, albeit a bit farfetched, like the following description of a riot on shipboard:

Expert pirates, predisposed for promoting pregnancy, primed for pornographic projects, furthered propinquity, provided privacy for paramours—Frauleins, pristine Priscillas, forward princesses—perhaps forestalled reproof projecting proper Presbyterians from prow, from forecastle, from previously prepared portals.

17. Technically, there is a difference between a *root* and a *base*, but for general use the distinction can be ignored. Another term, used especially in British books, is *etymon*. It will be noted that some PIE roots are so nearly identical that they appear in the same shape (e.g., **bhel-*[1], **bhel-*[2], and **bhel-*[3]). In most instances, such roots derive from a still earlier common root.

18. The *h* of the root represents aspiration lost in most European languages. Most of the other consonants can be treated as though they were phonemes in English.

*bhreg-(to break)—break, brake, fraction, fragment, frail, suffrage
*bhreu-(to boil)—brew, breed, breathe, ferment, fervent, phreatic
*deik-(to point)—toe, digit, diction, token, teach, preach, verdict, dictate
*deiw-(to shine)—Tuesday, deity, adieu, diary, journal, divine, psyche-delic
*dekm-(ten)—ten, hundred, decade, century, cent, reckon, dime, dozen, dean
*dek-(to take)—decent, doctor, dignity, dainty, docile, decorate
*del-(long)—long, language, longitude, oblong, dolichocephalic
*dem(e)-(house)—timber, toft, domestic, madam, don, dominion, despot
*deru-(be firm)—tree, true, tar, druid, duress, obdurate, rhododendron
*deuk-(to lead)—tug, tow, tie, abduct, duke, introduce, educate, team
*dhe-(to do)—do, deed, doom, fact, faction, modify, thesis, theme
*dheu-(to rise in a cloud)—dust, dizzy, down, fume, thyme, stew, typhus
*dwo-(two)—two, twelve, twist, double, diploma, binary, combine, doubt
*er-(to set in motion)—are, earnest, run, orient, orchestra, derive
*gel-¹(to form into a ball)—clod, clump, club, glue, ganglion, globe
*gel-²(cold)—cool, chill, jelly, gelatin, glacial, glance, congeal
*gen(e)-(to give birth)—king, kind, genus, degenerate, pregnant, malign
*ger-(crooked)—cramp, grape, curl, encroach, lacrosse, crumb, carp
*ghel-(to shine)—yellow, gold, jargon, gleam, glow, melancholy, gloat
*ghe(n)d-(to take)—get, guess, beget, apprehend, prison, prize, comprise
*gno-(to know)—can, know, notice, narrate, recognize, normal, diag-nosis
*gwei-(to live)—quick, vivid, vital, whiskey, hygiene, microbe, viper
*kar-(to grasp)—have, haven, heavy, capture, receive, chase, chassis
*kaput-(head)—head, capital, chapter, chief, cap, cape, mischief
*kel-¹(to shout)—claim, haul, low, calendar, clear, council, reclaim
*kel-²(to cover)—hall, hell, hull, conceal, clandestine, apocalypse
*ker-¹(horn)—hornet, horn, ginger, corn, cornea, cranium, carrot, runt
*ker-²(noise)—shriek, ring, raven, cricket, decrepit, retch, scream
*kerd-(heart)—heart, courage, concord, credit, grant, quarry, cardiac
*keu-(to bend)—hip, hop, hope, incumbent, cubicle, howitzer, cave, jail
*kwel-(to revolve)—wheel, collar, circle, colony, pulley, palindrome
*kwetwer-(four)—four, quarter, squad, quarantine, quire, firkin, quart
*kwo-, *kwi-(relative pronoun)—who, which, why, either, quote, quality
*leg-(to collect, to speak)—leech, elect, logic, legend, dialect, loyal
*leg(h)-(to lie)—lie, lay, low, law, litter, beleaguer, lair, lager

leuk-(brightness)—light, lea, luminous, illustrious, lynx, lunatic

magh-(to be able)—may, might, mechanism, machine, magic, dismay, Maud

med-(to do appropriately)—meet, must, medicine, moderate, mode, empty

meg-(big)—much, mad, mis-, molt, emigrate, amoeba, municipal

men-(to think)—mind, mental, maniac, mentor, mandarin, comment, maenad

ne-(not)—no, nothing, never, neuter, neglect, nihilism, annihilate

okw-(to see)—eye, ogle, oculist, inveigle, myopia, ophthalmologist

pa-(to feed)—feed, foster, pastor, pasture, companion, fodder, foray

ped-(foot)—foot, fetter, fetlock, pedestal, polyp, trapeze, pioneer

pel-(to fill)—fill, full, plenty, replenish, plebiscite, surplus

pele-(flat)—field, floor, veldt, explain, airplane, plasma, Poland

per-[1](forward)—for, far, purchase, approach, pro-, proof, primitive

per-[2](to lead)—fare, welfare, fjord, passage, porch, opportune, export

pet-(to fly)—feather, petal, compete, pen, propitious, ptero-

plat-(to spread)—flat, flatter, flounder, plant, plateau, piazza

pleu-(to flow)—flow, fly, float, plover, pneumonia, flotilla

pou-(small)—few, filly, paucity, pullet, page, paraffin, puerile

reg-(to go straight)—right, reckon, rectify, rogue, interrogate

rei-(to cut)—row, ripe, rift, river, arrive, ripple, reap, rope

sed-(to sit)—sit, saddle, soot, session, reside, cathedral, soil

sem-(one)—single, same, assemble, similar, simplicity, anomalous

seu-(self)—self, swain, suicide, ethic, swami, desolate, sober, secret

skei-(to cut, to know)—shiver, ski, schizo-, esquire, skit, schedule

skel-(to cut)—shoal, school, shell, scalp, sculpture, half, cutlass

skep-(to cut)—shape, shave, chap, capon, scapula, shabby, comma, kopek

(s)ker-[1](to cut)—share, shears, short, skirmish, incarnate, curt

(s)ker-[2](to bend)—shrink, curve, crest, circum-, arrange, crinoline

skeri-(to cut)—shrivel, crime, garble, describe, hypocrisy, Ukraine

skeu-(to cover)—skim, scum, hose, hide, cuticle, obscure, recoil

(s)pen-(to stretch)—spin, spider, span, ponder, pensive, pound, expend

sta-(to stand)—stand, stool, arrest, substitute, state, system, stoic

stel-(to put)—still, stall, instill, install, stalk, stout, stollen

ster-(stiff)—stare, stern, stork, cholesterol, start, torpedo, stereo-

steu-(to push)—steep, stood, stucco, stupid, stupendous, pierce, type

tel(e)-(to lift)—toll, tolerate, relate, tantalize, Atlas, dilate

ten-(to stretch)—tend, tenant, extend, tone, tense, tension, thin

*ter-(to rub)—throw, truant, threshold, diatribe, return, trite, trauma
*trei-(three)—three, triad, trio, riding, troika, testament, tertiary
*upo-(under)—up, above, evil, supine, subterfuge, hypo-, vassal, eaves
*wed-(wet)—water, winter, otter, hydrant, surround, undulate, vodka
*wegh-(to go)—away, weight, wagon, vehicle, convex, Norway, inveigh
*wei-(to see)—wise, guide, view, evident, history, penguin, idea
*wel-(to turn)—welter, walk, wallow, evolve, valve, helix, wallet
*wer(t)-(turn)—ward, worth, adverse, avert, briar, wrong, extrovert
*werg-(to do)—work, erg, energy, organ, liturgy, bulwark, wright, orgy

CHAPTER **IV**

GETTING WORDS IN A HURRY
Loans

The French borrowings were so extensive that they changed the whole balance of the language and prepared the way for the incomparable hospitality to words from other languages that English has shown ever since.

—L. M. Myers

1. The Nature of Linguistic Loans

In vocabulary, an obvious way to get many words in a hurry is to steal them—although we have a more genteel word for it, *borrowing*, and we call the liberated word a *loan*. Thus foreign languages provide one of the great banks of accessible vocabulary for English. If appropriating other people's words is criminal, then English speakers must be incomparable thugs, for they have amassed what would seem to be the largest vocabulary of all time. The bulk of NE terms are borrowed or have grown from loan words, as though once a language has a savings account of words, it starts receiving interest.

We have been dealing with borrowing, especially in the previous chapter, where all the elements we designated as nonnative or as cognate were also loans. But borrowing as a process is quite different from descent within the language, and I did not want to use the terms *borrowing* and *loan* until we had established the ways of descent. One of the peculiarities of English which makes its penchant for loans intriguing is that most loans into the language are also cognates, or they are made of compounded elements that include cognates. Not all cognates are loans, however, and not all loans are cognates, and accordingly we shall do well to make the distinction at once. For example, most of the commoner roots in PIE descended into both English and Sanskrit. The descendants of these roots are cognate with one another, having been "born together" in PIE. But most of these Sanskrit terms never became loans into English. On the other hand, *tomahawk* is a loan into English, since it was picked up by English-speaking colonists in America, but it is not a cognate. So far as we know, no American-Indian language descended from PIE. How and why so many loans into English are also cognates of English words will become clear as our discussion develops.

Linguistic borrowing may enrich the borrower but does not impoverish the borrowee. Nobody can borrow any linguistic bit and get what it was in another language, nor can he return it, if by *it* one means exactly what was borrowed. As we shall see in detail later, a loan word cannot be returned, even if there were any point in trying to do so, because it will have changed during the borrowing, and afterward.

Fortunately, linguistic loans need not be refunded, for the borrowee has lost nothing. A language can sometimes repossess a term, although such a reborrowing will always be something other than the original loan. Long ago English borrowed *camp* from Old French, meaning a place of military bivouac, but modern Frenchmen have now borrowed the term back as *camper* (a verb) and *camping* (a noun) with meanings similar to what *camp* and *camping* imply in American English. The French have reborrowed *sexy*, also; English had built it up from Old French *sexe* and Latin *sexus*, meaning males and females collectively, but the French now use the term in senses that approximate those that are often labeled slang or colloquial in American English. That such a borrowing is actually a reborrowing is quite accidental, of course. The French teenager who uses *sexy* today is likely to have no notion that it is a contortion of a French word that once had other uses.

Vocabularies keep growing. Tens of thousands of years ago there were no vocabularies; now there are hundreds of languages, each with thousands of words and some with hundreds of thousands, and yet so many tongues have vanished from the earth and so many terms have become obsolete that more words have died than are now living. During the eons that man has used languages, speakers were more or less industriously adding words to their vocabularies. They lost words, too, but usually they lost them quickly in great catastrophes. During the nineteenth century in North America, disease, starvation, and institutionalized murder combined to exterminate hundreds of Indian tribes. Their vocabularies, containing millions of words, were lost with them, but even while these Indians were being wiped out, they were borrowing words like *gun, pelt,* and *whiskey* from the exterminators. If languages die they usually die quickly, but while they live they grow, partly through loan words.

2. Why We Rob Word Banks: French Loans

All languages have means of developing their own words. English has used such devices, but it has also been a great importer of words—so much so that fully three-quarters of the words that appear as entries in most English dictionaries are borrowed. Why?

If we ask when and what, we may be able to guess why. We might examine a fair sample of sources, and perhaps the fairest of all would be French, since borrowing has gone on from French into English for more than a thousand years, and more words have been borrowed from that tongue than from any other body of speech. The following table, based on citations in the *Oxford English Dictionary* (hereafter referred to as OED), suggests when French loans came into English:[1]

Period of Time	Recorded Loans
Before 1050	2
1051–1100	3
1101–1150	3
1151–1200	26
1201–1250	103
1251–1300	249
1301–1350	238
1351–1400	349
1401–1450	139
1451–1500	144
1501–1550	164
1551–1600	180
1601–1650	132
1651–1700	82
1701–1750	56
1751–1800	49
1801–1850	48
1851–1900	16

1. The table is a composite of two studies based on the first occurrence of French loan words as they appear in the *Oxford English Dictionary*, a random sampling of some two thousand words. For details of the sampling procedures, see Otto Jespersen, *Growth and Structure of the English Language,* 9th ed. (Oxford: Blackwell, 1956); repr. Anchor Books, A 46; sec. 95.

These figures could now be somewhat revised, but they permit at least the following conclusions: borrowings before 1150 were few, even those counted for the totals above may have come directly from Latin or from Latin through OE. Loans started to increase faster in the twelfth century than these figures suggest, and the bulge in the late fourteenth century was less prominent than these totals imply—the OED relied heavily on literary documents, and Chaucer and Wycliffe lived in a time of literary efflorescence. The slump during the fifteenth century was not so pronounced as these figures indicate, since many words that the OED lists for the sixteenth century were common earlier.

With such revisions, we would get the following summary:

Before 1150—period of very limited borrowing from French
1150–1250—period of rapidly increasing borrowing
1250–1400—period of very great borrowing
1400–1650—period of continued, rather high borrowing, with some increase before and after 1600
1650–1700—decline in borrowing
1700–1850—continued but rather limited borrowing
1850–1900—further decline
1900-   —(estimate; not fully documented) sporadic borrowing, probably declining slowly

Below is a rough graph of borrowing from French into English.

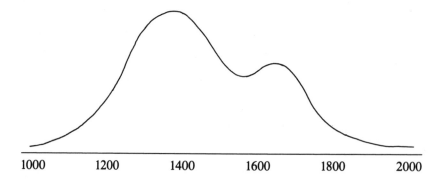

| 1000 | 1200 | 1400 | 1600 | 1800 | 2000 |

This pattern is too consistent to be accidental and too distinctive to be meaningless.

It does not seem to respond to the kind of dates that appear in history books as epochal. In 1066, William the Conqueror, a Norman whose people spoke French, overran the island of Britain. No great increase in borrowing followed immediately. In 1147 the great Second Crusade started; about this time borrowing was picking up, but the crusade could not have accounted for the shift. In 1215 the Magna Carta was signed; like the Crusades it might have been symptomatic. In 1362, in the time of greatest French borrowing, Parliament was opened for the first time in English, a shift that would seem to signal the decline of French in England. In 1415, the Battle of Agincourt, an English victory over the French, signaled neither increase nor decline in the borrowing of French words. Printing was introduced into England about 1485, but it occasioned no great immediate change in borrowing. In 1603 Queen Elizabeth I died after a prosperous reign, notable for increasing associations abroad; French borrowing apparently increased somewhat during this time. In 1660, after a revolution and an interregnum, the court returned from France, but French borrowing, instead of increasing, soon declined. In 1781 the American Revolution was completed with French help; French borrowing held steady. In 1876, when Queen Victoria became Empress of India, French borrowing was declining.

So much for the *when.* The graph above suggests that time is very important in the progress of borrowing from French, but whatever accounts for borrowing must work in other cycles—probably in longer cycles—than those indicated by individual dates, even a date such as 1066, when the English were overwhelmingly defeated and England was taken over by speakers of French. No marked increase in French borrowing can be detected for a century thereafter. Likewise, after 1660, when a king who had matured in France brought his court back to England, French loans went into a decline from which they never recovered.

Now we should consider the *what.* What words were borrowed when? What were they like, and what happened to them? A bit of background will be pertinent here. Civilization had thrived at the eastern end of the Mediterranean Sea and in river valleys and along the coasts to the south and east. This civilization moved west and then north, bringing with it new ideas, new products, better ways of learning and living, along with new terms for these cultural imports. Culture that had grown among Sumerians, Egyptians, Semites, and others had flowed west, notably through Greece, Rome, and Alexandria, and north through western Europe. For centuries, England was at the end of this channel. The flow continued, altered and sometimes impeded by all sorts of local shifts, but it was the dominant fact in cultural change among English-speaking peoples for nearly two thousand years, until England became the center of the British Empire and itself a great exporter of culture. The early known French loan words are part of this flow from the highly cultured Mediterranean lands to the relatively uncultured offshore islands of Britain.

To keep the record straight, we should note what I am counting as "French," since loans mentioned below are by no means the first borrowings from across the English Channel. During prehistory, what is now France had been lived in by many peoples. Our earliest written records show some Celts there, known as Gauls. The Romans subdued them and introduced Latin so extensively that little Celtic survives in Modern French. With the decline of the Roman Empire, as part of the same broad movement that brought Angles and Saxons to England, the Gallic lands were overrun by various Germanic-speaking peoples, notably by the Franks (whence the word *France*) and Burgundians (whence *Burgundy*). For some time what is now France must have been linguistic chaos. Unlettered Celts learned Vulgar Latin badly from peddlers and soldiers; they learned Germanic tongues badly from a welter of invaders; they jostled with all sorts of migrants, including Moors, although most of them were eventually driven back south. By the second Christian millennium various dialects were taking shape, which collectively we call Provençal and Old French. Accordingly, only loan words that seem to have crossed the Channel after about the year 1000 am I calling borrowings from French. Earlier borrowings came from speech we must call Latin, to be surveyed in the next chapter. In fact, the earliest words that may be French may equally well be Latin; *tur*, "tower," was recorded in the late tenth century, and *sott*, "foolish," was common enough in the eleventh century to have two forms, one Latin and one French. *Prud*, "pride," was almost as common for religious reasons and may be as early—Pride was the first of the deadly sins. A few others are clearly eleventh-century and clearly French: *capun*, "capon," *tumb* or *tumbere*, "dancer," *gingifer*, "ginger," *bacun*, "bacon."

By the late eleventh and early twelfth centuries French loans were frequent enough so that we can discern some patterns. Consider the following list: *arbalest, abbot, cardinal, castle, chancel, clerk, court, countess, duke, justice, market, miracle, legate, prior, prison, purse, rent, servant, service, standard, tower,* and *treasure.* These fall readily into a few groups: government (*castle, countess, court, duke, justice, legate, prison*, and probably some others like *clerk* and *service* that could be classified also under another heading); military affairs (*arbalest, castle, standard*); clergy and the church (*abbot, cardinal, chancel, clerk, miracle,* and *prior*); business (*market, rent,* and *treasure*). We know from other sources that the conquering Normans took over most of the key positions on the island. They became the rulers, the great churchmen, the landed gentry; many of the prominent Anglo-Saxons had died honorably on the field of battle at Hastings, and doubtless most of the rest disappeared ignominiously. But if we did not know this from documents, we could infer it from the Norman words that became English.

The words reveal how the Normans behaved in the land they had conquered and what words the natives learned in order to deal with them. *Service* meant the state of being in servitude; etymologically the word is related to *slave,* and a *servant,* a person in service, was probably not much better off than a slave. Safe in his *castle* the Norman conqueror could throw you into his *prison* or subject you to his *crucet-hus* (torture chamber), a word that appeared a little later, although probably the institution was early. Similarly, the imported words revealed a more elaborate administrative machinery than the native Anglo-Saxons had known. The English had their kings and their laws, but now there were *courts* and *legates* to administer *justice*. Norman fortifications could be assaulted with such elaborate machinery as an *arbalest*, a mechanical crossbow, and their attack was directed from a command post marked by a *standard*, sometimes consisting of a mast from an invading vessel, with flags on it. The natives, having more forthright ways of chopping heads off, had not known nor thought they needed such niceties.

Some words, such as *purse,* suggest more cultivated living. The Germanic tribesmen may have lacked containers for luggage; they brought with them from the Continent a Latin loan word, *sack,* and they had picked up *bag* from Old Norse. A sack was sewed up from cloth, and a bag, at least part of the time, was an animal stomach. A purse, the word meaning "made from leather," was probably a more elegant carry-all. Likewise, a *tower* was a splendid thing; the English had begun to build towers in the Norman manner prior to the Norman conquest, and after it such structures increased in number. There had been an Old English word *tor*—which comes from the same Latin word, *turris*, which had meant the walls of a fortified city, and this seems to have been the idea the Anglo-Saxons got from the Romans.

After a century or so of Norman occupation, after c. 1150, borrowing began to increase rather rapidly. Some of the new loans suggest the earlier ones: church words increased with *baptist, canon, cell, chaplain, grace, heretic, hermit, miracle, pilgrim, prophet, saint,* and *virgin.* Words for the new nobility increased: *dame, grandame, master, prince.*

There were more terms for government and business: *menster* (office), *poor, privilege, obedience, rich, warrant*. There were words for objects the English had not known before: *marble, lion, oil, rose*; new clothes: *ciclaton* (a mantle), *mantle* itself, *purpur* (purple silk), and *sandals*. Some words suggest more gracious homes: *carpenter, barber*, and *butcher*— people were living in professionally built homes, having their hair cut professionally, and preparing new foods.

Equally interesting are the words that were not borrowed. Anglo-Norman loans include few from untutored occupations, notably from farming. Farm laborers did not know French, and they probably had little contact with their own masters but dealt with bilingual overseers. In fact, early loans from French had so little to do with agriculture that Serjeantson, who divided the Anglo-Norman loans into categories, found no use for such a heading. In fact, she seldom included an agricultural term under her "Miscellaneous."[2] We can guess why the borrowing increased. After a few generations, the animosity against the hated Normans had cooled, and no doubt more of the natives were now bilingual and were able to live like the affluent descendants of the conquerors. As the two peoples fraternized more, as more people knew both languages, the words of everyday living drifted from one body of speech into the other.

3. What Do We Get When We Borrow?

Now we must ask ourselves what these loan words are, what they had been, and what they became in their new home. The terms "to borrow" and "loan" suggest that a locution was lifted from one body of speech and dumped unchanged into another. As we have noted above, however (Chapter IV.1), nothing of the sort is usual or even possible in language. Before a loan can be accepted as a word in another language, it must become the working property of hundreds or thousands of users. A lin-

---

2. Perhaps the most famous example concerns farm animals and their flesh. Tended by native herdsmen, beasts on the hoof retained the OE term: *ku* (cow), *calf, swin* (pig), *shepe*. Dressed by a cook and served on a great man's table, they became Anglo-French *boef, veal, porc*, and *mutton*. The lexicographer Nathaniel Bailey noticed the contrast and included it in the introduction to his dictionary (1721), whence it was apparently lifted by Sir Walter Scott and put in the mouth of Gurth, a swineherd in *Ivanhoe*. It is a revealing example, even though anachronistic with Scott; so far as our knowledge goes, the French terms were not used in English until a century or two after c. 1200 when Gurth flourished, even by cultured writers, not to mention illiterate swineherds.

guistic loan must pass through the minds of an alien people and be uttered by alien tongues. It has come from the language system of the lending body of speech and must enter into a different linguistic system that is native to the borrowing language. In obvious or subtle ways it will differ from the locution it came from.

Let us look at the word *castle*. We can only guess at some changes; every language and every dialect of a language has its own pattern of tones, but we do not know the tones of Norman French, or Anglo-Norman, or the various dialects of ME. We can only assume that the tone of saying *castle* changed. Of the pronunciation we can say a little more. It was borrowed with an accent on the last syllable, typical in words derived from Latin, but English had an accent on the first syllable, inherited from Germanic. One can still see the difference today: English *castle* has an accent on the first syllable, whereas French *chateau* has it on the last. This trend started when the word was borrowed and developed as ME changed. As a secondary result of this difference in stress, the consonant cluster /st/ developed differently in the two languages, becoming /s/ in English, /t/ in French *chateau*. Some speakers may even have pronounced the word with sounds of central Old French; at least some of the ME spellings start with *ch*, which suggests the sound /č/, not /k/. The grammar was different. Anglo-Norman *castele* would have lost its inflection inherited from Latin and taken its place along with other nouns in the English word-order patterns. For a time it acquired a ME dative plural with *-en*, but it soon lost that. It had been a noun and remained one, but it also became a verb, meaning "to provide defense by equipping with castles."

Shifts in meaning may not be more numerous, but they are easier to document. Superficially there was no change: in its basic use, *castel* has the ostensible referent. If a Norman duke built a combined home and means of defense on English soil, it would have been pretty much the same sort of building he and his kind built in Normandy, designed by the same architect. But it would not have been looked upon by the Saxons as was such a building on the Continental side of the English Channel. There castles were the means of opposing invaders and protecting the local people. They had been devised to stop Norse marauders, but in England a similar structure would be associated with a torture room, dungeons, the symbol of a government that had slaughtered members of the family, the home of a hated despot who might yet, by the grace of God, be overthrown.

Other uses are more obvious. OE had acquired *castrum* from Latin, it being the term Roman soldiers used for any fortified point. From thence it survives in place names with various spellings, *Lancaster, Chester, Worcester*, etc. This word apparently preserved some of the meaning in its Greek cognate, *kome*, "village," and thus alongside the Norman use for a defensive stone building another meaning thrived: any inhabited place, even a whole county. An invading Welsh army was said to have built a "castle" on the border, which may have been no more than earthworks on top of a hill. We are told that in India castles were "timbered" —no Norman baron ever timbered his castle—on top of elephants and stored with men to frighten the enemy. Pictures of such beasts and their burdens reflected the name for many an English "pub," *Elephant and Castle*, which is said to derive also by folk etymology from *Enfanta de Castile*. A castle could be a heraldic representation, or a movable tower used in sieges. The defensive part of a ship was called its castle, and any powerful man could become a "castle of strength." Figuratively, the human body was said to be the castle of the soul, and a castle could provide defense against sin, protection from any temptation, being especially a refuge for chastity. Taverns, presumed to be promoters of lechery and drunkenness, were called "the devil's castles." On the other hand, the meaning of a "rural palace" did not much develop in England, as it did in France.[3]

The changes were even greater in words that developed less specific uses. The *standard*, as we have seen, was a flag or set of flags, and for a Norman, a command post, a place to watch for orders, to rally to, and to defend at all costs. To an attacking Anglo-Saxon it was a hated symbol, the place of greatest danger, but an opportunity for sudden victory. One Scottish commander made it just that; in what came to be called the Battle of the Standard, he overran the place where the standard was set up, forced the opposing command to flee, and won a smashing victory.

Thus the word as it was borrowed was not precisely what the term had meant in French, and it has gone on changing differently in the two languages. In French, *standard* has, in effect, ceased to exist; flags are no longer used as they once were. But in English the word has thrived and ramified. It became "the king's standard," the official definition of a weight or measure. It became any kind of recognized belief, principle, or practice; products and labor are supposed to meet certain *standards*. A modern general who has a high *standard* may be quite different from

---

3. Uses like *castle* as a name for the rook in chess and "building castles in Spain" are too late to be thought of as associated with borrowing.

a Norman general with a high *standard*, or at least the same terms make quite different statements about the two officers. *Standard* has become a modifier; the most reliable reference volume is said to be the *standard* work, and to *standardize* has become a verb. The word has proliferated until any *standard* dictionary is likely to recognize two or more dozen uses of the term, along with a page or so of compounds: *standard English, standard time, standard error*, a *standard schnauzer*, even a *standard-wing*, which is a kind of bird of paradise that has an upright feather on each wing.

What, then, is a loan word? It is at least two things, neither of which is quite what its name might imply, or what the borrowers are likely to assume. It is a shape, that is, a sound or a spelling or both, which usually approximates the original, but the sound is inevitably altered, since it is now pronounced by persons with backgrounds different from those who used it in the lending language. It is also associated with some use, some meaning. This, again, is not and is likely never to be just what the use was in the lending language, and once this loan word finds a place in the borrowing body of speech, it starts growing in its own way, in accordance with the tongue and the life of the borrowing people. Inevitably, it drifts farther and farther from what its sister word was, and still farther from what its sister word will become. The borrowed term will be changing in accordance with another sort of life and another people, or even of other peoples—if English borrows a word today it is not likely to become the same term in British English, American English, Canadian English, and Australian English. In fact, a loan word becomes so readily a local product that it might better be called a "hint word," a suggestion for something new.

4. The Great Flood of French

Sometime after about A.D. 1250 borrowings from French changed pervasively in ways that should become evident if we examine some of the words. Here is a list:

ailetter, aventaile, bainberg, broigne, chamfron, cubitiere, genouil-liere, greave, heaume, hauberk, housing or huce, rerebrace, surcoat, vizor

Unless you are a specialist in these matters, you have never encountered most of these terms, and even if you do know a word like *vizor* you may be misinterpreting its use in a list like this, where it means a half-circlet of metal hinged to a helmet. Similarly, *housings* were heavy cloth coverings for a knight's charger. But by the fourteenth century French had become the fashionable language, so that military leaders, who came mostly from the upper classes, would have known some French and could pick up French terms readily. A new way of fighting on horseback was developing on the Continent, and the words above are some of the terms for a man and his horse that were in use before 1300 and were beginning to find their way into English, as insular knights learned the new techniques and acquired the new equipment. This list could be greatly expanded; soon more specialized terms were appearing, like *jamb* and *quiche* for two parts of leg protectors. More such terms for armor alone came into English in a few decades than had been borrowed from French in all areas during the centuries before the thirteenth.

Some of these loan words became common and brought with them related terms, or they developed families of such terms in England. Take *armor:* it is an ancient word, which had meant a joint and, in Latin, the shoulder, then what we call the *arm*, figuratively an arm as the defender of the body, and then a weapon used by the anatomical arm. It came into English spelled usually *armure* or *armour*, with the accent on the second syllable, and meaning weapons collectively. It was common enough so that it was used figuratively also; the priest's vestments were said to be his *armor* against the devil, and coverings of a head of grain were called its *armor* against "the biting of small birds and worms." *Armor* was the protective covering of the body, an offensive weapon, the trappings of a war horse, a body of troops, military equipment collectively, and the use of armed forces. These uses—I am surveying more than five wide columns devoted to the subject in the *Middle English Dictionary*—appeared so fast after about 1300 that we do not know which of them were borrowed from French and which developed through the sprightly life a French term acquired in England. Soon *armor* could mean heavy siege equipment, and related terms developed: *armorless, armorer*, and *armory*, which itself developed various uses, such as a storage house for arms or a place to repair arms.

Most surviving suits of armor are now preserved only in museums, and most terms for their parts are preserved only in specialized dictionaries and monographs. But many ME borrowings from French have become so much household terms that only close students can recognize them as loans:

abundance, air, alas, carry, chapter, chase, chief, claim, cost, cover, danger, double, easy, eager, faith, fault, gentle, grief, guard, guardian, guide, honest, and on through the alphabet.

Many of the loans from the thirteenth and fourteenth centuries fell into categories noticed above, including ecclesiastical words like *faith* and *grace*, along with military and governmental terms. *Govern* itself is one of them, soon followed by *governance, governor*, and *governess*, and by legal terms like *charge, convict* (v.), and *murder*. Especially there were names for more luxurious living, as for spices, including the word *spice* itself, soon followed by *spicery, spicy, to spice*, and *spicer*, who could be a druggist as well as a seller of spices. Loans implied more elaborate dwellings: *chamber, porch, parlor, chimney, cellar, pantry*; such places had *ceilings, curtains*, and *screens*. Words for the essential parts of a building—*floor, roof*, and *wall*—had come from OE. There were names for foods, including new ingredients and new dishes (*blancmange, gravy, toast, biscuit, salad, jelly, pastry, mortreux* (a kind of soup), and *galingale*); new implements (*cutlery, plate, saucer*); new means of preparing food (*broil, fry*, and *seethe*); and new names for known products (*mackerel, oyster, venison*). There were names for jewels, including *jewel* itself, along with *pearl, ruby, garnet*, and many more. There were conduct words like *courtesy, manners, flattery*, and *treachery*, and games like *chess*, with various terms; *chessmen* is changed from *chessmeinie*, that is, the company of those involved in chess, since a lord's *meinie* (however spelled) was his household of servants.

Words for learning increased: in the sciences and professions, *alchemy, astrolabe, vuket* (advocate), *surgeon*; in literature, *matter* (in the sense of *subject matter*), *tragedy, comedy*; in philosophy, *philosophy* itself, along with *reason, destiny*, and many more, including general words like *discussion* (or more frequently *disputisoun*, our word *disputation*), *argue*, and *altercation*. And there were fashions, in clothes, hairstyles, and everything else, for both sexes, along with all sorts of new gadgets. Chaucer, for example, distinguishes between the kind of timepiece an individual might own, called a *clock*, as opposed to *orloge* (horologe), any of the great clocks imported from Rouen that were placed in clock towers. In short, the flood of French words from about 1250 to about 1400 is so great—the above are only samples—that we can make no pretense toward describing it in detail without devoting a whole book to it.[4]

4. We cannot, with any exactitude, tell what words were borrowed when or whence. Contemporary persons may not know when a word is borrowed, and in the Middle Ages they would not have bothered to record the fact if they had noticed. What we know is that a word appears in a certain manuscript. Most manuscripts can be dated at least roughly, and

5. Why Borrow?

Now we should notice characteristics of this borrowing. First, borrowing increased, so that loans came in by the thousands. Englishmen were growing more prosperous; the wool trade gave them credit on the Continent, and they could import goods in quantities their ancestors would not have dreamed of. And with goods of any sort came words already associated with the imported items. Second, many imported words seemingly responded to a felt need, or if the word *need* is too strong, at least to a feeling that the loan was handy or desirable. Some terms referred to objects that had not existed among the Anglo-Saxons, or the Normans either, or were not previously known to exist. In the translation of a work about the Greek conqueror Alexander, the following passage occurs: "Olifauns and camelis weoren ycharged with vitailes" (Elephants and camels were loaded with food). Elephants were so little known that an illuminator, learning that the elephant had a trunk (probably spelled something like *tronc*), mistook this word for French *trompe*, our *trumpet*, and showed Hannibal's elephants blasting their way through the Alps with a long buglelike instrument sprouting from the forehead.

Other terms did not so obviously refer to new objects, although in reality they did. We might return to Chaucer's words *clock* and *orloge* for an example. No word has been recorded in OE for a timepiece, and until recent centuries most people got along by guessing the time from the heavenly bodies. The Mediterranean peoples had sundials and hourglasses, and Boethius in Rome may have invented a mechanical clock in the sixth century, but no such contraptions were to be found in northern Europe until much later. About 1300 Edward I imported a clockmaker

---

the form of the word may suggest its origin. Thus we can say that a given word was used in a specific form by at least one person by a certain time. We assume that by then the term had considerable currency. It could have been earlier, much earlier; we would assume it was at least somewhat earlier and had been around long enough to be familiar. Usually the known occurrence would not have been the first. What we have is a use that happens to have come from a certain person in a manuscript that happens to have survived, and the manuscript is one that was used by the readers for a dictionary (many manuscripts and even many works have not yet been so read). And we should note that little writing was done in English for two centuries after 1066, and still less of it has survived. Thus the evidence for any specific loan is likely to be no more than approximate, the date usually somewhat later, but not much, although it can be more than a century later. On the other hand, the evidence is now so extensive and so reliable that there can be little doubt in a general way about the extent of English borrowings from French.

from the Netherlands, and the word *clock* may be Dutch, although it is related to an OE word for a bell, and the instrument Chaucer called a clock was probably a small device for striking a bell. But the *orloge*, from Latin *horologium* from a Greek word meaning "something to tell the time," was a huge arrangement of weights, wheels, chains, and the like. Chaucer may have been thinking of the great horologe in St. Paul's Cathedral, that had mechanical figures to strike various bells; about 1400 a dial was added to it, apparently the first in England. Thus Chaucer probably thought of a *clock* and an *orloge* as two different sorts of things with a common purpose; they did not look alike, sound alike, or work in the same way. Or at a minimum he would have assumed the new French word was a more precise term for the object he had in mind; *clock* was a general term, or insofar as it meant a local, Dutch-inspired instrument, a name for a different referent.

Third, many loans answered to what we might call a "need," but they may better be thought of as the results of social and rhetorical pressures. Loans promoted economy and precision, especially in areas of rapid growth, where some native words existed, but more terms and more exact terms encouraged more exact thinking and clearer expression, as in medicine. *Sick* was a native word, and so was *evil*, used as a term for illness, and *ill* had been borrowed from Old Norse, but as medicine advanced, these terms were too few and too general to serve for diagnosis. One might notice Chaucer's description of the *Doctor* of *Physik* (both words are loans). I have italicized the loans, mostly from French:

In al this world ne was ther noon hym lik,
To speke of *phisik* and of *sourgerye*,
For he was grounded in *astronomye*.
He kepte his *pacient* a ful greet deel
In *houres* by his *magik natureel*.
Wel koude he *fortunen* the *ascendent*
Of his *ymages* for his *pacient*.
He knew the cause of everich *maladye*,
Were it of hoot, or coold, or *moiste*, or drye,
And where they *engendred*, and of what *humour*.
He was a *verray, parfit praktisour*.

Even *cold, hot*, and *dry*, although they are native words, are here used to embody imported meanings. Chaucer goes on to mention *apothecaries, drugs*, and *lettuaries*, all French loans, and yet this is a popular state-

ment. A technical treatise would contain many more, and more specialized, terms, although mostly in Latin, not French.

Some loans duplicated words already current; consider the following
lists—

avense	harefoot, herbe Bennett
comfrey	knitbone, boneset
ellebore	lungwort
euphrasie	eyebright
herb serpentine	dragonwort
herbe yve	ground pine, yellow bugle
motfelon	knappweed, hardhead
sanicle	self-heal
treyfoil	red clover

These are words used by English midwives and healers, the column to the
left being loans, presumably from French, and the synonyms to the right,
native words that had existed in OE. These herbs were all native, or
mostly so; they had been known for centuries to native speakers, who
had homey names for them. The healers would have had no trouble
making themselves understood if they mentioned *boneset* or *knitbone*,
and could have dispensed with the foreign word, *comfrey.*

This is sometimes called redundant borrowing, since the referent
identified by the borrowed word is already named by a native word. Such
examples of apparently unneeded loans can be found in all major fields,
and they sprang up like weeds in fourteenth-century vocabulary. Strictly
speaking, however, the loan was not redundant, if by redundancy we
mean that the new term could imply all that the old term could convey
and nothing more. Apparently languages will tolerate redundancy in
expression, but not in the use of individual words.

Given two terms with a single referent, the use of one term—and
usually of both terms—will shift so that the two are no longer exact
synonyms. The midwives and healers who preferred *comfrey* to *boneset*
and *treyfoil* to *red clover* may have had special reasons for doing so.
Doubtless their egos were cultivated by their knowledge of a rare and
foreign term, and their social and professional standing may have been
enhanced. What farmer or housewife would be impressed by an expensive medical preparation if the expert identified it as cow feed by calling it
red clover? But the fashion must have appealed more generally, as well,
not only to midwives in their professional capacity. Englishmen need not

have borrowed *language* (*langage* in Norman French, from Latin *lingua*, meaning *tongue*). English already possessed *speech, talk, tongue*, along with other terms like *spell* that could have been pressed into service, not to mention the innumerable possible compounds—OE already had *word hoard*, meaning "vocabulary," and by extension it could have served for *language* itself. Examples like this are legion.

6. New Sources, New Fashions in Borrowing

Borrowing, even what may seem redundant borrowing, reflected in part a shift in fashion. We have already seen that the Anglo-Saxons, needing a new term for a new thing, tended to grow a suitable name by finding a new use for an old term or by compounding native elements. Instead of adopting Latin *sanctus*, or its French derivative *seint, saint*, they used *halig* (a holy one), for the new sort of revered being. Instead of borrowing *baptist* they used *fulluhtere*, one who has been sanctified. *Altar* was not borrowed; instead *wigbed* served, meaning the table of worship, and an *idol* was identified as *deofolgylda*, an object for the worship of the devil. That seems to have been the habit, or perhaps we should say fad, among the speakers of OE, but by the fourteenth century compounding was no longer the fashion. The Normans by their very presence may have induced the change. Once most literate Englishmen were bilingual, knowing some of both English and French, adopting a French word was so natural as to be unconscious. Of course words already in the language acquired new meanings and were incorporated into compounds, but for whatever reason, borrowing now became customary.

Meanwhile, the source of loans shifted from Norman French to central French, especially the French of Paris. Often the source of these new loans can be identified by their form. Norman French had been an aberrant dialect, partly because it was the result of the Germanic-speaking Norsemen learning a Romance language. For example, Latin /k/, probably reinforced by a similar Old Norse sound, was retained in Norman, but not in the dialect of central France. Thus the word that was borrowed as *castel* in Norman, was borrowed later from central France as *chastel* and *chatelet*. Names that in Norman were *Carl* and *Carole* were paralleled later by *Charles* and feminine *Charlotte*. *Capital* with a /k/ was borrowed in Norman times, but terms from the same Latin word, *caput*, were later borrowed as *chapter* and *chief*, with the sound spelled in English as *ch* and written in phonemics /č/, and still later in *chef*, with the sound often written as *sh*, in phonemics /š/. Similarly, the sound that appeared as /w/ in Norman French appeared as /g/ in the French of Paris, so that we have *warrant* and *war* from Norman, *guarantee* and *guerrilla* (from *guerre*) through central French. There were many other differences, not all so readily described; *gentle, genteel,* and *jaunty* are successive borrowings from the same original.

Paris had long been an obscure village on a northern river, but by the thirteenth century, and more in the fourteenth, it was becoming a capital, a metropolis, and a center of trade. Accordingly, as the Middle Ages advanced, French goods, both material and cultural, came more and more from Paris, not through Normandy. At about the same time, the "French of Paris" became the fashionable standard; readers of *The Canterbury Tales* will recall that Chaucer has gentle fun with the Prioress, who was proud of her French, but she had been a provincial girl, and "Frensh of Paris was to hire unknowe." The new flood of French loans that started sometime about 1250 followed the new trade and culture routes through Paris to London, bringing non-Norman terms from central France.

7. French Loans Continue: Confusion, Resentment

For a time French loans continued to provide the best channel for English borrowing. During the fifteenth century loans declined somewhat, perhaps because both countries were involved in prolonged and exhausting wars. But the flow of culture west and especially north continued, and for England, much of it came through France, bringing new terms with it. Then, in the sixteenth century and into the early seventeenth, the borrowing of vocabulary quickened once more.

Some reasons for this are obvious. Europe experienced dynastic wars, but they troubled England relatively little, and the long reign of Queen Elizabeth I was a time of unprecedented prosperity. London became an important European capital, and Englishmen took part in the exploitation of the New World. Money increased; gold and silver poured in from Mexico and Peru, and the Italian bankers were learning to multiply investment capital by discovering modern finance. Printing, imported in the previous century, was now becoming common enough to have an impact. Trade with the Orient increased. Perhaps most notable of all was what we call the Renaissance, a complex of trends, new learning from the eastern Mediterranean, Classical works newly discovered, findings in science and the professions, new techniques in art, and new models in literature. As before, new culture tended to flow through Italy to France and thence into England, bringing loan words, which, however they may have got started—and some had come from the Near and even the Far East—arrived in the British Isles in French dress: *hegira* (from French, ultimately from Arabic *hijrah*); *magazine* (from French from Arabic *makhzan*, "storehouse").

A few of these loans seem to suggest new channels of borrowing. Travel increased greatly during this period, and now for the first time books in foreign tongues were readily available, books in French and Latin being printed in England by Caxton and others. Travel abroad and the reading of foreign books would have brought words. The following list includes terms likely to have come through such channels:

alloy, ambuscade, baluster, bigot, bizarre, bombast, coach, comrade, detail, duel, entrance, equip, equipage, essay, explore, genteel, mustache, postilion, progress, retrenchment, shock, surpass, talisman, ticket, tomato, vogue, and volunteer.

Likewise, exploration of the New World brought terms. New products inspired *tobacco, potato, maize, chocolate*, etc. Many such terms came from Indian languages like Nahuatl, transmitted through Spanish or Portuguese, but even so, many of them arrived in England tinged by French. England participated in explorations and colonizing, and hence mariner's terms increased, along with words in naval warfare, such as *frigate, navigation*, and *navigable*. *Compass*, which had been an earlier borrowing, was now used for the newly invented instrument that made far voyages possible. *Explore* and *exploration* themselves came in, at least partly through French, but many of the more technical nautical terms—*nautical* came from French in the sixteenth century—came through tongues other than French, such as Dutch, Spanish, and Portuguese.

Most of the new loans, however, fall into the old patterns, words for more luxurious living, for new foods, new clothing, new house furnishings; for learning and the professions, for government and war, along with the so-called redundant loans, new terms which had become fashionable and were drowning out synonyms already in the language. These new borrowings are so numerous they appear in almost all writers of the day. Shakespeare alone is said to provide the first appearance of some twenty words, including the following: *accommodation, apostrophe, assassination, dexterously, dislocate, frugal, indistinguishable, misanthrope, obscene, pedant, premeditated,* and *reliance.*

Curiously, as learning increased, channels of borrowing become harder to identify. During the sixteenth century education in England increased rapidly so that more people knew foreign languages, especially French and Latin. Encountering a word in French, and recognizing its Latin origin, they might replace it with the Latin as being more learned, more correct, or more fashionable. Likewise, a common body of European learning was growing, so that discoveries by the Polish astronomer Nicolaus Copernicus, which would be reported in Latin, might arrive in England in almost any European language, Dutch, Italian, Spanish, or French, or in several of them. Many words presumably Italian became known in England in French forms: *battalion, bankrupt, bastion, brusque, brigade, carat, cavalcade, charlatan,* and on through the alphabet. Similarly, from Spanish via French came *cavalier, escalade, grenade,* and *palisade.* Spanish, French, and Italian combined to give English *cochineal, gallery, galleon,* and *pistol.* A considerable number of Italian, Portuguese, and Spanish words came in, partly from the languages of the New World, but whether they filtered but little changed through French, or whether English exploration and trade brought them in directly, can often not be known: *armadillo, banana, cannibal, canoe, cocoa, corral, hammock, hurricane, maize, mosquito, mulatto, negro, potato, tobacco, yam,* and many others.

In fact, so many foreign words came into English during the Renaissance that the influx infuriated conservative persons. In *Romeo and Juliet* Mercutio ridicules the new manners and new terms for sword play—Italian styles of fencing were superseding French styles in Shakespeare's day, bringing new foil-work and new fencing terms. The passage reads (II, 4, lines 21–38):

MERCUTIO: Oh! he is a courageous captain of compliments! He fights as you sing prick-song, keeps time, distance, and proportion; rests me his minim, rest, one, two, and the third in your bosom; the very butcher of a silk button, a duellist, a duellist; a gentleman of the very first house, of the first and second cause. Ah! the immortal passado! the punto reverso! the hay!

BENVOLIO: The what!

MERCUTIO: The pox of such antic, lisping, affecting fantasticoes, these new tuners of accents!—"By Jesu, a very good blade!—a very tall man, a very good whore."—Why, is not this a lamentable thing, grandsire, that we should be thus afflicted with these strange flies, these fashion-mongers, these *pardonnez-mois*, who stand so much on the new form that they cannot sit at ease on the old bench? Oh, their *bons*, their *bons!*

Mercutio would not have known that in preferring the older fencing and its terms to the new French and Italian, he was only defending an earlier borrowing, in its day as fantastical as *fantastical.* Even *ease* is a French borrowing, as strange in 1200 as was *passado* by 1600.

Very numerous are the learned words, in philosophy, science, and scholarly studies, but by Queen Elizabeth's day, students of such subjects were likely to go directly to Latin or Greek, ignoring the words that had been or now could be borrowed from French. A man like Francis Bacon, though conversant with French, used it little for learned purposes; he entitled a work *Great Instauration*, taking the latter word from Latin, although *restore* and its relatives had been borrowed long ago through French. He used *Novum Organum*, again preferring the Latin, although *organ* and its relatives had been introduced earlier.

More significant is the enduring fact that basic words, terms handy for all serious discussion, and to this day lively items in the language, were still being borrowed in quantity. They include such terms as *adaptation, agile, alienation, anachronism, allurement, allusion, assassinate, benefit, denunciation, dexterity, expense*—the list could readily become a long one, especially since most of these words represent various mixings of influences from French and the Classical languages.

8. The Decline of French Loans

As our statistics showed, after about 1700 French loans declined from their second great period of popularity during the Renaissance, and by this time printing was common enough so that new words can be spotted rather quickly, and the forms of language were reproduced accurately enough so that we can tell French from Latin. This decline continued in spite of the fact that the French court under rulers like Louis XIV to Louis XVI was the most brilliant in Europe, that the French Empire became the dominant force in the world, and that French fashions penetrated even to Moscow and New Orleans. No doubt the recurrent French-English wars discouraged communication. Then France declined after the disaster of Napoleon, and England became the mother of the Industrial Revolution and the center of the great British Empire. Finally, when the balance of power shifted toward the United States and Russia, French declined so much as a source of English loans that, with occasional exceptions like *detente*, few but proper names are borrowed: *Gaulism* as politics, *Existentialism* as philosophy, *Mirage* and *Concorde* as airplanes, *Renault* and *Citroen* as automobiles, *Chanel* and *Brut* as cologne, and the like.

Thus French loans not only declined in number but changed in character. French loans were now almost exclusively specialized terms. By the eighteenth century, English no longer needed many names for familiar objects—however one defines *need*. The new terms, growing from some French speciality, were likely to have only a limited life. English fine ladies might wear their hair in *pompadour* styles, sit on a *pompadour chaise longue*, wear clothes in *pompadour colours*, and dine with a *cuisine a la pompadour*, but most of these terms have remained rather specialized or have disappeared. Likewise, military terms appeared: a fortress might contain an *abatis*, a *fraise*, a *banquette*, a *demilune redoubt*, and dozens of other refinements, and the *enceinte* ("body of the place") might be designed by the *caponier, tenailled*, or *bastioned* system. These terms are now no more part of the working English vocabulary than are words for the *barbules* that protected a knight's cheeks.

Some recent French words remain. Designations of food (*bouillabaisse, pâté de fois gras, omelet, soufflé, au gratin, Chateaubriand*) are likely to survive as long as the foods do, and more general terms like *dessert, sauté, à la carte, maître d'hôtel* (cut down to *maître d'*) are likely to be equally durable. Words like *chemise, cravat, beret*, and *chiffon* are probably in English to stay, but so many of the recent borrowings from French have been fads of the day that the modern influence of French on English, both American and British English, is easily overestimated; in fact the tide has now been reversed, and a modest number of Americanisms are finding their way into French.

9. Linguistically, All the World Are Borrowers

Not many patterns of borrowing can rival the French loans into English in number and extent, but we may plausibly expect all languages to borrow more or less all the time. Surviving American Indian languages have acquired hundreds of loan words from the whites who settled down beside them—*car, tire, spark plug, bus, bread, shoes*—terms for all sorts of things the natives did not have, along with terms like *job* and *school*, which provide a new way of looking at something long familiar. The whites borrowed a few terms like *poganip* and *chinook* for aspects of local weather, *teepee, wickiup*, and *hogan* for native architecture, *quahog* and *kinnikinnik* for local fauna and flora, *tomahawk* and *atlatl* for local weapons, *pemmican* and *maize* for local food. Similar trends are common in other parts of the world. An explorer in Australia recorded that the way was intercepted by "what the Major calls . . . anabranches of the river, but which the natives call billabongs, channells coming out of a stream and returning into it again." So now, while *anabranch* remains a technical term, *billabong*, which seemingly meant "dead water" in the native speech, is becoming an international term.

Or, to take another instance, with the great Jewish migrations of the late nineteenth and twentieth centuries, Russian and Polish words that had found their way scatteringly into Yiddish were imported as part of that language, terms like *paskudnyak* and its feminine *paskutstva*. Soon another sort of Russianism came; Russia became one of the leading world powers, expansive both politically and industrially, so that borrowings included words like *soviet, commissar, troika, nyet, MIG*, and *cosmonaut*, although many such loans were reborrowings of Western words from Greek, Latin, French, or German.

Similar loans can be observed for the Orient, of course. For centuries, a few words like *khan* and *tea* had been seeping west, with more specialized terms like *oolong* and *Lapsang Souchong*. Mostly they were closely tied to names for things—*chow mein, chow* dogs, and *Chou* dynasties—especially to importable things. In toto they were few, and mostly not well known. At this writing, with the growing detente between the United States and China, a new generation of words is coming and will probably increase. Today, more Americans could discuss *Maoism* than *Confucianism*, more could define a *wok* than a *Dutch oven*, and many are even picking up *yin* and *yang*.

We have noticed above that French loans always involved at least two parts: something of the lending language, something from the culture of the borrowers. We may now add that such mingling seems to be characteristic of borrowing as a practice: some borrowing is presumably going on all the time in all languages, more where contacts are close, less where they are not. Consider the word *Venice*. We got our term from the Old French form, which in France has now become *Venise*; in Latin the town was called *Venetia*, which became modern Italian *Venezia*, German *Venedig*, and many others in various languages. Consequently one could find dozens of terms for this famous city in the various languages of Asia and Africa, depending upon whether the Germans, English, French, Spanish, Dutchmen, or Portuguese spearheaded trade or colonization there, not to mention what the various sorts of Arabs, Bantus, Turks,

Jews, and Armenians have done to loans through various tongues.

Or we might notice English borrowings of *infant* and its relatives. The term was loaned into ME from Old French as *enfant*, with a nominal form *enfense*, which developed into *infancy*. It is made of two parts, Latin *in-*, meaning "not," and *fans*, meaning "speaking"; thus the word meant "not-speaking" and could apply to anybody who did not speak, for whatever reason. The word was borrowed again, this time probably straight from Latin, as one who could not speak legally—that is, a person younger than full legal age. Then the same shape was borrowed a third time, as *infantry*, the young men of the army (presumably the oldsters were officers or military specialists), again from French, although probably with assistance through Italian and Spanish. Soon the word was borrowed a fourth time, as *enfand*, meaning something so horrible that it should not be spoken about, a use now obsolete, although it lasted long enough to be carried to the New World. In a fifth borrowing *infante* and *infanta* from Spanish and Portuguese designated royal offspring. In Australian a foot soldier became an *infanteer* and a shop selling baby clothes either an *infanteen* or an *infantorium*. In American English an *infant* is a baby while in British English an infant may be up to seven years old. Meanwhile, English has been borrowing words related to *fans* from many sources: *fable, fate, preface, famous*, and *banish* from Latin; *prophet, telephone*, and *euphemism* from Greek; *bandit* from Italian; *ban, boon, abandon*, and others from various Germanic languages including Frankish and Old Norse, all somehow involving the idea of speech.

The American words *Yankee* and *Yank* are instructive. Neither is now much used in the land of its origin—it presumably comes from *Jan Kees* (that is, "John Cheese"), taken as a plural but actually a dialectal variant of *Jan Kaas*. It was a Dutch term for a scamp and it had some currency in colonial Manhattan as a term rather like *John Doe, Mack*, or *John Q. Public*, a term for anybody. *Yankee* is now used somewhat as an adjective, as in *Yankee ingenuity, Yankee school-marm*, or is associated with New England and New Englanders and with certain baseball players.

CHAPTER V

THE WORD EXPLOSION
Further Borrowings

All the great civilizations have contributed to our vocabulary. Indeed, the history of English is the history of our civilization in all its aspects.
　　—James Bradstreet Greenough and George Lyman Kittredge

1. Growth of the Word Stock

To the population explosion and the knowledge explosion, add the vocabulary explosion. When the language that is now English was brought to the British Isles, its speakers used some thousands of words. We have records of only a few thousand, but the whole body of writing in OE is small and limited in character—ecclesiastics wrote the bulk of it, and much was poetry. Even so, most of the common words must have survived, and many of the rare ones. A guess of 20,000–35,000 allows for a wide margin of local and specialized terms. We now believe that man has used language for at least 50,000 years and perhaps for 100,000 years or more.[1] During that time he has been acquiring and discarding words, and we must assume that the ancestors of the speakers of OE go back to the dawn of time, including the dawn of language. That is, the net result of at least 50,000 years of using vocabulary was fewer than 35,000 working words in English, an average gain of one word every year or two.

That was the state of the English treasury of words a little more than a thousand years ago, when our earliest manuscripts were written. Today,

---

1. We have archeological evidence that language was sophisticated by 35,000 B.C., and apparently culture started developing rapidly after about 100,000 B.C. The cause may have been language.

a so-called unabridged dictionary has a word list of nearly half a million, and these are words conceived to be more or less in general circulation. Most of the terms in specialized dictionaries, those for medicine, law, chemistry, and space travel, do not appear in dictionaries intended for general reference. Thus we may plausibly guess that English now uses more than a million terms leading to more than two million uses. That is, whereas the ancestors of English were picking up words at the net average of one every few years, English in recent times has been acquiring words at the rate of a thousand or more per year.

2. The Main Stream: Greek–Latin–French

Where did these words come from? They did not come mainly from the parent language. OE had no such plethora of words. Many, as we shall see in Chapter VI, came from the language-manufacturing aptitude of modern man, but many words relying on numerous new shapes arrived as loans from other languages. This downpour of words came about mainly in two ways, both implied in the previous chapter. Apparently, wherever peoples speaking different languages are in friendly contact for long periods of time, vocabulary will move from one to the other. During the recent centuries, users of English have associated with speakers of dozens of languages and have borrowed terms from all over the world. The other flood of terminology, although it too relies on contacts between peoples, is so distinctive and spectacular that it warrants special treatment.

England, as we have seen, was at the receiving end of a cornucopia of vocabulary that for centuries poured new loans on the users of English. The flow had its source in the Near East. A remarkable culture had grown in Athens. It drew from the earlier societies to the south and east and spawned an empire that for a time during the pre-Christian centuries dominated many of the Mediterranean and adjacent lands. When it was replaced by the Roman Empire, much Greek culture flowed west through Rome, very much as we have seen French culture flowing north into England, and of course it carried Greek terms with it. But Roman culture, and even the Roman language, flooded into the lands that became France. Meanwhile, this stream of words from the Classical languages moved into bodies of Romance speech other than French, and through these, also trickled into English. Thus this whole wave of borrowing becomes intricate as well as overwhelming. We might try to chart this channel of westbound words by tracing a few.

3. Oriental Terms into Greek

Camel comes from a North Semitic word (many Semites lived in the desert, unlike the Greeks) through either Hebrew or Phoenician *gamal.* From Greek *camelos* it moved west to become Latin *camelus*, and then north and west early enough to get into OE, where it was reinforced by reimportations from French, presumably Norman French, since the initial /k/ sound was retained—the Modern French word is *chameau* with initial /š/. It probably owes its wide dispersal to the necessity of having local words to translate the Bible; in English it became also a slang word for a hulking fellow, a designation for a type of coal, and a specialized name of a device for floating grounded vessels, but mainly it has remained as a name for its referent, the one- or two-humped "ship of the desert."

Tiger. The word first appears in Avestan meaning "to stick" or "to pierce," and is thus cognate with NE *stick*, and remotely to *etiquette*, a notion not much associated with tigers. It developed the meaning "swift," and was the word in Iranian for an arrow; the *Tigris River* is "the swift one." Apparently the word got into Greek when one of Alexander's generals sent him a tiger as a curiosity; it was called "the swift animal," and this designation continued in Latin, the Greek being translated literally as *felis tigris*, with *tigris* still a modifier. The term became the name for the beast early enough, however, so that most of the references in Latin use *tigris* as a noun. From Latin—and perhaps Greek—the word traveled north and got into OE, it being mentioned by Aelfric and others, and somewhat later it appears in a list of dangerous beasts: "Lyons, olifauns [elephants], Tigres, & dragouns, Vnces Grete [probably "river-walking serpents"] & leopards." In time the word became a powerful symbol (as in Blake's "Tiger, tiger, burning bright / In the forest of the night," where it must suggest something like primal cruelty) and entered into many compounds, including *tiger lily* and *tiger's eye*, a semiprecious stone.

Some words apparently came from as far east as India, including *candy* and *sugar*, although neither referred to anything sweet. The ancestor of *candy* probably meant *crystallized*, and the ancestor of *sugar* referred to sand or gravel. The total of these Oriental borrowings into Classical Greek was small; Sanskrit in India is usually credited with *chintz, indigo, loot, mandarin*, and *pepper*. Hebrew provides a few more terms because of the Bible: *alleluia, amen*, and *leviathan*. Hebrew also supplied personal names like *John, James, Elizabeth*; see Chapter II.3.

Near Eastern terms were later stimulated by the flourishing of Arabic science, and Far Eastern terms by medieval travel.

4. Greek into Latin

As we have seen in Chapter III.9, *organ* goes back to an ancient root *-werg-*, which meant "to do" and has become *work* in English. It became *ergon* in Greek, meaning "a tool, something to work with," and in Latin, *organum*, "a device to do work." These two were more or less fused and became the forebears of many meanings in English for *organ*—a musical instrument, a vital part of the body, and any sort of means, as in "an organ of the Federal government." From such uses have arisen some of the most widely used and rapidly growing words in the language: *organic, organize, organization. Orgasm, orgy*, and some others represent related borrowings from Greek. *Energy* is presumably a coinage by Aristotle from *en* plus *ergon*, meaning "at work." His meaning was somewhat misunderstood, so that Latin *energia* came to mean "vigor in speaking," "efficiency," and "power." The widespread current use, as in *the energy problem*—the difficulty of getting sufficient power from coal, oil, solar heat, atomic fission, and the like—is strictly modern.

Mathematics comes from Greek *mathema*, which means "something learned," that is, knowledge. It became specialized to science in a broad sense, well verified knowledge. It appears to come from a root meaning "to think," seen in our word *mind*. In various borrowings it probably reflects influence from Greek, Latin, and French, directly and indirectly, but it was still very general when it got to England. Astrologers were said to practice "the mathematick arte," and mathematics included music, optics, astronomy, and some other subjects. In the fourteenth century Wycliff referred to "matematik, or the lawes of kynde," that is, the laws of nature. For centuries the common use was "the mathematics," conceived as a plural, since it included various sciences. The present common use, treated as a singular meaning "the science of figures and symbols," is recent.

Philosopher, meaning "lover of wisdom," is apparently a coinage by Pythagorus, who for modesty did not wish to refer to himself as *sothos*, meaning "wise man." It quickly developed the ancestor of *philosophy*, and both words came into Latin, then French, and so into English. As studies became more specialized the word had to be qualified as in *moral philosopher, political philosopher*, and *natural philosopher*, the latter being what we would call a scientist.

Words directly or indirectly from Greek are so numerous that estimates of them run to as high as ten percent of the entire English vocabulary. They developed as soon as Mediterranean culture began to be felt as a learned and artistic influence in northern Europe, and they continued to come for more than a thousand years, mainly as a Greek-Latin-French channel, the impact of Greek thought being felt until about 1500, as tempered by French transmission. Thereafter, Englishmen were becoming learned enough to do much of their borrowing directly, or at least to revise the French loans by returning to Classical spellings and Classical meanings.

5. Latin into French

Proud was apparently compounded in Latin from *pro-*, meaning "for," and *esse*, "to be." Thus, *prodesse* meant "to be for somebody or something," and then "to have value," perhaps as a supporter. By the time it got into Old French as *prud* it meant "brave," "gallant," and later in English, "thinking highly of oneself." *Prude, pride, prudent*, and *prudery* are related borrowings. *Proud* was borrowed as a modifier, whereas loans generally tend to be nouns, names for new things. The reason French acquired an adjective is that *prut* or *prud* involved no borrowing nor can it be considered a loan word, because Old French grew from Latin, as NE has grown from OE. That is, *prud* developed from *prodesse* from within the Latin-French line of descent. *Prud* was one of the very early loans into OE, doubtless promoted by bilingual speakers and by the concern of the clergy with pride, the first of the seven deadly sins. Another term borrowed as a modifier is *sot*, which may be the past participle of a Hebrew verb "to be foolish." It entered English as a modifier meaning "foolish," but soon became a name for a foolish person, and was apparently so welcome to our ancestors that they borrowed it from both Latin with a short vowel and from French with a long one. In the *Proverbs of Alfred* we are advised, "ne gabbe þu . . . ne chid þu wyth none sotte." (Don't gossip or squabble with a fool.) The meaning "drunkard," someone drunk enough to be foolish, developed in English.

Dispute comes from Latin *dis-*, meaning "apart, away from," and *putare*, "to think, compute, discuss," which descended into French as *disputer* and was borrowed into English as *desputen* or *sputin*. As a saint's legend in ME has it, "nan swa deope ileæret þaet durste sputin wið us" (none so deeply learned that he dared to argue with us). The word has not been found in English much before the fourteenth century —the followers of William the Conqueror did not much bother to discuss affairs with the natives. The shape *desputen* appears later, when France was the channel through which all kinds of learned matter and learned activities arrived in England. Thus the loan mainly represents the second wave of French borrowing, stimulated by trade, not by settlement.

Oyster came into French through Latin *ostrea* or *ostreum*, and perhaps directly also from Greek *ostreon*, related to *osteon*, meaning "bone." It got to England, not by the Norman invasion, but by the later importation of French cuisine. The following is from a fifteenth-century cookbook, with the French terms, mostly by way of Latin, in italics:

> *Oysters* in *gravey.* Take *almondes*, and *blanche* hem, and grinde hem, and drawe hem þorgh a *streynour* with *wyne*, and with goode fressh broth into gode mylke, and sette hit on þe fire and lete *boyle*; and cast þereto *Maces, clowes, Sugar, pouder* of *Ginger*, and faire *parboyled onyons* my[n]*ced*; and þen take faire *oysters*, and *parboile* hem togidre in faire water; and then caste hem there-to, And let hem boyle togidre till þey ben ynowe cooked; and *serue* hem forth for gode *potage.*

English has thousands of such terms from Latin through French, or French combined with Latin.

Le, -el, etc. The French articles, *l', la, le,* and *les,* along with many prefixes and suffixes, come from Latin demonstratives like *illa, illos,* and *illum,* equivalents of English *this, that, these, those,* etc. In their grammatical uses these terms did not get much into English; we might remind ourselves that whereas vocabulary passes readily from one language to another, grammar is part of the structure of the language, which resists change, so that syntax and morphology as grammar are borrowed relatively little. *Le* and its relatives appear in a few words as a syllable, in *novel, tunnel,* and in some names: *Lejeun,* meaning "the young," *Lamoth,* "(at) the barns," *Atterbury* and *Attlebury,* that is, *at le burg,* meaning "in town."

6. Billabong Terms

A modest number of terms were borrowed from the Greek–Latin–French stream, through other Romance languages, such as Italian and

Spanish. *Clavier* survives from a large group of words that go back to a root meaning "to make round," which became *gloutos* in Greek, a buttock, *claw* in English (presumably from making a fist), and *clavis* in Latin, which gives us *key* and other terms like *clavicle*, a key-shaped bone. A *clavichordium* was a medieval stringed instrument, from which came Italian *clavicordio* and German *Klavichord*, the word meaning "a chord stopped with a key." Through one or both of these languages the word got back into the main stream through French *clavier*, in which form it moved into English, just as though it had never strayed from the main Greek–Latin–French stream.

Gringo, which probably means "gibberish," became attached to those who were thought to talk gibberish, that is, foreigners, and now exists in English as a contemptuous epithet visited by Mexicans and other Latin Americans on speakers of English, notably from the United States. Presumably the word is a corruption of Spanish *griego*, Greek, which in turn is probably from Latin *Graecus*, a term for Greek colonists in the Italian peninsula.[2] The history of vulgar and slang terms, since they live so much orally and so little in written form, are always hard to trace, but this would seem to be a "billabong term," one that has left the main stream and then returned to it.

Clan came into English from Scottish Gaelic, that is, from Celtic, as a term for a social group, something between what are commonly known as families and tribes. But it was not native Gaelic, having been borrowed early from Latin *planta*, meaning "sprouts," "whatever comes up." The word is related to English *flat*, and the Latin term presumably reflects the practice of tramping ground flat for planting. *Clan* sired derived terms like *clannish*. Borrowings from Celtic tongues are few, although some terms were borrowed from Gallic dialects into French, and some from Welsh, Scottish, Irish, Cornish, and even Breton speech into English. Words like *clan*, borrowed from the Latin–French–English stream and then reborrowed into it, are scarcer still, but even they have survived.

7. Italian Loans

As we have noticed (Chapter IV.7) most of the early loans from Italian came by way of French, in fact all of those before the sixteenth century—

---

2. A folk etymology supposes that *gringo* comes from a sailor singing "Green Grow the Lilacs," or a homesick Yankee soldier singing "Green grow the rashes, O," a line

florin from Italian *florino* influenced by Latin; *alarm*, French from Italian *allarme*, that is, *all' arme*, "to arms"; *Lombard*, which because of Italian banking became a term for any financial agent, and a few more. Even during the Renaissance, when England had direct connections with Italy, and there was some exchange of travelers, most of the terms took on a French form: *poltroon, artisan, cassock, ballot, garb*, and *concert:* a motley crew. Italian horsemanship and some military innovations brought more terms, again mostly in French dress: *cavalier, cavalcade, bandit, musket, pistol, salvo*, a few dozen in all. Business and shipping brought a few terms: *contraband, milliner, carat, frigate, skiff, argosy*, and specialized terms, now mostly lost, for pottery, cloth, and the like. Some of these words had traveled far; *artichoke*, although it arrived in England from Italy, had gone from Arabic into Old Spanish, and thence into the Greek–Latin–Romance stream. The spate of Italian borrowing, however, flowed from poetry, architecture, drawing and painting, but especially from music. These loans started in the sixteenth century, but most of them came later and in an approximation of their Italian shape: *soprano, concerto, prima donna, pizzicato, contrapuntal*—several hundred of them in all.

8. Words from Unwelcome Relatives: Scandinavian Loans

Off the east coast of northern England lies the holy island of Lindisfarne, where stood a famous abbey, sacked by pirates in A.D. 875. When the killing and looting were over, some of the monks, fearing this was only the first of many raids, took their most precious possessions and fled west to Ireland (northern England had first been Christianized by way of Ireland). They made it across the Irish Sea, but their fragile boat capsized, and they lost most of their goods, including an illuminated copy of the Gospels. The next morning, however, the manuscript was found washed up by the waves, a salvation believed to be a miracle, the Lord intervening to save his Word, for which reason the incident was thought worth recording. The *Lindisfarne Gospels*, surely one of the world's beautiful books, still survives in the British Museum.

The ninth-century monks were right. The sacking of Lindisfarne was only the prelude to more and more widespread marauding. The Danes

---

from a song by Robert Burns. Such fictions have long been discredited, but they are still being repeated in some reference books.

and Norwegians came in their long boats; they were often called *Vikings*, Creekmen, because they would row up a *vik* (Old Norse for estuary), and then burn, rob, murder, and rape until a local force was assembled, when they would leave, but only to go pillaging again in another estuary. Army after army overran the country, and the robbing and butchering went on, with interruptions, for more than a century. The English strategy was to bottle up a marauding army, induce them to settle down, and convert them to Christianity so that, should they forsake their oaths by breaking the peace, they could be threatened with Hell and damnation. With much backsliding, the tactic worked; the country was partitioned with the area north and east of a line running about from London to modern Liverpool becoming Danelaw, where there were considerable colonies of Scandinavians and where the Danish legal system was the law of the land. For a time even the English king was a Dane, *Knut*, in English spelling, *Canute*.

Thus borrowings from Scandinavian languages resemble loans from Norman French in that they came about through bilingual speakers and through others living side by side and speaking different tongues. Unlike the French, however, the pirates that sacked Lindisfarne brought with them no Classical or Oriental tradition of sophisticated elegance. French gives us terms like *Chateaubriand, filet mignon*, and *sirloin*, but Old Norse gives us *steak*, which meant "something roasted on a stick." When the Norse invaders were not warriors they tended to be fisher folk and dirt farmers, not the clerics and would-be landed gentry who had followed William the Conqueror. The Normans had been Vikings in their time (the word *Norman* is only the syncopation of *Norseman*), but by 1066 these Frenchified northerners had absorbed a degree of Mediterranean culture. The Danes and Norwegians who pillaged England were no devotees of book learning, but they were hard workers, and they seem even to have tried to be decent neighbors, taking up the marginal lands, not grabbing the best by force as the Normans were to do later. Once pacified they brought their women, or else married local girls.

The characteristics of Norse loans will appear in sample terms.

They, their, and *them* come from Old Norse, the Old English third person pronouns having been *hi, hierra, hiem* (in various spellings)—notice the form *hem*, modern *them*, consistently in the recipe quoted above (Chapter V.5) under *oyster*. As previously observed (see *le, -el*, etc. in Chapter V.5), influence from one language on the grammar of another is rare, and the importation of Norse pronoun forms into ME indicates a close relationship among speakers of the two tongues. As we have seen in Chapter III.4, Old Norse was a close relative of OE, and the similarity of the two tongues promoted borrowing from one into the other, and in many areas, notably in what are now Norfolk and Yorkshire, Norwegians and Danes outnumbered the descendants of Anglo-Saxons. The third personal singular ending -s on the verb is Northern and presumably from Old Norse.

Husband was one of the earliest borrowings, being made up of *hus*, the word for *house* in both Old Norse and OE, and *bondi*, a derivative of a verb something like *buan*, common in Germanic languages, which meant "to live, dwell." Hence *husband* meant a person who lives in and runs a household, and by extension the kind of person who looks after the needs of daily living. The meaning is apparent in a line of Chaucer's about the old woman in "The Nun's Priest's Tale," who managed to get along by "housbondrie of swich as God hire sent" (by looking after whatever God sent her), a meaning that survives in such a phrase as *to husband one's resources*. The common use of *husband* as a married man is later; the earliest known use occurs about 1250, as in *Teache me hou i sule don þat mine hosebonde me louian wolde* (Teach me how I should behave so that my husband will love me).

Skirt is a doublet of English *shirt*; that is, the words came from the same root in Proto-Germanic, probably related to our word *short*, so that *skirt* or *shirt* was a short garment, "the short one," from a still older word meaning "to cut (off)," seen in such words as *curt*. For a time both words were used side by side, but when both survived, *shirt* was specialized to mean the upper short garment, *skirt* the lower one. Such differences may remind us that some consonants changed in English: /k/ became /č/ as in *kirk* and *church*; /sk/ of Old Norse *skirt* survived, but a similar sound in OE *scirt* became /š/ in NE *shirt*. The example is typical. Thus the occurrence of the spellings *c, k, sk,* or *g* in Modern English usually represents borrowing, notably from Norman French or Old Norse.

More than fifty of the NE /sk/ words, from *scab* to *sky*, came from Old Norse or were influenced by it. *Scant* came from an Old Norse word meaning "short." It may be related to a number of other words like *skimp* (a variant of *scamp*) and *scrimp*; they never got into literary English, but look like Scandinavian words. As late as the eighteenth or even the nineteenth century Danish and Norwegian dialects continued to be spoken in coastal areas of northern Scotland, and in the Orkney and Shetland Islands (which are geographically close to Norway and Denmark), long called in Scandinavia the "[Norse] lands West over sea."

But early Norsemen, seafarers and tillers of the soil, did not write much, and when their descendants became educated they spoke and wrote English. The ancestry of thousands of dialectal words from Scandinavian is now hard to trace, harder even than *scrimp*.

This sort of thing has happened frequently. Terms for the same referent in rival languages may change enough in meaning so that each has its own use. *Ski*, which now means a length of wood for traveling on snow, formerly meant any stick of wood, and was a doublet of the English word *shide*, a thin board. More frequently still, one of the doublets has fallen out; usually in ME the disfavored term was the Old Norse, since it was likely to be restricted to a few rural dialects. Thus OE *bushy* has triumphed over Old Norse *bosky*. ME had at least two words that could be spelled *gate*, one from OE meaning about what *gate* does now, and another from Old Norse meaning "road." Thus Robert Mannyng tells us that a certain beggar going to a mansion *took the gate and went through the gate*. That is, he walked along the road and passed through the gate. But *gate* as a road or path now survives only in a few Northern English dialects. Sometimes OE and Old Norse terms fell together as in *dale*. Old Norse accounts for many names, including some as common as *beck* (stream), *thorp* (village or home), as well as lesser known terms like *haugr* (hill), as in *Svart How* (from *haugr*), meaning "Black Hill."

9. Words from All Over the World

As we have seen, when medieval Englishmen wanted the more sophisticated goods available on the Continent, they imported them from the handiest source, usually from France just across the English Channel. Often they borrowed the terms for the goods when they imported them. Likewise, when they got imports from the remainder of the world, whether tea from China or alfalfa from Arabia, speakers of English tended to use loan words, sometimes terms from the country of origin, sometimes in the language of an intermediary—*alfalfa* comes from Arabic, but through Spanish. And usually, the more intimate and extensive the associations, the greater the borrowing. A rundown may be useful for reference:

African Languages—Except for northern African languages, borrowings have been few and scattered; for Arabic tongues, see *Arabic*, below in this list. A few terms came in early from Egyptian, like *ebony, paper, ivory*, and *oasis*, probably through the Greek–Latin–French channel. More recently a few archeological terms like *canopic* have been picked up. From Black Africa have come a scattering of terms—*okra, chimpanzee, cola, gumbo, koodoo, tsetse, voodoo*, and a few more, mostly rare. Traders and missionaries probably brought some, but recent research suggests that the bulk of the terms associated with American Black English are a heritage from pidgin dialects that sprang up as part of the slave trade from northeast Africa to the Caribbean area and to North America.[3] From pidgins the loans got into what is called "Plantation Creole," a dialect of English learned by many blacks and by whites who dealt with them.

Amerindian—Amerindian terms have come mainly in two waves by two means. Explorers, conquerors, and early settlers in Central and South America, mostly Spanish and Portuguese, encountered new objects and picked up local terms for them—*potato, tomato, tobacco, cocoa, chocolate, maize, atlatl, peccary, piranha, armadillo, llama, cacique, petunia, vicuña*, etc.—a limited but considerable list. They came from tongues like Nahuatl, Quechua, and Carib and got into British English with various alterations. They were then reimported into the New World with English and French colonization of North America. Another set of Amerindian terms was picked up as white colonization moved west, some few through the French in Canada, a few more through Spaniards in the Southwest, but mostly these were European words used to identify something native: *lacrosse*, an Indian game, is presumably from *jeu de la crosse*, a game played with a crooked stick. Most of the Amerindian loans seeped into American speech as whites and the surviving aborigines settled down to living peacefully side by side—*chinook, hogan, menhaden, moccasin, moose, teepee, papoose, squaw, skunk, toboggan, wickiup*. More numerous are the Amerindian place names; see Chapter II.8. Unusually fruitful have been terms involving the natives in northern and western Canada. *Siwash* came from French *sauvage*, but applied to the aborigines it developed many compounds; a *Siwash camp* is made by scraping away the snow, a *Siwash berry* is the western blueberry, a *Siwash blanket* is a cloud cover, and *to Siwash* is to travel light.

Arabic—We have noticed that Greek permeated other European tongues because Greek became the channel through which Mediterranean culture moved west. With the decline of Greece, and then of the

3. J. L. Dillard, *Black English* (New York: Random House, 1972), pp. 18–38, 73–185. Dillard's theories as to the extent of the impact of pidgins on many vocabularies is exciting, but not accepted in all quarters.

Roman Empire, Jewish and Arabic scholars became intermediaries. During the Middle Ages much of what Christian Europe knew of great figures like Plato and Aristotle came through the mouths and the manuscripts of non-Christians. This traffic was enhanced through the presence of Arabs in the Hispanic peninsula for a thousand years. Many early scientific terms arrived from Arabic tinged with Spanish—*alchemy, algebra, alcohol, Almagest, alembic, alkali, cipher* (through French), *elixir, zero,* and many more—along with words in agriculture, like *artichoke, lemon, cotton*; in government and society, such as *caliph, salaam, harem,* and *fakir* (poor man); in religion, for instance *Koran, Allah,* and *genie*; and miscellaneous terms including food, such as *candy* and *sugar* from farther east; birds and animals, *albatross, gazelle,* etc. Many early loans begin with *al-* or *el-* because the borrowers did not recognize the Arabic definite article *al* as a separate word. Later, various other loans trickled in—*casbah, casaba, coffee* (influenced by Dutch), *ghoul, hookah,* etc.; perhaps a hundred million Arab speakers fringe European culture to the south, and with the recent rise of Egypt and oil-producing countries like Saudi Arabia more Arabic loans can be expected, along with Arab-inspired coinages like *petrodollars.*

Celtic (Irish, Scottish, Welsh, Cornish)—considering that the Celts were a great people who once occupied much of western Europe and included groups who lived adjacent to speakers of languages like English for hundreds of years, relatively few Celtic terms have gotten into other tongues, except through place names; see Chapter II.2 above. The first common-noun loan into English seems to be *ancor,* best known in *anchorite* (itself a loan from Greek), and probably *dry,* reborrowed as *druid.* In later centuries a scattering of terms were picked up, most notably from Scottish dialects—*bog, claymore, ingle, loch, plaid, ptarmigan, slogan,* and *whiskey. Menhir* is presumably the only English word surviving from Breton, and those from Welsh are few: *crag, coracle, cromlech, eisteddfod.* A few more, such as *gull* and *dolmen,* came from Cornish. Some Irish loans have become quite common: *brogue, galore, leprechaun, shamrock, spalpeen, shillelagh,* and *tory.* The latter came from a verb meaning "to chase," applied to people being chased, outlaws and bandits, and eventually was applied to the Tory party, and to any reactionaries with wide acres and bulging bank accounts.

Chinese—The Chinese people are the largest politico-ethnic group in the world, and Chinese speakers the largest linguistic group, but the impact of Chinese on English has been minute. A few words arrived in the Middle Ages by circuitous routes. *Silk* came through Latin *Siricum,* the name of an Oriental people, through a Greek word (seen also in *serge*), which had probably seeped through several Balkan and Slavic tongues from east Asiatic speech. *Tea* came from Portuguese *chaa*, by some devious route leading from Mandarin, and as a direct loan through Dutch from another Chinese dialect. A translation of an early Spanish *History of China* observes that "They haue a kinde of plummes that they doo call, Lechias," that is, *litchis*. Much later, when China was more open to trade, came names for individual kinds of tea, *bohea, pekoe, lapsang, oolong*, and the like. A smattering of other loans came as well, *sampan, ketchup* ("the brine of pickled fish"), *kowtow, pongee, tong* (in the sense of a secret society, from *t'ang*, meaning "a meeting place"), *chow-chow, chop suey*, and *China* itself. At this writing, with improved relationships between China and the outside world, loans can be expected to increase.

Dutch—We have noticed (see Chapter IV.2) that Mediterranean culture came to England especially through French, but some words passed down the Rhine River and arrived through Dutch. The Hollanders became such explorers and colonizers, and so many immigrants from the Netherlands arrived in London, that a trickle of Dutch words infiltrated English from the time *poll*, "head," arrived, probably before 1200. It may be another slang term for the human skull gone respectable, since Latin *bulla* can mean "bubble." It has many derivatives like *polling place*, and in the sense of a scientific sampling, is now one of the most vigorous American terms. Other loans include *boor, brandy, drum, isinglass, knapsack, sled*, and *wagon*. Nautical terms are common: *avast, boom, deck, dock, jib, skipper, sloop, yacht, yawl*, etc. A few Dutch terms have come through Afrikaans—*aardvark, spoor, trek, veld*, etc.

French—For the main stream of French borrowing, see Chapter IV. French exploration and colonization led to limited borrowings directly into American English. From Canada and French explorations and fur trading along the Great Lakes come terms like *portage, cache, parfleche, rapids*, and others that have remained mainly in French, like *coureurs de bois*, "runners of the woods," who carried trade goods and packs of fur. From New Orleans and the Mississippi River come *pirogue* (presumably from Caribbean Indian), *picayune, bayou, rotisserie, sazerac, sashay*, and perhaps a hundred more.[4]

German—German has become one of the great languages of the

---

4. For a longer list see Albert H. Marckwardt, *American English* (New York: Oxford U. P., 1958), pp. 34–40.

world, but in spite of its close relationship to English there seem to have been no early borrowings from it, and later loans can readily be over-estimated. Even *lobby* (borrowed by 1553) did not come directly, but probably through Late Latin *lobia*; the verb meaning "to try to influence legislation" and the corresponding noun are Americanisms from the nineteenth century. *Carouse*, borrowed at about the same time through French, is the remnant of *trinken gar aus*, "to drink all out," that is, to the last drop. Subsequent centuries brought a scattering of words—*cobalt, droll, meerschaum, plunder, pumpernickel, sauerkraut, shale*, and some others. Immigrants to America, especially the so-called Pennsylvania Dutch, brought some terms—*bock beer, delicatessen, Kris Kringle, liverwurst, noodle, phooey, turnverein*, and *wienerwurst*, perhaps fifty or so in all.[5]

Greek—For most Greek loans, see Chapter V.2 and V.3 above, but Greece was for a time the center of a great mercantile empire, exporting in all directions. Notably for English, the Christian religion moved north at least as readily as it moved west to Rome, and thus the Germanic ancestors of the Anglo-Saxons acquired on the Continent such religious terms as our *church*, from Greek *(doma) kurikon*, that is, "the house of the master." *Bishop* goes back to Greek *episkopos*, "an overseer"; the same word arrived through Latin as *episcopal*. *Angel* is somewhat confused; it probably comes from Greek *aggelos*, a messenger, and appears in OE with spellings something like *engel*, presumably through Germanic dialects, but was later "corrected" on the basis of Latin to *angel*.

During the last two centuries a different kind of borrowing, both learned and deliberate, has drawn terms from Greek and Latin. The practice stems from the Swedish botanist commonly known as Linnaeus. He endeavored to catalog the plants of the world by analyzing them on the basis of his descriptions, and for these he needed terms that would be international, could be defined objectively, and would not be clouded by popular, ambiguous uses. He solved his problem by coining words out of Latin roots, the so-called "Latin names" for the plants. Other scientists took up the idea; physicists, needing new terms, turned to Greek. Chemists, geologists, and inventors generally have turned to the Classical tongues to get new names for new products or discoveries. Thus a Greek term like *mega*, meaning "large," or "a million," can give rise to *megacephalic*, "having a large head," *megalocardia*, "having an

5. For a list, see Marckwardt, pp. 48–50.

enlarged heart," *megapod*, "a large-footed bird," *megadeath*, "one million dead persons," and even slang terms like *megabuck*, "a million dollars." *Prot-* or *proto-* implies "first," as in *protozoology*, "study of the earliest microscopic animals." In this book I have occasion to use such terms as Proto-Germanic, the earliest form of language that can be called Germanic. For more on Greek prefixes and suffixes, see Chapter IX.

Hawaiian, Malay, Melanesian, Micronesian, etc.—As Hawaii becomes one of the most important States, more words from the aborigines enter standard American speech, *aloha, lei, luau, muu muu*—a short but growing list. Apparently the first loan from a Pacific language was *sago* from Malay (attested 1555). Some words from this language have become quite familiar—*bamboo, bantam, caddy, cockatoo, gingham, gutta percha, gong, launch*, and *raffia*. A scattering of words have come from islands throughout the Pacific Ocean, and especially from Australia—*boomerang, dingo, kangaroo, koala, wombat*, and others not so well known.

Hebrew—Considering the worldwide importance of Hebraic and Aramaic writings, the number of loans has been few. In Asia Minor the Hebrews were not relatively important, politically or culturally. A few early loans came through Greek, like *jasper, balsam, lotus, abbot* (originally Syriac *abba*, father): see also *Greek*, above in this list. Some Hebrew words came into ME through French—*coral, cinnamon, emerald, endive, niter, myrtle*, and a few more, some of them loans from farther east. Names for some objects were picked up directly out of the Bible—*Mammon, babel, behemoth, leviathan, shibboleth*—many influenced by Latin through the Vulgate translation. Jews and Jewish studies have promoted a few words more recently—*cabala, kosher, midrash, torah, kibbutz, sabra*, etc. See also *Yiddish*, below in this list.

Indian Dialects, Sanskrit—Sanskrit was one of the few IE languages to be well recorded at an early date, from several centuries B.C. The wealth of the Indies was fabulous; jewels, spices, fine cloth, rare woods, and the like found their way west bringing their Sanskrit names with them. Most of the names are obscured in various languages, but some recognizable terms got to English—*pepper, panther, candy, sugar, sandal* (sandal wood), *sendal*, and *margarite* or "pearl," *meregrota* in OE. More recently a few Sanskrit words have come in from philosophy—*karma, maya, nirvana, yoga*. Subsequently, loans have arrived from Indian dialects, including those descending from Sanskrit, especially because of the residence of many Englishmen in India, first through the East India Company, then through the government of the British

Empire—*bandana, chintz, cot, chutney, cowrie, deodar, dinghy, gunny* (sack), *juggernaut, loot, mongoose, panda, pajamas, sari, shampoo,* and many more, most of them not well known.

Italian—Early Italian borrowings can often not be distinguished from late Latin, but words like *florin, million, ducat, brigand, mizzen, tunny,* and *bark* can be called Italian, although arriving in England mostly through French. By the sixteenth century, the stream of Italian culture north was deepening, and much of it went straight to England; see Chapter V.7. Loans continued in such a lively manner c. 1550–c. 1900 that they total many hundred, but recently they have declined.

Japanese—Few terms have come from Japanese into English, and none early, apparently because association with foreigners was discouraged or even forbidden for Japanese. *Bonze, shogun, kimono, sake, soy,* and *mikado* arrived before the nineteenth century, when borrowing picked up a bit with *harakiri, ginkgo, tycoon, jinricksha, samurai, geisha,* and a few more. With the burgeoning of Japan as a great commercial nation linguistic exchange can be expected to increase, but as yet Japan has been more a borrower of English, especially Americanisms like *baseball, business deal,* and *TV.*

Latin—For early Latin borrowings, see Chapter V.2–5 above. In the last two centuries Latin has contributed to tens of thousands of deliberate coinages used in science and invention, such as *quadriplegia* and *ultracentrifuge.* This is now one of the most rapidly growing areas of English vocabulary, and it will continue; see *Greek,* above in this list. Latin even contributed to coinages like *locofoco,* an early friction match whose inventor probably thought a Latin-sounding name would lend dignity to his product. The word then acquired a life of its own and became the name for the Democratic Party, or for any Democrat.

Portuguese—Portugal was not an influential country during the Middle Ages, and hence there are no known early Portuguese loans. Beginning with the sixteenth century, however, when the Portuguese took to exploration, and Portugal became the center of a world empire, a scattering of terms began to arrive, many through French: *tea* and *mandarin* from China, *bonze* from Japan, *caste* and *buffalo* from India, *palaver* from Africa, *typhoon* probably from Urdu merged with a Chinese word, *peccary, macaque, guinea,* and a few more from Amerindian languages in Brazil. Some words come from Portuguese itself, *dodo,* meaning "stupid," *sargasso,* meaning "gulf weed," *molasses, tank,* and a few more. With the collapse of the Portuguese empire, such loans have slowed, but since Portuguese-speaking Brazil promises to become one of the great nations, Portuguese probably has some future as a source of loans.

Russian—*Sable* is the only word known to have been borrowed from Russian into ME, but as part of sixteenth-century exploration, limited contacts led to *kvass, czar, caleche, steppe, mammoth, ukase, samovar, vodka, pogrom, astrakhan,* and a few more, some through French. Through the rise of communism in Russia came *soviet, bolshevik,* and *commissar,* and with Russian emergence as a world power and as one of the pioneers in space travel, borrowing has quickened, with *sputnik, cosmonaut,* and *cosmodrome,* along with a few general terms like *nyet* and *troika.* With the U.S.S.R. as one of the great powers, and one with expansionist projects, Russian loans can be expected to continue.

Sanskrit—See *Indian Dialects,* above in this list.

Spanish—Early Spanish loans are few; *cordewan,* "Spanish leather," and *cork* (probably from *alcorque* from the Arabic article *al* plus Latin *quercus,* "oak") came before 1500, and many Arabic terms were colored by Spanish; see *Arabic,* above in this list. Beginning in the sixteenth century the great Spanish explorations and colonizations brought words from Latin America and elsewhere—*mosquito, banana, palmetto, negro, cannibal, llama, chinchilla, avocado, barbecue, vanilla, pickaninny,* and others. Madrid became the capital of the Holy Roman Empire, and an exporter of military and cultural terms—*galleon, sonora, grandee, armada, comrade, matador, toreador, doubloon, sierra, embargo, junta, rancho, guitar, cockroach,* and hundreds more. Spanish became the growing language in much of Central and South America, and an exporter of terms, especially through Mexican holdings in what is now the southwestern United States—*bronco, bonanza, borracho, rodeo, stampede, pompano, adobe, serape, canyon, patio, tango,* and *cafeteria.* With the growth of Latin America, Spanish will continue as a great lending language.

Yiddish—Borrowings from Yiddish are mostly recent, but are numerous and perhaps increasing in American English because of the large number of Jews in American publishing and the arts and the charm of Jewish wit. Recent loans include the following—*chutzpah, haimish, schlemiel, bagel, lox,* and *nudnik.* Yiddish loans cannot always be distinguished from German, Russian, Polish, and some others.[6]

6. Many of the entries in Leo Rosten, *The Joys of Yiddish* (New York: McGraw-Hill, 1968), are loans.

10. PIE, Loans, and Vocabulary Learning

Now that we have established distinctions between descent within the language and borrowing from another language, we can put this knowledge to work. Clear thinking about language problems is impossible if the thinker confuses descent with borrowing, but that is what most students of language did for centuries, and many still do. As late as the Renaissance well-informed scholars believed that Latin was a debased form of Greek and that English was a debased form of Latin. So long as such notions persisted, serious thinking about the relationships of English to the Classical and Romance tongues was inevitably confused, and the understanding of the nature of the English vocabulary was muddled. Of course, no conversant scholar made such blunders, once the philologists had worked out the main relationships within the IE language family, but even the American lexicographer, Noah Webster, lived and died (in 1843) believing that English descended from some tongue spoken on the plains of Chaldee, or perhaps from Celtic. And even since etymology has been widely professed, relatively few laymen have ever heard of PIE, and fewer still could name as many as a half dozen PIE roots. Etymology, where it is taught at all in the public schools, is commonly limited to loans from Latin and Greek.[7]

Knowing something of the nature of man's greatest invention and one of his major means of becoming human is part of general culture. Knowing about man's language is part of knowing about man, but curiously, an awareness of PIE and of descent and borrowing has very practical, bread-and-butter uses. To see how this tool works, we might review some of what we have already surveyed, starting with the eleventh century. English, in the stage known as OE, was the basic speech of a well established, thriving people, adequate to their needs. In 1066 the more accessible parts of the island of Britain were overrun by Normans, who killed most of the educated people and made French the official speech for government, business, and everything professional or learned that was not conducted in Latin. English almost ceased to be written, and it was little used for any intellectual activity, including sophisticated

---

7. The teaching of language is improving, but slowly. Courses are sparse even in graduate schools; some colleges and universities require courses in linguistics, including historical linguistics, of certain majors, mostly in English and anthropology. Personally, I have yet to hear of a single course in any American public school, secondary or collegiate, that provides a sound basis in language, with the expectation that it will be taken by any large portion of the student population.

speech. Such practices continued for a couple of centuries or so, when English regained popularity and eventually crowded out French. By that time, two notable changes had altered the vocabulary: OE had been stripped of all but the most common words, the words used in humble homes, at work, for local gossip. Meanwhile, the lost words had been replaced by loan words, mostly from French, and the whole vocabulary had grown with the leavings from a great wave of borrowing. The result is that the English word stock is mainly of two sorts: a small body of short, tough native words that everybody knows, even small children, and great quantities of borrowed words, of which many are long, not very familiar in shape, and rare in use. Of course some of the borrowed words have become familiar—*church, government, wine*, and the like—but almost without exception rare and specialized words are loans. Corresponding OE words were mostly lost, some when their users were killed at Hastings and thereafter, more when native speakers did not need such terms in a world where Latin and French were the media of sophisticated discourse. Accordingly, through the accidents of geography and the phenomenal spread of IE languages, most of the loans into English were also cognates of native English terms.

The result is that most words a speaker of English may want to learn deliberately will be related to at least one word that is already known well, a native word. A few borrowings come from outside the IE tradition, but they are mostly so common they give no trouble—terms like *coffee, hashish*, and *tomahawk*. If they had not been much used they would not have been borrowed, or at best would not have survived. The great body of the uncommon words in English come as loans from other IE languages, and if they were popular enough to be borrowed, they were mostly popular enough to be represented by a native word, or by a word borrowed from another Germanic language like Old Norse or Dutch, so old in the English tradition and so much a part of daily life that it acts like a native term.

Let us see how this works. Assume that a speaker of English had encountered *patronymic* and either does not know the word or does not know enough about it. The dictionary I shall quote, here and elsewhere, *Webster's New World*, cited above, has the following etymology: "LL. *patronymicus* 〈 Gr. *patronymikos* 〈 *pater*, FATHER + *onyma*, NAME." This means that the word comes from Late Latin *patronymicus*, which in turn came from Greek *patronymikos*, which was a compound of *pater*, the Greek word for English *father*, plus the Greek word *onyma*, in English *name*. (The usual Greek form is *onoma*, but in this compound the variant is used.) Little more need be said; the word comes from the idea of the son taking the father's name. All this falls together; we have already seen that /f/ in English is likely to correspond to /p/ in Latin, that /n/ and /m/, being nasals, are similar in English and the Classical languages. A little acquaintance with languages will suggest that the loss of an initial vowel like /o/ is pretty common. If the searcher needs to know more, the fact that *father* and *name* are printed in capital letters means that one has only to look up those words to find more details, such as the IE root.

Now let us try a seemingly difficult word, involving roots less familiar than those for *father–paternal,* the medical term *apnea.* It means "temporary stoppage of breathing." It can be learned the hard way, as an isolated fact, but a better attack is to make it cousin to the knowledge you already have. It is composed of two parts: *a-,* reduced from *ab-,* "away from" or "without," which will be familiar through hundreds of words (*abstract, abduct*), and *-pnea,* from the PIE root **pneu-,* "to breathe," an echoic syllable made in imitation of sudden breath. Here the link to the English cognate is not so obvious. It is NE *sneeze,* which is a sudden use of breath, but *snee-* does not look much like *pneu-*. The explanation involves a blunder; /f/ was mistaken for /s/, the OE term for *to sneeze* being *fnesian.* But if that is too confusing, we can turn to other words from Greek, such as *pneumonia, pneumatic,* etc., all concerned with air or breathing, which will provide a ready link to *apnea.*

For some words a native speaker may get a bit of a runaround, going from cross-reference to cross-reference, but the journey will likely be worth it. Let us assume he starts with *maladroit.* It is made up of *mal-* and *adroit.* If the searcher does not already know that *mal-* means "bad" or "badly," it can be looked up. The cross-reference is to *direct,* where the searcher gets another cross-reference to *regal,* and there the IE root, **reg-,* which meant "straight." It has given us two common English words, *rich* and *right;* other related words are as varied as *rex, Reichstag, address, maharajah,* and *ergo.*

This list looks a bit confusing and will be hard to account for unless one notices that we have here to deal with a palatal, /g/, and that we have seen that palatals readily vary: **kerd-* gives us *heart, cordis*, and *cardiac;* **werg-* gives us *work, wright*, and *surgeon.* The fact is palatals are uncommonly unstable sounds. One reason for this is that they are movable. Try saying carefully, *meek talk.* You will find that you pronounce /k/ in *meek* farther forward than you pronounce the same phoneme in *talk.* The reason is that the vowel in *meek* is a front vowel (for the position of vowels see VII, 2) and the vowel in *talk* is a back vowel, and that palatals move with an adjacent vowel. Accordingly, the palatal /g/ of **reg-* became /kt/ in *direct,* /ks/ in *rex,* /ǰ/ in *incorrigible,* /ž/ in *regime,* /j/ in *royal,* /č/ in *rich,* and nothing at all in several sorts of words like *right, reign,* and *rule,* although it has left traces of older pronunciations in spellings like *gh* in *right* and *g* in *reign,* and even in *i* of the diphthong in *adroit.*

Now, anyone who wishes to pursue them is on the way to encountering thousands of uses stemming from the notion of "straight." One can learn any of these words that may be useful; they are part of a family and much more easily learned than *regicidium* and *corrigenda* would be without the central sound of IE **reg-.* Presumably **reg-* led to the word *right,* in the sense of "correct," because a *direct* line from one point to the other is a *correct* one, and to the sense of "right hand" because in a right-handed person the right hand is the more accurate. An administrator presumably did the "right thing," and thus he was *rex, regis,* Latin for king, and from that word came *regent, regime, regimen, regiment, interregnum,* and many more. Similarly, the king was the *ruler* enforcing the *rules* (cut down from *regnal*). Even a term like Indic *rajah* can be seen to develop from **reg-,* once we notice that the change in the vowel is slight and that the /j/ of *rajah* is only the affricated form of /g/. All of this and more can be worked out from a good dictionary having PIE roots, once the speaker of English has the key provided by Grimm's Law.[8]

11. Learning Hard Words Through PIE Roots

This device of learning strange or difficult words through PIE roots can be applied deliberately. As we have earlier observed, any loan from the Classical or other IE languages familiar enough to become a loan into English is likely to have come from a root common enough so that it has

---

8. Perhaps easiest to use is an etymological dictionary that has already worked out some of these relationships and provides some explanation, such as Eric Partridge, *Origins,* 2nd ed. (New York: Macmillan, 1959). *Webster's New World,* cited above, gives IE roots and indicates relationships. *The American Heritage Dictionary* (1969) has IE roots in an appendix, from which etymologies can be worked out. We now have two splendid etymological dictionaries for English: *The Oxford Dictionary of English Etymology,* ed. C. T. Onions (Oxford: Clarendon Press, 1966), and *A Comprehensive Etymological Dictionary of the English Language,* ed. Ernest Klein (Amsterdam: Elsevier Publishing Co., 1971). Onions has dates of borrowings; Klein is strong in borrowings from Oriental languages.

also descended into English. To see how this goes, let us glance at the list of common PIE roots in Chapter III.10 above. The first entry is as follows: "*ak-* (sharp)—egg (on), ear (of corn), acute, acumen, acrid, acrimony, vinegar, oxygen." Suppose a writer wishes to learn and remember the word *acumen.* The meaning of the root may be enough, once he is aware that the idea of *sharp* is here being used in the sense of sharpness of mind. If not, he certainly knows the word *ear* as it is used in the phrase *ear of corn,* and he can find out that *ear* is here being used in a common meaning, that associated with *spike.* The next entry in the list is "*ar-* (to fit together)—arm, art, article, articulate, armada, advice, logarithm." Let us assume that the writer wishes to remember *articulate;* once again, as soon as he knows that the root *ar-* means "to join or fit together," he probably will need nothing more, but if he does, he knows words like *arm* and *art,* and that the arm is joined to the body. The third entry reads "*bha-*[1] (to shine)—beckon, beacon, berry, banner, pant, fantasy, phosphorus." If the writer has here started with the word *phosphorescent,* he will need to relate it to *phosphorus,* recall that the sound for /f/ is spelled *ph* in Greek, and that /f/ is phonetically related to /b/ (see Chapter III.9 above). Thus *beacon* and *phosphorescent,* which at first glance do not look much alike, can be seen to be related through the PIE root, *bha-,* and they both refer to shining.

For a few words, usually rare ones, no cognate exists in English. The shape may have been lost from Germanic, or even from OE—change is unending in language, and some words disappear. Even so, a familiar cognate is likely to have survived in or through another IE tongue. Suppose that a medical student wishes to remember *endothelium.* His background in science will have taught him that *endo-* is a prefix meaning "within." The *-thele-* is the Greek word for "nipple." This may seem strange to him, but it will not be, once he knows that the root *dhei-* means "to suck," which through Latin provides the word *female,* which means in effect "she suckles." Awareness of the ways in which PIE roots stand back of most English terms, whether native or borrowed, plus the implications of Grimm's Law, the elements of English phonemics, and only a very little ingenuity will make vocabulary learning more fun and much easier.

CHAPTER VI

THE DO-IT-YOURSELF WAY
TO GET WORDS
Semantic Change

Words are like planets, each with its own gravitational pull.
— Kenneth Burke

1. Contexts and Meaning

A Sunday school song, according to a small boy, was about "the concentrated cross-eyed bear." The adults in the family were skeptical of this beast; apparently the original read about as follows: "the consecrated cross I'd bear."

The little boy's report follows a number of trends common in language. He replaced a strange word, *consecrated,* with one not so strange, *concentrated.* This is a minor if omnipresent practice in language, as when *asparagus* becomes *sparrow grass.* The word comes from Attic Greek *aspheregos,* probably meaning "sprout," from a verb implying "swell or burst," and anyone who has seen asparagus shoots almost leap from the ground will recognize its propriety. But the English cooks and gardeners who dealt with asparagus did not know Attic Greek. *Sparrow grass* looks and sounds familiar, and it makes a little sense, if not much. As an asparagus matures it becomes feathery and resembles such grasses as foxtails, and one can imagine sparrows eating the red berries, whether or not they do. Very similar is false or popular or folk etymology, which we have observed earlier. It occurs most frequently when a borrowing is misunderstood, but the youngster who replaced *consecrated* with *concentrated* was doing essentially the same thing. The vocabulary he was borrowing from was no more familiar to him than Greek would have been; *consecration* was probably no part of his experience, and *consecrated* not part of his working vocabulary.

117

He was having trouble, also, with *homonyms,* words having the same sound but different uses. *Cross-eyed* and *cross I'd* have identical sounds. In careful use *I would* has what is called a **juncture,** a break in speech, in this instance enough to separate two words. But junctures are much obscured in talk, and all three parts of the sequence, *cross I'd bear* differ in use depending upon the supposed purpose of the whole. As printed in the hymnbook, *cross* is the name of an object made of two sticks perpendicular to each other, carrying symbolic implications. In the child's version, *cross,* although derived from the noun, is part of a modifier, *cross-eyed. Eyed* is the remainder of the modifier, and that it is identical in sound with the contraction of *I would* is pure accident—there will always be a few of these chance identities in any language. *Bear* is, of course, a verb meaning "to carry" in the official text, but in the child's version the name of an animal.

Confusions like this are unusual in language, partly because of what is called **redundancy**, saying something more than once, and usually saying it in more than one way. For example, uses are commonly distinguished by grammar, sound or spelling, meaning, and even by circumstance. Take the terms *bear* as noun and verb, *bare* as modifier and verb. When Old Mother Hubbard found that "her cupboard was bare," no misunderstanding is possible. *Bear* cannot be used as a modifier, except in rare contexts such as "This is good bear country." Even if we assume a blunder, such as "The cupboard was a bear," we could still reject the sentence knowing that cupboards are not bears. On the other hand, in the phrase /bɛr bownz/ (either *bear bones* or *bare bones*) the requirements of both meaning and grammar are satisfied, and in speaking, if we are to be sure of the use, we must rely on context, which is usually sufficient—if not, we have the kind of puns that account for many of the more literate sallies in the comic strips.

But that is not the most fertile observation we can make about *bear,* noun, and *bear,* verb. The little boy, hearing the sound /bɛr/, had to use it in his own way. Bearing consecrated crosses was no part of his verbal experience. He was making language do something it had not done before. On the other hand, the speech was not, as a whole, any of his making; he was just trying to report as well as he could, and under the circumstances no doubt doing very well. The language as a whole has been made by society, and belongs to society as its creation, and in a broad way the little boy would have understood this. But the curious paradox is this: although language is the property of society, everybody uses it, and has to use it, as though it were his private possession. And when he uses it he is always changing it, however little.

2. Ask Not by Whom the Language is Made—It is Made by You

That is, everybody makes the language, and at least in a small way he makes it in his own image. Every word, as it exists at any one time, is what the users of the language have made it. One of the results, of course, is that language is always changing, partly because each human being is unique, partly because the users of language change, partly because linguistic systems overlap and shift, and partly because the world changes.

In what is perhaps the simplest sort of case, the use of a linguistic shape changes because the referent changes. We have already seen this happening in Chapters IV and V; we might use *ship* as an example. In OE the word was written *scip* (pronounced like our word *skip*), a term of uncertain origin, but probably related to the root *sgei-*, meaning "to cut." The ancestor of *scip* probably referred to the largest boat the people knew, in this instance, a dugout, a hollowed-out log. When the Danes and Norwegians overran England they came in *scipum*, long boats carrying a hundred men or more, and even small horses. The boats were made by expert carpenters, but they were still referred to by the term formerly used for a dugout. A thousand years or so later, Admiral Perry was quoted as saying, in his dying admonition, "Don't give up the ship." He was using the same word, slightly altered in sound, but it now referred to a man-of-war. More recently, a floating palace like the *Queen Mary* has been called a *ship*; an airplane can be called *the ship*; and an interplanetary module can be called a *ship*, or more frequently a *spaceship*.

Most instances are much more complex, because the shape itself is used to do more than name a referent. Take the word *man*. It formerly meant any human being, the male being called *wer man*, the female *wif man*. This meaning continued in OE, where we are told in a sermon of 971 that "the doors of heaven stand locked because of the first men," and *men* would have included Eve, who was often given at least half the blame. This use still exists, but *man* in this sense now means more than it did because we know more about mankind, about the history, nature, and probable future of *homo sapiens*. Man was once thought of as a sort of replica of God, and was for a time considered mainly important because his body was the prison of a soul. We now think of man as a creature so self-reproductive that he is making the world uninhabitable; we compare him to monkeys and contrast him with them.

This sort of drift has gone on and on, and doubtless will continue; *man* as a term for a human being has kept the same referent, but our concepts of the referent have shifted.

Meanwhile, new implications have developed. By 825, *man* could be used to designate the human race; a psalter of that date asks, *Hwet is mon* (What is man)? Soon, *man* could refer to a husband, as in *man* and *wife*, and it continues in such expressions as "her man." The term was used to summarize the nobler qualities of a human being; Hamlet says of his father, "He was a man, take him for all and all: / I shall not look vpon his like againe." A *man* was a servant, an employee, a member of the armed forces, an adult as in *man and boy*. It even became a euphemism to avoid a forbidden word like *God*, a use probably preserved in the current exclamation, *Man!* Many compounds developed like *man-of-war, to a man, man about town*, derivatives like *manly* and *manlike* (which are in origin the same), a verb *to man*, and proper names.

Here is change indeed. If we think of vocabulary as uses, not spellings like *m-a-n* or sounds like /mæn/, one word has been used to breed dozens. These are not borrowings; they are grown within the language by the users of the language. How has this come about? We are not likely to find the answer; the working of the mind is subtle and varied, but we can infer something if we notice how words have grown. We have already noticed that some stem from naming.

First, we might observe that in considering this growth within the language we are dealing with no trivial matter. We remarked above that OE had a vocabulary of fewer than 50,000 words. More than half of these have been lost, probably much more than half. A few tens of thousands of words have been borrowed, many with only one use. Frequently a name for something arrived; a verb or modifier might come, also, although not usually, but we have already estimated that we have records of more than two million named uses. English words are made up, then, of three sorts of shapes: (1) a few tens of thousands of native terms, plus (2) a few tens of thousands of loans, plus (3) hundreds of thousands of terms that have been made from these two sorts. All of English vocabulary has been made or altered by the users of English. What have been called (1) and (2) above, the native terms plus the borrowed terms, may have changed little; *man* can still mean any member of the human species, but speakers no longer mean quite what their ancestors did when they use *man*, nor do modern hearers react exactly as their predecessors would have. Even more, what I have called (3) are new meanings, somewhat related to the earlier meanings in most instances, but fresh mintings, new intellectual currency. Obviously, of these groups, the do-it-yourself products are much the most numerous.

Second, if by vocabulary we mean all the meaning-conveying units, we must go beyond what are popularly recognized as *words*. Consider the combination *pie in the sky*. It has its meaning, albeit a rather slangy one, that is something other than the total of the meanings of its components—*pie, in, the*, and *sky*. It has much the same use as it would have were it printed *pie-in-the-sky* or *pieinthesky*. Such phrasal sequences are being made by the ten thousand: *in bankruptcy, a Dear John letter, on purpose, double up, crime in the streets, survival of the fittest, the common good, limited access, by night, white backlash*, etc. English speech is highly fluid in many ways, and not least in such combinations. They are changing, and the state of many of them is uncertain, but they need not appear first as slang. *At the summit*, identifying a meeting of heads of state, was probably respectable from the hour of its coining. If a cowboy *shot up the town*, the sequence means something different than *shot up* means in the following: the cowboy shot straight up; the cowboy ran like a rabbit, ducked around the corner, and shot up the alley. But often distinctions are not so sharp. *Under contract* is becoming a set having its own identity, but many users of the language would insist that we think of it as a prepositional phrase, with *under* having a somewhat figurative meaning. Similarly, *under no obligations, under the ground, under a false name*, and dozens of others can be thought of as new terms, as *underground, underfoot*, and *undergraduate* certainly have become new terms. Or they may be treated as phrases, a combination that is part of a sentence, not an entity within a sentence. The question is complex (see Chapter IX) but we might notice that the phrase-making sense in NE is a great miller of meaning, that phrasal combinations are part of our working vocabulary.

3. Words and the Imagination: Mundane Meanings

Meanings grow through figures of speech, most commonly the simplest sorts, called **metaphors** and **similes** since they are based on comparisons. Actually, they might better be called analogy, since they usually compare referents that are alike in one particular but different in others. We have already noticed that the Latin or Greek equivalent of *foot* can be applied to objects that, like *feet*, can appear at the bottom, or like a foot can serve as something to stand on. The same simple analogies have worked with the native word, as in the *foot* of the bed, the *foot* of the page, the *foot* of the line, which can lead to *footing* the bill. A *foot* soldier is one who goes on *foot*, a *foothill* one at the *foot* of a range, a *footbridge* one intended for pedestrians. A linear standard was as long as the king's *foot*, and a *foot* in verse probably derives from this unit of measurement. The *foot* of a sewing machine is shaped like a foot, and anyone fighting for something may gain a *foothold*. The OED recognizes some fifty main meanings for *foot*, with many subdivisions and hundreds of compounds, many of them figurative.

Most of the more familiar parts of the body have provided figurative meanings. An *arm* of the sea may reach past a *headland*, connected by a *neck* to the *body* of an island, of which the *backbone* leads to a *shoulder*. A man may have to *toe* the mark, a fish may be a *fingerling*, a sharp angle in a golf fairway may be a *dogleg*, a tree will have various *limbs* as well as a *trunk*, a storm may have an *eye*, a river a *mouth*, legislation may have *teeth* in it, a chimney has a *throat*, a cup a *lip*, and a language is a *tongue*. We may be unable to *stomach* something and be *ribbed* for it, or have a *bone* of contention but make a clean *breast* of the matter. We may be saved by the *skin* of our teeth, or a *hair's-breadth*. A roof may have a *hip*, almost anything may have a *waist*, a brace may be a *knee*, and a man may be the *brains* of a gang, may *muscle* in, and have *guts*, more politely known as *intestinal* fortitude, and in the *womb* of time may still go to Abraham's *bosom*—so many analogies that an Englishman might call it *bloody* confusing. Some words, like *belly, chest*, and *rib* have gone back and forth from the anatomical so much that one may be uncertain which use is figurative.

Some figures move in the opposite direction. Calling a human head a *pan* is as old as Aristophanes. The French word for head, *tête*, comes from Latin *testa*, a pot, particularly a broken pot, and in the United States a crazy or misguided person can be a *crackpot*. *Cranium, cerebrum*, and cerebellum are presumably all related to our word *horn* through Latin and Greek. *Skull* probably stems from Old Norse *skoltr*, a bowl, and heads have been called *domes, cabbages, bubbles, balloons, pumpkins, squashes, nuts*, and almost anything round, especially if hollow or solid, as in *bonehead*. The word also enters into compounds like *bullheaded, pigheaded*, and *hophead*. Nor have man's more private parts been neglected; testicles are called *balls, nuts, berries, seeds, stones*, and *twins*; a penis is a *prick, prod, meat, tail*, or *reamer*; the female pudendum a *bag, fish pond, hot box, monkey, cat bin, pussy, slot*, and *tail*. The mountainous portions of America were once well scattered with twin peaks known as *Squaw's Ass*, terms now mainly expurgated by the

Forest Service and the U.S. Postal Service.

In fact, figures of speech so permeate word-building that some students have said that all words come from dead metaphors. Such an assertion probably lays claim to too much, but without doubt comparison and analogy enter in one way or another into most words that have any extensive history. Many recent terms are obviously figurative, and the figure gives words their charm; if a woman is called *peach, tomato, lemon, skirt, broad, doll, hen, heifer, chicken, white meat, a hank of hair*, a figure gave rise to the use and has preserved it. Older terms may rest equally on figures, although custom has dulled our awareness; a word as hackneyed as *circumstances* means whatever is standing around, and terms like *out-standing, under-standing, use-ful, extra-ordinary* take on new impact once we look at their parts.

Figures of speech come in many sorts, some utilizing mainly meaning, some relying on sound, and some combining both. Particular languages promote them more than do others. For various reasons, Latin and Greek were readily adapted to figures of speech, and Classical rhetoricians have identified dozens of sorts. Distinctions among them are fine, and the various sorts may seem to overlap when they are applied to vocabulary building, but in addition to metaphor, at least one other sort of figure may be revealing, **synecdoche**, taking a part for the whole or the whole for a part. The principle becomes apparent in the *crossbow*, in which a bow does cross a stock, but this idea of crossing is not the essential fact of the instrument. It had a more accurately descriptive name in Latin *acroballista*, "an engine of war utilizing an arc or bow." By false etymology the word got into German as *Armbrust*, which would seem to mean an "arm breast," using a different "part for the whole," portions of the body involved in firing the weapon. In another false etymology the term became *arrow blast*, which has nothing to do with either of the Latin roots that went into the word, but uses a different "part," the arrow and the force of its firing.

At least one other activity has given us a harvest of meanings, the love of making sounds. Babies use their bodies gleefully, wiggling their toes and whacking with their arms and legs, and since they can make noises with their vocal equipment, they do, cooing to themselves and babbling in sentence patterns in imitation of adults. When locomotives still made chuffing sounds, children called them *choo-choos*, and these days youngsters are adept at making chattery sounds in imitation of a *burp gun* when they *zap* or *zonk* you. Many nonliterate peoples have been fond of imitating the sounds about them and will call an owl an *uhu*, a Canada goose an *ongk-ongk*. Nor need we go to children and nonliterates to discover the adult love of making imitative sounds; the song about the various noises on Old Macdonald's farm is a perennial favorite, and it was adults who named an antiaircraft gun an *ack-ack* and a machine gun a *pom-pom*, along with the *bobwhite, whippoorwill,* and *peewee.*

Words for sounds are so characteristically **echoic** (the technical term is **onomatopoeia**, Greek for "making a name") that one can scarcely doubt we are dealing with more than coincidence in *peep, pipe, fife, clink, clunk, chink, chunk, boom, bang, whoop, whisper, slither, swish, swoosh, murmur, mumble, clatter, clack, chatter, mutter, chug, rattle, sputter, splutter, thud, bump, clang, ring, blubber, shush, bubble, tingle, sough, plop, ping, twitter, twang, ding, quack, honk,* and dozens more. Significantly, many of these words cannot be traced back very far; they occur in few languages, and hence we believe they sprang up after PIE times. We must assume, however, that PIE had its own echoic terms, many of them now obscured by changes in sound or meaning. If so, such terms may be much more numerous than they at first appear. Those that are obviously echoic like *shush, whinney, psst!* and *ack-ack* are sparse, while those that are apparently echoic like *murmur, whine,* and *whistle* are more plentiful—as we would expect them to be if this sort of thing has been going on for thousands of years.

But language changes. The older words have altered so much that we can only guess how they got started. Consider **wer-*. This root is so widespread that etymologists recognize more than ten archaic uses[1] of it in words as varied as *wart, liverwurst, rhomboid, apéritif,* and *extrovert,* more than a thousand shapes in English alone and thousands more in related languages. But suppose the ancestor of these shapes comes from one primeval echoic coinage? That it does is not improbable. Much evidence suggests that the earliest linguistic shapes were made from three sounds, a consonant plus a vowel plus a consonant, and a good percentage of these consonants would have been semivowels like /w/ and

---

1. The question is complex; authorities agree in general but differ in detail. Watkins, following but revising Pokorny, recognizes eleven roots taking the shape **wer-*. These may or may not stem from the same morpheme. His **wer-*[3], having the central meaning "to turn or bend," is surely the "base of various Indo-European roots." It alone accounts for nine subdivisions, most of which in turn have sub-subdivisions. One of these includes the Latin *vertere,* "to turn," which alone has dozens of cognates in English from *avert* to *universe.* Clearly we cannot here do more than suggest the wealth of loans involving **wer-*, whether or not we are dealing with a single original term.

/r/. A syllable like /woo-ah/, /way-ər/ is quite to be expected, as an imitation of the wind, for example. And as a matter of fact, *wer- tends to carry meanings like "turn," "twist," and "make a sound," ideas that could readily develop from a name for the blowing of the wind. That this *could* have happened is not a proof, but considering how prevalent echoic syllables are among all peoples—perhaps especially among those who live close to external nature and rely immediately upon it for food and shelter, as early IE peoples did—we must assume that at least a moderate number of the primeval morphemes came from the imitations of natural sounds. If so, hundreds of thousands, probably millions of modern words go back to echoic roots.

4. Caution: Minds at Work

Some uses of words grow from more intellectual processes. An example should supply evidence; we may elect *cross* and its relatives. The word is what is sometimes called o. o. o. (of obscure origin); some scholars derive it from *ker-, seen in our word *curve*, but it could have come from Phoenicia to Carthage and thence to Rome (a rare but not impossible route). If so, since nobody knows Carthaginian, we can only guess what it meant. It appeared in Latin as a word for a form made by fastening one stick across another. The term was but little used in early Latin; later, it was the name for a gibbet, since execution by fastening to crosses was not uncommon in the Roman Empire, especially in the Near East. Then it became "the cross," the name of the gibbet on which Jesus was presumably hung. With that attribution the word ballooned.

The *crucial* shape was the Latin, *crux, crucis*. It led to *crucify*, with derivatives like *crucifixion*, but it went from that to a general word for "to torture," with derivatives like *excruciating*, then "to torture to the extremity," that is, to death; and thus anything decisive became the *crux* of the matter, leading to *crucial* decisions, *crucial* evidence, and *crucial* actions. The word got into French as *croix*, and thence into Spanish, where a coin with a cross was a *crusado*; those who took the cross became *crusaders*, their military ventures *the Crusades*. So the word came into English with little change. In German a crusader was a *Kreutzer*, which became a family name, and English was invaded once more by *The Kreutzer Sonata*.

Meanwhile, some words from Latin seem to have preserved the idea of two sticks, one across the other, and thus many uses developed involving ideas like "opposing," "traversing," and "being angry." The word got into Dutch and presumably gives us *to cruise*, along with *cruiser*, and *cruise ship*; lumbermen *cruise* a stand of timber to determine its content in board feet. The word went north to other peoples, including the Irish, but the Norsemen overran Ireland even before they dominated England. Both Celtic and Old Norse uses supplemented those that came from the Classical and Romance tongues. The shape probably came in as Norman French *cruks* and certainly as central French *crois*, a pronunciation presumably supplemented by Irish *cros*, Welsh *croes*. Danish or Swedish *kors* became Scottish *corse*. Thus ME *cross* is a normalization of terms that followed various channels.

You can *go across* or *come across* or just *cross* the ocean, or a mountain range, and your action becomes a *crossing*, but a *crossing* can also be a place at which one thing seems to cross another, as in a *railroad crossing*. You can *cross* someone by opposing him, and work at *cross* purposes. You may *cross* animals or plants by interbreeding them, swear to the truth by *crossing your heart*, cancel something by *crossing* it *out* or *off*, and bribe by *crossing someone's palm*. You may become as *cross as two sticks*, in which phrase the word has combined a recent meaning with the earliest use we know.

Cross has gone into hundreds of compounds. The *crossbow* was an early weapon, and *crossbones* became part of the symbol of death. People run *cross-country* races, drown in *cross currents*, use *cross hairs* to aim a weapon, or die in a *crossfire*. Recent terms include *cross-index, cross-file, cross-reference, cross-examine* or *cross-question, cross section, crosswalk*, and *cross-town*. American English has accounted for dozens of such compounds, *crossties* on the railroad, a *cross-staked pole fence*, a type of structure favored by some rail-fence builders, and the *double cross-hop*, a frontier dance routine during which the male participant flung himself into the air and crossed his legs before he came down. His lady had to restrain herself to a *cross-shuffle*. Meanwhile, lumbermen used a *crosscut* saw; rustlers stole cattle and *cross-branded* them; farmers *cross-hoed* corn, partly to kill the *cross-leavers*, or wild licorice, and fashionable ladies fancied *cross-legged* furniture. Since then, *double-cross* has developed many meanings and has spawned *Double-Crostic*, a type of word puzzle.

Such listings could go on and on, but we should ask ourselves: what are minds up to when they devise such uses? One answer must be obvious: meanings are going from the specific to the general and back again from the general to the specific. The earliest meaning we know for *crux, crucis*, is moderately specific: two sticks crossed, for whatever purpose. The term became more specific, the designation of a pole set up with the crossbar near the upper end, intended as a gibbet for persons condemned to execution. Then it became very specific, in fact so limited that the term referred to only one object—the process is technically called *particularization*.[2]

Soon the term became general again. One finds such definitions as the following in dictionaries: "representation of a cross in any of various recognized forms, as a symbol of the crucifixion of Jesus, and hence of the Christian religion" . . . "any trouble or affliction that one has to bear" . . . "anything that thwarts or frustrates" . . . "any crossing or mixing" . . . "to go counter to, to thwart, or oppose." Such general meanings can immediately start giving birth to more specific terms, such as *crosshatching* and *cross-stitch*. And at any time, any of these words can become more or less specific as occasion warrants, and any of these uses may involve figures of speech. *Crossroad* carries perhaps medium specificity, and in a phrase like *mankind at the crossroads* it has become very general, but in *Crossroads*, a village in northern Donegal, it has become a proper name for one small place, which is about as specific as you can get. Almost any attempt to follow the streams of meaning associated with the main uses of *cross* will lead to varying degrees and various reversals of specificity and generality. Many scholars have called these two trends *widening* and *narrowing* of meaning.

A word about the two may be in order. They are basic ways of using the mind, at all times and everywhere. So far as language is concerned, this has not always been the assumption. In the day when the nature of language was a subject for philosophers to think about, before it became a field for investigators to work in patiently, specificity was associated with ignorance and being "primitive." The belief was that nonliterate peoples could name things, but were too stupid to generalize about them. Thus, if they were Eskimos, they might have dozens of names for different sorts of white stuff that fell during the cold weather, but would have no general word for snow. For them, wet snow falling gently, hard snow driven by a blizzard, snow heaped in drifts, and snow so packed as to be usable as building material might be four sorts of things, not one thing in different states. For good reasons, including his need for sur-

2. It is interesting to speculate what might have happened to the English language, and many other tongues, if Jesus had been stoned to death instead of fastened to a cross, as he might well have been, had the execution been carried out by the local folk instead of the Roman administration.

vival, the Eskimo thinks of snow not as one sort of thing that can appear with several variations, but as various sorts of things distinguished from one another by form, use, origin, and the like.

That an Amazonian Indian has more than a hundred terms for various conditions of his staple diet, the potato, but has no generic term for *Solanum tuberosum* is no evidence of his stupidity, any more than the lack in American English of a generic term for the various sorts of wounds that can be made with stone axes is evidence that white men are all morons. The notion that cultured Europeans could generalize but that savage Africans could not, that the ability to generalize was the test of intellectual maturity, was flattering to the philosopher and his countrymen, but it finds little support in fact, either technological or linguistic.

The idea was plausible for western Europe. We have noticed that Anglo-Saxons did not debate philosophical questions much; nor did their contemporaries, whose descendants now speak French, German, or Russian. When professional and academic questions engaged more minds, students did the obvious thing: they imported both concepts and the names for them from the Greeks and Romans, whose thinkers had learned to deal with ideas and had developed the terminology to do so. Thus many means of generalizing were loans from the Classical tongues, and such borrowing was enhanced by the use of Latin as the international language of learned discussion. Borrowing Classical terms was widespread and unconscious, and without doubt the Greeks and Romans had been subtle and learned people. Consequently, if an explorer found no equivalent of a Latin general term in the speech of Trobrianders or Chickasaw Indians, a plausible explanation was that the Greeks were sophisticated enough to generalize, but the Trobrianders and Chickasaws were not.

A closer look at life and language would have suggested that such ready generalities are not well-founded. Being specific is surely as difficult, as culturally advanced, as is generalizing. We might recall that the infant chimpanzee, Washoe, had no trouble generalizing; that small children can do it, and morons often speak in generalities. On the other hand, any scientist can tell you that being precise and specific is difficult enough to require long training and an extensive, finely sharpened vocabulary. There may have been a time when proto-humans could name objects but could not make observations about them, although this seems improbable. An aboriginal mother was surely as likely to have one signal for warning against almost everything dangerous as she was to have different shrieks for various predators. She probably did not lack the power of generalizing about danger. If she did, her descendants acquired such resources long before they learned any language of which we have record.

This is not to suggest that sophisticated life does not promote generalization. We should expect it would. Peoples, like those in western Europe and some other places, who have leisure and a dialectic tradition that promotes dealing with abstract principles and problems, may well generalize more than do people who live by dragging fish out of their native element or grinding pine nuts, people who must spend most of their working hours filling the overriding need for food. We would expect them to have more terms for generalized thinking. But they are likely to have more terms for specifics, too. The fact is, they have more terms of all sorts.

5. Can We Generalize about Generalization and Be Specific about Specificity?

The question is not which is the more sophisticated, being general or being specific; these means are native to both mind and language. A better question is this: can we analyze either generalization or specification more exactly? They can be kept apart, since they go in opposite directions. We may have difficulty saying how general a generality is, as we would have difficulty setting up any exact scale of specificity, but we can probably all agree that in going from *crux* as a name for the crossing of two sticks—any two sticks—to *crux* as the name of the unique cross used as a gibbet for Jesus we are moving from the general toward the specific, from the broad to the narrow. Similarly, in going from the cross of Christ to Christian faith, we are moving toward generality. But many mental processes are not so easily distinguished, partly because we find difficulty in identifying opposite poles, or isolating parallel trends.

We might consider parallel trends by having a closer look at *cross*. The word did not develop in OE, probably because Anglo-Saxons tended to adapt their own terms to imported objects; they called the cross the *Rood* (our word *rod*), using the compound *seglrod*, "sailyard," the crossbar on the mast. Terms like this are sometimes called **calque loans** (a *calque* being an exact replica), substituting a local word for its synonym in another language. This word *rood* had a lively life of its own in English, giving us *rood screen*, the screen that separates the choir from the remainder of an English cathedral, *Rood Day*, "Ascension

Day,'' and other terms associated with the symbol of the Crucifixion. But in time the nonreligious uses of *cross* as a verb appeared, either through borrowing from French or by a parallel development, so that before 1400 Chaucer could say that "over-thwart this line . . . there crosses another line.''

In the next few centuries the verb *cross* is used in various senses suggesting that something exists or moves athwart something else. We have noticed above that a traveler could *cross* the seas, a farmer could *cross-plow*, and a hare could *cross* one's path. How are we to say that these uses are more or less specific than one line crossing another? Each is somewhat different, and some figurative use may be possible, but the growth is better described by what scholars have called **transfer,** that is, a shape like *cross* was transferred from the concept of one line lying athwart another to a traveler's line of voyage lying athwart the sea. Or, to describe the act from the opposite point of view, the idea of "voyaging upon the ocean to a foreseen destination,'' is transferred to the word *cross*.

Such transfers can be numerous and varied. If we conceive that two ingredients are involved, the *name*, or shape, as opposed to the *sense*, the meaning or use, four sorts of transfer are possible—

1) *Name similarity* and *sense similarity:* the word *hard*, meaning "difficult'' leads readily to *hardly*, so difficult as to be unlikely.

2) *Name similarity* and *sense contiguity:* the word *belfry* presumably comes from *berfroi*, a tower for defense, but since towers were often graced with bells, *belfry* became a natural transfer.

3) *Name contiguity* and *sense similarity:* a traditional example is the Latin set phrase, *equites peditesque*, "riders and walkers''; when the riders became a social class, the knights, *pedites* became the name for common men, as opposed to knights.

4) *Name contiguity* and *sense contiguity:* an Indian who lived on the *plains* became a *Plains Indian*, those in the forest, *Woods Indians*, who practiced a *woods* culture.

Distinctions like these, useful in semantics as a study, become hard to delineate, and the corresponding terms impossible to restrict to only one sort of relationship. Apparently almost any kind of transfer is possible, if two words are related to one another in shape and two senses are related to one another by cause, position in space, similarity of idea, or whatever. If we are interested in working with words, to understand and to use them, not mainly to account for the psychological processes back of them, perhaps we need observe no more than this: that words and meanings shift readily to anything that is close to them in any way. Or, to phrase this confusion differently, the relationships within language are so extensive and varied that dozens of transfers are always possible, and any one transfer will utilize whatever relationship seems to arise naturally.

6. Making Words by Pattern and the Feel of the Language

Language lives by patterns and responds to the feelings of its users. Inevitably, these subtle drifts color the impact of words, even occasionally account for shapes and uses. The role of pattern in word formation is tricky to measure; speakers of the language have a feel for it and never create words in contrast to the native patterns. No new coinages begin with spellings like *phth* or end with strong stress on the last syllable because these are not characteristic of NE.

On the other hand, users constantly shape the language toward established conventions. Loans from languages having strange patterns are unconsciously modified toward local speech. Borrowed terms are more or less Anglicized, shifted in innumerable small ways to seem like English. *Paris*, France, is likely to be pronounced in the United States like *Paris, Kentucky*, although the accent and most of the individual sounds will thereby differ from French. Sooner or later most borrowed nouns are provided with English plurals; Latin *circus*, which had a plural *circi*, long ago became *circuses*, and *agenda*, a Latin plural, looks like an English singular and has been equipped with a new plural, *agendas*. Such bits can be pinned down, but the broader pressure of patterns and the temper of societies beggar analysis, although changes accumulate with the centuries. Measuring these drifts is not easy, partly because they are varied and subtle, partly because nobody, not even those of us who presume to write about language, has been able to describe the pattern of any body of speech completely and precisely. Mention of a few trends must suffice.

The tendency toward filling gaps is one of these. Minds are orderly, if not very orderly, and we like to feel there are no gaps in the vocabulary. We like, for example, to have antonyms. Some words by their nature have no antonyms—what is the antonym of *nose*, of *Atlantic Ocean?* And for some we had so many antonyms that no more were needed; having *small, little, baby, not big*, and the like, we have felt no need for *unbig*. But we have developed a remarkable number of words prefixed with *in-* or *un-*, although in most instances we already had some other way of expressing a negative. *Safe* soon developed *unsafe* (by about 1600), even though *dangerous* had acquired this meaning some two centuries earlier. Even a word like *crossed* in the sense of "signed with the cross" or "wearing a cross" prompted a derived antonym before *cross* itself had developed many related meanings; a tract of 1560 reads: *What a swarme of popyshe shauelyngs brought he forth . . . some crossed, some vncrossed."* We even developed *uncross-examinable*.

After the manner of language, most such coinages and derivatives insinuate themselves unnoticed, but occasionally one becomes an issue. Take *couth*. It was the past participle of an Old English verb meaning "to know," *cunnan, can, cunon, couthe*, which became an auxiliary, our word *can*, and there being no use for the past participle of an auxiliary, *couth* atrophied except in our past form, *could*. *Can* in the sense "to know" dropped out of the standard languages—it accounts for *ken* in Scottish and some other dialects. But *uncouth* in the older sense was already common; both King Alfred and the Venerable Bede point out that certain historical details are *uncuðe*, that is, "unknown." The word grew; a person who was unknown in a community was likely to be a foreigner, or to have come from the back country, and behave in strange, untutored, even boorish ways. Thus *uncouth* came to mean "crude," "socially inept." Then a few years ago a fad developed of noticing lapses in the language, and using the term *couth* became something of a joke, but it got started. At this writing it can be observed in serious use to mean "knowing how to handle oneself socially." *Inept* is now siring *ept*, and *disgruntled* is said to be producing a new noun, a *disgrunt*.[3]

Another trend is economy. Whether from a sober sense of parsimony in language, or laziness, or a deep love of revolt, we try to shorten things. The tendency can be observed in many languages; we borrowed *fruit* from French, but it was already cut down from Latin *fructus* before it became a loan. We cut *laboratory* down to *lab* and *being under the influence of alcohol* to *being under the influence*. Such reduction may lead to other changes; *professor* becomes *prof*, and the two shapes can have the same referent, refer to the same sort of person or even to the same individual, but the user of the terms is implying rather different attitudes with each, and the impact of the two on readers or hearers will differ. Or take the slang term *headshrinker*. It became a derogatory term for a psychiatrist, especially a psychoanalyst. It was cut down to *shrinker*

---

3. Many of these coinages are what we have called above *back-formations*.

and eventually to *shrink,* and can now be used in slang context for almost any medical attendant. The latter term is now common enough to appear in up-to-date American dictionaries, although *shrink* as a noun with any meaning was so rare as to find no place in the OED.

Common, and perhaps unusually common in recent American English, is ellipsis, that is, leaving out something presumably understood. Thus *railroad track* becomes *track,* a *pickup truck* becomes a *pickup,* a *law enforcement* or *police officer* or an *officer of the law* becomes just an *officer. Tie* has in effect replaced *cross-tie.* Such combinations readily combine a name and a modifier, but after ellipsis either the name or the modifier can remain as a noun; a *long-distance telephone call* can be a *long-distance call,* or just *long-distance,* a term in common use although not recognized in all dictionaries. *Gearshift* can become either *gears* or *shift.* A *six-pack of beer* becomes a *six-pack* and even a *six.* Lately, *hind,* practically unknown in American English as a noun, has become the name for the after part of a bird or animal so butchered as to be sold in two pieces, the term probably cut down from something like *hind quarters.* Such terms are now being made rapidly and must already exist by the tens of thousands.

Somewhat related are abbreviations and acronyms. These last are initial letters or syllables which, if they fall into customary English patterns, readily become words. Few people now think of *Jeep,* a trade name, as having any association with army slang for *G.P.,* General Purpose Vehicle; and ZIP, now often written *zip,* from *Zone Improvement Plan,* has developed *zip code* as a phrase, *zip-code* as a verb, *zip-coded* as a modifier, and even *zip* as a verb, "to provide with zip-code numbers." Acronyms have become routine in certain areas, including military and hospital use, so much so that a layman may be unable to understand the talk of army officers or even of practical nurses. A few acronyms, like *radar* (radio detecting and ranging), *sonar* (sound navigation and ranging), *CAT scan* (computerized axial tomography), have entered the common vocabulary, but most remain esoteric.

The devising of organization names that will provide amusing or attention-grabbing acronyms has become a minor sport. SCOOP, which addresses itself to people who walk dogs, stands for *Stop Crapping On Our Property,* and GASP denominates *Group Against Smog and Pollution.* Students have been uncommonly fertile in picturesque acronyms, producing STOP for *Students Tired of Pollution.* Many activists have contrived to name themselves to produce a sprightly acronym; thus, the National Organization for Women becomes NOW. *Mutual Assured*

Destruction produced MAD, and the San Francisco prostitutes must have felt some community with another outcast when they organized to promote better social acceptance and called themselves COYOTE from *Call Off Your Old Tired Ethics.*

Somewhat similar are what are called blends, or portmanteau words, since they do promote economy, although they are probably prompted by the will to be novel or amusing. Words having at least a common sound or letter are run together, as in *brunch* from *breakfast* and *lunch, smog* from *smoke* and *fog, rubbage* from *rubbish* and *garbage.* Some blends have become so common that they have crowded out most synonyms; *motel* from *motor hotel,* unknown a few decades ago, is routine in the United States, having replaced *cabins, motor court,* and several others, and is finding its way into England. The universal city envisioned by some planners becomes *ecumenopolis* for *ecumenical metropolis. Subtopia,* from *suburban utopia,* is ironical, suggesting that life among the hamburger stands can be less than idyllic. Some blends are so syncopated as to be hardly recognizable; a *moped* is presumably a "motor-assisted pedal-cycle." Even *bastitch* may call for explication; it designates a bastard who is also an SOB.

7. Taboos, Euphemisms, and Naughty Words

The explorer Captain James Cook, returning from the South Seas, reported that at a certain season, "Since every thing, very soon, would be *tabu,* if any of our people, or their own, were found walking about, they would be knocked down with clubs." The idea seems to have been that somebody or something, including as in this instance a period of time, was holy or consecrated to the goddess, to the King, or to whatever power. From the idea of being consecrated grew that of being forbidden, and from forbidden to hidden, in order that consecration might be preserved. Thus language comes in, because one way to obscure was to hide through the anonymity of having no name.

Not everywhere have taboos been so rigorous that anyone "found walking about" was knocked down with clubs, but taboos are and have been widespread. Christians have as many words as they do for the supreme deity because Jews were forbidden to name Jehovah—a practice widespread in folklore. *Jehovah* itself results from an attempt to obscure the original name, supposed to have been something like *Javeh.* Many a folk hero has boasted that he never refused to tell any man his name; the assumption was that knowing a person's name could give an enemy magical or other control, and giving your name was the last word in courage.

In modern Western societies, taboos have frequently implied "disapproved" rather than "forbidden," and they were directed not so much toward supernatural powers as toward sex, scatology, and a few subjects like death and cancer. Usually the taboo led to no more than **euphemisms** (from words that mean "good" and "voice" in Greek, and related to our word *fame*). Thus in some social contexts persons do not die; they *pass on, leave us, go to their reward,* or *depart.* They may even *go to Abraham's bosom* or *join the angels. Cancer* and *cancerous* are avoided; malignant growths are called *carcinogenic, carcinomatous,* or *sarcomatous,* and tumors that are not malign are said to be "benign" as though noncancerous growths are actually beneficial. For many terms the problem was solved by using Latin, which children would not be able to read. Thus in medicalese, answering a call of nature after going to bed is called a *nocturna,* a term that formerly meant a nocturnal religious service. The female orifice becomes a *vagina* (in Latin, "a sheath"), or a *pudendum,* from a Latin word for "something to be ashamed of," perhaps significantly here given the neuter gender, which was not usual in Latin. An English circumlocution, *private parts,* which was reduced by ellipsis to *privates,* allowed Shakespeare a handsome pun. Hamlet is greeting his former schoolmates, and has asked them how they are getting on—

GUILDENSTERN: . . . on Fortunes Cap, we are not the very Button. [Lady Fortuna was a Classical goddess who had survived from the Middle Ages.]
HAMLET: Nor the Soales of her Shoo?
ROSENCRANTZ: Neither my Lord.
HAMLET: Then you liue [live] about her waste, or in the middle of her fauour [favor]?
GUILDENSTERN: Faith, her Priuates, we.
HAMLET: In the secret parts of Fortune? Oh, most true: she is a strumpet.

Euphemism, substituting an innocuous term for one felt to be offensive, has altered locutions for reasons of politeness, prudence, and even fear. Since using a less honorific title than a person has earned may be insulting, many people deliberately exalt any rank above the one they assume to be warranted. Thus for a time the Southern States were seeded with colonels who had never advanced beyond sergeant, or had never used a firearm except to go hunting. Our ancestors called a large, lumbering brute whom they feared in battle "the brown one," our word *bear*. The weasel, since it was believed to suck the blood of sleeping persons, acquired dozens of flattering titles. In English it was *the fairy;* in French, *belette,* "beautiful little woman"; in Portuguese, *doninha,* "little lady"; in Spanish, *comadreja,* "good lady friend"; in Italian, *donola,* "lovely lady." In Denmark the weasel could be the equivalent of *bride* or *charming girl*, in Sweden, *pretty little girl*, in Albania and Greece, *sister-in-law*.

Impudent or raucous behavior has provided another evasion. As almost any child can demonstrate, impudence is a bastion of the abused, at once self-satisfying and difficult to identify objectively enough to justify punishment. The use of what has been called "foul" or "filthy language," for which children formerly had their mouths washed out with soapsuds, may have seemed an uncommonly fitting retort. No sound is dirty of itself. As beauty is in the eye of the beholder, so the foulness of language is in the ear of the listener, however much a similar sentiment may have been in the intent of the speaker. Earthy speech may seem the proper retort to the self-righteous, especially if the earthiness can mask as innocence. Thus pornographic and scatological terms have been promoted by native perversity, especially when taboo was coupled with prudery. Vulgar language can also be a ticket of admission, or a badge of membership in a society from which at least some others are excluded. Ability to use "four-letter words" could be a sort of male puberty rite.

8. Some Taboo Terms

Estimating the importance of all this for language is a bit hazardous, because much scatology and pornography has gone unprinted or has been ignored and glossed over in dictionaries. *Ass* should provide a revealing example. Historically, the word in English is *arse,* from OE *ears,* which comes from a root meaning "to wet," "to shoot out semen." It was a name for *dew* and is seen in our words *rosemary* and *rhubarb*. It early had several meanings in English and it could indicate the buttocks. To *beg breeches* from *a bare-arsed man* was the epitome of being ridiculous. It could mean the rectum; one of Chaucer's less sedate characters tells us that *twenty thousand freres* (friars) could be driven *out of the deueles ers* (devil's arse). In OE, an *ersgang* (arse-going) was a bowel movement, and an *erswisp* the equivalent of modern toilet tissue.

Ass could mean the vulva or coitus or probably both—as it does today in American slang. One manuscript of *Piers Plowman* reads: *For an hore of hure ers-wynnyng may hardiloker tythe pan an erraunt vsurer* (From an hour of her arse-winnings she can pay tithes better than can a downright usurer). The meaning "the male organ," found in current American slang, has not been attested for British English; it may be a recent parallel development, or it may preserve the original association of *erse* with insemination, in a meaning obscured by the reticence of scribes and lexicographers. The form *arse* is still common in British English and has been transplanted to Australia, where an unwanted question about somebody's whereabouts can be turned away by saying he is *up the camel's arse looking for an oasis.*

In the United States the word *arse* is mainly restricted to a few intellectuals given to fun, it being unknown to most persons trying to be naughty. It is written *ass* and pronounced /æs/, to rhyme with *mass.* The earliest recorded use having this spelling comes from the *Seaman's Catechism* of 1860, referring to "the ass of the block." The meaning of the term is made clear by an entry in Bailey's dictionary of 1721: ARSE, among sailors: the Arse of a Block or Pulley, through which any Rope runs, in the lower end of it." The OED labels the form "vulgar and dialectal spelling and pronunciation of ARSE," and since the editors did not usually give such attention to a term so rare as to warrant only one citation, one surmises they had a good many more, uses not so readily restricted as being "among sailors." The use probably came to the American colonies along with a good many other locutions common on the streets but frowned upon in the parlor. And it may have been influenced by the fact that many British dialects, including Received Pronunciation, obscures medial /r/, so that /ars/ would readily become /as/ or /æs/.

As a shape, the word *ass* was confused with the name of a beast of burden, which came from Latin *asinus,* perhaps through Celtic. It was probably popularized by its frequent use in Biblical translations. Since asinine quadrupeds are not common in England, the term is now mostly used there as a derogation for males, as in *silly ass, that young ass,* or *a complete ass.* In the United States, *ass,* from British English *arse,* impeded the use of the *ass* that named a beast of burden. The rare term *donkey,* apparently from eighteenth-century slang, was made respectable, and *burro* was borrowed from Spanish *burrito.* Meanwhile, even *jackass* was reduced in polite speech to *jack*—although not always among workingmen. Prospectors labeled many a bit of pasturage in the desert West *Jackass Flat,* and one such place name has been restored to respectability by becoming a nuclear proving ground. In the United States, in polite language, the term has been mainly restricted to strange foreign beasts, like the *Wild Ass of Persia.* The name *The Two Asses,* which can designate stars in the constellation Cancer and refers to *equus asinus,* not to an assortment of human buttocks, has never been much used in America.

But as slang and vulgate the word has been fruitful in English. *Ass-kisser* is a common term for a toady, and if you are dejected you may *have your ass in a sling.* I was delighted to hear an automobile mechanic say of an unenterprising garage, *Them guys better get their ass in gear.* An *ass man* or *big ass man* is defined in the *Dictionary of American Slang* as "a youth or man who devotes much time to coitus," and the editors comment upon it, "Often used with envy or admiration, esp. by students; seldom used in moral reprimand." Until recently all such uses were taboo. Then for a time you might hear a nice girl say *bassackwards* instead of *assbackwards*; she had not quite said the word, and had tried to reduce it to what W. S. Gilbert called "innocent merriment." Recently, there has been a minor revolution in usage, so that *ass* and most other taboo terms may be heard almost anywhere, emanating from almost anyone.

Similar erratic histories characterize many "four-letter words." The terms are mostly old, or moderately old, but have been only sketchily recorded. *Piss* comes from Middle English *pissen,* from Old French *pissier,* probably echoic slang. Chaucer knew the word *shitten,* and contrasted a *shitten* shepherd to *a clene shepe* (a clean sheep), to the advantage of the latter. The implication is that a decent layman is better than a corrupt ecclesiastic. The word is recorded once in OE, meaning "to defecate," probably with the underlying notion of separating oneself from something, since the root idea is to cut or divide. It has hundreds of relatives in various languages, including *schizophrenia, science, shin, schedule, shiver, ski, escutcheon, rescind*—an eminently respectable family tree. Eric Partridge, *Dictionary of Slang and Unconventional English*, treats the word, and gives numerous compounds and phrases from his years in Australia, such as *you could shit a brick*, to celebrate something astonishing. He says *shit* is widely used among cultured people "down under," and even more in Canada.

Chaucer used the word *cunt,* but he may have considered it somewhat suspect, since the Wife of Bath calls her organ of increase her *bele chose* (beautiful thing). It is not attested in OE, although it probably existed there: it appears in low Germanic and has relatives in several Germanic tongues, giving us *cod, cobalt, cottage, goblin, keel, chitterling*, etc. It apparently goes back to a root having the idea of a mound or enclosure, and may stem from the *mons veneris*, "mound of love."

Curiously, the word *cock*, a term for the male organ—and also *cock* as in *haycock* but not as a designation for a rooster—goes back to the same root. The words are not easily traced in English, because both are ignored, even by the OED,[4] as well as by most other dictionaries, but the editors of the *Supplement* to the OED are endeavoring to redress such oversights. They imply the existence of *cock* by including such compounds as *cockstand*, "an erection," and *cock-teaser*, "a sexually provocative woman who evades or refuses intercourse." *Cunt* is made an entry in the *Supplement* with many citations, the first a London street name, *Gropecuntelane*, recorded about 1230. Such a jocular reference implies wide currency. *Fuck* also gets its first extensive treatment in dictionaries in the same *Supplement*, and in Eric Partridge, mentioned above. They cite the following definition from Florio's *Worlde of Wordes* (1598), "*Fottere*, to iape [to deceive], to sard, to fucke, to swive, to occupy."

Most of these verbs are not well described, but *swive* is discussed in the OED. A satirical song of about 1300 charges that Richard the Lion-Hearted, "whil that he was kyng, He spende al his tresour opon swyving." The word occurs several times in Chaucer; in one of his unfinished tales a rowdy apprentice has a girlfriend who kept a shop for show and *swived* for their living. The word is related to Old English *swifan*, "to swivel." So far as I can observe, the taboo word that is now most rapidly losing its status as a taboo in the United States is the compound that refers to intercourse with a female parent.

9. Pejoration and Amelioration

The terms pejoration and amelioration should be mentioned, since they get into most surveys of semantic change, but in actuality they have been implied in such shifts as those described in the discussion of *ship*, above. **Pejoration** implies worsening; **amelioration**, change for the bet-

---

4. The editor labored over the problem, soliciting learned advice, while himself proposing to include a few questionable items, "especially those whose history shows them to have been originally reputable words debased by later usage." He was warned that *condum* was "too utterly obscene" to be included, and the letter including the advice was left in its envelope, marked *Private*. The same correspondent thought that excluding

ter. We have already observed that the referents of words may change, and when they change, inevitably some will grow worse in the sense that they will decline in the social scale, will be less admired, and the like, at least part of the time, and some will improve.

An example frequently cited is *marshal*. The word is an old compound, using a term that has survived as NE *mare*, meaning "a horse," and the earlier form of OE *scealc*, "a servant." Thus the term implied a groom, although we should add that possession of a horse presumed wealth. In subsequent centuries, *marshal* came to designate an exalted personage in government or the armed forces, and in some societies the *field marshal* is the highest military officer. This is surely amelioration. Contrarily, NE *knave*, "a rascal," meant merely "a boy" in OE *cnafu*, as it still does in German *Knabe*. The term became the name of a playing card before this pejoration took place; we are told that "the knave of hearts . . . stole some tarts," but that was presumably no more than a boyish prank. The phrase *an arrant knave* suggests the modern impact of the word.

Much nomenclature has drifted in both directions, for example, PIE **gwen-*, meaning "a woman." It has retained its impartial coloring in *gynecology* and other scientific and professional terms like *polygyny*, but it also turns up in Old Irish *banshee*, a female spirit that could be either a goddess or a wailing sort of female devil. Presumably there were expressions like "the king and his woman," his **gwen*, which in English became *queen*. But a man's "woman" might as well be a gangster's moll, and this implication is preserved in the spelling *queane*, a prostitute. In most groups of words amelioration and pejoration have not been so extreme, but we can safely assume that no body of common words in any language has ever been without some suggestion of one or the other. Considering the extent to which both language and society waver, any other condition is probably impossible.

10. Overstatement, Understatement, Debased Terms

"And I'm reading *trillions* of books," a student wrote home. She did not mean this, of course, but her chatter inclined to be what is often

---

pudendum would be cowardly and suggested it "might be curtly dismissed—of course, without a quotation—a thing presque introuvable." K. M. Elizabeth Murray, *Caught in the Web of Words: J. A. H. Murray and the "Oxford English Dictionary"* (New Haven, Conn.: Yale University Press, 1977), p. 195.

called "emotive." It ministered to her own feelings, not much to her parents' information. **Exaggeration** of this sort, formally called **hyperbole**, is said to be more than normally characteristic of many Americans and their speech. The opposite inclination, **understatement**, or **litotes**, is prevalent in England, and of course among reserved people everywhere. Beowulf provides a classic example. When he offers to invite an attack from the monster Grendel, he says in effect to his host, "I will not trouble you overmuch. If I lose you will not need to give me breakfast." He is implying that long before breakfast time he would have been devoured to the last morsel. The two trends together account for only a few words, but they do something to extend the range of language. Mark Twain made more deliberate use of both devices, side by side, than has any other distinguished writer of English. His journalism teems with exaggeration, but he is perhaps best known for observing once that reports of his death had been greatly exaggerated.

Some terms have been used so much and so thoughtlessly that they have lost all meaning and serve only to give the speaker the sense that he is saying something. At this writing, columnists all over the country are complaining that some speakers, mostly young, will throw in *you know* at every pause, as though it is oral punctuation. At hearings, speakers will say *exactly*, while trying to phrase a question that has nothing to do with exactitude in the expected answer. *More or less* has become so debased that recently a legislator complained, "That was the straw that more or less broke the camel's back." Some situations promote the debasing of terms, one being a promise of prompt action. *Anon* formerly had several fairly clear meanings involved in oneness, but it came to be a promise of quick action. Now *anon* is obsolete in all its senses. Currently such terms as *at once, immediately, right away, in a minute*, and *just a second* are losing meaning.

11. Word Formation by Whim and Blunder

A few minor sorts of word formation reflect man's confusion. *Backformation,* mentioned above, seems to be a transfer, except that there never was anything to be transferred. A commonly cited example is the word *edit. Editor* is presumably a loan from Latin, the past participle of *edere,* made up of *ex-,* "out," plus *dare,* "to give," something issued and, by transfer, the one who issues something. But by analogy with combinations like *farm, farmer*, and *work, worker*, the existence of editors seemed to presume the occupation *to edit* (it may have been somewhat influenced by the French *editer*). The earliest citation in the OED is late (1793). Some cases are clearer; presumably W. S. Gilbert coined *to buttle* from *butler* to amuse people, and *sculpt* is a handy word to name what *sculptors* do.

A set of words resulting from blunder has been mentioned earlier, called **false etymology**, less appropriately **folk** or **popular etymology**— the mistakes do grow from ignorance, but not only from the ignorance of the illiterate. With anything as complex as language, even the learned make mistakes, especially since no one can know all tongues. An *advocate*, a lawyer, is historically not one who *advocates* the cause of his client. He was one who called a witness. The word got from Latin into French as *avocat* and in ME was cut down to *voket*, but an approximation of the Latin form was restored by learned influence, *ad* plus *vocare*, to call forward. *Controller* is often spelled *comptroller*, and pronounced with an /mp/, since Latinists derived it from *comptare*, "to count." We now know it comes from Anglo-Norman *contre-roller*, that is, one who checked the rolls, or official records. Langland used the word before 1400 (the spelling *comptroller* comes from after 1500) with such spellings as *conterroller*, *contrerouler*, or *countrorouler* in the various manuscripts —the usual variety, but none spelled with *mp*.

Likewise, the apostrophe in the NE possessive results from a learned lapse. ME had a rare possessive, an ornate phrase pretty much restricted to a complimentary term, *the King, his daughter*. ME also had forms like *Kings daughter, Kinges daughter*, and *Kingis daughter*, variant spellings of the possessive. Later, the spelling *Kingis daughter* was supposed to be a contraction of the more formal form, *the King, his daughter*, and an apostrophe was inserted to recognize the omission. The practice spread, and we now have an unhistorical apostrophe in *the king's daughter*.

Inevitably, such growths stem most frequently from uninformed people. We earlier noticed (Chapter VI.1) a small boy confusing *consecrated* and *concentrated*. Similarly, a farm hand of my acquaintance, having encountered *recuperate*, rendered it *recruit up*, which sounded all right to him and fitted the apparent meaning pretty well. He was following a long tradition; *bridegroom* is a compound of OE *bryd*, "bride" and *guma*, "man," the latter warped into *groom* when *guma* was no longer recognizable. Similarly, *crayfish* and *crawfish* represent attempts to reproduce ME *scrayfisse*, from Old French, seen in Modern French *écrevisse*, a freshwater lobster. Shakespeare has one of his clowns say his father is "sand blind, nay gravel blind"; the earlier form was *samblind*, the equivalent of our *semiblind*, but the *sam-* was changed to *sand*. Currently, composition teachers are complaining that students who want to write *take it for granted* are producing *take it for granite.*

Northern England and Scotland are seeded with place names that had meaning in Danish or Norwegian and have now been twisted to resemble something in English. Old Norse *Skogarfell,* "wooded mountain," becomes *Skye Hill.* Old Norse *stakkr* meant a columnar stone, and since such pinnacles rise along various coasts, *Heigh Stakkr* (High Rock) was a frequent place name, not very well represented in its modernization, *Haystack.* The name of the *St. Kilda Isles* in the Hebrides has no pious origin, but presumably stems from Norse *skildir,* "shields."

In the United States, French and Spanish names were misunderstood, so that *Choupique,* a French spelling for an Indian term meaning "muddy" or "mud fish," becomes *Shoe Peg. Tête de Mort,* named for a skull on a pole, became *Tiddymor,* and then *Teddy Moore,* presumably named for a pioneer who, however, never existed. *Bois Brulé,* "a burned forest," becomes *Bob Ruley,* likewise nonexistent. *L'Eau Froid,* "cold water," for a creek, becomes *Low Freight. Tia Juana* is supposed to be Spanish for Aunt Jane, although there is no record of any early woman Juana ever having lived there; but an Indian term, *tee-ah-ja-wanna* apparently means "where the waves break."

The potentialities for blunder are almost infinite. Singulars and plurals have not always been recognized. *Pease* was a singular, but it sounded like a plural, and accordingly it was supplied with a new singular, *pea. Phenomena,* a plural, is engendering *phenomenas.* Confusion between *a* and *an* has disrupted a few words: *a numpire,* meaning a "nonpeer," a third party brought in to settle a dispute, has become *an umpire,* and *a nadder* has become *an adder. A napron,* "tablecloth," related to *map,* has become *an apron.* By reversing the process, an /n/ was added where none had been. *An eke name,* "an extra name," since *eke* means "also," became *a nickname,* and *an ewt* becomes *a newt.* One of the more recent innovations has given us *nother,* as when *another thing* becomes *a (whole) nother thing.*

Rather curiously, however, the words and meanings in English that have stemmed from ignorance or blunders are relatively few, nothing like the great body of words that reflect the orderly or playful working of the human mind. We are told, for example, that the fondness for what are sometimes called "sandwich words" is today growing, especially in England, with locutions like *inde-goddamned-pendent* and *abso-bloody-lutely.*

CHAPTER **VII**

THE SHAPE OF WORDS

Words are wind and fire, but those are difficult articles to collect.
—Ivor Brown

1. Sound Affects Sense

The late Frank Luther Mott, historian of magazines, tells the following story about his father, a man who tried to use language well, but who had come from a linguistic minority and inevitably had problems. When young Frank Luther came home from college, he endeavored to correct his father, pointing out that *dufference* was not a proper pronunciation of *difference*. The elder Mott tried to take this disciplining in good part, but he was also a bit irked—he had himself been accustomed to do the correcting—and he might occasionally be heard remarking somewhat testily, "I don't see the dufference atween *dufference* and *dufference!*"

Of course there wasn't any. The fact is that most people, even trained observers, cannot hear sharply. Especially, they cannot hear themselves. They think they say what they mean to say. I once had as a colleague a native German, who was deeply anti-Semitic, and when a distinguished German Jewish scientist came to our campus as a refugee my colleague had trouble being polite. He was too sophisticated to make obviously unkind remarks about the university's guest, being aware that such discourtesy would not have been admired in our academic community, but he got some satisfaction from casting veiled aspersions. On one occasion he said to me, as though deeply sympathetic because of the trouble of his former countryman, "Ah, dat Max! He hass a awful time wiz his English. He iss fon of zose Dzharmans zat cannot say *t-h*." Learning as an adult to speak a second language impeccably is extremely rare if not impossible. But obviously my colleague could not hear himself, although as a teacher of languages he had been trained to catch the nuances in

145

speech sound. The sounds we make are never the same as the sounds we intend to make. With most of us the divergence is not so great as it was with my German colleague, but the two are never identical, and each has its impact on all other language use. Specifically, the way we say words has something to do with the making of words, the use of words, and the meaning of words.

Obviously, phonetic and phonemic sounds affect the shapes of words. As the PIE voiceless labial plosive became the corresponding fricative, Englishmen learned to say *foot, father,* and *fish,* rather than *poot, pather,* and *pish,* as they would have if the sound had descended into English as it descended into Latin. This difference alters both what we say and what we print. Furthermore, these changes in sound have side effects in sense, for language is a system of which words are a part, and when you change one part of the whole complex you inevitably alter the working of other parts of the complex, even though in minor ways. When such changes go on through thousands of years they become encysted in a working language, and the effects build.

2. Voiced Breath: Vowels

You might start by saying the word *see,* putting your fingers in your ears and trying to be aware of what you do to make the word.

If you have now done this, you made two sounds, changing your mouth very little as you did so. You started by directing a narrow shaft of air at your upper teeth to produce /s/. To shift to the second sound you changed the direction of this flow of air enough so that it ceased to hit your teeth and you started voicing (for the voicing of consonants see Chapter III.8 above). In English—and in most known languages— a vowel is a voiced column of air not stopped or much restricted. If you do not voice the column of air you will get a whisper, as you may prove to yourself by saying *sis,* first in a normal way of speaking, then in a whisper. In the spoken *sis* you should hear a brief voicing, the vowel in the middle of the word. In the whispered *sis* you should hear no voicing.

You can produce various sounds with this vowel if you want to. You can keep the noise going so long as you have breath, making it become such sounds as you would associate with *a-a-a, u-u-u,* letting your jaw drop, rounding your lips, making the tone higher or lower, more or less forceful, and the like. That is, a vowel sound can be continuous and varied; it is not pinned down to a certain place, as a consonant is likely to be and it includes no sequence of actions that give it a predetermined length. One vowel can fade into another without a clear end to one or an identifiable beginning of another, as in *yowl*, which may be something like /jɪaʊl/.

But we can set up measuring posts. Say *see-saw*. When you pronounced the second syllable your jaw lowered, and you produced a much deeper vowel for *saw* than you did for *see*. And if you listened carefully, you probably noticed that whereas the vowel of *see* seemed to come from high up in your mouth and to the front, near to the sound of /s/ and hence at your upper teeth, the sound of the vowel in *saw* seemed to come from farther back and lower. This apparent positioning of the sound in the mouth is not entirely imagination. The node in the vibrating column of air shifts, and the shift is brought about by various changes in the mouth, especially by changes in the place and shape assumed by the tongue.

The tongue is an amazing coordination of muscle. It can so contort itself as to change the mouth cavity into a variety of sizes and shapes, and since the mouth is the principal resonating chamber for the vibrations set up by the vocal cords, the tongue can do much to shape the quality of the vowel. It is assisted by the jaw, lips, cheeks, glottis, and nasal passages, but it is so much the determining agent that vowels can be identified with some objectivity by describing the position of the tongue in their formation. On the whole, it thrusts forward to make a front vowel like that in *see*, and pulls back for a vowel like that in *saw*. It can be intermediate in a vowel like that in *some*. Thus phoneticians speak of **front, central,** and **back** vowels. The tongue also rises for the high vowels and sinks for the low ones, so that with a three-point spread we can speak of **high, mid** (to avoid confusion with *middle*), and **low** vowels. Vowels can be roughly distinguished by combining these two descriptions of tongue position; a mid front vowel would not be confused with a low back vowel.

We can set up more categories. To demonstrate, pronounce *say-so*. The vowels will differ in several ways, but notably in the action of the lips. For *say*, the lips are slightly parted but not rounded; for *so* the lips are rounded. We can then observe that the sound spelled *a* in *say-so* is unrounded, that for *o* rounded. And if you are an American speaker, you probably had a glide after each vowel, a front glide for *a*, a back glide for *o*. And there can be both ingoing and outgoing glides, as well as tones—Chinese recognizes five. The sound of *a* will be more stressed in *say* than will the sound of *o* in so, and will be less checked than the sound of *o*, but longer. There are also concepts like *open/close* and *timbre*.

This proliferation could readily become confusing. If we limit ourselves to front/back, high/low, we arrive at a simple chart like the following:

back		front	
so, dope	soon, tune	see, need	*higher*
put, good	sun, supper	sell, said	
saw, awful	sob, calm	sand, calf	*lower*

This is an inadequate representation, but if we started to map all the qualities of vowels, there would be no end to it.

But no language needs, or has any ever used, more than a few vowels as phonemes, and only a few vowel qualities—one, or at most two or three—have phonemic value in the senses that they are needed to distinguish one phoneme from another. Others will enter into the sounds of the language, but will vary without our needing to use them to distinguish phonemes. We can tell /i/ from /u/ by noticing that /u/ is farther back than /i/; it is also rounded, longer, closer, higher in pitch, and more checked, and it may have an ingoing rather than an outgoing glide. These details may be interesting for many reasons, but the two phonemes can be distinguished on the difference between central and front alone. In English, length has more to do with sentence patterns than with vowel phonemes. And so with other qualities of vowels; they could be used for phonemic distinctions, and in some languages they may be, but in no language will many of these possibilities be so used.

Accordingly, a simple pigeonhole system for vowels will suffice. The one above, with a little doctoring, will be elaborate enough for immediate purposes. It will not describe the vowels fully, but it will serve to keep them apart. I have reproduced a revised version of the chart below, with phonemic symbols added. I have also included a few variants to account for vowels that most obviously utilize glides (become diphthongs), or employ rounding. This diagram is not absolute truth; all of these sounds could be described in other ways. For example, I have elected—and it is a widespread practice if not the only good one—to treat the vowel in *hate* as /e/ and to distinguish it from the lower, slack, checked vowel of *tell* by writing *tell* /tɛl/. I could as well have written *tell* /tel/, as many writers on language do, and distinguish the vowel of *hate* by adding a glide /ej/, but there is no universally accepted system, and this will be as handy for us as any.

A few explanations will prevent misunderstandings in the table that follows. We need first to deal with the concept of the **allophone**. Consider the word for a white liquid spelled *m-i-l-k*. I shall assume that the vowel phoneme is /ɪ/, since I surmise that most speakers of American English approximate a relatively high, front, unrounded vowel, and believe that they make this sound rhyming *milk* with *silk*. But I have heard speakers pronounce *milk* so that it would rhyme with either *elk* or *talc*. I have also heard two other vowels in the word which I cannot isolate by rhyme: (1) a diphthong that starts out with a low front vowel like the phoneme /a/ and ends with a schwa glide (written /ə/); (2) a relatively pure vowel that is a little lower and farther back than the highest vowel associated with /ɪ/.

That is, for /ɪ/ as it appears in *milk*, I can identify at least five allophones, but since the subject of this book is words and their use, not phonetics, I can deal most of the time only with phonemes. If I have to refer to sounds treated as allophones, I shall use the phonetic alphabet, in which sounds are identified by being put within square brackets [ ]. That is, for the allophone highest and farthest front I shall use [ɪ]. (This is the sound I have associated above with *silk* and *him*; there is a sound higher and farther front which I have identified below as /i/ as in *see*, but I have never heard anybody say /milk/.) The sound slightly lower and farther back, which frequently can be heard in *hill* and *hid*, is [i]. The sound that rhymes with *elk* is [ɛ], the sound that rhymes with *talc* [æ], and the diphthong related to it is [æə]. All vowel phonemes, and many consonant phonemes, have allophones; the list given here is intended as a sample of the way sound works and of our devices for distinguishing sounds. We observed above that a phoneme is a spread of sound; we can now say that a phoneme is a spread of sound that comprises all its allophones. An allophone, likewise, is a spread of sound, but a much narrower spread, a spread roughly as broad as the human ear will distinguish.

With that introduction, here is one way to depict American English vowel phonemes:

/o/ *dope* /ow/ *so* (rounded; often with a glide)	/u/ *Sioux, soon* (rounded) (often /ɪu/ as in [nu:z] or [nɪuz])	/i/ *meek* /iy/ *see* /ɪ/ *hit* [ɨ] (lower and farther back)
/ʊ/ *put* (may be central and higher; alternate with [u] or [ə], as in *soot*)	/ə/ *some, other* (when stressed, often written [ʌ] as in *hull, done*)	/e/ *make* /ey/ *say* /ɛ/ *sell, head*
/ɔ/ *saw, awk* /ɔy/ *oil, void*	/ay/ *my, aisle* /a/ *odd, psalm* (in British English, often higher, farther back, and a diphthong)	/æ/ *sand, and* (often a diphthong [æə])

3. Sound into Sense: Sense into Sound

We can now return to sounds and what they have done to words. They started early, presumably as early as there was anything we would call language, and even before, when communication was limited to signs. Probably the most plausible guess about the origin of language is something like this: some of our ancestors developed a sizable body of signs (some monkeys have thirty-five or more—more signs than many languages have phonemes), probably both auditory and visual, such as are now used in sign language. They learned to use their signs as symbols. With that change, signs could proliferate into systems, could develop ramified meanings, and could be used in grammar. This complex provided a two-way communications system so much better than a collection of unrelated signs that many of the bipeds that had brains enough to use it learned it. The new tool, coupled with superior brains, provided these bipeds with the means of making themselves human.

These new techniques spread rapidly, so that there was for a time something almost approaching a universal language. It had qualities which we now think of as **language universals,** some of which have been preserved in many, perhaps in all languages. For example, all languages we know include both consonants and vowels, they all have meaningful units, and they have some means of combining these units; that is, they have what we call *vocabulary* and *grammar*. One of these universals probably concerns the form of meaningful units, that they were made of three sounds, a consonant plus a vowel plus a consonant. If so, PIE was near enough to this primeval language so that many of the IE roots we have been able to reconstruct are of this sort, roots like **dek-*, "to accept" and **man-*, "a hand."[1] Of course, some roots have been syncopated—some have lost parts and others have gained parts, but the sequence CVC is so common it must mean something. By contrast, affixes —prefixes, suffixes, and infixes—tend to be two sounds, a vowel plus a consonant or a consonant plus a vowel, as we shall notice in Chapter IX.

All that is theory and learned guesswork, albeit well-grounded guesswork, but with PIE our knowledge becomes so extensive and so consistent that we can call many of our conjectures "facts," especially since we have had to learn that even our most objective conclusions are relative. Thus, granted that all human knowledge is fallible, most of what we think we know about PIE and its descendants can be accepted and used. In fact, such has been the success of etymological method that even some of the wilder guesses have been confirmed.

About a century ago a brilliant young Frenchman, Antoine Meillet, proposed what was long called "laryngeal theory." He noticed that apparently aberrant changes in various IE languages could be explained if we postulate several sounds along the roof of the mouth and back into the larynx, and if we further assume that these sounds had caused changes and had then disappeared.[2] He called these hypothetical sounds "laryngeals," and his thesis was so plausible that it attracted wide support but had to be considered no more than a theory founded on indirect evidence. Then, when Meillet was an old man, scholars learned to read Hittite, probably the earliest IE language preserved in written form, and there, imprinted in the clay tablets, were some of Meillet's laryngeals.

As a matter of course, we do not know PIE as we know a modern

---

1. The reader should not be misled by spelling: even a sequence like **bhergh-*, "to hide," is essentially a consonant plus a vowel plus a consonant, even though such a consonant may include aspiration and may even be a consonant cluster.

2. We have noticed that palatals tend to be unstable, that English, for example, has lost /x/.

language, still spoken, available in all the richness of its detail, and subject to as many checks as we want to make. PIE has been built up from valid but incomplete evidence, rather like the sketch of a suspect put together by a police artist who must rely on evidence supplied by witnesses whose observations are inexact and whose memories are fragmentary. Thus our version of PIE is more regularized than in fact the language would have been, but we know it in a broad way, and we even know something of its dialects.

These dialects must extend well back of 3500 B.C. and account in part for the differences among the daughter languages. Various things that happened before the IE dispersal must account for the fact that many languages to the east use a word like *satem* (from Avestan) for "one hundred," whereas many languages to the west use something like *centum* (from Latin). Some events must account for a whole series of changes that made Proto-Germanic different from all other daughter languages, and something broke up the old basic PIE vowel and provided the basis for thousands of distinctions preserved in the differences between native English words and loans, and among the loans themselves.

PIE inherited a mid front vowel, written *e* in reconstructed roots, which had at least two variations. The root with *e* is called **full grade**, as in **dent-*, but it also developed a form with a vowel farther back and rounded, **dont-*, the two giving us *dentist* through Latin and *orthodontist* through Greek. Similarly, **ped-*, which gives us *pedestrian* and many more through Latin, developed a form with /o/, called **o-grade**, that came through Common Germanic and gives us *foot*. Then there was a **zero grade**, without vowel—vowels readily fall out or a sequence of sounds is simplified, especially if a word shrinks into fewer syllables; the English word *lord* comes from *hlafweard*, and *church* comes from early OE *cyrice* from Greek *kuriakon*—three or four syllables down to one. This sort of thing occurred the more readily if one of the consonants adjacent to the vowel was a resonant, like /m/, /l/, or /r/, which could become somewhat vocalized. Thus **pele-*, which gives us both *field* and *floor* from the full and zero grades in English, becomes *Poland* from full grade and *plane, planet,* and *plasma* in loans, with the vowel gone from zero grade that once stood between /p/ and /l/.[3]

Meanwhile, vowels could be nasalized, lengthened, or shortened, and the root could be built up with prefixes or suffixes. Several of these

---

3. Probably in all languages the line between vowels and consonants is not sharp for some sounds. PIE, which seems to have been weak in vowels, was rich in phonemes

changes could take place in a single root. Actually, *foot*, mentioned above, is both o-grade and lengthened. Likewise, the root **mer-*, "to rub away," "to harm," survives in English as night*mare*, but in zero grade it provides *mortar* through Latin, and in suffixed zero grade OE **mur-thra*, NE *murder*. With zero grade and another suffix we have *mortuary* and *mortgage* through Latin, and with a different suffix, *ambrosia* through Greek. That is, a few hundred PIE roots, when varied by three vowel grades, altered by such changes as lengthening, shortening, and nasalization, and augmented with dozens of affixes—which in turn might influence the vowels and provide new consonants—become thousands of working roots that provide millions of words.

A question now arises, especially when we remind ourselves that a word is at least two things, a shape (sound and eventually written and other forms) and use (including meaning). Did these shapes come into existence by the working of sound laws, and once the shapes existed, did users of the language find some use for them? Or did the reverse happen? Since shapes were falling heir to so many uses that they became ambiguous, did the language provide more shapes so that each would not have to carry so many burdens of meaning?

This sounds like an egg-hen question, and probably it is. No doubt shape and use interacted. We know that in many instances, when two shapes exist side by side through a loan, the words have tended to split the job of use between them. As we have seen, *scyrte*, which meant a short garment of any sort, became a doublet of a similar Old Norse word brought in by the Danes, so that we now have *shirt* for the upper garment and *skirt* for the lower. And this splitting can probably be carried back a step farther into Germanic, and account for our adjective *short* in contrast to the nouns *shirt/skirt*. On the other hand, we know that new shapes have been made to serve grammatical distinctions; *attend* leads to *attention*, with changes in consonants and accentuation; *invade* leads to *invasion*; three different syllables take the stress in re*cite'*, reci*ta'*-tion, and recita*tive'*. English has hundreds of such variations; especially

---

called **resonants**, sounds that had some consonant qualities but could be used like vowels to form syllables. In some modern writing systems the vowel quality of certain consonants is recognized, as in the name of the professor-statesman Brzezinski and the European city *Brno*. In NE, sounds treated as consonants are closer to being vowels than consonants in some words, /j/ as in *young*, /l/ as in *pull*—where it combines with a preceding vowel to form a diphthong with a down glide—and /r/ in most American English western dialects, when terminal and in words like *bird*. For PIE phonology see Winfred P. Lehmann, *Proto-Indo-European Phonology* (Austin, Texas: University of Texas Press, 1952).

common is the distinction between a noun like *rec'*ord, with the stress on the first syllable, and a verb like re*cord'*, with the stress on the second.

This much we can perhaps conclude. Man developed; as he had more experiences, accumulated more knowledge, and elaborated his understanding of himself and his world, he needed more word-use, more names for things and more uses of terms. At the same time, as he learned more sounds and more ways of combining them, he had more linguistic shapes available. Doubtless each of these helped the other. The fact that users of language had jobs for new shapes would have helped preserve the shapes, whether or not the need generated them. And the fact that man had more and more shapes available would have helped him to refine and employ new uses. Sound and sense in language have probably always worked together, each supporting the other, although we might have trouble determining just what and how much either of them did.

4. Patterns of Change

Tracing sound is no simple pursuit. We need to come down from some thousands of years B.C. into English, and from the same thousands of years into the languages from which English has borrowed. We must assume at least small changes working at all times in all languages, but a few patterns of growth in English and its ancestors have so altered the word stock that we must have a closer look at them.

First we should remind ourselves that a sound may be altered by its surroundings. A voiceless sound between or among voiced sounds may become voiced; to put this briefly and physically, if we start voicing, and expect more voicing to be called for soon, we may let the voicing go on, rather like idling a motor in order not to have to stop it and start it again. Thus *excursion* pronounced with some voiceless consonants as /ɛkskəršən/ may become all voiced as /ɛgzgəržən/. A similar change seems to be taking place in American English today, with the voiceless /t/ becoming voiced /d/ in certain positions. *Rotten* in some dialects is becoming /rad'n/ and *meeting* close to /midən/. In Ontario, one can even hear all the vowels of *potato* voiced into /bədedə/. The same change is not unknown in British English; Professor Charles Barber of Leeds University reports hearing a British Broadcasting Company announcer—than whom there are no more impeccable speakers—pronouncing *British* as /brɪdɪš/, and similar reports come from Australia and other areas where English is used. Similarly, a stop sound may become a fricative—sometimes called a *continuant*—by blending into the continuing flow of adjacent vowels, and a fricative that becomes terminal may shift toward a stop.

Beginning with Common Germanic and continuing into some of the daughter languages, a whole series of changes took place. Pure vowels became diphthongs, diphthongs were simplified into single vowels, vowels were lengthened or shortened and consonants doubled, and sound pulled forward or backward, up or down, voiced or unvoiced. All this is too complicated to survey here, but we can notice that the verbs, especially, were affected, being subject to vowel gradation and to suffixing because of the various tenses. The results can still be seen in the language in sequences like *sing, sang, sung; write, wrote, written; hang, hung, hung* beside *hang, hanged, hanged*. Most of these forms have long ago been lost; our word *fall* could appear as *feallan, fylth, feolath, feoll, feallen* or *gefeallen*, and in several more forms, of which we now have *fall, fell, fallen*.

Some changes created new consonants, or altered existing consonants. OE had two palatal stops, voiceless /k/ and its voiced equivalent /g/, written *c* and *g* respectively and scatteringly preserved in NE; OE *can* becomes NE /kan/, /kæn/, /kən/ without much change and OE *gan* stands back of *go*. OE also had the fricatives corresponding to these, the voiceless /x/ and a voiced equivalent. These sounds were probably about what you might produce if you start with /k/ and /g/, but try to keep the sound going instead of letting it stop. The first of these /x/ was written *h* in OE, so that our word *might* could be spelled *miht*, pronounced /mɪxt/. The voiced fricative was also written *h* or *g* or *gg* or something else—scribes had trouble because they used the Latin alphabet to write OE, and Latin had no such sounds nor any letters for them.

During the course of the centuries, all four of these sounds tended to disappear, some absorbed into adjacent sounds, some preserved scatteringly. They survived best when adjacent to back vowels—especially if supported by a similar sound in Old Norse—and became vocalized or vanished when adjacent to front vowels. We have already noticed that palatals move with an adjacent vowel; during this time, as we shall see below, some vowels were moving forward, and as a guttural consonant is pulled forward it becomes more and more difficult to pronounce in the flow of speech.

Of these sounds, /k/ survived irregularly. It was little changed in *caught, call, cat* (which was probably helped by Old Norse *kotte*); many of the sounds now spelled *a* were pronounced farther back than they are now in American English, or even in British English. Nonetheless, most words that now begin with /k/ in NE have been borrowed, notably from Old Norse *(crook)*, Norman French *(court)*, or Latin *(concord)* after OE times. Many of the /k/ sounds in OE became the affricate /č/ as in *church* /čərč/ from late OE *circ*, especially in the Southern dialects, from which come American English, Australian English, mainly Canadian English, and much of British English. This change did not take place in the North and in Lowland Scotland so that we have Scottish *kirk* /kirk/. Latin *castrum*, which became *Chester* in the South, remained but little changed in the North in *Lancaster, Doncaster*.

The corresponding fricative /x/ never survived, except in some Scottish dialects where it appears in the so-called "burr." But like the PIE laryngeals, it left evidences behind it. Consider the OE word *burh* /burx/, which meant some kind of inhabited place, later a walled town. In some dialects it became the corresponding voiced stop /g/, as in *burg*, now defined as an Americanism, "a city, town, or village, especially one regarded as quiet, unexciting, etc."[4] Most frequently the /x/ of *burh* became some kind of vowel, as in *borough* and a few other words and in many place names, *Edinburgh, Canterbury*. In a few instances /x/ became the voiceless labio-dental fricative /f/, as in *Brough-under-Stainmoor*, "town below the stony moor," pronounced /brəf/, and in a few common nouns like *enough* from OE *enoh* /ɪnəx/ and *tough* from OE *toh* /təx/. In some words it became the corresponding stop, as in NE *work* /wərk/ from OE *weorh* /werx/, /weərx/. It vanished from many words after helping to lengthen a vowel, leaving behind the spelling *gh*, as in *night* from OE *niht* /nɪxt/, *thought* from OE *poht* /θɔxt/, *through* from OE *purh* /θurχ/, and many more.

The voiced stop /g/ also had various fates, including that of becoming part of a diphthong. Occasionally it survived before a back vowel as in *god, good*, and *goat*. Sometimes it was saved by a similar sound in an Old Norse word, where palatals were less disturbed; thus our word *give* comes from OE *geſun*, which in ME was often spelled with an initial y or jod, that is, ʒ, as in ME *yeve* or *ʒeve*. Both spellings presume the sound /j/. But the Old Norse verb apparently survived in Yorkshire and elsewhere in the North, and was reimported into London speech. Most frequently /g/ blended into an adjacent vowel, became part of a diphthong, and then disappeared in a closed syllable, leaving behind some evidence in spelling. Thus OE *maegden* became *maid, saegde* became

---

4. This survival as /g/ may represent the voiced fricative which was often a dialectal variant of /x/, or it may preserve Norse influence.

said. In an open syllable the /g/ may be preserved as a glide, as in *day* /dey/ from OE *daga* or *daeg*. Much the same thing happened in *law*, probably from Old Norse **lagu* and in *lie, lay,* from Germanic /lag/.[5]

5. The Great English Vowel Shift

Another wide-ranging change affected some vowels. For example, our word *he* /hi/ changed from a sound that had formerly approximated our word *hay* /he/. At the same time *me*, formerly pronounced like our word *may*, became /mi/, and our word *seem*, formerly pronounced like NE *same*, became /sim/. Many changes are involved here; the vowel is becoming longer, less checked, and closer. But these qualities do not have phonemic value in English; that is, they do not distinguish phonemes. Length did distinguish phonemes in Latin—hence the popular terminology of "long" and "short" vowels—but in English, length reflects sentence patterns more than it does phonemes. But /i/ is also higher and farther forward than /e/, and height and position forward or back do distinguish phonemes.

Something similar happened to several other vowels: they moved upward or forward or both. Thus sounds /a/ to /æ/ became /e/, as in ME *mak* /mak/ which became *make* /mek/; ME *gat* /gɔt/ became *goat* /got/; ME *fod* /fod/ became NE *food* /fud/. Two sounds that were already high and forward lowered and became diphthongs: *write*, pronounced /rit/, with a vowel as high and far forward as it could go, lowered and became a diphthong, /rayt/. *House*, pronounced with a high central vowel /hus/, also lowered and became a diphthong /haʊs/.

This is what is called in language a **drift**. In IE languages, the changes called Grimm's Law constituted a drift among consonants. This later change was a drift among vowels, called the **Great English Vowel Shift**.

---

5. Very similar things happened to various Latin words on their way into English, and these sounds are preserved in various borrowings. Presumably, Latin *caesar* was pronounced with an initial /k/, a sound preserved in German *Kaiser*. It became /s/ in Late and Vulgar Latin, so that NE *caesar* survived as /sizər/ and *czar* with an initial /z/. We have noted above variations in the initial /k/ in *caput*. It was borrowed late enough to survive with little change in *caption*; it was borrowed early enough through Norman to become *chief* with initial /č/, and later from central France with initial /š/ in *chef*. Often the Latin /k/ shared the fate of its English counterpart, blending into a diphthong and then disappearing; thus Latin *fructum* gives us *fruit*, with the *i*-spelling reflecting the earlier /k/ spelled *c* in Latin. Similarly through French we have *bruit* from Latin **brugere* (related to *bray*), *cuisine* from Latin *coquina*, and many more with the palatal changing or dropping out.

We know more about how drifts work than we do about why they start or stop. A change will begin in at least one dialect of a language. This change has linguistic qualities and can be described linguistically—voiceless stops will become voiceless fricatives, as when PIE *ped- and *peter- changed so that speakers of English said *foot* and *father*; or, vowels will move forward and upward so that ME *dede* /dedə/ became NE *deed* /did/, ME *rad* /rɔd/ became NE *road* /rod/.

The English Vowel Shift apparently started in the fourteenth century and was mostly complete by the sixteenth, but in some dialects it may still be going on. The change from /i/ to /ay/ was late; Pope, and even later poets, rhymed NE *obliged* /əblaɪdžd/ with Continental words recently borrowed having /i/ rather than /aɪ/. And there is still great variety between /ay/ and /i/ in British and American pronunciations, so that the lingering echoes of the Vowel Shift may account for our uncertainty as to whether we should pronounce *iodine* with /ay/, /i/, or /ɪ/ in the last syllable. Meanwhile, some sounds moved farther and faster: ME *mete* /met/ became Modern English *meet* /mit/, but the word for *flesh* went from /mæt/ to /met/ to /mit/ so that *meet* and *meat* are now pronounced alike.

The Vowel Shift did not affect all vowels; ME *get* remained NE *get*, with the /ɛ/ but little changed, and ME *hil* or *hul*, /hɪl/ or /hʊl/ remained in NE *hill*, pronounced /hɪl/ or /hɨl/, with little change. We wonder why, and must assume that the vowels that drifted had something in common, as did those that remained with little change. On the whole, the sounds that changed are those popularly called "long," even though length does not have phonemic value in English. But /o/, /u/, /a/, /e/, and /i/ are also relatively tense vowels, and /ɛ/ and /ɪ/ are slack vowels (/æ/ is complicated, since it had both tense and slack grades). Thus a good guess is that tenseness made the difference; on the whole, high front vowels are tenser than low back vowels, and thus we can reasonably assume that tense vowels moved so that they became tenser.

Meanwhile, other changes were taking place, which may be involved in the Great Vowel Shift, but are not readily linked to it. One vowel disappeared. ME had a slack, checked, central vowel, somewhat below /o/ and /u/ and between them, used in words like *god, hot*. This sound tended to lower, and was in effect lost, combining with /a/ so that *god* is now pronounced /gad/ or /gəd/. A similar sound, the spelling reflected in NE *world*, also lowered to schwa or in some dialects /e/; *world* can now be pronounced /world/, /wʌrld/, or /werld/. An /l/ might blend into an adjacent vowel and seem to be lost, although it doubtless changed the quality of the vowel, and might even be preserved in spelling; ME *wolde* /woldə/ became *would* /wʊd/, *sholde* /šoldə/ became /šʊd/. ME *talken* /talkən/, /tɔlkən/ became NE *talk* /tɔk/. Meanwhile, the etymological /l/ in the ancestral term remains in *tell* and *tale*.

The varied results of all this can be summarized as follows. Some consonants, notably palatals, were lost or became involved in other sounds, mainly diphthongs. At least one vowel was lost, a sound still represented in the spelling of words like *god* and *hot*, along with various diphthongs, notably those made by vanishing palatals, some reflected in spellings like *said* and *eye*. Meanwhile, vowels shifted variously, with movements forward and upward in tense vowels predominating; a few new diphthongs were developing, /ay/ as in *ride*, /ɔi/ as in *boil*, /aʊ/ as in *house*, along with /oʊ/ as in *bow*, /ey/ as in *day*, and quite a variety having /ə/, so that *head* can be pronounced /heəd/, and *floor* /floə/, in some dialects /flo/.

Two other shifts, syncopation and the forward movement of the stress in borrowed words, reduced the number of vowels and altered the quality of some of them. Vowels maintain their quality best if they are stressed, that is, if they function as the only vowel in a strongly spoken word, or if they are the vowels in accented syllables in words of more than one syllable.[6] OE had inherited endings for many words, so that most nouns, verbs, adjectives, and some other words had two syllables or more. English generally carries a stress on the first syllable not a prefix, and this stress has increased, while most of the endings wore away, becoming first schwa and then nothing. Sounds within words, vowels or consonants or both, could be slurred and dropped; OE *hlafweard* (loaf-guardian) became NE *lord*.

Meanwhile, borrowing was increasing, and as we have seen, these borrowed words tended to be Latin or Greek, or terms from these languages filtered through French. Most of these loans were polysyllabic, and in Classical languages the accent was placed far on in the word, on the second or third syllable from the last. These Classical long vowels became stressed vowels in Old French, and when the same words came into English, the accent was usually shifted forward, so that vowels that had once been stressed were now unstressed. NE *labor* was borrowed

---

6. In English, even a vowel in a one-syllable word will weaken in an unstressed position in a sentence. The word *the* may be pronounced /ði/ in "He is *the* man for the job" but would become /ðə/ in "*The* man went home."

with a sound rather like *la-boor* /læbuər/. But when the accent was shifted forward the pronunciation became /lebər/ or /lebə/. Bethlehem /bɛθlɛhɛm/ became *bedlam* /bɛdləm/; thus doublets appeared from within the language, *Bethlehem* being scrupulously preserved as a word precious in religion, while the syncopated *bedlam* became a word for confusion because the Hospital of St. Mary of Bethlehem, originally established as a hospice for bishops and canons, was transformed into an insane asylum. The word *bedlam* represents both syncopation and forward movement of the stress. The word *government* was borrowed as four syllables, something like /go-ver-ne-mɛnt/. Now the word is never more than three syllables /gʌ-vərn-mənt/, frequently two /gʌv-mənt/. Vowels that had been quite distinctive have become schwa or have vanished entirely. In fact, so many stressed vowels have been reduced to schwa, or have been dropped out, that by all odds /ə/ is now the most widely used sound in English, particularly in American English. And in one way or another, most words, whether native or borrowed, that got into English with more than one syllable were reduced.

6. Sound Change: Drifts

Why do sounds change? Once they have changed in one dialect why do they then appear in other dialects? Why and how does a whole sequence of changes develop and move so that we have the patterns of speech suggested in Grimm's Law and the Great English Vowel Shift? These have long been mysteries, and they still are, although much thought and research has recently gone into such questions, and we are now getting plausible guesses as to what some of the answers may be.

First we might notice that students of language long deluded themselves by thinking of languages as entities, rather than collections of dialects, which are all equally respectable as language, whatever their status may be in fashion. English is not coterminous with Received Pronunciation; the speech of a Yorkshire salesman is as much the English language as is the tongue used at Oxford University, although it may have less impact on the English of the future. Much of speech develops by communities, and is represented by dialects of which a "standard" idiom is only one of many, and not necessarily the most influential, so that apparent change may be no more than borrowing from one dialect into another.

Furthermore, change is inherent in speech because of the way it is transmitted. Here we must distinguish between sounds that are inherited because the oral equipment is inherited and language that persists because it is always being learned. For the first, consider the sound made by cats, spelled in English *meow*. The sound will vary from cat to cat but not from generation to generation because kittens do not learn to meow from their mothers. They make the sound because they inherited the vocal equipment that will make it, and they will not make the kind of barks that the vocal equipment of dogs produces. Children, however, inherit vocal machinery that is neither so restricted nor so restrictive. They can make, or can learn to make, an almost infinite range of sounds, and they start imitating whatever they hear from their parents. That is, the sounds of language are learned, and nothing can ever be learned perfectly. Here, surely, is one of the reasons languages are always changing.

Scholars now know enough about language learning to describe in some detail the way transmission entails alteration. For the first few years of a normal child's life the infant learns language from its parents or from the parents plus the siblings, who started to learn, usually, from the same parents. During this time the child is acquiring mountains of facts, most of it disorganized so far as the learner is concerned, except as he becomes his own organizer. Inevitably, everything the child acquires is learned inaccurately. Gradually, this source of new information shifts from the parents to the other children in the neighborhood, at play, in school, or wherever. With a new source of knowledge come new standards. In part the infant had learned by imitation, imitation of the parents or those who had learned from the parents, and in part by inculcation. The child was corrected and told what to say and what not to say, but from an early date, perhaps after age five or even earlier, the child is subjected to a new set of standards, those of his peer group. If these new standards are not anywhere described, they are clearly evident to each child, and they are likely to be scrupulously enforced with the most potent of social sanctions, ridicule and group approval or disapproval. As a result, every generation speaks differently than did its parents.

That is, languages change always, because new speakers are always entering into the speech community, and all language must be learned by each child in its own way with its own inadequacies. The twittering and warbling of wrens does not change much from generation to generation, because the offspring does not learn from the mother. The baby wren has the anatomical means of twittering and warbling, and it makes the sounds its mother makes, not because it learns from the mother, but because its sound-making apparatus is in effect identical with that of the parents, and when the young wren is old enough, it starts using this equipment.[7] We have no transcripts of bird calls a thousand years ago, but presumably calls have not changed much. On the other hand, no language, we have reason to believe, ever continued so much as a century without changes; and whatever the reasons may be, one is this—it had to be learned, and learning is not and presumably cannot be precise.

Changes in sound are much slower than those in meaning and until recently have not been much observed. Caxton, the most prominent of the early English printers, realized that English had changed and was in his day fractured by dialects; he saw manuscripts, presumably English, which he could scarcely read, and he tells the story of a man who had trouble getting anything to eat because of confusions in language. A customer asked for *egges*, but the landlady said she knew no French. She volunteered, however, that she had some *eier* (a loan word for *eggs*, probably from Dutch). The man said, sorry, he didn't know French either. So, Caxton asks, which word should a translator use, *egges* or *eier?* So much he noticed, but if he recognized that the Great English Vowel Shift was in progress he gives no clue, although he lived in the middle of it, when the vowels were changing the most rapidly. Doubtless, drifts are the less notable because they do not necessarily work at the same time in all dialects, and changes that might otherwise be apparent are missed because converse changes obscure them.

In the past we have been handicapped in our study of sound change because we had no accurate records. We can guess that if Chaucer, who died in 1400, could have talked with Shakespeare two centuries later they would have had trouble understanding each other. By various devices, spellings, rhymes, loans from other languages, and the like, we can roughly reconstruct the speech of each of them. Mechanical recordings are only a few decades old, and even phonetic transcription dates mainly from the late nineteenth century, but now we are getting accurate records, and some of the evidence is highly revealing.

During the 1930s, in preparation for the *Linguistic Atlas of New England* (Providence: Brown University, 1939–43), trained linguists conducted interviews throughout the Northeast. That was nearly two generations ago (allowing twenty-five years for a generation). Recent checks of these same communities show measurable growths. For example, in Martha's Vineyard, an island off the southern coast of New England,

---

7. Recent research suggests that at least some birds that have several calls try to teach distinctions among them to their offspring, but I gather behaviorists would agree that most nonhuman sounds are inherited, not learned.

marked changes can be recorded, and these changes fall into patterns, the sort of patterns that constitute drifts. The island was settled early by whalers and other mariners, and for a time the population was relatively stable. Then more settlers arrived, dwellers on the mainland and Portuguese immigrants. By this time the older families, descendants of the original settlers, held much of the land and the more important positions, and their dialect, although by no means Standard American English, became the prestige speech. The newcomers did not much acquire the older local dialect, but their children did. The young people naturally wanted to succeed in their society, and apparently without making formal decisions on these matters, they knew that learning the prestige dialect of the old-timers would help. Similar research in New York, using the sampling techniques familiar to sociologists, has shown that shopgirls, apprentices, and various less privileged persons were acquiring, partly deliberately but partly unconsciously, the prestige dialects of the more affluent districts.[8]

We do not yet understand drifts, of course. How does a tendency to continue in one direction, a direction that can be described in such linguistic terms as voicing, stress, affrication, etc., alter so that changes will go on in one or a few directions, in many dialects, for centuries? We have no comprehensive answer, but now we can at least say that changes can be effected in a few generations, and that if a large part of the population wants a certain sort of change, the changes can be remarkably consistent.

All this raises the question: are some great drifts now in progress? Other generations could not detect drifts in their own time; only after the Great English Vowel Shift was over did anyone appear to notice it. But now we have better means of studying language, and one bit of evidence is suggestive. In area after area of English speakers—in England, Canada, the United States, Australia, and elsewhere—observers are recording that some consonants, including /p/, /t/, and /k/ are being voiced and becoming their corresponding voiced stops /b/, /d/, and /g/.

8. Such research is only in its infancy. The following is a seminal essay: Uriel Weinreich, William Labov, and Marvin I. Herzog, "Empirical Foundations for a Theory of Language Change," *Directions for Historical Linguistics*, ed. W. P. Lehmann and Yakov Malkiel (Austin: University of Texas Press, 1968), pp. 95–188. Further research is being pursued vigorously by Labov and his students, Weinreich having died prematurely. In England, somewhat similar results are being obtained with the methods of historical linguistics; see M. L. Samuels, *Linguistic Evolution, Cambridge Studies in Linguistics*, 5 (Cambridge: Cambridge University Press, 1972).

Of course we are in no position to announce a new drift; our evidence covers too short a period of time and is much too scanty, but at least we have here a suggestion of the sort of thing that may be happening in our time.

7. Miscellany: Rhyme, Alliteration, Atavism, Poetry, Blunder

Sound altered shape and sense in dozens of ways, many of them affecting but few words. We have already noticed that blunders in separating words turned *a numpire* into *an umpire*, and that false etymologies could augment such mistakes. NE *island* goes back to an OE word variously recorded *yllond, egland, iegland*, and the like, which probably meant something like "land in the middle of water." But the Latin was *insula*, and by whatever intellectual gymnastics, the notion arose that an *s* belonged in the English word, which should accordingly be spelled *is-land*, so called because it "is land." Such vagaries are legion, mostly individual.

But art played a part, too, and more consistently. Some words were initiated, or at least preserved, partly because they have pleasing sounds. They rhyme—*hodgepodge, namby-pamby, nitty-gritty, higgledy-piggledy, hillbilly.* They have a good ring—*backslapper, pipsqueak, dunderhead, goon squad, eager beaver, gas guzzler, dead of night.* They alliterate—*dead as a doornail, highhanded, hophead, shipshape, dapper Dan, dirty dog, too little too late, birdbrained.* They may blend such qualities —*wishy-washy, dillydally.* Sounds may combine with figures of speech as in *ants in your pants.*

Sound has played its part in the wide use of memorable phrases— *of the people, by the people, for the people; whatever is, is right; to be, or not to be; put up or shut up; The Song of Songs; Give me liberty, or give me death; call a spade a spade; cotton is king; art for art's sake; forgive them, for they know not what they do; saecula saeculorum (ages of ages; world without end); saints and sinners; faith, hope, and charity.*

By contrast, a few sounds, both vowels and consonants, have crept into individual words. English speakers do not welcome extended consonant clusters and may break them up with a vowel; *athlete*, from Greek *athletes*, has become a word that few athletes can spell, since they endeavor to reproduce their own pronunciation with an intrusive vowel, /æθəlit/. The preference for alternate vowels and consonants probably accounts for *rigmarole* becoming *rigamarole* in speech. An intrusion may result as a secondary reaction to an earlier change. In Latin *elmus* the consecutive consonants gave no trouble, because each was part of its own syllable, but when the ending was lost, and the word became English *elm*, many speakers broke the sequence of consonants with a schwa and produced /ɛləm/. Similarly, French *cheminee* became English *chimney*, bringing two nasals together. The nasal /m/ must be stopped before the nasal /n/ can begin, and accordingly the /m/ was often closed with the corresponding plosive /b/. This did not help enough; the flow of sound must break going from the bilabial /b/ to the palatal /n/, and a liquid was introduced, making the word in some dialects *chimbly* /čɪmblɪ/. Intrusive /r/ is said to be increasing in England. It has long existed after a terminal vowel in some dialects on both sides of the Atlantic, *idea* becoming /aydiər/. Now, we are told, it is becoming intrusive (in effect restored) before a word beginning with a vowel, so that although *father* may be pronounced /faðə/, *father and mother* become /faðər ənd məðə/.

The use of sounds has shifted with populations. The American east coast was settled mainly from southern and southeastern England, by lower middle-class folk, including many from debtors' prisons. The speech of these immigrants differed markedly from the fashionable dialect of the court, which was to become the basis of Received Pronunciation. For example, the sort of Englishmen who emigrated used /æ/ as against /a/ in many words, and when these immigrants became leaders in the New World, they said /ænt/ rather than /ant/ or /ɔnt/ for *aunt*. As the population of the United States surpassed that of the mother country, the use of /æ/ increased. Likewise, the immigrants into the Middle Atlantic States tended to pronounce final /r/ in words like *worker* and *doctor*. The Middle West and Far West were populated largely with these speakers who used /r/. In the twentieth century the Western States have grown mightily, while the British Isles and New England remained more nearly static. Thus *doctor* pronounced with schwa plus /r/ has increased relative to the same word pronounced only with schwa /daktə/. And there are quirks. Apparently from a very minor dialect north of London comes the pronunciation /ɔy/ as against the more common /ay/ and /ər/ as against /ɔy/. But this dialect found a foothold in New York City, and there are probably now more speakers in Greater New York who pronounce *oil* /ərl/ and *die* /dɔy/ than in all of the British Isles.

Changes of this sort are most noticeable in the United States, but not restricted to it. In several London dialects, including Cockney, and some dialects to the north and west, including municipal Cambridge, /e/ has developed a glide and become /ay/, so that *mate* is pronounced like

American *might*, and *way* sounds like the pronunciation of the letter *y*. This dialect, considering where it flourished, must have been brought to the American colonies, but it seems to have died out. Meanwhile, it thrived in Australia, which was founded as a prison colony, fed especially from the Old Bailey in London. There are now many more /ay/ speakers in Australia than there ever were within the sound of Bow Bells, and considering the great future of Australia this pronunciation is sure to increase.

Inevitably, social pressures and individual taste alter the spread of sounds. At times in the United States the dropping of final /r/ was a prestige pronunciation. The older families in Boston's Back Bay said /daktə/ for *doctor*, whereas the newly arrived "bogtrotters" said /daktər/ or even /dɔktər/. The /r/-less pronunciation was natural with some and affected with others. Meanwhile, we are told that in New York City and some other parts of the Northeast, the pronunciation with /r/ is becoming the prestige pronunciation again, perhaps being assumed to be "correct" because of the spelling. Likewise, at this writing British commentators are observing that American speech is being imitated in Britain by the more recalcitrant young and by rowdyish persons generally, who have heard gangsters talking American English on television. Understandably, many parents disapprove.

Theories that sound and sense reflect each other have been many, but mostly they are not well-grounded. It is an engaging notion that the namable parts of the real world embody some essential quality, so that the sound of a word will inevitably reflect the meaning, if only we have the wit to see the relationship. Some evidence can be found, but in anything as varied and subtle as language, some evidence can be found for almost anything.

There is, at a minimum, echoism. We have seen that some words imitate sounds; if such an echoic term was early, it could account for hundreds of descendants. In English we have many *fl-* words suggestive of flowing water: *flow, fly, flee, float, flight, fleet, flotsam, flotilla, flutter, flue, flood*, and many more. By Grimm's Law these equate with *plover, pluvious, plutocrat* (whose wealth is overflowing), *Pluto, pyelitis*, and *pneumonia* (the lungs being floaters). But all these words go back to PIE **pleu-*, so that if they are echoic they are only descendants of an early example of echoism.

Not all words having similarities are so readily accounted for. Consider the *sn-* words: *sniveling, snot, snout, sneak, snide, snake, snag, snail, sneeze, snore, snatch, snarl, snap, snippy, snub, snook, snort*—

they run for columns in any dictionary. Some can be accounted for by descent; *sniff, snub, snoop, schnozzle, snatch* and a few others come from a Germanic root—not a PIE one—that refers to the nose. Some, including *snorkel, sneak,* and *snore,* come from another Germanic root —once more, *not* PIE—*sner-,* which seems to refer to making noises. Another Germanic root, **sner-,* meaning "to twist," gives us *snare;* Germanic **sneg-* gives *snake,* and **sneit-,* "to cut," probably gives us *snickersnee.* But these words come from many sources, not from just one PIE root, and an uncommonly large percentage of them, like *snide, snob,* and *snub,* come from no language we can now identify.

These *sn-* words are so distinctive that they have long attracted comment, and at least two guesses about them might engage us. They do not come from a common PIE root, but one guess is that they may come from a still older term, in a language that stood back of PIE and is its ancestor and the ancestors of other languages, including some now extinct. The other suggestion relies on the observation that many of these words refer to unpleasant things—*snot, sneak, snide,* and the like—and that *sl-* words *(slander, slobber, slums), sm-* words *(smear, smirk, small),* and many others beginning with /s/ plus a consonant refer to distasteful objects and actions. If these words did not have a common origin, perhaps they owe their survival, among all the millions of words that have been lost, to the fact that they rely on a common feeling. Since /sn/ was an unpleasant sound, users may have felt it was suitable for words associated with unpleasant things. The thesis can probably never be proved, but it is an engaging guess. It makes one wonder what sounds might be associated with the concepts of *courage, beauty, goodness, industry,* and *faithfulness.*

8. Enter the Alphabet

Quite possibly the most fruitful inventions of all time have been language, the wheel, and the alphabet. These three inventions were slow in developing. Men probably talked for a million years before they developed anything like the vocabulary that has made the modern world possible. The wheel was known for thousands of years before it revolutionized society. Writing, as something more than iconic pictures, is some thousands of years old, but only in recent centuries has it been used as an ingredient of daily living. For millennia it was little more than a device for preserving laws and sacred texts, marking burials, keeping notes to aid the memory, identifying objects, and the like—the earliest

Germanic inscription occurs on a drinking vessel, "I Lingast the Holting made this horn," and an early Latin inscription on a brooch reads, "Manius made me for Numasius." The earliest extensive writing we know, that of the Sumerians, was a professional skill limited to a few priests and government servants. Later, writing was used also for business records.

But once writing developed into a generally usable tool, it changed men's minds and the face of the earth. We have only to notice that the seats of power, the areas associated with what we think of as modern civilization, are 95 percent literate: most of the United States and the dominant countries of Europe, Japan, the heavily populated portions of Canada and Australia. The areas moving into power are gravitating toward literacy: China, India, the Arab nations, a few others. Generally, the have-not nations are only 50 percent literate or less. Much of Africa and the more backward parts of Asia and Latin America may have less than 10 percent literacy.

For most of the million years or so that man has used language he talked, and when writing developed it grew from oral speech. Now all that has changed so much that many people think of the printed word as the authoritarian language, with talk as the secondary and less correct means of communication; and occasional individuals—editors, professional writers, computer programmers, a few executives, some judges—may live, work, and think more in printed language than in oral speech. At a minimum, the two now interact, and also have their unique ways of working. Whether writing affects talk more than speech affects written language we need not ask; each has impact on the other, enough to warrant a close look.

Writing sprang up as a human byproduct. Accordingly, we may expect it to reflect human good sense, human ingenuity, and human aptitude for lethargy and blunder. It will be in part inadequate to its great calling. We can use it better if we understand it, and we can understand it better if we know something of how it grew.

Written language came from pictures. Children draw pictures, stick men and stick doggies, and primitive men must also have done so. The artists, very far from being primitive, who decorated such caves as those at Altamira in Spain were imaginative craftsmen, even artists, but most nonliterate peoples have left only such crude representations as those in petroglyphs pecked into rocks by North American Indians. Such icons readily became stylized, and as more of these simplified forms were recognized, the possibilities for communication grew. In at least one system, these signs became symbols.

Let us assume that a large round dot is accepted as the sun. It is still a simplified picture; but suppose the same sort of dot can be used to suggest a round circle used in a religious service, or the head of a decapitated soldier and hence a dead man. Thus a dot has now become a symbol; it suggests something of which it is not a picture, such as a shield or a corpse. This intellectual leap was probably made many times, but certainly once. Writing systems using symbols existed thousands of years ago in at least three fertile valleys, those in central China, the Indo-Gangetic valleys in India, and the Tigris-Euphrates in Asia Minor. They are enough alike so that they may have had a common ancestor, but they need not; we might remind ourselves that children have symbol sense, which they do not have to be taught, and that the chimpanzee Washoe could use symbols. Symbols embodying ideas are called *ideographs*. Symbols may also be thought of as *logograms*, if they represent words (Greek *logos*, "word").

To continue our imaginary case, let us assume that the dot, a logogram for *sun*, is thought of as sound, so that (in English) the dot could also represent *son*. As a sort of shorthand, this sound could stand for its conspicuous parts, /sn/, and hence could represent any wording starting that way: *snipe, snow, sneak*, and the like. The writing system has now become what we call a syllabary, using a system much like that practiced by players of charades, who, if they have to act out *syllabary*, might indicate a window sill for *syl-*, raise a finger for *one* or *-a-*, and pretend to bury a corpse for *-bary*. Such a system was highly developed by the Sumerians, bequeathed to the Akkadians and Hittites, and became involved in the picture writing of the Egyptians in the Nile valley. The North Semites, living along the eastern end of the Mediterranean Sea, found out about the Egyptian system, and being great traders carried it to Crete, Cyprus, mainland Greece, and elsewhere.

How the next step, from a syllabary to an alphabet, became possible is not certain. What did the North Semites borrow from the Egyptians, and what did they disseminate? Egyptian writing included signs—many of them obviously stylized pictures, which could serve either as words or syllables. Some of these syllables represented only one sound, and thus were in effect letters, but the best guess is that the Egyptians did not think of them as letters. At least they did not standardize them into an alphabet. The Semites, especially the Phoenicians, may have. We have already observed that the early language that presumably stands behind many or all subsequent languages had at first only one vowel. Variously languages developed more vowels, some many, some few. Proto-Arabic developed few, so few that the Phoenicians did not bother to write them

—writing was still mainly a mnemonic device anyhow, used by specialists who needed only a hint at the intended message.[9] That is, the Phoenicians wrote a series of consonants, each presuming at least one vowel, as though I were to write *s* for *so* and *sd* for *sod*. In doing this I might be writing *s* as a letter, as a symbol for /s/. I might also be writing *s* as a symbol for a syllable, that is /sow/. Arguments can be made either way, but this much is clear: as the Phoenicians exported a writing system west, they provided only consonants.

The Greeks used this system as an alphabet, but they had too few vowels. In fact they inherited none, but they may not have known this. The word they called *alpha*, our letter A, was a consonant in Semitic, but represented a sound not found in Greek; the Greeks thought it was either a vowel or a letter that had no use and accordingly they gave it one as a vowel. In various ways they developed five vowels, roughly our *a, e, i, o*, and *u*. These were not enough, but the Greeks made do with them since Classical Greek was not so rich in vowel sounds as is NE, and thus five vowels served better in Athens than they would now in Paris or New York. Nobody has devised any pure vowel signs since then for the Latin alphabet, although St. Cyril added a few to the Russian alphabet.

The forms of the letter bring with them remnants of the Levant. *A* is presumably from *aleph*, "ox"; *B* is supposedly *beth*, "house"; *C* (or *G*) is *gimel*, "camel," and so on. The original signs may have been stylized pictures of the named objects—*B* was formerly two boxlike objects, one on top of the other—or they may be names given for a stylized object because they seemed appropriate, as an amphibian tank may be dubbed a *duck*. However these forms got started, they were juggled about. Writing from left to right and with lines going from top to bottom soon became common, but other directions were also used and, of course, inscriptions had to fit the space available, very much as RESTAURANT may run from the top to the bottom of a building, to conform with laws governing advertising on city streets. Thus some of the designs were tipped sideways or otherwise rotated; if *alpha* is indeed the head of an ox, his face and two horns, he was turned upside down, ⊬ becoming *A*.

The Greek alphabet has sired most modern alphabets, probably all of them, although Korean may be an exception. Some alphabets, like Arabic, may be based on a local syllabary but have borrowed the idea

---

9. Later Semitic writers learned to indicate vowels with diacritical marks, one of which is the ancestor of our apostrophe.

of an alphabet. Many descend directly. The Greek letters moved north, and were adapted for religious use as Old Church Slavic, Modern Russian, and some other Slavic systems. The Greek alphabet fathered several scripts in the Italic peninsula—Etruscan, Oscan, and Umbrian, in addition to Roman, which became the Latin alphabet, which was spread by the Roman Empire and the Christian church so widely that it is the nearest thing we have to a universal writing system.

As it grew in Latin and in Western European vernaculars, the Latin alphabet underwent small changes too numerous to be surveyed here, although individual ones will be mentioned when they become pertinent. For example, Greek had θ, theta, for the voiceless velar fricative, but Latin had no such sound and it died out of Western alphabets. English scribes revived a Germanic symbol for it, þ, called *thorn*, and later another symbol, crossed d, ð, was imported, and both were used almost indiscriminately for the voiceless and the voiced consonants. All these signs were unfamiliar to Norman scribes, who tended to treat the sounds as an aspirated /t/, giving us the modern *th*. Greek upsilon, composed of two upright strokes, was linked at the bottom with a curve for convenience when written with a brush or a quill, becoming our *u*; linked without a curve, for convenience when carved in stone or wood, it became our *v*. Thus the alphabet got one more letter. Doubled, it provided another letter, *w*, called "double-u" and in German more appropriately "double-v." The alphabet got another letter from the scribal habit of adding a tail to a final *i*, as in the Roman form for the figure *8*, which became *viij*, and thus *j* was born. We have noted above that various signs, including the revived Irish *z*, became involved in the shifting palatals.

9. Too Few Vowels to Go Around

One broad problem was never solved, and it has plagued English spelling to this day. The Greeks had supplied too few vowels, and nobody with power enough tried to overhaul the vowels in the Western vernaculars. Scribes made some attempts (apparently they understood the desirability of letters representing sounds), but they had troubles. English was much fractured by dialect, and the transcribing was further confused by Norman copyists trying to write it with alphabetic traditions that had grown in Continental languages. Individual scriptoria endeavored to establish reasonable practices, but each writing school was a law unto itself. There was no national standard, and not all manuscripts were the product of well-regulated bodies of scribes. Many scribes inclined to represent pronunciations in their native shires, tempered by their own idiosyncracies. The confusion in writing and spelling in ME was not so great as it inevitably seems to a modern reader, but the written records are far from orderly.

In spite of this bedlam, scribes developed one practice which, although it was never applied with entire consistency, did much to solve the vowel problem. Latin had become much more reliant on stress than on length, but even so a written *a* stood for two sounds, one long-stressed, one short-unstressed. On the Continent, standardizers of language used diacritical marks variously; French now has *e, é,* and *è* (not to mention *ê,* which has a different use), but in England scribes tended to pick up this idea of two sounds for a vowel. Theoretically this system could have given English two times five, or ten phonemes, and consistent use of *y* would have given two more. This system would have been about right, since analyses of English mostly call for ten to a dozen vowel phonemes, but the device was haphazardly applied.

In general, the procedure was this: if a vowel was to be marked as long, an extra vowel would be added; if it was to be marked as short, a subsequent consonant would be doubled. Thus the word for high ground was spelled *hill* to show that the *i* represented a short, unstressed sound, and the animal grazing on the hill was spelled something like *shepe* or *sheep* to show that the *e* represented a long, stressed sound. But this system was not worked out carefully and applied rigidly. Some scribes seldom doubled anything; others apparently doubled by whim or habit. And many scribes did not bother to use these devices if they assumed the reader would know anyhow; thus in the same manuscript *get* may have one *t,* whereas the infinitive *getten* has two. Likewise, some long vowels were seldom doubled; *he* was not much spelled *hee,* or *hei,* or *hey,* as it might have been. Nor was there any agreement as to where these extra vowels would appear, or what they would be. Some of the resulting variations have survived, so that we spell *moor* and *Muir; jail* and *gaol; house* and *howl; seas, sees,* and *seize.* In Northern spelling *i* or *y* was regularly used for the extra vowel, but these letters were used also for the glide left by a palatal, so that we have *may* from *maeg* and *sail* from *segl,* but also *mail* where there was no palatal. As the OE endings were being dropped and reduced to schwa as an interim stage (spelled *e*), a final *e* might represent a sound, an indication of a preceding stressed vowel, or almost nothing, since many scribes got the habit of writing final *e* and would add it where no *e* had ever been. In ME the spelling *mete* could be the equivalent of *meet,* with the extra *e* to mark a long vowel appearing after the consonant; or it could be a reduction of OE *mettan*, indicating two syllables /metə/, or it could reflect a spelling convention, or the habit of a scribe. Even so, the practice was common enough so that it could be of more use than it is, particularly since a few centuries later printers recognized it, and somewhat normalized the practice.

10. Spelling Becomes Conventional

Effective standardization of English spelling began in the time of Elizabeth I. I have elected to reproduce Shakespeare in this book from the *First Folio*, partly for accuracy, partly to remind the reader that standardized English spelling is fewer than two hundred years old. The printers deserve considerable credit; they must have understood that if a language is much fractured by dialects, regular spelling becomes possible only by being arbitrary. They apparently took into account the writing of college professors like Roger Ascham in the *Scholemaster* and his *Letters*, but they combined his principles with printing practices that had become established.

Thus the "correct" spelling today often represents some kind of compromise. The initial consonant clusters *wr (wrong)* and *kn (knife)* represent old sounds which were soon reduced to /r/ and /n/, but the silent *w* and *k* had continued to be written, and printing standardized them. On the other hand, NE *laugh* was written in OE, with good reason, as something like *hliehhan*. But these palatals, *hl* and *hh*, did not endure, so that Shakespeare wrote, "the whole quire [choir] hold their hips and loffe [laughed]." The printers standardized the word as *laughed*, which had been common with many writers. NE *to, too*, and *two* have different ancestries, and although they have now fallen together in sound, they probably maintained distinct pronunciations in Shakespeare's time, as they do in some dialects today.

Printers established other conventions, most of them, like punctuation, not pertinent to the study of words, but capitalization has been refined into a very good tool for identifying proper names. Modern English *may* is not *May*, *will* is not *Will*, and the capital letter serves nicely to keep them apart. The refinement took centuries. As late as 1771 the philosopher and grammarian James Harris printed the following:

Now the POWERS OF THE SOUL (over and above meer nutritive) may be included all of them in those of PERCEPTION. By the Powers of PERCEPTION, I mean the *Senses* and the intellect;

by Powers of VOLITION, I mean an extended sense, not only the
Will, but the several *Passions* and *Appetites*.

This sort of printing provides a handsome variety of type faces, but it
does not promote meaning. Harris writes "POWERS" and "Powers,"
and elsewhere he writes "powers"; he writes "Senses" and "sense."
If his capital letters imply any use or meaning, the reader is entitled to
wonder what it is. But a better system had already been found. A *Pocket
Dictionary* (1753) reads as follows:

> Thus the English tongue, which was anciently pure British or
> Welsh, became a mixture of a little British, a great deal of Latin,
> a yet far greater part of Anglo-Saxon, some Danish, and abun-
> dance of Norman French: But since that time the revival of arts and
> sciences has added greatly to its imbellishment.

This could almost be PDE. The capital letter is here used to distinguish
a proper noun, and nothing else except the beginning of a sentence or
major clause. The text is not cluttered with needless capitals, and italic
type is freed for other purposes. As a result, capital letters have taken on
meaning. If we read "I heard an Angel recording," we know that someone heard a record issued by a well-known record company, but if we
read "I heard an angel recording," we must assume we have here a statement about a quite improbable miracle.

11. Reverse English: Spelling Makes Sound

For centuries spelling was little honored, but it became a system, and
now it is venerated in some quarters, especially in the United States, as
though it were eternal truth. There are as many spellings of Shakespeare's
name as there are autographs, none of them the currently accepted
orthography. The late Miles Hanley, checking early New England letters
and town records, noticed more than fifty spellings for forms of *receive*,
including *receyve, resaived, recued, recieveing,* and *receaued.* Now
young Americans are refused admission to the better universities unless
they can spell in accordance with a rigid system, and purists may become
furious unless one admits that a pronunciation that seems to reflect a
spelling is the only "correct" one.

Sounds change and, particularly, words are compressed, in English
mostly by dropping an ending or syncopating within the word. In some

languages initial sounds are dropped, but not much in NE. OE had a prefix *ge-*, of which the only survivor is supposed to be the initial *a-*, pronounced /ə/, as in *abuilding*. Some aspiration has been lost from NE; when *why* is pronounced like the name of the letter *y*, the change represents loss of an initial sound, since the value of *wh-* is actually /hw/. But such examples are few. On the other hand, the loss of endings has been widespread, but that was mostly centuries ago, and will be best treated under *grammar* in the next chapter.

The word *often*, long pronounced as one syllable, /afn/ or /ɔfn/, can be heard widely in the United States and Canada as two syllables, /aftən/ or /ɔftən/. Curiously, this word was never pronounced /ɔftɛn/, as many revisionists assume it was. In OE it was commonly *oft*; like so many other words it was frequently written with a final *e* in ME and it got the *n* possibly by analogy with *selden*, NE *seldom*. The cluster /ftn/ simplified to /fn/. Meanwhile, most such shifts in sound pass unnoticed, partly because speakers do not usually hear themselves. Many speakers, on both sides of the Atlantic, pronounce *wicked* as though it were a term associated with a British sport, *wicket*, but thousands of such variations can be heard everywhere without their creating doublets like *shirt* and *skirt*. Some New Yorkers will speak of *boying a ticket* but their auditors soon learn to replace *boying* with *buying*. Thus, seldom do variations in pronunciation lead to new words or to much confusion in using the old ones.

12. The Values of the Letters

Ideally, each letter in an alphabet should represent only one sound, and every sound would be suggested by only one symbol. By this standard the English alphabet is far from ideal. No one-for-one alphabet exists—except for arbitrarily constructed systems such as that used in Esperanto—and a little speculating on the subject will suggest that such an alphabet might not work so well as my term *ideally* suggests. One wonders, for example, what would happen when sounds change and all the printed books would become wrong, and who would decide when a new "letter" was needed, and what would the new symbol be? For better or for worse, we do not have that kind of alphabet and are not likely to.

As a matter of fact, a natural alphabet, with all its redundancies and contradictions, may work as well as any other. The human mind will tolerate a deal of inconsistency and be but little bothered by ambiguities and irregularities; we have no trouble dealing with words having many meanings, and we are surely better off with our sort of vocabulary than we would be with the clumsy collection of terms we would require if a word could have only one use. Children who learn the language as natives are able to match sounds to alphabetic symbols and do most of it unconsciously, although spelling becomes a problem, as it is not with many languages, Spanish and German for example. Even so, a survey of the letters and what they can do may be useful for reference. Following are the commoner values in American English:

a As we have seen, this letter was made over from a consonant. Presumably it is either long or short, stressed or unstressed. When stressed it may have the sound of /e/. This is usually marked by an additional vowel, most frequently *e (gate)*, but sometimes *i (gait)* or *y (gayly)*. In American English the most common short sound is /æ/ *(hat)*, but *a* can serve for any sound along the lower length of the mouth from /ɔ/ *(gawk)* forward, and even the mid front vowel /ɛ/ *(any)*. When it suggests the sound /ɔ/ it is usually accompanied by another vowel or semivowel *(talk, hawk)*. Like all other vowels, especially in American English, it can become /ə/ in unstressed syllables *(about)*. It can mark a preceding long vowel *(boat)*.

b A voiced stop, /b/ corresponds to the voiceless stop /p/, the voiced fricative /v/, and the voiceless fricative /f/. These sounds can readily interchange. PIE **bher-*, "to carry," gives us *bear, bier*, and *bore*, by direct descent, and /f/ in Latin *transfer, suffer*, and with the spelling *ph, amphora, metaphor*, etc. from Greek. PIE **beu-* gives us both *bosom* and *pout* as native words, *pocket* and *bowl* as loans. As a variant, /v/ is less common, but does occur; *scribe, shrive, scrivener, scarify*, and *serif* all come from **skeri-*, "to cut," a *scribe* having once been a person who cut or scratched in wood or stone. Occasionally an intervocalic /b/ became /v/, not necessarily in loans; OE *libban* became *live*, but the spelling *bb* may indicate an affricate. The PIE bilabial voiced stop was frequently aspirated as /bh/, but this heavy breath was preserved mainly in Sanskrit, from which English has borrowed only sparingly, and usually indirectly.

c This is a Latin spelling, used in NE for both /k/ and /s/. The regular spelling for /k/ in OE was *c*, and it has survived in some words like *can, camp*; see also *ch* and *k*, below. When *c* has the sound of /k/ it most frequently comes from a Norman word *(court)*, or Old Norse influence *(score)*, or it represents IE /k/ as preserved through Latin *(conclave)* or Greek through Latin *(cardiac)*. It has the sound of /s/ through French *(cent)*, often for sounds that have come from PIE /k/.

ch This digraph usually represents /č/ in native words *(church)* and in loans from Norman French *(Charles)* or /š/ in terms from later French *(chivalry)*. In loans from Greek it may stand for /k/ *(psychology)*. For other consonants and vowels that may be cognate with sounds spelled *ch*, see *g*, below.

d This is a voiced velar stop, corresponding to voiceless /t/ and the fricatives, usually spelled *th*, voiceless as /θ/, voiced as /ð/. Thus it readily relates to any of these three sounds. PIE **deru-* becomes *tree* and *truth* in native words, *durable* through Latin, *philodendron* through Greek, and *deodar* through Sanskrit. PIE **dhe-* becomes *doom* and *deem* in native words, but is borrowed from Greek as *theme* /θijm/, *hypothesis*, and many more. Since the /d/ was aspirated in IE it can become /f/ in Latin, in such loans as *fact, fashion*, and *profit*.

e This is the most common letter in English, notably because it is so frequently what is called "silent." It serves as a marker to indicate that another vowel is long *(hide, heed)*. In OE and ME it served as an inflectional ending, or part of one. Some final *e*'s may be remnants of such endings, but they are hard to identify, and some result from analogy, since so many words ended with an *e* having no phonetic value. It is also, in effect, silent when terminal in French loans *(castle, etiquette)*. Long it is regularly /i/ *(she)*, the sound having moved forward from /e/ in the Great English Vowel Shift. Short it is regularly /ɛ/ *(get)*, or /ɪ/ *(houses)*. In the digraph *ea* it may stand for /i/, having moved from /æ/ in ME *(meat)*. If the sound shortens, the digraph may represent /ɛ/ *(health)*. In digraphs it may participate in any of several sounds: /e/ *(neighbor)*, /i/ *(brief)*, /aɪ/ *(Cheyenne)*, etc. In combinations with *r* it shows great dialectal variety, being a retroflex vowel (the tongue flips back), schwa, or nothing. It may represent schwa /ə/ or have no value in unstressed syllables *(even)* or when a syllable is lost by syncopation *(tired)*. It may be a remnant in various loans *(valley, value)*.

f A voiceless fricative corresponding to the stop /p/. This variation occurs frequently in English, as we saw when comparing English *father, foot* and Latin *pater, pes*. For /v/ and other related sounds see *b* above.

g A voiced palatal stop *g* is a spelling for /g/ *(get)*, /ǰ/ *(age)*, and /ž/ *(garage*, American pronunciation), the latter two usually through French and often spelled as *dg (ledge)*. As a sound /g/ was common in early OE, and survives in words like *hog, gold*, but was mainly lost, sometimes leaving behind the spelling *gh (high)*. It often survives as /k/, spelled *c*, as in *club* and *clutter* from PIE **gel-*. When it represents the sound /g/ it most frequently occurs in loans from Norman, Latin,

Greek, or Old Norse *(guardian, geyser, globe).* It occasionally became a vowel or part of a diphthong, as in *law* from *lagu, day* from *daga.* For some suggestion of the variety of changes that can overtake a palatal, see the discussion of **kerd-, *reg-,* and **werg-* in Chapter III.9.

h   The sign of aspiration in English, it may represent a native sound or one borrowed with little change, but frequently it comes from /k/ in a PIE root, which may be preserved with little change in loans from Greek or Latin, although spelled *c* in Latin, and becoming /s/ although still spelled *c* through French; English *hundred,* Latin-French *century,* from **dekm-;* English *home, hide, haunt,* Latin-French *civic,* and Latin *incunabulum* from **kei-.* For other palatals that may be represented by *h* see *c, ch, g,* above.

i   When long, this vowel most frequently becomes a diphthong /aɪ/ *(hide)* from earlier /i/ as part of the Great English Vowel Shift. In loans after the shift it may retain /i/ or /ɪ/ *(machine).* Short it is regularly /ɪ/ or /ɨ/ *(it, hill).* In digraphs it usually represents the Northern practice of using it as a marker for a long vowel *(Muir)* or it represents a palatal that has become a vowel and then was lost *(maid).*

j   As a spelling, *j* usually represents /ǰ/ *(judge).* In loans from Spanish it is /h/ *(Jai-alai);* in some Germanic loans it is /j/ *(jarl).*

k   In loans it may equate with *c* in Latin, *ch, k,* or *x* in words from Greek. As a sound, /k/ is the voiceless stop corresponding to /g/; see *g* above. As a spelling, *k* represents /k/, a sound more frequently signaled by *c* and sometimes *q(u).* It can represent a /k/ unchanged from OE, as in *king,* but more frequently it results from a borrowing *(kindle* from Old Norse, *court* from Norman French, *kremlin* from Russian, *kangaroo* from an unidentified Australian language, etc.). In a modest number of words it represents /g/ or /q/ in an IE root; English *kind, kin,* etc. from IE **gen-* or **gene-* are cognate with many loans from Latin, *gender, genus, germ, pregnant,* etc., and some from Greek, *genealogy, genesis, gonad,* etc. In native words it can represent a sound in OE that is no longer pronounced *(knife, know).* For more that can happen to palatals like /k/ and /g/, see *c, ch,* and *g,* above.

l   As a spelling, *l* represents the liquid or semivowel /l/. It can be absorbed in a vowel and disappear or can interchange with /r/, but is not much involved in orderly IE change and is often preserved. It has become silent in a few words *(chalk, would, palm).*

m, n   These are the nasals in English, and as may be observed by checking the cognates in Chapter III.7 above, they are not much involved in orderly drifts among IE languages. Alternation between /n/ and /ŋ/ is common dialectally in English, especially in gerunds and present participles as evidenced in spellings like *goin', singin', nothin'*. Only recently has /ŋ/ in such terms been promoted as "correct," whereas /n/ is condemned as "wrong." The history of these variations is not clear, but on the whole, in contrast with the popular assumption, /n/ seems to enjoy a more respectable genealogy than does /ŋ/.

o When long, this vowel has the sound /o/ *(go)* or any of several diphthongs /ow/, /oʊ/, etc. Doubled, it can stand for any of several sounds: /u/ *(cool)*, /ʊ/ *(hood)*, /o/ *(brooch)*, etc. In the digraph *ou* it is often part of the sound /u/ in French loans *(routine)*, in either *ou* or *ow* as part of /aʊ/, /æʊ/, etc. in native terms from an earlier /u/ *(house, cow)*. Short, it represented a rather high central vowel, which lowered and became either /a/ or /ɔ/ *(god)*.

p This is the voiceless bilabial plosive, corresponding to the voiced /b/ and the fricative /f/. Characteristically, it appears in cognates where /f/ occurs in English *(for, fore; per-, pre-, pro-)*. When it occurs in native words it may descend from PIE /b/, which sound may be preserved in cognates (NE *lip, lap*; Latin *labial, slob*). In words from Greek, *ph* is the spelling for /f/. In other digraphs, *p* usually represents a spelling, not a sound; *pn* is a Greek spelling *(pneumatic)* pronounced /n/ in NE; *ps* is a transliteration of Greek *psi*, pronounced /s/ *(psychic)*.

q(u) This is a French spelling, pronounced /k/ *(physique)* or /kw/ *(quick)*. It is found in French words borrowed from Paris and central France, not in Norman French, and was but little used in English until the spelling reform that began in the sixteenth century.

r This is a spelling for a variety of sounds, mostly glides, some trilled, some retroflex (formed by a backward flip of the tongue). Sounds represented by *r* vary widely dialectally, but not much in the drifts described in Grimm's Law. It has mainly disappeared as a terminal consonant in Received Pronunciation, in many southern English dialects, in many northeastern and southern American speech areas, where it can be dropped or can survive in a diphthong, *floor* becoming /flo/ or /floə/. In Scottish speech it may be trilled. It may interchange with /l/ in what is called a rhotacism or transpose with a vowel in metathesis. Chaucer wrote *brid* where NE has *bird*, and many Scotsmen say what sounds like *gerdel* or *girdle* for an implement that farther south is called a *griddle*.

s This is a voiceless sibilant, made with a narrowed flow of air directed at the upper teeth, corresponding to the voiced sibilant /z/ and roughly to the voiceless /š/ and the voiced /ž/, made with a flow of air spread by the raised and contracted tongue. The shifts among these related sounds are not much involved in IE relationships. Changes in English involving shifts in accent and absorption of adjacent vowels are too numerous and complex to analyze here; NE *tissue*, ME /tisiu/, is now mainly /tɪšu/; ME *vision*, ME /viziun/, is now mainly /vɪžn/. When /k/ was palatalized during late OE times, /sk/ spelled *sc* usually became /š/ spelled *sh* (OE *scip* became NE *ship*). In French loans it may combine with *c (descent)*.

sh This digraph is the common spelling for /š/, and may represent OE /sk/, French *ch*, German *sch*, or some other borrowing. See also *s* above.
t This is the voiceless consonant corresponding to voiced /d/; see *d* above. It regularly descended from PIE /d/, as in **deru-*, from which came *tree, true*, corresponding to /d/ in cognates *(duress, obdurate)*. It is usually preserved in cognates descending from PIE /t/, which regularly became a sound represented by *th* in NE (*three* and *thumb* in English, *trio* and *tumor* from Latin). See also *th*.
th This digraph is used for two sounds in English, the voiceless fricative /θ/ *(think)* corresponding to /t/ and the voiced fricative /ð/ *(this)* corresponding to /d/; see *d*. Either sound may descend from IE /t/, as in *there, they, think* from **to-* and **tong-*. Cognates are likely to have /t/ *(tandem, triad, trinity*, etc.). The spelling *th* may represent the Greek theta, θ, the symbol used for the English voiceless fricative, as in *theme, theater*, a sound which may correspond to /d/ in ME, as in *deem, doom*.
u This vowel is usually /u/ or /ɪu/ *(use)*. It can combine with *o* in diphthongs and digraphs: see *o*. It usually follows *q* in French loans (see *q* above in this list) and may mark *g* as /g/ *(guess)*.
v This is the voiced fricative corresponding to voiceless /f/; see *f* above. Because it was not much used, if at all, in PIE, it is not very useful for distinguishing languages. As spelling, it was long a variant form of *u*. In loans, /v/ may have developed from /w/; **wes-* gives *was, were, wear* in English, *vest, invest, travesty* in loans from Latin.
w Insofar as /w/ is a consonant, it is mostly a rounding of what would otherwise be a vowel. Thus it readily merges with an adjacent vowel; IE **werg-* descends as English *work* but was borrowed as Greek *ergon*, Latin *organ*. It may alternate with /v/, as in English *wine*, Latin *vino*; English *was, were, wear*, Latin loans *vestal, vest, travesty*, etc. It may combine with another vowel in a digraph *(show, new)*, may imply that a preceding *a* is pronounced /ɔ/ *(hawk)*, and can combine with a vowel to make the diphthong /aʊ/ *(dowse)*. It is silent in a few old spellings *(wrong)*.
x Medially and terminally *x* as a spelling is the reverse of a digraph,

being one symbol for two sounds, /ks/ voiceless and /gz/ voiced; see *k* and *g* above. Initially as a spelling it may represent Greek *xi* and be pronounced /z/ *(Xantippe, xylophone)*.

y As a consonant *y* is pronounced /j/, and may equate with the spelling *j* in Latin having the sound /j/ or /ĭ/: English *youth, yoke*; Latin loans *juvenile, subjugate*. It links with a few other palatal and aspirate sounds, not very consistently. It is mainly a vowel, medially a transliteration of Greek upsilon *(physics, psychology)*, and terminally as an alternate spelling of *i (very, slowly)*.

z As a sound /z/ is the voiced correspondent of the sibilant /s/ (see *s* above), and may be spelled *s (devise, times)*, often because /s/ has become /z/ in English. As a sound it is not much involved in IE relationships. In loans it may represent Greek *zeta*.

CHAPTER VIII

GRAMMAR IN WORDS
AND WORDS IN GRAMMAR

Grammarians are accustomed to humiliation. It is their heritage.
They are dry, they are plodding, they are mere: at their funeral no
one weeps. . . . Yet not even a grammarian should always be meek.
Like a rat-catcher a word-catcher has worked hard to master the
secrets of his trade. Not every man can catch a rat or define a noun.
—James Sledd

1. The Grammar of English

"That's a good school," Nelson Antrim Crawford quoted one of his neighbors as saying. "They don't teach no goddamned grammar there."

Doomed to perdition or not, NE grammar is not much comprehended by users of English, and it must be if we are to trace the imprint of grammar on vocabulary in any detail. The doctors do not agree, at this writing, as to what NE grammar may be, but they do agree on enough for our purposes, and the linguistic machinery they describe is probably not what Crawford's neighbor meant by "goddamned grammar." He probably referred to a system, drawn mainly from grammatical descriptions of Latin, that has long been taught in American schools. It has some relevance for English, but not enough, and it has perpetuated irrelevance we could do without.

A fundamental statement about grammar may here be in order. All languages comprise at least two sorts of elements: (1) linguistic particles that, whatever else they do, are notably concerned with meaning, and (2) various devices for dealing with these units. The first is technically the *lexicon*, which I have been calling vocabulary; in English it is composed mainly of phrases, words, and syllables. The second, called *grammar*, provides means of enlarging and refining the working of the vocabulary items, in English notably by building them into sentences and larger units of discourse. In the two sentences *Fire the help* and *Help the fire*, the words seem to be the same, but the meanings of the sentences are quite different because the grammar is different. Even the meanings of individual words change with the grammar, *fire* in the first sentence means to discharge, in the second it means a conflagration. *Help* can mean either the body of employees or to give assistance, depending on the grammar, and if the term were used without any other words it would acquire a still different implication, as in "Help!" Many more uses are possible, depending in part on the grammar, as in *They fire at the fire truck, He could not help helping.*

Grammar, then, from one point of view, is a way of handling meaningful units to enhance their meaning. With units of language, two things can be done; they can be put together or they can be kept apart, and either can be handled in various ways for various purposes. We use the first of these means somewhat in English; we can put *look*, a verb, together with *out*, a particle or an adverb, and get *lookout*, a noun, as in *Look out for the lookout*. Words used in such combinations may lose most of their meaning and become almost purely grammatical signals. Our syllable *-ize* meant in Greek "to act in a certain way," but it can now be attached to a word like *standard* (usually a noun or a modifier) to make *standardize*, a verb. By adding another syllable, *-ed*, the verb can be thrown into a past tense or turned into a verbal or a different modifier, *standardized*.[1] Numerous bodies of speech rely heavily on this device of attaching affixes to key words or roots; they may be called **inflectional** because in them so many words have endings to reveal the grammar, or **synthetic** because the grammar works by synthesis, by putting things together. Classical Latin and Greek were such languages.

No grammar relies on only one principle, but as will be apparent from the paragraphs above, NE grammar works extensively on a principle opposite to combining elements, that is by keeping words apart. Whatever makes *Fire the help* different from *Help the fire* is grammar, and at least superficially the difference stems from a changed word order. We might consider a more complex example; the following headline occurred in a local paper: PLAYER TAMES GREENS TO LEAD U.S.

---

1. This principle of combining syllables can be pushed so far as to provide whole words —or in some languages whole sentences—from elements that cannot stand alone. In English we can build a few words like *illiterate*, made of *il-*, *-lit-*, *-er-*, and *-ate*, but the device is minor in English grammar.

OPEN. Presumably this sequence had meaning for contemporary sports fans; it meant that a golfer named Player was winning a tournament played over a troublesome course. But these words, with some inflection, could mean something—perhaps as much as they did in the original— in almost any order: U.S. OPENS GREENS TO TAME PLAYERS, GREEN LEADS U.S. TO TAME OPEN PLAYERS, GREEN PLAYERS LEAD U.S. TO TAME OPEN, on and on. Obviously much of this shifting amalgam of grammar and meaning relies on order, but some inflectional change is involved, too; the grammatical signal *s* has to be added or removed variously, and *to*, although it is called a word and must occasionally be shifted, is not much more than a grammatical signal as it is used here. That is, for our purposes we can think of NE grammar as functioning mainly by word order, supplemented with some other devices. It keeps linguistic units apart, doing this in recognized patterns, some of them quite rigid, a device technically known as **analysis** or **distribution**. English makes so much use of this device that, speaking roughly, we can call it an analytic language and Latin or Greek a synthetic language.

2. Grammar at Work

As we have seen, most English words trigger meaning, and are usually thought of as carrying meaning—if we accept a liberal definition of meaning we can probably say that all of them, even *of*, *'twas* as we observed it in Chapter I, and *to* as the sign of an infinitive, have meaning. In addition to meaning, English semantic units are all involved in grammar in at least two ways: (1) every word has a use in grammar, and (2) every word is involved in the grammar generated through other words.

We might look at two similar sentences. For a time, in the United States, rented automobiles came mostly from two companies, one of which was older, bigger, and much better known than the other. The smaller company made a virtue of this handicap, advertising, "We Try Harder," explaining that since they were smaller and less well known, they had to treat their customers better in order to compete. They used this slogan so extensively that all literate people in the country knew it and its associations. Some time later, a company that sold concrete advertised its product by printing on its trucks, "We Dry Harder."

Phonetically, these sentences are similar; in fact in the mouths of many American speakers they would be identical, since the voiceless /t/ and the voiced /d/ are often confused in current speech. Even formally the difference is slight, that between the initial voiceless consonant of *try* and the corresponding voiced consonant of *dry*. But this slight difference in shape changes the grammar of the sentence and the meaning of all words in it. Each word participates in the grammar, and superficially in the same way in each sentence. *We* is the subject, a noun; *try* or *dry* is the verb, working in nexus with the subject to make a sentence. *Harder* is some kind of complement or modifier, completing or altering the predication implied by *we* plus a verb. But only superficially is the grammar the same. In "We Try Harder" the *we* is presumably the employees of the company, the embodied policy of the company, or something of the sort. That is, *we* is here part of a sort of sentence common in English, in which the subject names an actor, the verb an action, and the complement (if there is one) a goal. But in the sentence with *dry* the subject is not an actor. In "We Dry Harder" the executives of the company are not petrifying. The subject is not an actor; it is being acted upon, and it is probably not even plural. The *we* here is the company's product, presumably singular—structural concrete.

Similarly, the verb is not only different in meaning; it also differs in grammar. *Try* can serve as the verb in the actor-action-goal sequences: a judge can try a case, a cook can try lard, a pestiferous pupil may try a teacher's patience, but *try*, as the shape is used here, is a sort of auxiliary. It may be followed by an infinitive, as in "I will try to win," or the main verb may appear in another sentence: "Miss Jones, can you get this letter typed before closing time?" "I'll try." Or, as in the sentence in question, a main verb and even a complement may be omitted as being roughly understood, as though the slogan were "We try harder to please you," or "to satisfy our customers."

We might notice here that grammar is becoming involved in vocabulary and meaning. The verb *try*, as against the verb *dry*, alters the meaning of the adjacent word, *we*, and at the same time the grammatical functioning of *try* determines which of the various possible uses of the word will be triggered in this sentence. *Try* must here mean something like *endeavor to*; it cannot mean "determine right or wrong," "reduce by heating," or "see if it's locked" (as in *try the door*).

Likewise, both the meaning and grammar of *harder* vary with the grammar of the sentence. In "We Try Harder" it presumably serves as an adverb, indicating the degree of the trying done by the employees. In "We Dry Harder" the same shape can be thought of as a modifier, an adjective, also a complement, since it extends the idea of the verb *dry* and describes the subject *we*—presumably concrete—after the drying process is complete. Once more, the meaning of *harder* is selected by the grammatical functioning of the word and of other words in the sentence, and it fits into the grammar of the whole sentence in such a way as to influence the use, and hence the meaning, of both of the other words. The grammar, of course, does not determine the meaning; it cannot provide a new meaning for *harder*—it cannot make *harder* trigger the concept *green*—but it can select the meaning appropriate to this sentence, the particular meaning being selected from the various uses of the symbol h-a-r-d-e-r or /hardər/.

In English, complements tend especially to determine meanings of words by selecting which of the various possible uses of another word in the sentence—notably the subject or verb—is here the actual use. One might notice what happens to *put out* in the following sentences as the complement changes:

1) She put out the fire.
2) She put out the cat.
3) She put out the runner.
4) She put out the information.
5) She put out her best china.
6) She put out that her murdered husband had gone fishing.
7) She was put out by his impudence.
8) She was not putting out.

In each sentence *put out* would have a distinctive definition, and if the meaning of the complement is ambiguous, the verb is also, as in sentence 3. In "She put out the runner," the combination *put out* has one meaning if the runner is a baseball player, another if it is a long rug, and a third if the complement is a road runner, a kind of bird. Sentence 7 can work only in the passive, and sentence 8 requires that the verb have no complement.

3. Grammatical Fluidity: Conversion

All this fluidity is enhanced by another characteristic of many analytic grammars, including that of English, a susceptibility to what is called **conversion**, the process by which a term having one grammatical use is converted to another. For example, *bicycle* usually refers to a two-wheeled vehicle, but recently a new use has developed. A broadcasting company may receive a tape to be used by several studios in the community. The broadcaster plays the tape and sends it on to the next station on the list; this sequence is called *bicycling the tape*, probably because for prompt and sure delivery it was sometimes sent by a courier on a bicycle. That is, a noun has developed use as a verb.

This process is so pervasive in English vocabulary that common words regularly have various grammatical uses. The IE equivalent of *man* referred to a male human being, but we can *man* a boat. The etymon for *land* referred to earth, but we can now *land* a plane or the plane can *land*, and the term *land* can be used as various sorts of modifiers. On the other hand, words like *stand* and *stop* started as verbs but have developed dozens of uses as nouns and modifiers. In fact, in English, any common word that serves as a noun, verb, or modifier is likely soon to become the other two also, sometimes with change of form—*live* became *life* and *alive*. Such changes can take place rapidly and may occasion little notice. Recently a rail transportation system has been developed called AMTRAK; today, one can say, "That is an AMTRAK device," without most people questioning the usage. For this term to become a verb will probably take a bit longer. I have yet to hear the following conversation: "Going to drive?" "No, we plan to AMTRAK," but if passenger rail-roading continues to grow, one soon will hear it, and probably few purists will object.

What are sometimes called "full" or "lexical" words—notably nouns, verbs, and modifiers, which are mainly freighted with meaning—undergo conversion very readily. But words showing relationship change slowly. They are mainly grammatical signals, and changing signals can be tricky. We have been hundreds, even thousands of years developing enough grammatical particles so that an analytic language can work, and we are still growing new ones. Most of these relationship words—prepositions, conjunctions, and the like—were formerly full words, especially abverbs, now converted to new purposes. *By* was formerly an adverb of place; *of* was an adverb that meant "away from"; *to* meant "up toward"; *over* is probably an old comparative of *up*, meaning more up than *up*. These relationship terms are common words and have been for centuries—either native words or borrowings so early they had lost any foreign flavor.

Apparently unconscious conversion or resistance to conversion becomes a part of most languages, a sense for propriety that the users of the language feel. An inflectional or synthetic language is likely to resist conversion; if the language includes an elaborate paradigm of endings to be added to nouns, shifting one part of speech to another will entail many changes. Careful speakers will feel that these changes are "wrong," and children will be taught not to use them. But if a word has no endings, if it appears in the same form whatever its grammatical use—*fast* can be noun, verb, adjective, or adverb—a new grammatical usage is not likely to attract much attention. Thus, if we borrow the word *blitz* as part of the German noun *Blitzkrieg*, meaning lightning war, we need not be surprised that one fighter defeats another by blitzing him.

4. The Old and the New in Sentences

Communication can be thought of as going from what is sometimes called the "old" to the "new." Even on the simplest levels, the communicants must have something in common, something that has grown out of previous experience. If a dog wags its tail we know it is at least somewhat friendly, but if a cat lashes its tail we surmise it is not. We make such assumptions because we know something about cats and dogs. We have something that is "old" in this special sense. In communication through language, all this gets involved in grammar, and in English the "old" and the "new" appear in sentence structure. To communicate, two speakers must agree, at least tacitly, on the subject, and this subject of the conversation tends to become the grammatical subject of sentences. That is, in a sentence having the familiar pattern identified above as actor-action-goal (or subject-verb-complement), the grammatical subject is the part known to both speaker and hearer, the "old" in the sentence. The "new" is the predicate, whatever is said about the subject, the verb and what goes with it, along with the complement if there is one and what goes with that.

In the sentence, "God protects drunks, fools, and American foreign policy," the "old" part is *God*, the grammatical subject. We may not know who or what God is, but the notion of a deity is familiar to us, and we know enough about the concept of God so that we can accept it and go on from there. It is "old" to both speaker and listener. The remainder of the sentence, *protects* and *drunks, fools, and American foreign policy*, respectively the verb and the complement, are "new." The "new" part may not be true, of course, but presumably the speaker thinks it is, or has some reason for using these semantic counters. He may want only to be amusing, but whatever his motives, this "new" part provides the reason for this sentence existing at all. The speaker assumes that the hearer does not know this truth, or he has not heard it expressed in just this way, or something. The assumptions may be unfounded; the listener may have heard this same remark from some loquacious person who was fond of mouthing it, but in that case there is no communication, only boredom, because the supposedly "new" matter was not new to the listener. It, too, was "old," although the speaker did not know this, or admit to himself that it was old.

5. Choosing Subjects

This fact of there being "old" and "new" in any good English sentence has implications, the more because of the way our grammar works. In English, some words or groups of words can be used to identify the "old," that is the subject. They are nouns or nounlike terms, but whether or not a user of English can define nouns and identify them, every native speaker of English knows which terms can be used as subjects and which cannot. *God, you,* and *ectoplasm* can be used as subjects; *abusively, of,* and *the* cannot be—except in very special circumstances. (Shakespeare made *but* a noun by having Falstaff say, "But me no buts," but Falstaff was having fun, distorting the language.) Every child knows this, long before he knows what *ectoplasm* is.

One of the central facts in the pattern of English is this: *The first word in a sentence that can be the subject becomes the subject unless we are signaled that it will not be.* In the sentences above, we know at once that *God* is the subject; it is the kind of word that can be a subject, and we are given no signal that in this sentence *God* will not be the subject. But suppose the sentence read, *Knowing that God protects drunks, fools, and American foreign policy, the Secretary decided to get drunk, act like a fool, and take a long weekend.* A word like *knowing* could be a subject; *seeing* is the subject in the proverb, *Seeing is believing.* But the combination *knowing that* would almost never be a subject; on the other hand, the sequence is familiar as a signal that this sentence will start with a subordinate structure, and that the subject will not be along until after the structure is complete. The comma marks the end of this structure, and in speech the pitch of the voice would provide the same clue. The next word is *the.* This word cannot normally be a subject, but it usually precedes the kind of term that can be. Accordingly, we recognize that the true subject is *Secretary.*

Now we should notice another fact about English grammatical patterns. If the grammatical subject of a sentence establishes precisely the subject of the conversation—if it adequately embodies the "old," as *God* does in the sentence about the deity's penchant for protecting those who cannot protect themselves—the sentence usually runs well. But the first word in a sentence that can be the subject becomes the subject, whether it comprises the "old" or not. And if the "old" is never established, if the term that becomes the subject cannot do the job of the subject, the ensuing sentence will almost inevitably be a disaster.

Let us see how this works. Let us assume that a speaker is hemming and hawing, trying to get started, or a writer is facing a blank sheet of paper, knowing something must be written down. He starts with whatever rises spontaneously, which will be something familiar, probably something general, a word like *reason*. So he writes "The reason." He did not mean to choose the subject for a sentence, but he has, because *reason* can be a subject and we have not been warned that it will not be. So the writer goes on, but not much can follow "The reason" except a structure based on the verb *to be*, which will inevitably lead to other words, whether the writer wants them or not: "The reason a lawyer is needed is because, there being in this country a ruling about not using a building that is not up to code for the marketing of petroleum products." By now our writer has not even produced a sentence, but worse, he has concocted a jumble because he did not get started with a grammatical subject that represented essentially the actual subject of the sentence, the "old" that could be followed by the "new," what the writer wanted to say.

The writer might have started, "I need a lawyer because . . ." "A lawyer could probably get us out of this by . . ." "My business needs a lawyer to . . ." We might note that Crawford's neighboring farmer, with whom we started this chapter, emitted clear, strong sentences, at least partly because he knew how to choose good subjects: "That's a good school. They don't teach no goddamned grammar there." He used pronouns for subjects, and particularly in familiar prose they make good subjects if they are well selected, since they refer to somebody or something specific. Proper names make good subjects, too; notice the sentence beginning *God*. Specific nouns and concrete phrases make good subjects; notice the sentence having "the Secretary" as subject. General terms and blanket terms like *reason, factor*, and *circumstances* usually make poor subjects, and even more dangerous are expletives like *there* and *it*: There is always the reason that . . . ; It is what I was trying to say . . . . Of course, *it* can be a pronoun (It's a boy), *there* can be a demonstrative (*There* is your answer), and even *reason* can be a specific name (The *reason*, as a mental process, exists in primates other than man), but usually such terms make unlikely candidates for good subjects leading to vigorous use of language, because they do not provide concrete, specific subjects.

6. Modification and Word Choice

As we have seen, words do much of their work in sentences. Each word provides a meaning and implies a sound that fits into the pattern of the sentence. But it also carries out part of its job by interacting with other words and combinations of words in its sentence, and to a lesser extent with other sentences. The central structure of any sentence is usually a blending of the old and the new, the subject and its predicate, and in simple communication, such as the remark of the farmer about the local school, a sentence may contain little more—*That* (subject) *is a good school* (predicate, verb plus complement). But much writing—and much speaking, too—in the complex, highly professionalized, elaborately technical world we know, deals with questions much more subtle and elaborate than whether a farmer does or does not like what happens in a local school. Most of what gets communicated is not carried by the two or three terms that are likely to provide the core of the sentence, the actor-action-goal sequence, or a similar sequence that states a fact: *That is a good school.* Most of the words in many sentences are not part of such a core; they are appended in one way or another to this SVC skeleton.

Consider the paragraph you have just read. It has transitional sentences at the opening and close, and transitional sentences are usually rather simple. The three sentences that constitute the body of the paragraph might be broken down as follows: (1) *structure . . . is . . . a blending*, plus more than fifty other words; (2) *writing . . . deals* with . . . *questions*, plus nearly forty other words; (3) *most . . . is . . . carried by terms*, plus some thirty words. The results could be altered slightly depending on our grammatical analysis: is the verb in the second sentence *deals* or *deals with?* In the last sentence, is the verb *is* or *is carried*, and is the sequence beginning with *by* subject, complement, or modifier? But the total result could not be changed much, and the answer is obvious: most of the words in these sentences are not part of the actor-action-goal sequence, when pared to its essentials. They flesh out this central skeleton.

They are attached in two ways, called **coordination** and **subordination**. The first of these devices is relatively simple. In the first sentence *old* and *new* are coordinated by running them one after the other and joining them with *and*; in the second sentence units in the sequence that begins with *complex* are made coordinate by placing one after the other and separating them with commas. This device is important in the sense that it is basic grammar, but it does not require much vocabulary. We have a few coordinating conjunctions—*and, or,* and *but*—along with some other words not quite so clearly coordinative, like *for* and *however.* These terms have varied and subtle uses, and they warrant close study, but there are not many of them.

Subordination in English, however, is panoplied, complex, and shifting—so complex that I shall make no attempt to analyze it here. Grammar, as such, is not what we are dealing with. But it also involves a considerable vocabulary, and words are our business here. In the passage above, and in any similar piece of prose, two major means of subordination appear, paralleling the two devices for coordination. Some terms are subordinated (that is, they modify) by position; in *good school, good* is made to modify *school* (if it is not part of a compound or phrasal term *good school*) by being placed immediately before *school.* The same device appears in *no goddamned grammar* and elsewhere. Not all subordinated matter follows this pattern; the modifying clause, *that states a fact,* follows the word it modifies, *sequence.* And we could find modifying structures that are separated from the terms they attach to. Much of the modification in this or any passage, however, is signaled by words like *by, in, with, of,* etc. We employ dozens of such single words, along with phrasal sequences like *as soon as,* or *in accordance with.* Although they are few compared to the mainly meaningful words, they carry a great burden in the language, and since they seem to be insignificant they warrant acute attention.

Consider the following sentences:

1. *Until* she was married, she lived in a hotel.
2. *After* she was married, she lived in a hotel.
3. *While* she was married, she lived in a hotel.
4. *Although* she was married, she lived in a hotel.
5. *Because* she was married, she lived in a hotel.
6. *Since* she was married, she lived in a hotel.
7. *Even though* she was married, she lived in a hotel.
8. *As soon as* she was married, she lived in a hotel.
9. *Whenever* she was married, she lived in a hotel.
10. *If* she was married, she lived in a hotel.

Obviously, we have more than different meanings, with all sorts of possible innuendos, depending upon the choice of one of a number of words, in this instance what are called **relatives,** or **relative** or **subordi-**

nating conjunctions. We might notice, also, that some sentences are ambiguous because the relative has more than one meaning. Sentence 3, for example, may imply "During the time she was married," or "Although she was married."

Such words are highly useful, but they are also treacherous. They are useful because the language could not work without them, and they are treacherous because they provide such unsure footing, being at once varied, specialized, and shifting. They are mostly native, and they have all been adapted from words that once had quite different uses. They have been jostling for centuries and they are still jostling, making room for an occasional newcomer, fighting for old semantic territories, and moving into new ones as the culture and the language expand—an exciting but difficult body of words. To appreciate their propensities we shall need a bit of background.

7. The Growth of Relationship Words

Presumably, PIE had no such terms. I write *presumably* because, in theory, we can never say that something did not exist in a reconstructed language, but here the evidence is so good that in effect we know: (1) IE had such an elaborate inflectional system that no such units were needed, and (2) no evidences of them have survived, whereas if a language relies on such terms they tend to be very common. As for conjunctions, even by OE times subordinate clauses were rare, at least in the verse, and we have no early prose. Apposition was common, but juxtaposition sufficed for that. Nouns and verbs—with a few modifiers—constituted the bulk of the PIE vocabulary, and they were practically all built on a root, which provided the basic meaning, one or more suffixes which make the stem, plus an inflectional ending. The stem marked the part of speech. Calvert Watkins provides the following example:[2]

Thus a single root like *prek- (variant of **perk-**[2]) could, depending on the suffix, form a verb *prk-sko-, "to ask" (Latin *poscere*), a

---

2. In his appendix, p. 1497, to *The American Heritage Dictionary* cited above. Many of the older books on language, based exclusively on IE languages, assumed that this was the pattern of all languages, and that modern tongues are inferior because they have been corrupted from the Classical languages, Latin and Greek, which preserve much evidence of this type of structure. The recording of unwritten speech, notably by anthropologists, has destroyed the myth that the Classical tongues provide the best of all possible linguistic devices in the best of all possible language.

noun *prek-*, "prayer," (Latin *preces*), and an adjective *prok-o-*, "asking" (underlying Latin *procus*, "suitor"). Note that *prek-*, *prok-*, and *prk-* have, respectively, e- [often called *full grade*], o-, and zero grade.

Conjugations and inflections were numerous and elaborate. Watkins describes the verb as follows:

> Verbs had different endings for the different persons (first, second, and third) and numbers (singular, plural, dual), for the voices, active and passive (or middle, a sort of reflexive), as well as special affixes for a rich variety of tenses, moods, and such categories as causative-transitive and stative-intransitive verbs.

Obviously, with such an array of forms, IE had little use for such auxiliaries as *have* in *have gone*, for modals such as *might*, or phrasal combinations like *catch a cold* or *blunder onto*. Similarly, nouns were so elaborately inflected that prepositions would not have been needed.

Some relationship words must have been developing among IE dialects. *Kwo-* must have had a meaning in the sense that it had a referent, for it has descended into Persian meaning "something"—it appears in English in the slang sense of *cheese* in *the big cheese*. It is known in Latin, where it sired *qui*, "who," *quam*, "than," *ubi*, "where," etc., and a few nonrelatives, *quantity, quality, quote*, etc. It must have been functioning with grammatical uses in Common Germanic, because it existed in enough dialects so that several forms have been reconstructed, *hwa*, with inflections, NE *who, whom*, etc. Another was *hwatharaz*, NE *whether, neither*. There was also a phrase, *aiwo gihwatharaz*, "ever each of two," OE *aeghwaether*, NE *either*. The root provided a number of other relatives and pronouns in OE, NE *what, why, how, when*, etc.

This drift continued. Following are the first lines of *Beowulf*; usually dated somewhat after A.D. 700, it is the oldest extant extensive example of any language descending from West Germanic:

> HWAET. We Gar-Dena in geardagum
> þeodcynynga þrym gefrunon
> hu þa æþelingas ellen fremedon

Hwaet is NE *what*, but we can ignore it; it is something like a toastmaster rapping on a glass for silence. *We* is NE *we*, the nominative plural, part of an inflectional system. *Gar-Dena* is a hyphenated noun with a genitive plural ending, meaning "of the Spear-Danes." *In* is NE *in*; this must have been a new use, since this is the only occurrence in the poem in which the word refers to time. The common use, spatial, occurs thirty-six times, as in (line 731) *in sele paem hean,* "in the high hall." *In*, from PIE **en-*, had been a modifier having several meanings; it survives in both Greek and Latin as a word having a referent, *entrails* in Latin, *intestines* in Greek, and several others involving the idea of interiors, including *interior* itself. Its extensive occurrence in *Beowulf*, however, indicates that by early OE times it was well established as a preposition. *Geardagum* is another compound, literally *year day*, meaning something like "olden days," with a dative plural ending. Here the two grammatical devices are combined, since *in* and the dative ending both indicate that the word stands in an oblique relationship (here the time) to the remainder of the sentence. *peodcynynga* is another compound with a genitive plural ending, so that the whole means "of the kings of the people."[3] The noun *prym,* meaning something like "power," must be accusative singular. It is not marked by an ending, but since all nouns in its class had endings for all but the nominative and accusative cases, we should think of this word as having zero ending. *Gefrunon* is the first person plural of the verb *frignan,* "to ask," with the appropriate ending. The *ge-* prefix often implied continuing until a result is achieved, so that *gefrignan* means "to go on asking until one gets the answer," that is, "to hear about." *Hu* is NE *how*, a relative conjunction; see the discussion above (Chapter VIII.6). The particle *pa* can be translated something like *those*; it is the nominative plural of a declined demonstrative, which was beginning to act like a definite article. The plural nominative declined noun *æpelingas*, the subject of the clause, can mean "heroes," "princes." *Ellen* can be modernized as "deeds of valor." It is inflected for the accusative singular, the word meaning "courage," but by implication it can imply numerous instances of courage. *Fremedon* is third person preterit plural of the verb *fremman,* "to do," here something like "achieved."

Surveying the whole, we can say that the use of most of the terms is

---

3. Actually, the compound means no more than *kings*, but *cynyng* enters into many redundant compounds, probably out of respect for the sovereign or for the exigencies of the verse.

made clear by some synthetic device, mainly endings. *Hu* and *þa* suggest the growth of analytic devices to reveal grammar, but they are being used in ways uncommon enough in OE so that we would assume they were moving into new ways. In one instance we have redundant use, with both the preposition *in* and the inflectional ending *-um* having the same force. That is, this passage stands perhaps midway between PIE and NE so far as grammar is concerned.

By way of contrast we might look at the opening lines of *The Canterbury Tales*, written by Chaucer a little before 1400. I have italicized the words that probably would not appear if the passage had been composed in OE:

> *Whan that* Aprill *with* his shoures soote
> *The* droghte *of* March *hath* perced *to the* roote,
> And bathed every veyne in swich licour
> *Of which* vertu engendred is *the* flour;
> *Whan* Zephirus eek *with* his sweete breeth
> Inspired *hath in* everyy holt and heeth
> *The* tendre croppes and *the* yonge sonne
> *Hath in the* Ram his halve course yronne,
> *And* smale fowles maken melodye
> *That* slepen all *the* nyght *with* open eye
> So priketh hem nature in hir courages

Many terms could be argued about. I have italicized half the occurrences of *and* and *in*. Both occur in *Beowulf*, but Chaucer employs them for uses not found in OE and with greater frequency. They are rather sparse in OE, but here each occurs four times in eleven lines. Obviously, the relationship words have increased greatly in a few hundred years. In fact, word order and relationship words here carry most of the burden of the grammar. Except for the inflected personal pronouns, the ending *d* indicative of a past tense, and *s* indicating the plural of nouns, the passage could be read with no inflection or conjugation at all.

That is, in the course of a few millennia the old grammar wasted away. Either synthesis died because analysis was assuming more and more of the grammatical job, or analysis moved in to fill the gap as synthesis declined. Which caused which we need not argue at the moment, but the obvious fact is that the old grammar worked less and less, and the new grammar needed new relationship words. It had inherited few if any from IE.[4] On the whole, English acquired the necessary terms by turning old units to new purposes.

8. How to Make New Relatives

Consider *while*, which for some centuries was a relative, and now—in spite of learned abhorrence—is becoming a coordinating conjunction. It started like any other meaningful word, coming from IE **kweye-*, which had to do with rest, as descendant words through Latin, such as *quiet* and *quiescent* still do. In Old Norse, *hvila* was a "bed," literally a resting place, and from "rest" the cognates in Persian and Avestan in Asia developed the idea of "joy." Going into Germanic the root picked up a suffix *-lo*, which presumably supplied the idea of time, so that what was "a period of rest" became OE *hwile*, "a segment of time." (We might recall that the palatal plosive /k/ from PIE became the aspirate /h/ by Grimm's Law in English, and the resulting /hw/ is rather inaccurately spelled *wh* in later English; meanwhile, the sound did not change much going into Latin, but the /kw/ is spelled *qu*, as in *quiet*.) The *Blickling Homilies* (before A.D. 1000) has "Hwilce hwile hine wille Drihten her on worlde laetan" (For such a length of time the Lord permits him [man] here in the world). This concept, probably helped along by the genitive *hwiles*, "of a time," developed adverbially as in the OE hymn, "Hwile mid weorc, while mide worde, while mid pohte" (Sometimes with work, sometimes with words, sometimes with thought). It developed compounds that have given us *awhile* (from *one hwile*), *meanwhile,* and *whilom* from the dative form of *hwile*, "at times." It became a conjunction by being linked with words like *pat* (later *that*) as in "To hwiles that his bodi lai in the graue" (During the time that his body lay in the grave).

More centuries were to elapse before the use developed which was eventually to have the common implication that one event takes place at the same time as another, as in "A very good move for while it brings the Queen into a more attacking position, it at the same time defends White's Queen's Pawn." And now the word is becoming a coordinating conjunction, as in the following from a current newspaper, "Eckerhard won the hundred-yard dash and placed second in the two-twenty, while he was able to garner only a fourth in the discus." Here *while* could be replaced

---

4. Observers would differ as to the boundaries of *relationship*, which is not objectively definable, but the broad outlines are clear enough.

with either *and* or *but*, and careful writers would say it should be. If we allow only the older usage, Eckerhard did remarkably well to place at all in the discus at the same time that he was running two races, but the fact is that *while* is now often merely a colorless coordinating conjunction.

Like and *as* have been battling each other for centuries, but not until after they became relationship words. Both were Germanic terms, possibly picked up from tribes the Germans overran, and were at first used mainly for their meanings. *Like* comes from OE *lic*, meaning a body, either living or dead. As *lich* it survives as an obsolete equivalent of *body*, as in *lichfield*, a cemetery, literally a "body-field," but already *gelic* had appeared, our word *alike*, meaning "of like body." A ship breaking through the waves, with froth at the prow, is said to be *flota famiheals* (a floater foamy-necked) *fugle gelicost* (most like to a bird). The word expanded tremendously; as part of a compound it sired most adverbs in NE, *lic* becoming *-ly*, as in *mostly, firmly, slowly*, and some adjectives like *goodly* and *homely* (from *ham lic*). Once it had become a modifier meaning "like in body," it soon served as a relative conjunction; Lydgate wrote, *Thou* [the goddess Fortune] *brougtest men in trouble . . . Lik a corsour makth coltis . . . With spore & whippe to be tame & mylde* (You have brought men into trouble, like a horseman makes colts to be tame and mild with spur and whip).

Meanwhile, *as* was developing. Apparently it started as **swo-*, NE *so*, which was a demonstrative pronoun, meaning about what *that* means now as a pronoun, as in *That is true*. It early combined with *lic* to form OE *swylc*, NE *such*. It developed into a preposition, as in *swa beorht swa gold* (as bright as gold), and soon into a relative conjunction; a thirteenth-century sermon has, *Hwi ne fele ich þe in mi breostes swa swote as þu art?* (Why do I not feel you in my breast, so sweet as you are?). But the form continued to be cut down; the language was losing endings like /o/, even when they were not declensional, and /l/ is especially vulnerable after a mid vowel (as in *talk* and *palm*). Thus OE *ælswa*, NE *also*, was cut down to *as*.

So now there were two relative conjunctions, *like* and *as*, both having to do with the idea of similarity. Of the two, *like* was for a time much the more widely used, but *as* increased, especially when used with other words, such as *how* and *that*. Smollett in the eighteenth century has one of his characters say, *I believe as how your man deals with the devil*. By the nineteenth century *as* was triumphing, and the supposed misuse of *like* as a conjunction had become almost a moral issue. The Evanses have an account:

During the nineteenth century literary gentlemen felt strongly about this question. Those whose education had been chiefly Greek and Latin said that the use of *like* as a conjunction was a vulgarism. But [F. J.] Furnivall, the foremost English language scholar of the period, defended it. He tells on one occasion, "having to answer some ignorant in a weekly about the use of *like*, I said to Morris [probably Furnivall's editor, Richard Morris, rather than the poet William Morris]: 'Have you ever used *like* as a conjunction?' 'Certainly I have,' answered Morris, 'constantly.' 'But you know there's a set of prigs who declare it's vulgar and unhistorical.' 'Yes, I know. They're a lot of fools.'" But Tennyson belonged to the other camp. He told Furnivall, "It's a modern vulgarism that I've seen grow up within the last thirty years; and when Prince Albert used it in my drawing room I pulled him up for it, in the presence of the Queen, and told him he never ought to use it again."[5]

In the United States, both of the great lexicographers, Webster and Worcester, shunned *like* as a conjunction while admitting *as*—they both tended to exclude terms felt to be in bad odor. The more hospitable *Century Dictionary* defined *like* "as, as if," and added, "This use is commonly condemned as incorrect," but the editors add that the construction occurs several times in Shakespeare, and they cited Darwin and the following from James Russell Lowell:

> *Like* for *as* is never used in New England, but is universal in the South and West. It has on its side the authority of two kings . . . Henry VIII and Charles I. This were ample without throwing into the scale the scholar and poet Daniel.

Then came a widely disseminated advertisement, "Winston tastes good like a cigarette should." Whether this slogan rode the crest of a wave or produced the wave, the locution is now heard everywhere. For some years I have amused myself—particularly in dull committee meetings—trying to detect anyone, even one of my fellow English teachers, using *as* as a conjunction. I seldom do. Apparently *as* survives in England, but in the United States only a few old fuddy-duddies like the author of this book still use *as* as a conjunction out of habit, although an

5. Bergen Evans and Cornelia Evans, *A Dictionary of Contemporary American Usage* (New York: Random House, 1957), under *like; as.*

occasional purist is still battling against *like*: ". . . the ad writer who dreamed up the Winston commercial should be jailed . . . Let's form a wall against advertising corruption of the language . . . I think we can win this one if we fight on. This is pure vulgate . . . It is not a popular evolution out of common speech, but a deliberate vulgarism by hucksters to whom I will not surrender easily . . . this monster is omnipresent . . . illiteracy imposed by commercial persuaders," and so on and on.[6]

Thus the seesaw goes, with *as* taking over comparative relations from *like* in one century, only to have them redeemed by *like* in the next century. At the moment, *like* is triumphing over *as* as a relative conjunction in parts of the United States, but not in many other parts of the English-speaking world. Meanwhile, *as* is expanding mightily in the newer phrasal subordinaters like *as soon as, as far as*, along with idioms like *as is* and *as of*, where as yet *like* has invaded but little. Something of this fluidity and flexibility can be observed in many of the conjunctions and prepositions, probably in all of them.

9. The Mighty Midgets of English

The conjunctions and prepositions are not alone in being diminutive but potent in English. Notice the following, which appeared in a local printing of a wire report:

Shortly thereafter, Meier resigned from the Hughes staff. He is not being sued by the Hughes organization for his involvement in the purchase of mining properties for the eccentric billionaire. Meier is also under indictment on a tax evasion charge.

The second sentence is ambiguous: is Meier being sued or isn't he, and why or why not? The confusion probably grows out of a typographical error, a change of one letter in a three-letter word. No doubt the sentence should read, "He is *now* (not *not*) being sued, etc." Few words can alter meaning so radically as do the negatives, *no* and *not,* but they are not alone.

In fact, old words tend to be short. As we have noticed above, by the current theory, the once universal language, from which all subsequent languages are believed to have sprung, was composed of two sorts of

---

6. William and Mary Morris, *Harper Dictionary of Contemporary Usage* (New York: Harper, 1975), under *like/as*.

semantic units, both of them small.[7] Furthermore, grammatical terms tend to be old—grammar changes slowly when compared with other aspects of language. In many languages, especially in inflectional languages, grammatical units tended to be attached to meaningful bases, but in English, as we have seen, inflectional endings were mainly lost, and many old words remained about as they were, with little added to them. Thus, characteristically, short and inconspicuous words tend to be powerful, permeating a phrase, a clause, a whole sentence, even an idea that may spread over several sentences. This fact promotes vigor and economy in English, but it also places a burden on the reader or listener; the smallest, most obscure words may be those that do the most. In fact, we might take a suggestion from the highway department and put up a sign over our writing desks:

CAUTION: SMALL ENGLISH WORDS AT WORK

7. There were roots or bases, composed mainly of three sounds, consonant-vowel-consonant, like /bab/, and additives composed of two sounds, consonant-vowel or vowel-consonant, like /ed/ or /de/. All longer words or phrases were made from combinations of these.

CHAPTER **IX**

PUTTING THE PARTS TOGETHER
Compounds, Affixes, Phrases

*That vast aggregate of words and phrases which constitutes the
Vocabulary of English-speaking men presents, to the mind that en-
deavours to grasp it as a definite whole, the aspect of one of those
nebulous masses familiar to the astronomer, in which a clear and
unmistakable nucleus shades off on all sides, through zones of de-
creasing brightness, to a dim marginal film that seems to end no-
where, but to lose itself imperceptibly in the surrounding darkness.*
—J. A. H. Murray

1. Coining New Terms

To make something you need, bring together what you already have,
even opposites. At least, that is one way; life grows from the conjunction
of the sexes, earth is made of land and water. We have seen similar
growth in language. When our Germanic ancestors moved west, they encountered such linguistically upsetting incentives as the sea, Christianity,
and Roman civilization. They needed new names for new things and new
ways. They got names in part by borrowing, but even more they devised
terms by combining bits of their own language. They encountered the
Bible, but even ecclesiastics were slow to pick up this strange Greek
word,[1] preferring to put two native words together to make *god-spel*,
"good news," which was eventually misunderstood as meaning "God's
word," and synocopated into *gospel*.

Similar compounding characterized Old Norse—and as we have seen,

---

1. *Byblos* is Semitic in origin, being the name of a Levantine city, famous for its papyrus
volumes; the place name became a term for the city's product, for a scroll or roll and hence
a book, but the word came into English through Greek and Latin.

many Norse words were accepted as native. The Indo-Europeans had apparently made houses with daubed wattles, a construction that provided little space for windows. When speakers of Old Norse got more sophisticated dwellings they used a native compound to name the openings, *vind-auge*, "eye for the wind," NE *window*.

2. Compounding: Confusion Confounded

This making of language will be clearer if we look at an ordinary sentence. The following is from a sermon dating *c.* 1200:

> No man þe sineged haueth ne mai wiðuten þese wedes holi husel underfon; bute to eche harme his soule and lichame and ech man þe it underfoð wiðuten eiðer þese wedes shal ben shameliche driuen ut of þis holi gestninge, and bunden togedere his honden and his fet, and worpen in to þe ateliche pit of helle bi ure drihtenes word þe seith to swich men.

Compounding permeates it. In *no man, man* is impersonal, not a designation of a male being, and the sequence is one of several in ME: *no man, no body, no one, no thing*, and the like, of which *nobody* and *nothing* are now thought of as words. *No man* and *no one* have remained two words, *no one* probably because *noone* was a common spelling for *noon*, but *no man* must be partly happenstance. Similarly, *sineged haueth* (has sinned), would formerly have been one word, *singod* or *singed*, but the patterns of verbs were changing. The new form might as well have been spelled *singedhaveth*, or in ME *singedhas*, but this sequence never caught on. One reason for not so combining may appear in *mai . . . underfon* (may receive), since a verb that is essentially a compound has the direct object *(holi husel)* within it. *Wiðuten þese wedes* (without these clothes—the use of *wedes* is here figurative, meaning "protection") is a compound idea, a modifier made of three parts: a subordinating word, NE *without*; a qualifier, NE *these*; and a noun, *weeds*, meaning "clothes," now archaic except in "widow's weeds." *Holi husel* (*holy wafer*, used as a sacrament) we can ignore since it is a modifier plus a noun, but *underfon* is a compound, made up of our word *under* plus *fon*, the infinitive of a verb meaning "to grasp." This figurative compound does not occur in early OE, and it was later replaced by *understand, undertake*, and the like. It is, in short, one of thousands of combinations devised to fill the need for new vocabulary, most of which have been lost in the welter that new expressions must survive if they are to become part of standard usage.

The variety of development continues. The next words mean something like "But for each sin," which leads to the interesting phrase *his soule and lichame*, "to his soul and body." We have since reversed this pair, as in "to keep body and soul together," as a loose sort of phrase. Within the sequence is a compound we have since lost, *lichame*, which is a blending of *lic*, "body," and *hame*, "home," the body being conceived as the home of the soul. Then, *and eche man þe it underfoð*, "and each man who receives it," leads to an expansion of the phrase we have seen before, *wiðuten eiðer þese wedes*, "without either of these protections." These are here a sequence of four words that have a single use as a modifier. Once more we have a compound within a compound: *with*, meaning "against" or "toward," *ut*, meaning "the outside," plus an ending. The verb may be thought of as *shal ben driuen* or *shal ben driuen ut of*, "shall be driven out of."

Here we have one of those verbs that have been drawing into themselves various sorts of particles—whether these particles are modifiers or prepositions we need not argue at the moment—to produce thousands of new phraselike verbs. Whether we analyze this sequence as a verb *(shall be driven)* plus a preposition introducing the modifying prepositional phrase *ut of þis holi gestninge*, "out of this holy banquet," or whether we call the verb *shall be driven out of*, followed by the complement *holy banquet*, makes little difference. In either description we have a sequence of words falling into what amount to undistinguished phrasal sequences, either a long phrasal verb plus a complement, or a shorter phrasal verb plus a phrasal modifier. And within this compounding of words into phrases is a compound, *shameliche*, "shamelike," that is, "shamefully." *Shameliche* should have given us the modifier *shamely*, as *hamlich* gave us *homely* and *manlic* gave us *manly*. Indeed it did, but the word never became popular and was last heard of when a contemporary of Shakespeare condemned anyone "who shamely doth." Likewise *gestninge* is a word of two parts, being made up of our word *guest* plus an *-inge* ending, that is, a "guesting," a party, a banquet.

The passage continues: *and bunden togedere his honden and his fet*, "and bound together his hands and his feet." Is "hands and feet" a phrase, or are they simply the four prominent human appendages? They approach being a phrase, that is, a combination of words that work as a unit, and they handsomely illustrate that no sharply defined line can be drawn between phrases and a string of words that function in the main independently. *Togedere*, modern *together*, is a compound, made up of *to-* plus *gedere*, "fellowship," "a gathering," the whole meaning something like "as a community." The sentence continues: *and worpen in to pe ateliche pit of helle*, "and thrown into the horrible pit of hell." Here again we have one of those emerging verbs: is it *thrown into* plus a complement *pit of hell*, or is it the verb *thrown* plus an adverbial phrase *into the pit of hell?* We need not decide, and perhaps could not, since the constructions are bafflingly fluid, but we can notice that earlier the verb would have been one word and the idea of *into* would be involved in an inflectional ending on *hell*—and there would probably have been no such sequence as *pit of hell*. *Ateliche*, from *atol* plus *lic* meant "horrible" by this time, but it had probably come from a compound that we can modernize as *fiendlike*.

The remainder of the sentence is made up of two sequences, what we would call a prepositional phrase *bi ure drihtenes word*, "by the word (or better, *order*) of our Lord," and a clause, *pe seith to swich men*, "who says to such men." Once more, four words (the equivalent of "by the order of" or "according to the word of our Lord") have become a single modifier, and within this sequence is a compound. *Drihten* is a common word *lord*, but it is related to our archaic word *dree*, "to suffer," and means "the one who endures." In the clause is a verb that blends into a particle and into a noun that may be either a complement or part of a phrase. In deciding which, we might notice that *seith to* means more than "says"; it means "tells."

3. Compounding: the Underlying Good Sense

Superficially we have confusion rampant here, with varying degrees of bringing things together, with inconsistent means of indicating compounding, even when the compounding seems to be one sort of thing rather than several. But looked at more broadly, the whole welter becomes the working of one simple trend. We noticed in the last chapter that the dialects that have given us NE underwent a broad grammatical shift. PIE had been a strongly synthetic language; that is, the uses of words, their grammatical functions and interrelationships, were revealed by changes in the shape of the individual terms. During, before, and after OE times most of these grammatical syllables atrophied. Grammar —that is, the job of building semantic units into larger meanings through phrasal combinations, sentences, and paragraphs—was more and more generated through the order of words and the patterns of semantic units.

At the same time that this shift in grammar was taking place, our ancestors also had unexpected use for new terms. As we have seen, they encountered such physical phenomena as the sea and seashore living, along with new social and intellectual notions that cried out for additional vocabulary—Christianity, bureaucratic government, urban development, professional and industrial services. Thus, at the same time that they acquired a grammar that had new uses for existing words, they found themselves in a world that demanded new semantic units. This dual need for new uses and new meanings worked together—*use* and *meaning* are after all two ways of looking at the same thing—so that English became, and has remained, a language notable for bringing old bits together to make new meaningful terms.

This tradition goes back to OE, and is at least partly rooted in the Germanic verse form, which relied on alliteration. The poet had to alliterate at least one stressed syllable in one half-line with a stressed syllable in the second half-line, and accordingly, what are called kennings became convenient devices. Poets had great numbers of compounds, which could be used to name familiar objects and at the same time to get the needed alliterative sounds. For example, the sea could be called *the gannet's bath*, and thus alliterate with words beginning with /g/ or /b/, or it could be called *hronrad*, "the road for whales," and could alliterate with *hrether*, meaning "heart," with *hring*, meaning "ring," or *hrim*, meaning "frost," and the like. Trusting to the influence upon language of anything so esoteric as poetry may sound a bit dangerous, but we might recall that this verse entered into the daily lives of people in charms, prayers, proverbs, and the like. A charm to capture a swarm of bees goes in part as follows:

Forweorp ofer greot, þonne he swirman, and cweð:
    Sitte ge, sigewif sigað to eorpan
    nafre ge wilde to wudu fleogan!
Throw over them dust, when they swarm, and say:
    Sit ye down, triumphant woman settle to the earth
    Don't ever like a wild thing fly off to the woods!

The term *sigewif*, literally "victory woman," was probably flattery to the queen bee, or possibly to each individual in the swarm of females, but it also had the virtue of alliterating with *sitte* and *sigað*. And the formula would have been known by heart by the farmer and most of his family; honey supplied the only sweet, and the most concentrated source of alcohol, mead.

This is only one of a number of heathen charms, somewhat colored by

Christian sentiments, that survived among OE country folk. At a more sophisticated level, recitals of verse were a form of public entertainment; *Beowulf*, instinct with kennings, quoted in the previous chapter, served that purpose. Verse also catered to intermediate tastes. A considerable body of alliterative riddles has survived, and they all utilize kennings. In several, solving the riddle requires seeing figures of speech implied in metaphoric language. One begins: *Ic waes waepenwiga*, "I was a weapon warrior." The riddle develops by enumerating various feats this "weapon warrior" can achieve, one being that it may *flyman feondsceapan*, "put devil-criminals to flight," that is, rout the enemy. The final half line can be modernized, "What am I called?" And the answer is supposed to be a horn. Of course we can only surmise how much this versifying affected the word-making, but it may have been considerable. At least, the evidence that has survived suggests that OE persons, from the king to the cowherd, lived more in the presence of compounds, many of them rooted in figures of speech, than have most peoples.

The practice continued, as we have seen in the sentence from the sermon above (Chapter IX.2), where *underfon, lichame, wiðuten, gestninge, togedere, ateliche*, and *drihtenes* are all compounds, mostly of words stuck together. The practice was favored in OE, and if it declined relative to borrowing during the Middle Ages, it continued in a lively manner. Consider the *out-* words; following are those beginning outa- and outb- with the earliest dates given in the OED:

outact (1644)
outake, out-take, to withdraw, make an exception of (1300)
outalien (1667)
out and out, out-and-out (1325)
outargue (1748)
outask (1719)
outbabble (1649)
outbalance (1644)
outbawl (1648)
outbeam (1797)
outbear (1530)
outbeard (1611)
outbearing (1350)
outbelch (1573)
outbellow (1623)
outbent (1601)
outbid (1597)

outbirth (1663)
outblaze (1711)
outbleed, in the sense "shed blood" (1430)
outblossom (1695)
outblot (1549)
outblown (1851)
outblush (1634)
outbluster (1748)
outboard (1823)
outbond (1842)
outbook (1882)
outborn (1450)
outbound (1596)
outbowed (1627)
outbrag (1565)
outbraid, drawn, as of a sword (1390)
outbranch (1835)
outbrave (1589)
outbray (1558)
outbrazen (1681)
outbreak (1000)
outbreast (1622)
outbreathe (1559)
outbring (1200)
outbudding (1840)
outbuild (1742)
outbulk (1652)
outbully (1708)
outburn (1597)
outburst (1400)
outbutting (1730)
outbuy (1608)
outby (1400–1450)
This is probably a fair sample.[2] The most obvious generalization is

2. I have arbitrarily thrown out some marginal entries like cross-references and the nonce word, *out-Achitophel*, along with derived forms.They would not much alter the pattern. One should recall that the OED cuts off at 1900, so that the great recent drifts toward compounding are not represented. One can be sure, also, that once the *Middle English Dictionary* reaches *O* most ME entries will be dated somewhat earlier, and some Early Modern English will appear as ME.

probably this: compounding is and always has been a lively force in the growth of English vocabulary.

The development of the hyphen promoted compounding. Greek had a hyphen—our word is adopted from Greek—a curved line, but it was not used as is the modern symbol, and most older manuscripts do not employ it. Renaissance grammars and handbooks describe the hyphen about as do modern writers, but the printers did not use hyphens much, except to mark words broken at the end of a line. Writers who used them were very inconsistent; Webster used *father-in-law* with a hyphen as an entry word, but *father in law*, in italic type and without hyphens, in his definition. *The American Universal Geography*, as late as 1819 in its seventh edition, used *New-York, New-Jersey, New-Haven, North-Carolina*, and even *West-Jersey* with hyphens. But by the twentieth century the use of hyphens in compounding had become pretty well standardized, so that the device now provides a more orderly progression from two words to a compound recognized as a new word.

Space, in the sense of "outer space," will provide an example. *The Century Dictionary*, edited in the 1890s, found no occasion to use *space* in this sense in any compounds and, presented with the concept of a space-traveling device, would surely have written it as two words, the noun *ship*, preceded by a modifier naming its qualifications: *space ship*. Something more than a quarter century later the *New International*, second edition, was beginning to hyphenate some compounds, in *space-world* and *space-time* (this last a somewhat different use of *space*). In another quarter century the *Webster's New World* was recording *spaceship* as one word, although some dictionaries were more cautious with *space-ship*. With the second edition of the *New World, spacecraft, spaceport*, and even *spacewalk* were recognized as compounds that can be written solid, although *Space Age* remained as two words, presumably because it is a proper name.

In American English, compounding has grown from a need to something approaching a habit. We have noticed in a previous chapter (Chapter II.4) that the demand to name the flora and fauna of the New World brought a flood of compound terms like *buffalo chip* and *buffaloheaded duck*. This practice continues, although somewhat changed; natural phenomena are still being discovered, but the objects tend now to be so minute or obscure that they inspire mainly esoteric scientific terms. Meanwhile, as we saw when we surveyed classical borrowings, modern Western languages, especially American English, are developing tens of thousands of terms conglomerated from Latin and

Greek words and roots for new inventions like *isogeotherm* (*iso-*, "the same," plus *geo-*, "the earth," plus *therme*, "heat") meaning "an imaginary line or curved plane connecting points beneath the earth's surface that have the same average temperature," or *hydrogasification,* a method of converting coal into gas, the word being a compound of two earlier compounds, *hydrogen* and *gasification.* This process will continue, and may well increase. The phrase *knowledge explosion* seems to imply a sudden blooming, like an atomic mushroom cloud. But not so. More and more, knowledge is the modern way of life, and the enduring custom of American English is to label new finds with coined compounds, built mostly of Latin and Greek elements.

Abetting this flood of technical and professional nomenclature is a shower of humble compounds, less conspicuous because they utilize mainly native elements or loans already well established in familiar English. They are of two sorts, although neither can be sharply delineated. Some are technical and industrial, the new terms for automobile parts *(overhead camshaft),* for business terms *(kilowatt-hour),* and the like. Others are so much a part of daily living that they arise almost unnoticed *(stop-and-go, snowplow, self-service).* One of the recent sets of coinages involved *hop;* whether or not the fad stems from *island-hopping* during the Pacific War, pupils can now *grade-hop* and debtors can *payment-hop,* at least so far as the language is concerned. Compounds of these sorts are so much involved with phrases, however, that they will best be presented below.

4. Affixes and Cognates

Here we can use a concept that does not as yet have wide currency, that of the **bound morpheme** as against the **free morpheme**. A morpheme is a unit of meaning. It may be a word; *word* is a morpheme, because it has a meaning as a unit, and if you break it up you get meaningless parts. But *words* is two morphemes, *word* plus *s* (pronounced /z/), each of which has meaning, since *word*, singular without the ending, refers to one word, to more than one word if it has the ending, *s* or /z/. Of these two morphemes, *word* is a *free* morpheme; it can be used alone. The *s* or /z/ is a *bound* morpheme; it must be attached to something else— usually a free morpheme like *word*, although there are a few exceptions —or it is unusable.

Various sorts of bound morphemes are possible in language, but in English we have mainly two: inflectional endings and affixes. The inflections are remnants of once-elaborate paradigms that revealed grammar —*s* and /z/, along with a few others like -*d* and -*ed*, as in use*d* and depart*ed*. Affixes are not part of any inflectional system, current or historical, and they may reveal grammar, meaning, or both. They comprise three sorts. If you are attaching a bound morpheme, you can put it in front of, within, or after something else. In English we have prefixes and suffixes; the *pre-* of *prefix* is a prefix; *pre-* means "before" and *prefix* "something that is attached before another element." In *fixation* the -*ation* is a suffix. English formerly had a few affixes inserted within words, that is, *infixes*, but they are no longer used. Some, and probably all, of our affixes have once been words, and for a few we have identical shapes surviving as both a word and an affix. *In* as in *in the house* and *it fell in* is historically a survivor of the same root that has given us the *in-* that appears in *inward* and *inside*. Similarly *by, to*, and a few others may occur as either words or affixes, but the two should be thought of as variant descendants of a common ancestor.

Some of the commonest native prefixes have cognates that have become loan prefixes, including *for*. We have already noticed that often where /f/ occurs in English, we may expect /p/ in non-Germanic IE words because the sound would have been /p/ in the root. The root of *for* has been reconstructed as *per-, one of the most fruitful syllables in the world (see Chapter III.9, above). It means something like "forward," "through," and developed a variety of derived meanings in many languages suggestive of "early" or "first in time" and, in space, "against," "toward," and "associated with." In English, *for* as an entity developed as a preposition and a conjunction (rarely as an adjective) in dozens of uses, some now obsolete. OE used *for* as an intensive, *forwel* meaning "very well," and Chaucer says, "As any ravens fether it shoon forblack," (It shone black as any raven's feather, *as . . . forblack* seeming to mean "as black as"). It entered into many sorts of compounds. In *forbidden*, it earlier meant "spoken against." In *forget*, it seems to involve the idea of losing one's hold on something past—the idea appears in other languages, in German as *vergessen*. In *forlorn*, it means "totally lost"; in *forsake*, it formerly meant "to accuse," "to quarrel with," OE *saccu* having denoted a crime, a legal accusation. In *forswear*, it meant "to swear against" before it came to mean "to swear falsely." When the prefix means "first" or "ahead" it is usually spelled *fore*, as in *foregone, forelock, forenoon, forestall*, and many more. The expansion of *for, for-*, and *fore-* go on; *foreseeable future* is one of the fastest growing current phrases, although it is apparently little more than a half century old, and a nest of slang terms, *for free, for real,* and the like, is maturing in the United States. In England a *foreloader* is a loader attached to the front of a tractor or other vehicle; in South Africa a *forelooper* is a boy who runs with a lead team to guide or goad them; and in Australia a *forehand turn* is a turn made by a surfer when he faces a wave as he angles across it. A few descendants of **per-* are developing as post-particles,[3] as in *what for, good for,* and the nonstandard *worth for.*

Meanwhile, PIE **per-* has entered into many languages and in many forms. In Latin it sometimes remained as *per-,* with many of the meanings found under *for* in English, and was extensively borrowed as in *perfect, pervade, perdition, perhaps,* and dozens more. Like many affixes and relationship words its uses are fluid. It can remain a preposition, as in *per head, per capita,* or *per diem; peradventure* was still a phrase in ME, where it is likely to appear as *par aventure,* meaning "by chance." The assimilation has been completed in *peroxide,* which means "containing as much oxide as possible," but the consolidation is still going on in *per cent* which is also spelled *per-cent* and *percent.*

With a change of vowel as in *par-, para-* and appropriate changes in pronunciation, the same root appears in *parable, paradox, parabola, parallel,* some through Latin and some through Greek, but mostly involving ideas similar to those expressed in English by *for-* or *fore-.* *Paradox* formerly meant a thesis or tenet apparently opposed to previously accepted doctrine or belief, but *paragraph* means a "mark beside." With a somewhat different vowel the prefix becomes *por-,* as in *portrait,* and more remotely enters into a variety of *port-* words, even including *portulaca.* With shift of accent, the prefix *per-* lost its vowel and became *pre-, pri-, pro-, prae-,* and the like. With the spelling *pre-* the prefix usually implies "before," as in *prewriting, preposition, preparation, preliminary;* "early" or "first" as in *preeminent, preferred, predisposed, precocious, preponderant, preposterous;* along with a number that combine and confuse such ideas, *prerequisite, prerogative;* or just "more" as in *preponderant.* With the spelling *pro-,* the prefix usually implies support—the equivalent of *for* in "being for something," as in *propose, propaganda, profess, protect,* and *pro* as in *pro* and *con,* but a scattering of *pro-* words can involve a number of ideas such as being ahead in time, space, height, or depth, as in *program, profound, produce, proclivity, procreate, profile.* *Pro-* becomes obscured within a

---

3. The term will be readily understood if it is contrasted with *preposition.*

variety of words such as *approach, reciprocal* (meaning "back and forth"), *approximate*. It entered into Latin *probare*, which gives us such terms as *probably* and *probe*, and with changes into English, *prove* and its flock of derivatives like *provable, approve*, and even *proof*. As a prefix, *pri-* and *pir-* have given us *prime, primitive, private, privilege, pirate*, but the syllable in this form never became a prefix active in English. One could write a considerable book about what has grown out of *for* and its relatives.[4]

The family of *in* is similar in many ways, but more complicated. Here we have prefixes that take the same shape, but have different, even almost opposite meaning. Some prefixes have contrasting shapes, but have identical origins and similar meanings. Still other prefixes seem to be different, but are essentially the same. Then, as if this were not enough, we have a flock of independent words and affixes from the same sources.

We can find some order in the welter. First are the words having *in-* prefixes that seem to be alike but may be almost opposite in meaning, including *induct*, which means "to bring in," and *impede*, which means "to obstruct or delay." Similar contrasts arise between *influential* and *incompetent*, between *included* and *inadmissible, inactive* and *increase*, and many more. On the other hand *unable* and *incapable* are synonyms, as are *uneatable* and *inedible*. The explanation stems from one basic confusion: PIE had two roots, each with its own meanings and its own descendants, which changed with the millennia and the various languages into which they descended, sometimes growing more like each other, sometimes choosing their own vagrant ways.

One of these roots was **en-*, made of /n/ preceded by the common PIE vowel, usually written *e*, which could become any of several modern vowels. It descended into English without much change in shape, giving us *in* as a preposition (*in* time), an adverb or particle (go *in*), a noun (spelled *inn*), an adjective (an *in* group), and formerly a verb—Chaucer says that a duke "inned" his guests, took them *in* or put them up at *inns*. It also survived as a prefix in words like *inside, inmost*, and *inwards*, which has become *innards*. The same root descended into Latin without much change, as in the Latin etymons of *inflame*, "make burst into flame" (the word can also be spelled *enflame*), *induct*, "to bring in," and *inspect*, "to look into."

Another IE root, **ne, *na*, descended into OE with both variations—

---

4. For other words involving **per-*, including some from Sanskrit, Persian, Old Norse, Dutch, etc., see chapter V.11 above.

and since in the Great English Vowel Shift, sounds associated with *a* were later often spelled with *o*, NE has this variation also. The syllable was a negative—in fact, the words *negate* and *negative* come from it. In English it appears as *no, naught, not, nothing, none, never*, and others. ME also had a negative *ne*, which could be thrown in to convert any clause to a negative, but we have lost that convenient syllable, except in dialectal isolates like *wilna* and *dinna ye*. The PIE *ne* was reduced as a combining form—combining forms, being unstressed, readily lose a vowel—but when it was combined it developed a new vowel at the front, so that PIE *ne* became English *un-*, the initial syllable in a whole host of words from *unabating* to *unyouthful*. The editors of *The Century Dictionary*, after noting that there are thousands of these that are self-explanatory, went on to devote more than a hundred long columns to *un-* words they thought deserving of comment, from *unabashed* to *unzoned*. Hundreds more must have been added in the twentieth century, terms like *unfissionable, unpeople*, and *unperson*, "officially not recognized as existing"; *unstrikable*, "not legally subject to a strike by workers," along with increased use of old *un-* words—like *unreconstructed*, a term used of individuals who refused to accept the consequences of the American Civil War. It was later revived, humorously, and is now used proudly by all sorts of dissenters, North as well as South. *Un-* is now one of the most useful and flexible prefixes; it can be attached as a coinage to almost any modifier, even of such nonce words as *un-Hollywoodlike* and *un-Churchillean.*

Meanwhile, the PIE *ne* had gone into Italic and thence into Latin, where it lost its vowel—as its cognate did in English—and acquired a vowel before the /n/. But the Latin vowel was different, spelled *i* rather than *u*. (Actually, at the time, the vowels now spelled *u* in English and *i* in Latin were not very different in sound, but the English vowel has since moved back in the mouth so that the two differ markedly in NE.) Thus Latin acquired two prefixes spelled *in-*, the one from PIE *en* meaning "in" or "into," the other from PIE *ne*, meaning "no" or "not." The second, cognate with English *un-* and having about the same use and meaning, was much the more popular, at least among words that were borrowed, directly or indirectly, into English. There are thousands of them—*inability, inabstinence, inabstracted, inabusively*, and on through the alphabet to *invulnerably* and *invultuation*. And if *un-* can be freely prefixed to many native words, *in-* as a negative can be prefixed to even more borrowed words.

In addition to the *for-/per-* and *un-/in-* pairs noted above, a few

English prefixes are linked with cognates. PIE *ambhi- became OE *ymb*, "around," a word that has not survived, though it existed once as a preposition, adverb, and combining form, as in *ymbsittan*, "to sit around," and hence "to besiege." Curtailed, it gives us two English prefixes: *be-*, as in *befriend, befuddle*, and *by-*, as in *bystander, byblow* (a child born out of wedlock). In Latin the prefix appears as *ambi-*, meaning "both," as in *ambidextrous*, and in Greek as *amphi-* with a similar meaning, as in *amphibian, amphitheater. Off-* in English, with the usual pairing of /f/ and /p/, comes from PIE *apo-*, which appears in Greek words with various meanings from *apocalypse* to *apotheosis*. In Latin with voicing of /p/ to /b/ it appears as *ab-*, in *abash, abate*, and hundreds more, and can appear as *a-*, *au-*, or *abs-*, depending on the context (for an explanation of such phonetic changes see *en-*, above in this section). Likewise, the prefix *over-*, as in *overpower*, helps to explain cognates. It stems from PIE *upo-*, voiced fricative /v/ being represented in the voiceless plosive /p/, that is retained in Latin *super-*, and with rough breathing (that is, with aspiration) in Greek *hyper-*, in a few common terms like *hypercritical*, and in dozens of technical terms like *hyperthyroid. Under-* from PIE *ndra-* appears as a common English prefix, as in *understand* and *undertake*. It is cognate with Latin *infra-*, a prefix that found but little favor among the Romans and still less as a loan, *infrared, infrasonic*, and *infrastructure* being among the exceptions.

5. Native Prefixes

The borrowed prefixes, however prevalent they may be in loans already part of the vocabulary, cannot rival the native prefixes as creative parts of the word stock. A copybook rule—where it came from might be hard to say—requires that native prefixes should be used with native words but borrowed prefixes must accompany borrowed roots, Latin with Latin, Greek with Greek. The rule has not always been honored in the past and is now almost expunged. Speakers who do not know Latin and Greek feel uncomfortable attaching most of the borrowed prefixes to anything. A recent American coinage is *technopolitan*, referring to a society dominated by technology; if a negative of this modifier were called for, most speakers would hesitate to produce *intechnopolitan*.

Furthermore, there are complications, and to understand these, we should recall that a sound may alter an adjacent sound. We noticed, for example, that *nonpeer* became modern *umpire* through several changes, one being that the palatal /n/ changed to a bilabial nasal before a bilabial stop. In many words an /n/ changed to /m/, or blended into an /m/ that was already present; thus *in* plus *mature* becomes *immature*; *in* plus *possibilis* becomes NE *impossible*. Similar changes occurred before some other initial sounds in the root; before the initial /r/ the *in-* drifted toward that sound so that we have *irreligious, irresponsible*. If the initial sound of the word to be prefixed began with /l/, again the /n/ drifted so that we have *illegal, illiterate*. Before some sounds, with which /n/ could not readily fuse, it disappeared, as in *ignoble* from *in-* plus *gnobilis*, and *ignorant*, from *in-* plus a term related to *gnostic*, which is related to English *knowledge*. The same prefix, coming to English through Greek, may appear as *a-*, *an-*, and likewise can be expected to adjust to a following consonant, as in *atom, amorphous, anarchy, agnostic*. Thus, if the base word begins with a sound that does not readily blend with /n/, speakers of English would be even less likely to employ the borrowed form of the prefix; probably no speaker would produce *impsychedelic, ir-Raphaelitic,* or *illunilogical,* meaning "having nothing to do with the study of the moon." Faced with the necessity of coining a negative, most speakers of English would turn readily to the native elements, *un-* and *not*. The loan *non-* is an exception; it is from Latin, although most speakers of English would neither know that nor care. They have probably never heard of the rule that bans miscegenation among affixes and roots, and they could not apply it if they did. But they know what terms they feel comfortable with; *non-* is among them, but *ir-* and *il-* are not.

Among the native prefixes still active in word formation is *out-*. Both *out* and *out-* descend from PIE **ud-*, but the root has few surviving relatives outside the Germanic family, although the nearer cousins are fairly numerous and provide *carouse* from Old High German, *outlander* and *utter* from Dutch, and more recent terms like *ersatz* from German. Latin *uterus* is presumably related, and from Greek, so are *hysteria* and *hysterics*, since these disturbances were supposed to come from disorders of the womb. Coming into English the voiced /d/ of **ud-* became voiceless, as many such sounds did, and the vowel /u/ became the diphthong /aʊ/ in accordance with the English Vowel Shift, providing for the NE spelling *out*. Once established as an English prefix it grew rapidly, with specialized meanings. It can be spatial, *outside, outdoors*; it can be something concrete and spatial, *outskirts, outhouse, outback*; it can refer to things from the outside, *outpatient, outline*; it can suggest superiority, *outlast, outgeneral,* and it can enter into a variety of related concepts like *outlay* and *outlook.*[5]

NE *mis-* has many cognates, and may seem to have a parallel prefix from Latin, but does not. It descends into English from PIE **mei-,* meaning "to change," and many of the Latin and Greek descendants of that base maintain this meaning, as in *migrate, transmute,* or they represent a derived meaning, as in *communicate, mutual,* but **mei-* seems not to have become a prefix in Latin or Greek. In English, words from **mei-* interpreted the idea of "change" as a change for the worse, even so much worse that **mei-* has become NE *mad*—which meant "insane," "having lost one's wits," before it came to mean "angry." The prefixing form *mis-* means "bad," "badly," and although an identical form has been borrowed from Old Norse, as in *mistake,* the words from Romance languages that take this shape have a different history. They are mostly from Latin *minus.* This prefix came into Old French usually spelled with an *e,* as in *meschefe* and *mesnommer.* Here Old French *mes-* has a meaning similar to English *mis-,* and purists with a zeal for spelling "corrected" these two words on the basis of the English words and made them, respectively, *mischief* and *misnomer.* As a creative prefix, *mis-* seems now to be restricted to learned coinages, as in *misorient* (1970), but in the past it has been so active that more than five hundred surviving terms incorporate it.

With- has grown from obscure origins to be one of the most varied terms in English. It has not been traced beyond Common Germanic, so that we must assume it did not exist in PIE, but was picked up somewhere by the Germanic peoples in their migrations. It is related to *wither* and apparently meant "against," but it also developed early the notion of association in space, represented in combinations like *within, without,* which led to association in purpose. This duality is apparent in the phrase *fight with,* which can mean either "to oppose" or the opposite, "to mutually receive and extend help in fighting." As a prefix the two ideas appear in combinations like *withhold, withdraw, withstand.* It seems to have fallen heir to ideas that in ME went with *mid,* comparable to German *mit,* perhaps through Old Norse *vith,* and it became the way to translate Latin *cum.* Thus it acquired meanings involving an agent, more in phrases than in compounds, *to cut with a knife,* and the like.

---

5. *Out* can be a word as well as a prefix, and hence has been treated also in compounding; see Chapter IX.3 above.

And the prefix is still growing with concepts like *withholding tax.* The ways it has developed are suggested by the following joke, which utilizes an earlier use now threatened with obsolescence:

"A lady waits without, my Lord."
"Without what?"
"Without food or clothing, my Lord."
"Give her something to eat and send her in."

Another of the active native prefixes is *over-.* The *Barnhart Dictionary of New English Since 1963* recorded thirty-three new terms formed with that prefix in a single decade, 1963–1973, from *overachieve* to *over-technologize*, including such common words as *overkill* and *overoccupied.* Like *upon*, it descends from **uper-*, and is cognate with *super-* in Latin and *hyper-* in Greek, which have similar meanings. It formerly had a variety of uses, including being physically higher, extending across, dominating, and damaging, but as an active prefix it seems now to be limited to a meaning "in excess." Likewise, *a-*, from *on-*, was known in several senses, but is now uncommon, used in the single sense of "not." For the same period, 1963–1973, Barnhart found only one coinage, *ahemeral*, "not constituting a full day," a scientific coinage apparently rare even in learned circles.

6. Loan Prefixes

The great body of prefixes are loans from the Classical tongues, Latin alone supplying some fifty—the total is uncertain because some initial syllables may or may not be prefixes.[6] Relationships among them can be

6. For ready reference, the following are some of the more common prefixes, mostly Latin, a few Greek, and some both—

ab- (abs-)	com- (co-, col-,	in- (il-, im-, ir-)
ad- (ac-, af-, ag-,	con-, cor-)	inter-
al-, an-, ap-,	contra-	intra-
ar-, as-, at-)	de-	intro-
ambi- (ambo-)	di- (dis-)	mal-
ante-	en-	mega-
anti- (ant-)	epi-	meta-
arch-	ex- (e-, ef-, ec-)	multi-
bi-	extra-	neo-
cata-	hyper-	non-
circum-	hypo-	ob- (oc-, of-, op-)

complex. We have already noticed that many have cognates in English, and the same is true of the Classical tongues. *Pro-*, for example, has been borrowed from both Latin and Greek, the former often meaning "for," "instead of," as in *proconsul, pronoun*, whereas many of the Greek loans embody the idea of "earlier," "primitive," as in *prologue, prophet* ("one who goes before"). Some prefixes have developed opposites, as have *super-* and *supra-*. They come from the same root, **upo-*, which has also provided what seem to be their antonyms, *sub-*, as in *subterranean, subbasement, submarine, substandard* and not so obviously opposite, as in *substitute, substantial*, and *subject*. As we can see, if we apply the analysis of sounds in Chapter VII, the /p/ of *super-* is merely the voiceless form of the /b/ of *sub-*. The voiced and voiceless forms existed, and they specialized, each becoming the trigger for a different meaning, as frequently happens with doublets. As for the meaning, the key is given by the English word *up*. The root **upo-* means both "under" and "up from under," and thus the English words *above, under*, and *up* all come from the same root, as do the Latin cognate prefixes, *sub-* and *super-*.

Many borrowed affixes enter actively into word-formation, and some seem to be increasing. We have noticed *in-* and *per-* above (see Chapter IX.4). The supplement to the *Third New International Dictionary*[7] has some four pages of entries for the period 1955–1971 beginning *de-*, most of them utilizing the prefix. They include terms as common as *defog, de-escalate, deorbit*, and *devolatilize*, although we should notice that some entries rely only on new uses of old words, such as *destruct* in the sense "self-destruct." Coinages with *anti-* during the same period are almost as numerous, *antidepressant, antihero, antisexist*, and *antismog*. Following are random samples of loan prefixes still active:

> *counter-* (as in *counterproductive*, 1963), *dis-* (as in *disinvestment*, 1938), *inter-* (as in *intermedia*, 1967, *interpopulation*, 1971), *extra-*

para-	pseudo-	super-, supra-
per-	re-	syn- (sy-, syl-, sym-)
peri-	retro-	trans-
post-	se-	tri-
pre-	semi-	uni-
pro-	sub- (suc-, suf-, sug-,	vice-
proto-	sum-, sup-, sur-, sus-)	

7. *6,000 Words* (Springfield, Mass.: G. & C. Merriam, 1976).

(as in *extra-special*, recent U.S. slang), *multi-* (as in *multilingualism*, 1968, *multiprogramming*, 1970), *re-* ("again" as in *recycle*, 1970, *recombinant*, 1976); *semi-* ("half" as in *semiquotes, semifinalist*), *super-* ("improved" as in *superjet*, 1964, *superwater*, 1969); *ultra-* ("exceedingly" as in *ultraminiature*, 1968, *ultraleft*, 1970); *tri-* (as in *trijet*, 1970, *trimaran*, 1965).

The most productive Greek prefix in current American English is *ex-* (or *e-*) in the sense of "former," which can be applied to almost anything, even newly coined or borrowed words—*ex-cosmonaut, ex-stringer*, "a former part-time local journalistic correspondent," *ex-ombudsman*, and the like. The prefix has become so common in *ex-wife* and *ex-husband* that colloquially one can hear a one-time spouse referred to as "my ex." The prefix *ex-*, meaning "out of" *(exclude)*, "completely" *(exasperate)*, "beyond" *(exceed)* is no longer active.

Almost any Greek prefix can be used in scientific and technical coinages; I have had occasion to use *Proto-Indo-European* in this book, and if the ancestor of Basque should ever be discovered it could be called *Proto-Basque*. We have already noticed the **meg-* which has descended to OE as *mycel*, NE *much*. From the suffixed form **mag-no-* we have NE *magnify, magnificent*, etc. through Latin *magnus*, "great." From the suffixed form **mag-yos-* we get NE *mayor, majority*, etc. through Latin *major*, "greater." From the suffixed superlative **mag-samo-* NE has *maximum, maxim*, etc. through Latin *maximus*, "greatest." From the suffixed form **mag-to-* NE has *matador* from Latin *mactus*, "made great," through Spanish, and from the suffixed feminine **mag-ya-* the name of the Latin goddess *Maia*, NE *May*. From the suffixed form **meg-al-* NE has the prefix *meg-*through Greek in many words, *megaton, megacycle*, etc.; and from a variant form through Sanskrit *mahatma, maharajah*, etc. Most common PIE roots have some such variety of offspring through various suffixes, but this generation of word making is part of the growth of PIE vocabulary, not that of English proper. The practice of suffixing was well established in the IE tradition, however, and English has its own tradition of vocabulary making by suffix.

7. Suffixes: Native

The native suffixes are rather more numerous than the prefixes, presumably seventeen in all, but they enter less into the creative part of the language. The following are usually called suffixes: *-ard*, "characterizing someone," *(coward)*; -*dom*, "quality, condition" *(wisdom)*; -*en*, "to make," "made of" *(wooden)*; -*er*, -*or*, "one who," *(worker)*; -*ful*, "full (of)" *(helpful)*; -*hood*, "quality," "state" *(motherhood)*; -*ish*, "having the quality of" *(childish)*; -*el*, -*le*, "agent" *(handle)*; -*less*, "without" *(useless)*; -*ly*, a syllable to make modifiers, now mainly adverbs *(ungainly, awkwardly)*; -*ness*, "state or condition" *(eagerness)* (concrete variants have developed, such as *witness*, or *wilderness*); -*ock*, a diminutive *(hummock)*; -*ship*, "state or condition" *(hardship)* (concrete variants have developed, like *your Lordship*); -*some*, "having the quality," *(winsome)*; -*ster* "one who" *(punster)*; -*ward(s)*, "toward" *(toward, to* having formerly indicated motion); -*y*, -*i*- (when followed by a second suffix), "having a quality" *(guilty)*. Several of these suffixes, like -*ard*, -*el*, -*en*, -*some*, and -*ock*, survive but sparsely and have long since ceased to be active. Most users of English would not imagine that such syllables had ever been suffixes.

A number can still be resurrected, but usually are not. The suffix -*dom* can be used, especially humorously, but seldom is; *teenagedom* is possible, but has not been recorded by lexicographers. The suffix -*hood* is similar to -*dom* (*teenagehood* and *tycoonhood* would be understandable but unexpected); while -*ish*, semantically the equivalent of -*y*, once common, is now mainly jocular or derogatory, but can be used with approximate times (We'll expect you *sixish*) and in nonce words *(Faulknerish)*. The suffix -*ship* is not very active; *musicianship* has developed, but *surgeonship* has not; -*ster* is possible, as in *gangster* and *pollster*, but rare: no *pollutster* or *skister* appears in dictionaries, although the latter would avoid the awkward *skier*. The suffix -*ward(s)* can be used as a nonce word or humorously *(Boston-ward)*, but *spaceward* has not developed. A few are now obscured by changes in sense or meaning or both. *Buxom* comes from *bow some*—the /k/ is the remnant of an old palatal, and *some* was often spelled *sum*. Thus the term meant "zealous to bow," and accordingly "obedient," which developed as "pleasant" or "pleasantly plump" or, now especially, "bosomy."

Thus the native suffixes that can now be used readily for devised terms are few. Remarkable is -*er*, which has little ancestry but wide modern currency. It may have been borrowed from Latin -*arius*, which has a similar use, or it may go back to a common ancestor not very certainly pinned down, but it can now be attached to almost any action where it makes sense *(trampoliner, bootlegger)*, or to a functioning agent *(atomizer, Breathalyzer)*, and the like. It can refer to an object utilized for a special purpose: a *sleeper* can be a timber in use, somebody sleeping, a place to sleep (e.g., a Pullman car), or, as an Americanism, anything abnormally inactive (a stock or real estate that does not sell). And related uses may develop from any of these; an exhausted person may, in informal terms, "take a *breather*." Similarly, *-y* can be applied to almost any appropriate word. *Goof*, in the sense "an incompetent person," was recorded by 1916; by 1921 it was converted to *goofy*, and by 1932 it had also become a verb. As a suffix, *-y* has multiple origins, some uses from IE *-ig*, from Common Germanic *-iga*, some from various loans, including Latin *-aria* and *-ate*. As a suffix *-ful*, from IE *pel-*, can be added to many nouns *(useful, merciful, cupful)*, and it has cognates in the Classical languages, but none that are suffixes. By Grimm's Law we should expect the English /f/ to be parallel with Latin /p/, and it is, in such words as *plural, plenty, plenipotentiary, plebiscite, complete, compliment*, and many more that grow from the PIE base *pel-*, meaning "to fill." Likewise, a few have been borrowed from Greek, such as *plethora, pleonasm*, and *Pleistocene*, but no affixes from either tongue.

Two of the most fruitful suffixes cannot be traced to Indo-European, although they are widespread in Germanic tongues, *-ness* and *-like*. The first can be attached to almost any modifier to make it a noun meaning "having the quality of," as in *goofiness*, in *funkiness*, and in *peppiness*, which is a little older; *pep* was slang about 1915. *Like* has a more complex history; as we have seen in OE *gelic*, it meant "having the body or form of." It developed as a way of making modifiers, as in OE *freond (ge)lice*, that is, *friendlike*, which became *friendly* during the general word shortening that took place in ME. With time this truncated ending, *-ly*, became recognized as an adverbial ending, so that for centuries we have made only adverbs with it: *beautifully, smugly, urbanely*, etc., thousands of them, and *-ly* has become so much the sign of the adverb that speakers now feel uncomfortable using an adverb without it. Hence we are making old words that were adverbs in their own right to fit the new norm. OE *sleaw*, which became *slow*, is becoming *slowly*, as the OE adverbs *full* and *sare* have already become *fully* and *sorely*.

8. Suffixes: Greek

Borrowed Greek suffixes are few but flourishing. Consider *-ize*, also spelled *-ise*, especially in England, for words borrowed from French as against those coined in English. The syllable comes from Greek *-izein*, a term of limited application, indicating that a person does a particular sort of thing. It appeared in *barbarizein*; in Greek use any non-Greek was a barbarian, and thus *barbarizein* was "to act like or take the side of foreigners." The suffix was picked up to make verbs out of nouns for the Christian religion, when that became popular, as in *baptizein* (baptize), and NE *evangelize, catechize*, and the like. No doubt being associated with religion and the church promoted the suffix for all sorts of learned purposes. *Critic* had sprung from a PIE root **skeri-*, to cut, seen also in *crisis*, but soon the activity of a *critic* became to *criticize*. The suffix was added to many words, especially learned and solemn words: *philosophize, civilize, etymologize*. In more recent tongues, the suffix could be added to proper names: when McAdam invented a new kind of road, the verb was *macadamize*; when Mesmer devised a technique for hypnotism, the verb was *mesmerize*, and when Thomas Bowdler tried to remove the supposedly naughty words from Shakespeare he gave rise to *bowdlerize*. This sort of coinage grew to be so common that the addition of *-ize* will turn almost anything into a verb, perhaps especially in the United States and Australia. The pattern of analysis is now so much the pattern of grammar in English, and conversion from one grammatical use to another so unconscious, that many new nouns can be used as verbs without change, or may give rise to a back-formation. As we noticed above, *goof*, a noun, sired "to goof," a verb. *Laser* (an acronym from *(l)ight (a)mplification by (s)timulated (e)mission of (r)adiation*) promptly sired a verb, *to lase*, which can work like any other English verb; *lased seeds* are said to germinate rapidly. And when the time comes that requires a verb meaning "to provide with a laser," the word will probably be *laserize*.

Meanwhile, *-ize* had engendered two suffixes to make nouns, *-ism* to designate an action or an activity *(baptism, criticism)*, a doctrine, belief, or faith *(Communism)*, anything characterized by a quality *(truism, fundamentalism)*, and many others. A practitioner can be designated by *-ist (arsonist, botanist, mechanist)*, but both these terms, *-ism* and *-ist*, tend to retain something of their learned and patrician ancestry. A person working with metropolitan problems can be called a *city planner*, the term being made of the homey (although borrowed) words *city* and *plan* plus the native suffix *-er*. In more professional and more academic phraseology the same person may be an *urbanist*, pursuing *urbanism*. On the other hand, one who "goofs off" would not be called a *goofist*, partly because *-ist* implies deliberate application in something approaching professional persistence, and thus *goofist* would in effect be a contradiction in terms. Also, *-ist* is a generally commendatory term, not to be sullied by a slangy epithet like *goof*. Thus, within the limits of propriety *-ize, -ism*, and *-ist* have become standard devices for making verbs and nouns in NE; they were greatly popularized through French and Latin, but they all stem from Greek.

Two other Greek suffixes, *-ic(s)* and *-oid*, have some currency in English but are now used to generate new words only in learned circles. Of these, *-ic* and *-oid* identify modifiers; they appear in familiar words like *angelic* and *volcanic* and in learned words like *spheroid, schizoid*, and *anthropoid*. They can still be used in scientific coinages stemming from Greek roots, but *bikic*, as a term to refer to motorcycles, is unthinkable, and *golfic* is at least unlikely. The suffix *-ics* appears in nouns, *mathematics, mechanics, gymnastics*, and the like, which now look like plurals because they end with *-s*, although the nouns were singular in Greek and remain so when borrowed. A number of Greek words like *logos*, "word," have been so handy making compounds in the learned world that, although they were not suffixes in Greek, they have in effect become suffixes in English. Any new study can become an *-ology* (*paleolimnology*, the study of freshwater lakes in geologic times), and any new instrument for looking can be a *-scope* (*laparoscope*, an optical instrument inserted through the abdominal wall, composed of Greek *lapara*, "flank," plus *-scope*).

9. Suffixes: Latin

More than half of all NE suffixes come from Latin, and they include many of the most active. We have already noticed that the commonest suffixes from Greek were popularized through Latin. In addition, Latin suffixes and Latin grammatical endings include many of the most-used affixes, including many still active, although mainly in learned coinages. More than forty can be identified, which include *-(a)tion*, *-ant* and *-ent*, *-ance* and *-ence*, and *-ment*. Only a few of the more common can be considered here.

Most words ending in *-ate* come from a class of Latin verbs that have a past participle ending in *-atus* (*designate, alternate, masticate*, hundreds of them). Nouns related to these verbs could have an ending *-ionis*, which in English has regularly become *-(a)tion* (*designation, alternation, mastication*, etc.). This became so much the pattern for nouns growing from Latin verbs that *-(a)tion* endings developed for derivatives from verbs that never had had an *-ate* ending (*application* from *apply, publication* from *publish, modification* from *modify*), and the analogy was extended to nouns built on words that seem to have become verbs in English (*causation* from *cause, formation* from *form, starvation* from *starve*, a native word, etc.). These terms preserve the *t* of the Latin spelling, although usually not the pronunciation, the *t* having been restored by pedants or others who knew Latin—Chaucer writes *predication* as *predicacioun* (the second *c* was pronounced /s/, and the /sɪ/ has since been simplified to /š/). Other similar Latin verbs produced similar English words. Verbs having participles ending *-itus* and *-issus* have produced nouns like *rendition* and *remission*. Meanwhile, these words were being borrowed into French and then further borrowed into English, bringing with them the developments already established in French. Words with similar endings derive from some Latin nouns, and thus we have words from a variety of sources with similar pronunciations (*ascension, persuasion, reversion*, etc.).

There are others. A Latin nominal ending *-antia* provides words like *informant*, and through French, *appearance*. Like some similar endings, it was applied to non-Latin verbs, *riddance, forbearance, utterance*, and the like. The suffix *-ancia* could also produce *-ancy* (*necromancy, redundancy*, etc.). Closely related are the nouns that stemmed from Latin *-atia, -acia*, and *atus*, giving *delicacy, papacy, accuracy, advocacy*, etc. Another Latin ending *-entia* (later *-antia*) provided abstract nouns, with endings through French *-ence* and *-ance* (*presence, temperance, absence*, etc.). And as always there were blunders; a plural like *excellences* sounded so much like plurals from *-y*, spelled in English *ie*, that *their Excellencies* developed. Meanwhile, modifiers sprang from the present participles, the equivalents of forms like *riding* and *sketching* in English, which in Latin regularly ended *-ant* or *-ent*. These account for thousands of adjectives like *intent, instant, confident*, etc., and these have in turn led to abstractions and to various animate objects *(student, agent, current, coefficient)*. In the plural, these terms are identical in sound with the abstract nouns that have developed with the *-ence, -ance* suffixes; the two uses can be kept apart by remembering a sentence like "This doctor's *patients* need *patience*."

Another fruitful ending was the Latin *-mentum*, which could be added to verbs to imply a noun that was the result of the action, as in *fragmentum* from the verb *frangere*, "to break." This ending became *-ment* in French, where it also developed as an active suffix, to make a noun out of almost any verb. Thus we have *government, atonement*, both *compliment* and *complement*, and the like.

Most Latin suffixes have not become very active in either English or French, and hence survive in only a modest number of loans. Latin *-aticum*, another ending attached to *-ate* verbs, provides through French *-age* such words as *portage, damage, marriage*, etc. Latin *-alis* has been reduced to *-al*, attached especially to modifiers, including those meaning "having the quality of," as in *liberal, literal, annual*. The suffix became somewhat active, and nouns could be developed, with or without an additional ending (*principal, signal, nationality*, etc.). Likewise, *-ary* from Latin *-arius* includes modifiers based on the idea "related to" or "referring to" *(contrary, necessary, voluntary)*; words in this stream borrowed late from French are likely to appear with *-air(e)*, as in *legionnaire*. Words ending *-cy* can come from a great variety of brief endings in both Latin and Greek, including *-ia* and *-tia*, designating a state or condition (*secrecy, prophecy, captaincy*, etc.). The suffix *-(i)ous*, with or without a preceding vowel, provided a large number of modifiers *(glorious, atrocious, aqueous, covetous)*. The Latin *-tude* is roughly equivalent to the English *-ness (altitude, pulchritude, magnitude)*. NE *-ure* from Latin *-ura* may imply an action or process, or the result of these *(figure, culture, creature)*. The ending *-y*, noticed under native suffixes, can come from a variety of foreign sources, including *-ity* from *-(i)tas*, providing *purity, amity, piety*, etc.

10. Loose-jointed Compounds: Phrases or Chains

As we have seen, new ideas or uses can be given convenient handles by sticking two semantic units together and treating them as one word *(highway)*, by linking them with a hyphen *(high-pressure)*, or placing them in an invisible chainlike sequence *(high school)* in which they are linked forward and backward through a sense for grammar. Such a string of words has been called a **phrase**. Unfortunately, that term has been used also in various special ways—as we shall see below. And as a matter of fact, it is not very descriptive anyhow. The Greeks used it to mean "speech," "manner of speaking." To avoid confusion associated with *phrase* some grammarians have used the Latin term for a sequence of interacting words, *catena*, from which we get our word *chain*. So let us use *chain*, which everybody knows, since it does effectively describe these linked uses.

We are here discussing no minor matter, particularly not in PDE. In the hope of obtaining a random sample I have transcribed the entry words in the first column of pages 100, 200, 300, 400, and 500 in *The Barnhart Dictionary of New English Since 1963*, which is, for the decade 1963–1973, the most extensive list available of very recent English.[8]

8. For economy I have skeletonized or rephrased most of the definitions. A few may be uncertain: is *relaxor* a new use of an old word, *relaxer*, or a new coinage with a different suffix, *-or*?

computerese—the jargon of scientists working with computers.
computer graphics—art or design produced on computers.
computerizable—capable of being programmed.
computerization—the use of computers.
computerize—to equip with computers.
harambee—Swahili word meaning "pull together."
hard-core—a person considered part of the nucleus of a group.
hard drug—a drug considered addictive.
hard-edge—a form of abstract painting.
hard-edger—painter of the above.
hardened—military term meaning "protected against missiles or bombs."
monoamine oxidase—a tranquilizing enzyme.
monocrystal—a strong, synthetic filament.
monocrystalline—composed of the above.
monohull—sailing vessel having one hull.
monokini—one-piece bikini.
rejectant—a repellent using ingredients insects reject.
rejection—the human body's refusal to accept transplants.
rejective art—a school of art that rejects nonessentials.
rejectivist—related to the above.
relativistic—term in physics referring to very high speeds.
relaxor—a substance that loosens or slackens tightly curled hair.
wealth tax—a tax based on wealth regardless of income.
Weatherman—member of a militant youth organization.
wedel—back-formation from Wedeln.
Wedeln—skiing maneuver, derived from German *wedeln*, "to wag the tail."
weepie or **weepy**—British slang for an overly sentimental book, movie, etc.

The sample, obviously inadequate, may still be revealing. The entries may be classified as follows: compounds made of free morphemes, 1 *(Weatherman)*; hyphenated compounds, 3 *(hard-core, hard-edge, hard-edger)*; loans, 3 (one a back-formation: *harambee, wedel, Wedeln)*; different uses of recognized words, 5 *(hardened, rejection, relativistic, relaxor, weepie)*; chains or phrases, 5 *(computer graphics, hard drug, monoamine oxidase, rejective art, wealth tax)*; coinages utilizing affixes, 10 (all the remainder). That is, if this sample is valid, building new words by utilizing affixes is the most widely used device for acquiring new terms in PDE, closely followed by the conversion of an old word to a new use. Except for these devices, developing chains or phrases is as common as any, with one sixth of this sample. This is no measly proportion, but there is reason to believe it too small. The principal weakness of the Barnhart dictionary, in my opinion, is that it treats phrasal sequences too lightly. For example, it includes almost none of the verbal chains called *verb sets*, like *go public* and *let it all hang out*, of which thousands have been developed in this century. That the practice has so declined that none were made after 1963 is unthinkable. One might plausibly guess that if the editors of a dictionary of NE were as hospitable to phrasal sequences as are the *Supplement* to the OED, *New International*, or *Webster's New World*, the coinages by chains would be roughly equal to the coinages by affixes, accounting for perhaps a third of the semantic developments. For the validity of such an estimate I shall offer more evidence below, but at a minimum this device of making new semantic units by building a chain of words is clearly to be reckoned with in NE terminology.

We have noticed that the line between compounds and phrasal chains is not sharp, that in part the distinction grows from the whims of spelling. Broad principles can be traced. Speakers of English do not like extremely long words. English has no such place names as the Welsh term cited above (Chapter II.1); even a community like *Cold Spring on Hudson* is not written *Coldspringonhudson*. German speakers can build up modifiers like *the-down-the-street-going man*, and such structures have a degree of economy, briefer than *the man who was going down the street*, but English avoids both long compounds written solid and extensive use of hyphens. Even terms like *mother-in-law, Book-of-the-Month Club*, and *pay-as-you-go policy* are rare. When a term was needed for a camera that would take pictures in dim light, the term was *available-light camera*, not *available-light-camera*.

To further this end we have several devices, one being to keep separate those words whose relationship is revealed by grammar. We do not write the subject and verb solid, although some languages do, and we tend not to make compounds within the patterns of modification. Usually the sequence, determiner + modifier(s) + noun, is not broken up; *the old man* is written as three words. This practice is maintained, even if the sequence is clearly a semantic unit. Consider the sentence: *The young men may be mostly concerned with sex, but the old men are more likely to be interested in their health.* Here the subjects of the two clauses are clearly not *men*. If we remove the words *young* and *old* the sentence makes no sense. These words are more than modifiers; they are essential components of the subject. *The young men* and *the old men* are semantic units, even though their elements are kept apart, as though they are parts of two chains.

This practice may be illogical, but it is workable. *Old* and *young* can be modifiers, and nothing more, as in *There was an old man, and a young man, and a whole flock of children*. But the borderline between the use of words like *old* and *young* as modifiers, and words having the same shape as integral parts of a semantic unit is hard to draw. And compounding is arbitrary; you either do or you don't. Accordingly, sequences like *the old man* are never compounded, and we are slow to compound any modifier and its head word. There are exceptions; we write *black bird* and *blackbird, black board* and *blackboard*. Here the compounding serves a real purpose; a *blackbird* is a black bird (although it may have wings partially red or yellow) but not all black birds are blackbirds. Likewise, what used to be a blackboard can now be gray slate, painted plaster, or suitable plastic of whatever color. Thus, arbitrarily, most modifier-noun sequences are kept without compounding. Many obviously could be compounded with no harm and with added precision, such as *bigcity, smalltown, pavedroad*, etc., but *almost any silk screen printing process* would be nearly unreadable printed as *almostanysilkscreenprintingprocess*. By sensible practice we avoid such compounds. We are more likely to hyphenate or compound two nouns, as in *railroad, bullfight, bullpen*, etc. (although not *bull session*, perhaps because no bulls are or ever have been involved, and *bull* here seems more like a modifier than a name).

Similarly, some chains tend not to be compounded into single words if they seem to be held together by grammar, even though with time they may become more semantic units than grammatical constructions. One of these is the so-called prepositional phrase, sequences like *in the car, behind the door*, etc. We may conceive—although we need not—that each of these words is an integer, calling up a meaning associated with itself, working within a grammatical structure. *In* and *behind* would here be called prepositions, introducing prepositional phrases, but the same shapes can also serve in other ways. (The doctor is *in*. The runner was *behind*.) Many of these same shapes, on the other hand, can appear as affixes and be written solid in elaborate compounds like *inhalability*. Some older combinations have become compounds, relationship words like *into* and *although*, but the chain *as though* has not been treated as one word, and some chains would become confusing if they were. Many chains now work as new semantic units even when they have other entities like nouns and verbs within them, and some are so long that they would readily be confusing written solid: *in consideration of, as a matter of fact, at the end of, on a par with*, etc.

11. The Scale of Idiomacy

As we have seen, language works by means of meaningful units and the grammar that develops among them. In English, and probably in all languages, these two, grammar and meaning as it is triggered by semantic units, blend into each other and are constantly changing. Part of both the fluidity and the change appears in chains of words, which may be quite clearly grammatical structures, or idiomatic sequences each of which works in all ways like so many words, or something between.

An example may be instructive. Consider the sequence *get a job*. We have two semantic parts here, *get* and *a job*, having a grammatical relationship that enlarges the meaning of the sequence. We can demonstrate that this relationship is grammatical; we can replace *a job* with synonyms and still have meaningful sequences: *get employment, get something to do, get a way of making a living.* We can replace *a job* with other nominal terms and have a sequence acceptable to native speakers: *get a wife, get a book, get a wholesome outlook on life.* Likewise, we could substitute synonyms for *get* and have grammatically acceptable sequences: *find a job, acquire a job, accept a job.* Now let us take another example: *get over a cold.* Here we have something different, for if we start replacing words with synonyms we have only nonsense left, as in *acquire over a cold, get above a cold, find something on top of a cold.* That is, the relationship between *get* and *over* in this sequence is not grammatical. Here *get* and *over* are as much one word as though they were written *get-over* or *getover*, and they have synonyms for the pair, not for the separate words, terms like *recover from, get well after having had.* That is, *get over* with the sense appearing in *get over a cold* is what is commonly called an idiom, although to understand what is happening we need only think of *get over* as working like one word rather than two.

Not all cases are so clear. Consider various uses of *take off.* In *take off your clothes*, *take* and *off* look rather like a verb and an adverb. *Clothes* can be replaced with *shoes, shirt,* or even *the top book on the stack* or *the cover.* In *take off a dollar from the price*, the complement *a dollar* can be replaced with *a dime, fifty cents,* and the like, but the complement is now much restricted; apparently it must be a unit of money, as though this *take off* is what we might call a *half-way idiom.* Some other instances are quite clearly idioms: *the plane took off, the mimic took off the President.* Others are not quite so idiomatic; if a plane *takes off* it can *depart from* (an airport), *for* (Chicago), but the idea involves rising into the air, a part of the meaning understood in the idiom, but not expressed. If the sentence is, *I grabbed my bag and took off for the office,* the *taking off* may involve a helicopter but is not presumed to do so. That is, as we saw when we examined words and grammar, other words in the sentence, or a known subject of discussion, may select among the uses of a word, and may determine the degree and kind of idiom-making that appears in any sentence. If the sentence is *I took off five pounds,* the use is not idiomatic if the subject of discussion is weights on one pan of a balance scale and the speaker is reporting that he removed weights. But the chain is much more idiomatic if the speaker is a Briton and he is taking off pounds to reduce a price, or if the speaker is describing the effect of a diet.

How do these changes come about? We do not know for sure, partly because we have not tried very hard to find out. Laymen have frequently assumed that idioms are rather like acts of God; their existence has been recognized, but being exceptions—the usual example is "The sun sets"— they need not be inquired into. Laymen will dismiss such locutions with a shrug and say, "But that's an idiom." Students of language have certainly known better, that idioms are very much the creation of man and must represent some sort of group consciousness, one of man's ways of building communication, but scholars have not studied idioms very persistently as phenomena. In the evolution of some idioms, gradual changes over long periods of time have been involved. We can conceive that *to give away,* in the sense of offering as charity or a gift, could have developed one use after another until the chain *a dead giveaway* became an understood phrase, a new idiom. On the other hand, some new uses must represent leaps in meaning, as figurative terms usually do. Consider *get down off your high horse* in the sense, "Stop being so self-important." This chain could have been uttered as a literal request to dismount, particularly in the time when equestrians were more prevalent than they are today, but the idiom is now so much more current than any meaning depending upon the literal use of each word, that few people who use the expression would assume it involves any four-footed object, either a tall Percheron or lofty piece of gymnastic equipment.

The results of this fluidity have been noticed in the best study of idiomatic use in English to date,[9] where the editors suggest that instead

---

9. *Oxford Dictionary of Current Idiomatic English,* eds. A. P. Cowie and R. Mackin (London: Oxford U. P., 1975–   ), projected in two volumes, of which vol. I treats what I have been calling *verb sets.*

of recognizing some chains that are idioms and some that are not, "We shall do better to think in terms of a *scale* of idiomaticity."[10] The term well identifies the human inclination—perhaps especially in NE—to turn old terms into new, highly specialized uses, by using various devices in varying ways, including sticking units together, attaching affixes, and linking terms into phrasal chains. Perhaps especially when linked to a new fad, new sequences can grow rapidly; to *gift-wrap,* leading to *gift-wrapped,* is now extremely common in American English, but so recent that the *Supplement* to the *OED* missed it, as did most, but not all, American dictionaries.

Some of these chains have earlier been quotations (*Let there be light, Methinks the lady doth protest too much*). They maintain the shape of the original, but they acquire their own semantic use, which may be more or less than their one-time use in context. They may even reverse an original sense, if some of the words change meaning. "The exception that proves the rule" is now widely taken to imply the idiotic belief that a rule is valid if, and only if, the rule has exceptions. The interpretation that makes sense reflects the day when *to prove* more frequently meant "to put to the proof," or "to test," which implied that if a rule has too many exceptions it has only limited worth.

We might notice three steps on this scale of idiomacy. First are clusters that have a meaning as a whole, but rely on an unperverted standard use of each unit in the chain. *Into the house* is a unit of sorts. Taken as a whole it can tell where someone has gone, but to have this use, each of the parts of the chain works in a normal way; *into* means what it usually does, and so with the other terms. Furthermore, the speaker probably used the chain because it implied what he had to say; he was not following any tradition, recalling consciously or unconsciously a recognized unit, and if circumstances had warranted the sequence, he would readily have said *out of the house, behind the bar,* or *over the cuckoo's nest.* That is, this chain of words has a shape that could be that of an idiom, but the sequence is not idiomatic. It relies on the syntax of the language.

By contrast, at the top of the scale of idiomacy are those chains composed mainly or wholly of terms so employed that they do not suggest any of the uses normally associated with them. In *heavens to Betsy* the word *heavens* refers in no way to the sky or eternity, nor could one substitute *Algernon* or *Gretchen* for *Betsy.* Similarly, nothing can be done to *struck all of a heap. To call a doughnut a doughnut* would seem

---

10. The name seems to me needlessly cumbersome; *idiomacy* is bad enough.

to have no meaning, but *to call a spade a spade* does have meaning, although nothing that is associated particularly with horticulture.

Between are chains that include words which trigger something of their accustomed meaning, but have become part of a traditional pattern that maintains its own existence, sequences like *high and mighty, death and taxes, for God and country, the jig is up, a comedy of errors, money to burn, tricks of the trade, give someone a piece of one's mind.* These can be interpreted by accepting something approaching normal uses of the individual words, but few terms can be inserted or left out, and they tend not to tolerate substituted synonyms except for humorous purposes. Instead of *for God and country* we could say *for the Lord and my native land,* and a writer might do this, but if he did he would do it as a deliberate piece of composition. It would not be a chain that comes to him as a predetermined entirety. Some of these sequences involve more or less figurative use, as in *to have a bee in one's bonnet;* bonnets are out of date, but one cannot replace the term with *cap, hat,* or *beret,* and a *wasp, hornet,* or any other biting or stinging insect cannot be substituted for *bee* in normal, nonchalant use.

Notable among these chains that stand rather low in the idiomatic scale are sequences commonly called verb phrases, terms like *will go* and *have been going.* Formerly, the verbs that have become English were all, or mainly, one-word verbs. The pattern of PIE grammar was that the shapes of a word were changed to show their various uses. These syllables that were attached as affixes had no doubt been semantic units at an earlier stage in the language, but by IE times they had become standardized into bound morphemes, and eventually into patterns of these, which we call the "endings" in the paradigms of verb conjugations. The Germanic speakers whose dialects were to become English ceased making such shape-changing verbs before they came to the British Isles, and they continued the new practice in their new home. These speakers of OE—and the later speakers of ME—indicated the various uses of verbs by developing chains of words. The process was slow. For example: OE had no future tense, but used the present as a future. It did, however, contain verbal combinations. Anglo-Saxons could say they would like to do something by using the word *wyllan,* which means "to wish," "to want," and adding to it the infinitive of a verb indicating what they wanted. But wants are always in the future. The forms from *wyllan* have become one of our futures, whether or not conditional, as in *I would go, I will go.* A similar development changed *scealt,* implying a duty, into *shall,* which was built into other chains that provided futures. Meanwhile—although the process took centuries—*go* from OE *gan* was developing into a future. If you are going, are on your way in order to do something, you are "going to do it," which has become the commonest future in NE, except for oral *'ll.*

This means of making grammar has continued, until now the majority of verbs in American colloquial English are composed of two or more words, and these phrasal combinations are common wherever English is used, whether spoken or written. They are like the other moderately idiomatic sequences in that they have a standard choice of words and a rigid sequence, and most of the individual words have a commonly recognized meaning, but the total adds up to something more or less than the total of the meanings of the words in the chain. A sequence like *I should have liked to have been able to hear the lecture* fits roughly the total meaning that the speaker, at some time in the past, wanted to hear but presumably did not, a lecture that was then in the future but has now become past. That is a tolerably subtle idea, not so readily expressed in most languages by the use of an inflected verb.

12. Verb Sets, Merged Verbs, Phrasal Verbs

Currently, the most active of these chains high on the idiomatic scale are a growing body of multi-word verbs. We have sampled them above; they are combinations like *take off,* "to imitate"; *get down to* (work), "to start seriously"; *run into,* "to encounter"; *put by,* "to save," and the like. Each contains a verb plus one or more other words, and the sequence has use as a whole that is not the use of any of the parts. A boy who is *put by* a girl—by somebody handling the seating arrangements, let us say—sits beside her. Such a sequence is not a phrase; the verb is *put* and *by* is a preposition. But money that is *put by* is not situated beside anything named; it is put into a savings account or a strongbox or is invested. Likewise, if a person *gets down to* something he does not assume a lower position; he may even be higher, since he may have to *get up,* that is, leave his horizontal position on a bed, in order to *get down to work.* Similarly, if a plane *blows up* it does not go up nor does it blow; it falls. If you *run into* Mary in a parking lot you presumably do not batter her with your car bumper or pin her against a wall; you meet and probably talk with her. If you *look out* a window, you look, and your looking goes out, but if you *look out for* something, a locomotive or a falling rock, you are guarding against being hit.

These are among the most intriguing of all developments in English.

They fit, of course, into the general pattern of moving from long, inflected words toward spreading an idea or a use over a number of words, most of them short. These chains started early in English; a few can be found in OE, but most of them at that time were enough like verbs followed by a prepositional phrase so that determining which is an idiom and which is not can pose problems. OE had an expression *leornian aet,* which had presumably been used so that it was followed by a word meaning "church" or "school," or "the priest's place." That is, someone learned *at a place.* But King Alfred writes that he translated *swa swa ic hie geliornode aet Plegmunde minum aercebiscepe* (as I had learned them [works in Latin] at [or from] Plegmund, my archbishop). Presumably the *aet* here means "from," but a less exalted learner than the king might well have learned "at," that is, at the feet of the archbishop, or at his place of residence. There comes a time when *aet,* though it continues to mean "at" in most uses, has clearly shifted to be an idiomatic equivalent of *from* in a particular chain, but for a time the meaning may be uncertain.

Such growths in use must have affected thousands of word sequences during the past two millennia. Publishers of the *Oxford Dictionary of Current Idiomatic English,* cited above, say that their book will contain twenty thousand idioms, and of the two volumes, one is composed only of such verbs.[11] Idioms like these appear in some of the earliest OE we have, but they were then rare.[12] They are somewhat more common in ME, and by Shakespeare's day they were being developed rapidly in popular speech. The "rude mechanicals" in *A Midsummer Night's Dream* use such verbs habitually, but the Duke and his aristocratic guests eschew them. Doubtless the terms were vulgar. By the eighteenth century, however, they are common in edited, informal writing, and speakers of English have been making them in lively fashion ever since. Nor do they seem to be declining in slang, a good sign that coming generations will go on generating them. There is some reason to believe that at present they are growing fastest in the United States and Australia, somewhat slower in Britain and Canada, still more slowly in India, Scotland, Wales, Ireland, New Zealand, and South Africa; and even bilingual speakers who use English as a second language seem to be making them.[13]

11. Furthermore, the volume is based exclusively on British authors and periodicals. It does not include thousands more of these verbs from other sorts of English.

12. They do not appear much, if at all, in *Beowulf,* although we should add that the poem represents highly formal prosody, courtly composition, certainly conservative and perhaps even archaic. We have no colloquial OE.

13. These are guesses; I know of no adequate comparative studies.

These verbal chains have other peculiarities. They are made, at a minimum, of a meaningful verb followed by one or more free morphemes, which may be identical in shape with adverbs, prepositions, or affixes, words like *out (stand out), off (keep off), over (take over)*, etc. They may involve more than one particle *(to catch up with, to get out of, to back off from, to be hard at work on)*. A particle may follow the verb immediately, as in *stand out*, or in some sequences the particle may follow later, after a complement, or even at the end of a long clause *(look up a book, look a book up; I got to the bottom of it, this is the question that we all want to get to the bottom of)*. They can be involved in the extremely complex predicates that are characteristic of NE, as in *They pinned their hope on a revival of tourist trade; It was by the lawyer they were put on to selling everything off*. Perhaps the extreme example is that of the child who objected to a particular bedtime story, saying, "Why did you bring that book I don't like *to be read to out of up for?*" By a kind of back-formation, hyphenated adjectives have grown out of these verbal combinations: *a badly gotten-out brochure, a trumped-up charge*, along with somewhat fewer nominal sequences, mostly compounded *(splashdown, ripoff, runaround, playback, print-out)* or hyphenated terms *(a run-through, the go-ahead, a make-up)*, or written as two words, at least in printing colloquial uses *(He needs some checking up on)*.

What should we call these verbal chains? Although they are attracting growing attention, no term for them has been agreed upon. C. T. Onions, in a little book that has been a standard text in England for most of the century, calls them "verbs constructed with a fixed preposition."[14] Whatever they are, this they are not. The particle is not well called a "preposition"; it follows the verb, not precedes it, and the misnomer has probably led to the ridiculous copybook injunction "a sentence should not be ended with a preposition." And they are not fixed, as Onions himself pointed out (p. 27), citing " 'Call off the hounds' or 'Call the hounds off.' " In this country, one of the first to describe verbal chains was Arthur Garfield Kennedy, who debated what they should be named and chose "verb-adverb combination." This has not found favor, perhaps partly because these particles do not act like adverbs, although some of them have been. Margaret M. Bryant called them "merged verbs," not a bad title, although it tells us little. On the basis of German "verbs

14. *An Advanced English Syntax* (London: Routlege and Kegan Paul, 1st ed., 1904; 2nd ed., 1927), frequently reprinted; Onions had been preparing a new edition when he died in 1965, which the publishers imply will be completed and issued.

with separable prefixes," I proposed "verbs with separable suffixes," but the name was cumbersome. The editors of the *Oxford Dictionary of Current Idiomatic English*, cited above, call them "phrasal verbs." This term seems to me unfortunate, since it is so close to the title "verb phrases," already established, and because, at least in this country, sequences like *have gone* are often called "phrasal verbs." Since this *Oxford Dictionary* will be the nearest thing we have to a standard work at least for a long time, *phrasal verbs* is likely to be used by many grammarians. On the analogy of the use of *set* by mathematicians, many writers in this country now call such chains *verb sets*, which may be as good a name as any—hence my heading above. It is brief, made of familiar units, and has not been preempted. But the fact is that we have no generally accepted terminology.

One more sort of verbal construction should engage us. Like the verb sets, it is taking over crucial areas of English use and meaning. Such a chain is made up of a relatively colorless verb—*to be,* an auxiliary like *to have,* or any of what have been called quasi-auxiliaries, verbs like *get, take,* and *put,* plus something else, usually an adjective or a noun. The result is a chain like *get well.* These combinations are filling what would otherwise be gaps in our vocabulary. As we have noticed, we do not usually make words out of nothing; we may borrow, attach an affix, or convert an old word to a new use: *sterfan,* which meant "to die" has become specialized to mean "to suffer from lack of food," to *starve.* Or we devise a phrasal chain, a device which seems to be particularly congenial to speakers of NE. For example, consider verbs referring to one's personal health. We have no one-word verb that means to be ill, except for the somewhat old-fashioned *ail,* which now usually connotes poor health over a period of time. We say, "I have a cold," "I feel bad," "I am not feeling well," "I picked up a bug somewhere," "I woke up with a cough," "I'm going into the hospital because of my spleen," "I got an infection," "It became infected," but we have no common one-word way of saying we are suffering from a disease or some physical disability. In fact, I have had to use such circumlocutions in writing this paragraph, just to say we have no good, single word.

And so with other observations about health. For relatively formal uses, when the subject is already known, we can say we *are improving* or *recovering,* more usually *recovering from,* but the workhorse terms are *get better, get well, be all better, get over (something), be cured,* and the like. Similarly, we have no one-word, trouble-free way of saying that a patient gets worse. ME had the word *sicken*; about 1200 Orm wrote that someone was *hefigliche secnedd* (heavily sickened), and the word has continued, but it seems to have declined, perhaps partly because in England *sick* implies vomiting. Even in the United States, where *sick* may suggest no more than *ill*, *sicken* has become poetic, academic, or stilted —anyhow, little used. *Ill*, common almost everywhere, (it is somewhat more formal in the United States than *sick*, but current), has never developed an intransitive verb, as it might have been expected to (colloquially, in England, it became a transitive verb, *to ill* [*something*], "to make it worse," but that use never thrived either). Logically, we would expect *sicken* to become popular, or *illen* to develop and become standard, but neither did. For some reason, speakers of English have preferred to devise new phrasal chains.

This tendency permeates NE. In one basic area of communication after another, although a Latinate locution may serve formal purposes, the workhorse terms are verb sets or combinations of a relatively colorless verb with a noun, an adjective, or something else shanghaied to do the job.

13. The English Speaker's Urge to Put Things Together

The fondness for putting things together into such chains as *putting things together* is hard to overestimate in the building of vocabulary. The practice began early; as we have seen, an early ancestor of English employed building blocks composed of a vowel plus one or two consonants. These primitive syllables would have been few, probably numbered in the hundreds—somewhat more than a thousand roots have been identified in PIE, which was later, already considerably elaborated. When two of these "words"—if we can call them that—were put together, one would usually be subordinate to the other, would be less stressed, and would lose the consonant adjacent to the stressed root. Thus CVC + CVC would become either CV + CVC or CVC + VC, depending on whether the first or the second root was stressed, and CVC + CVC + CVC would become CV + CVC + VC, and so on, a string of alternate consonants and vowels. Thus roots of words tend to be made up of three sounds, CVC, but affixes tend to be made up of two or even one: CV, VC, or only V or C. Of course this system of combining became complicated, as we have seen, with fricatives and affricates, with single consonants becoming consonant clusters—as /s/ plus /t/ became /st/—with pure vowels becoming diphthongs, and the like. But essentially the process is simple. Semantic units were brought together, and changes took place as the units were more or less run together.

By PIE times, somewhat more than 5,000 years ago, this system of "putting-together" was well advanced. At the same time, vowels were being differentiated—sounds can be distinguished that now are written *a* and *o*, along with the old universal vowel, now written *e*, varied with color and stress, and many more consonants had developed. We have surveyed PIE vocabulary building above (see Chapter IX.4) but to have all this freshly before us we may as well look again at the root *per-*, which produced NE *for* and *fore*. It was used unchanged, as in *period;* in what is called *zero grade* (that is, it had lost its vowel), we have *prandial* from Latin; with change of vowel we have prefixes like *pri-*, *pre-*, and *pro-*, some of these being encouraged by suffixes.

Presumably *pro-*, as seen in *probable, proof*, comes from *pro-* plus *bhwo-*, meaning "straight," the whole meaning "straight forward." An extended form, *pres-*, provides the basis of *Presbyterian*, and another extended form, *preti-o-*, appears in *price* and *depreciate*. Another verbal root, *per-*, rang the changes on *par-* and *por-*, which with a suffixed form gives *ford* in English, *emporium* from Greek, *pan* from Sanskrit, and with another suffix in Latin, *-to-*, provides *port*, *portage*, etc. Another suffixed zero grade form, with *-si* added, becomes *heifer* in English and through Dutch, *farrow*. Another verbal root, *pere-* or *per-*, meaning "to give," "to allot," accounts for *parade, repair,* etc. A different suffixed root, *per-yo-*, appears in *peril, expert*, etc. A sixth form, with a nasal added, survives in *pregnant, imprint*, etc., and a seventh verbal root, *per-et*, meaning "to traffic in," appears in *prostitute* and *pornography*. That is, a common root like *per-* finds place in thousands of words in dozens of languages, partly because it was growing by affixing and compounding, certainly in PIE, probably also in whatever language preceded it.

As we have seen, especially in the loans from Classical languages, this process continued. More prefixes and suffixes were added in Latin and Greek, and while some of these were eroded in French and ME, more new ones were added. In short, we can now see why words borrowed into English from Latin and Greek tend to be longer than the native words. Grammar accounts for part of the difference; Classical tongues used grammars that relied on paradigms of endings, whereas English mostly discarded its endings. But word length involves the patterns of word building, also. The Roman and Athenian cultures were much more sophisticated than were the life styles of any Germanic peoples; accordingly, Romans and Greeks needed more terms, and they got them by affixing. When English became the medium of a sophisticated people, fashions had changed. English did not need to build up so many complex words; it could borrow them from Latin and Greek. And when speakers of English wanted terms they could not borrow, or devise from their own much less numerous affixes, they utilized the now popular analytic devices and built chains of words.

These processes have continued, until probably the liveliest source of word coinge today is the stringing together of old roots and affixes to make the new words that science and technology are demanding. Meanwhile, English, responding to the need for new names in new lands, had developed the practice of naming by coining chains, producing *sidewinders, diamond-backed rattlers*, and the like. During the same centuries, English shifted from synthetic patterns in grammar toward analytic patterns, and whether vocabulary-making was influenced by analogy, or whether some deeper sense of need led to similar devices for both grammatical and semantic purposes, the same sort of practice thrived in vocabulary. Speakers of English developed more and more chains, some falling into conventionally recognized patterns called *verb phrases, prepositional phrases,* and the like, some into chains less commonly noticed, *verb sets*, and a great variety of other idioms.

CHAPTER X

FASHIONS IN WORDS
Dialects, Usage

A dialect is not a degraded literary language; a literary language is an elevated dialect.

—Greenough and Kittredge

1. The Problem of Usage

Language is always in flux, and when it changes, it grows. Especially, a medium like the one that serves the English-speaking peoples, who are expanding geographically and socially, will every year add hundreds of new terms, new combinations of terms, and new uses for old terms. These new linguistic counters will be few when compared to the total word stock, a fraction of one percent a year; but even so, words and phrases in the various bodies of English speech—those in the British Isles, in Australia and New Zealand, in Canada and the United States, in South Africa and India, to mention only the largest—run into thousands of new locutions. Furthermore, many of these emergent uses, having been initiated through urgent need, will balloon and become much-used terms. A locution like *petrodollars* or *Camp David Accord* was used thousands of times within weeks of its coinage, and as we have seen in the previous chapter, combinations like *get by, get out, get better, give up, give in,* which were never used until recently, are now the common coin of everyone speaking American English.

Anything new will stir mixed reactions, including new vocabulary. Renaissance divines inveighed against Englishmen because they were so *newfangle*—a newfangled term that meant that they would grab at any new thing—but on the contrary, any confirmed Tory could be expected to reject anything recent, if for no other sin than recency. And new things are more likely to be condemned if they are thought to be different. Each

243

new term has its own experience. The life of a locution is unique, but some patterns can be observed; some trends in word coining can be broadly isolated, and some of the ways in which terms are welcomed or spurned can be studied.

2. The Speaker of English and His Verbs

Consider what happened to English verbs. Traditionally, they followed the general IE pattern in the bodies of speech that were to sire English, that is, the dialects of Germanic that had descended from PIE, but had not as yet been isolated in the British Isles. The verbs showed by their form how they were used; sounds that suggested past, plural, aspect, or person were incorporated within the verb and became part of its form, while sounds were introduced to give the verb another use, to work as a verbal, in what we might call verb-nouns or verb-modifiers.

Some verbs have preserved these sequences enough so that we can see what they were like. Many followed regular patterns: *sing, sang, sung; ring, rang, rung; write, wrote, written; ride, rode, ridden; give, gave, given.* The habit of expanding verbs in this way was lost, but for some centuries before and after the Germanic invasion of Britain the speakers in the English stream of language had unusual need for new verbs. During this time, new ways of making verbs were springing up, and the words and phrases needed to describe new experiences, and to adapt new borrowings, followed these new patterns. Various changes blended together. The old verbs lost some of their forms. Typically, *to carry* had the principal parts *beron, baer, baeron, boren;*[1] conjugation for person and number added such forms as *ber, beranne, berende, birest, bere, berab, baeren, birþ, birep.* Of these NE has left *bear, bears, bearing, bore, born.* *To come* appeared as *cuman, com, comon, cumen, cymþ, cymep,* and several more, but of these we have only *come, comes, coming, came.* These shifts have been made without trouble, but not so in all verb sequences. *Don, dyde, gedon* survives as *do, did, done,* but for centuries many speakers have not used *did,* but say *he done it,* as well as *he has done it.* There is nothing irregular in this; many verb forms have been dropped, and the survivors have picked up the uses of the lost forms, but here there is no agreement as to whether *did* can or cannot be superseded by *done.* Or rather, there is agreement among those who

---

1. They reveal the vowel changes in the root; with these basic forms the user of OE could derive all actual forms by grammatical rules.

decide what is right and what is wrong, but not among all users of the language. Similarly, *to drink* appeared as *drincan, dranc, druncon, druncen,* and survives as *drink, drank, drunk* or *drunken.* But do you say *have drank* or *have drunk,* and when can you use *drunken?*—not to mention regional forms like *drucken.*

Meanwhile new verbs were growing. With chivalry the word *squire* came into the language as meaning the young servant of a knight. To make this term into a verb, English used the noun form with no change (except the conjugation for person), so that Chaucer could have one of his ladies complain to her husband "because he [her youthful lover] squires me up and down you have caught a false suspicion." Past tenses were devised with a model of simplicity, by adding one of the commonest plosives, adapted to fit individual circumstances. In a word like *squire,* where the ending followed a voiced sound, it was the voiced /d/, *squired,* but if it followed a voiceless sound, it would appear as the corresponding voiceless /t/; and if a whole syllable was needed, the final plosive was preceded by a slack vowel—/ɪ/ or /ə/—written as modern *-ed,* so that the French noun *market* produced the verb *to market, marketed.* And this single new form served all uses referring to the past so that *squired* served for both *He squired her* and *He had squired her.* In modern pronunciation, many of these syllables have been reduced, and the voiced sound has become voiceless as in *escaped* /ɛskept/, *guessed* /gɛst/.

Thousands of such verbs were made in English or adapted to English; by themselves they gave no trouble. They were easy to make, easy to use, easy to remember, and the human mind is adaptable enough so that speakers of English knew, without being told, that there were two verb systems, one that added /d/ or some variation of it, and another that was somewhat irregular. But the trouble arose because, when there are differences and possible choices, not everyone will agree as to the choices to be made, and some alternatives will be more fashionable than others. These variants became the more confused because the new type of verbs increased so mightily that many of the native OE verbs seemed old-fashioned, or were thought of as crude or vulgar, and disappeared. These included many of the commonest OE shapes, like *fon,* "to seize," *niman,* "to take," and *weorthan,* "to become" or "to happen."

Many words were shifted from the old system to the new, and during the process—and in some instances today—one form would be "preferred," while the other (which might be either the new or the old form) was frowned on but survived. Among the verbs successfully shifted to the new style was OE *helpan, healp, hulpon, holpen,* meaning "to help," but even as late as 1600 Shakespeare was using *holp* as the past tense, while some of his younger contemporaries were writing *helped* or *helpt*. *Drink* was partially changed over, and then slipped back, leaving behind the form *drinked*, which is now thought to be "bad grammar" although in fact it is only a fashionable form that did not stay fashionable long enough to become standard. OE *dyfan* gives us both *dived* and *dove*; the new form *dived* became the only accepted form in the English court, but *dove* survived in the provinces, and was transported by immigrants to the American colonies. It was for a time considered dialectal or colloquial, but it is now recovering as a dignified term. One of the most confused is the modern word *think, thought*, which apparently preserves parts of two OE verbs jumbled together, *pencan* and *pyncan*. They developed forms after the new pattern, but these did not become popular enough, so that we have had *thinked, thunk,* and several others that have never become anything more than "bad grammar."[2]

Meanwhile, the fashion was developing to make what are called **periphrastic verbs**, sequences formed by combining a verbal form, such as *(to) study, studying,* or *studied*, with some common verb form used as an auxiliary. These auxiliaries included *shall* and *will*, forms of *to be* and *to have*, and modals (*may, might; can, could; ought (to)*, *would, could,* etc.), along with a great variety of phrasal combinations *to be going to, to be about to, to expect to, to start to, to be in a position to,* etc. Most of these new forms have slipped inconspicuously into the language, but not all of them.

2. The most fruitful in confusion has been the verb *to be*, presumably because it has been both the most common NE verb and the most irregular, the detritus from four old roots. It is as though the job of linking a subject to a complement was so onerous it wore out the words, and reserves had to be poured into the breach. The census is about as follows:

1) PIE *es-*, meaning "to exist," gives *am, is* (compare Sanskrit *asmi*); curiously, seen also in *sin*, "what one does."
2) *ar-*, Germanic form of unknown origin, gives *are*.
3) PIE *bheu-*, a widespread root that meant originally "to grow" and hence "to become," seen also in *husband, beam*, and many others, native and borrowed; it gives *be, been*.
4) PIE *wes-*, had an original meaning "to dwell." It gives *was, were. Wassail* is *wes hal*, "be whole," "healthy."

The most troublesome form is the contraction *ain't*. For a time, usually spelled *an't*, it enjoyed considerable respectability, more in the colonies than in the mother country. Fanny Burney used it in England and both Emerson and Thoreau in New England, and it was standard among the fashionable set in Charleston, S.C. In the United States today it is probably the most widely attacked locution. Some commentators accept *ain't I?* rather than the British *aren't I? Wan't*, formerly regional vulgate for *wasn't*, appears to be moribund. For an objective discussion, with bibliography, see Margaret M. Bryant, *Current American Usage* (New York: Funk & Wagnalls, 1962).

Do is instructive. It was a verb meaning "to perform," "to behave." Beowulf says, *Swa scal man don*, "So should a man behave." It developed various auxiliary uses: *do on* and *do off* have given us *don* and *doff* respectively. It has developed a wide variety of uses: as a substitute verb (She wanted to win and she *did*), in asking questions (*Do* you really mean that?), and as various sorts of intensives or concessives; notice the differences between *I did tell the truth* and *I did occasionally tell the truth*. *Do* and *did* were formerly used as auxiliaries indicating "to finish something" or "to order it finished," including finishing the life, killing, but this use mainly died out (the verb set *to do somebody in* may be an exception). In some bodies of speech, especially American Black English, both *did* and *done* developed auxiliary uses not always condoned. The old song has it, "People keep a-comin' an' de train *done* gone," which could be a descriptive preterite or a perfective, but it has not been accepted. Likewise, *be* appears in some British dialects where *is, am*, or *are* is standard and this use has been transplanted to some American— especially Black—speech, as in *They be mixed up all kinds of way.*[3] *Have you?* as against *Do you have?* has varied acceptance, and there is no agreement between Americans and Britons, even in supposedly standard usage, as to *get, got*, and *gotten* as they enter into periphrastic verb forms.

3. From Idiolects to Dialects

Everybody's life is unique, and every person's collection of terms, his understanding of them, his use of them, will have grown from his experiences, which will not exactly parallel the experiences of any other person; even if they could, he will have made different use of them because he is a distinctive organism. Thus everyone has a unique way of using language, which is called an **idiolect**. It will be a complex, of course, including pronunciation, grammar, words and phrases, and the individual's feeling for these. Here we are interested in idiolects insofar as they comprise vocabulary.

Idiolects may be analyzed roughly as being composed of two elements: (1) the results of whatever the individual does and has done because he is unique, and (2) the combination of dialects that have gone into this body of speech, which will again be a unique combination.

3. Cited with much other evidence in Ralph W. Fasold, *Tense Marking in Black English* (Arlington, Va.: Center for Applied Linguistics, 1972), p. 151.

A **dialect**, as I am using the term here, is a subdivision of language, a combination of language components selected through some outside forces and circumstances.

There are, for example, **regional dialects**. In A.D. 872 one Harold Fairhair, a Scandinavian ruler, defeated a number of his rivals and established himself as king of what is now Norway. Many of the disgruntled noblemen, with their adherents, left for an island that had been discovered to the west, now known as Iceland. Inevitably, they took with them their ways of speaking Old Norse. As we have noticed repeatedly, language always changes, and every body of language will change in many ways, in many directions. These two bodies of Old Norse were no exceptions, so that the total drift of the two was apart. After some generations, the Norse spoken in Iceland differed enough from that spoken in the mother country, Norway, so that the two bodies of speech became what we may call two regional dialects of North Germanic.[4] After a thousand years more of divergence we think of the two bodies of speech as two languages, although closely related, Norwegian and Icelandic.

This sort of divergence goes on constantly, everywhere. The physical distribution of human beings emphasizes the difference between one body of idiolects and another, although the break is not always as sharp and enduring as that between seagirt Iceland and continental Norway. The more sharply the two are isolated and the longer the separation continues, the more the ways of speaking will diverge.

When settlement from England built up in the colonies on the eastern coast of what is now the United States, culture tended to center on a few ports; those in New England, notably Boston and New York; those to the south, notably Philadelphia; and those farther south, on the Jamestown peninsula and Chesapeake Bay, and eventually to Charlestown and Savannah. Hinterlands tended to look toward these coastal population centers. Roads were few and not conducive to heavy hauling, but a river like the Hudson served to link the port city to the rural areas, north and west, and the ports were in touch both with one another and with the world at large. Thus the relative isolation of the settlements on the Atlantic coast tended to shelter each from its neighbors and to promote dialects, but in this conservation the terrain was only preserving and abetting what the patterns of immigration had established.

4. As so frequently in anything as complex as language, simple cases are rare. Here the development was regional, but variant social dialects must have been operative in the origin of the two bodies of speech. Harold's followers included many landed folk; the Icelanders included patrician families and their servants.

The immigrants brought different dialects with them. Those that centered respectively on Massachusetts Bay and Chesapeake Bay both came from the south of England, but from different parts of southern England and from different social strata. Lord Baltimore brought Catholics to Maryland, and the tobacco of Virginia attracted big planters along with the lower-class artisans that moneyed people needed, notably from London, even from the London jails. New England drew many Protestants, and Niueu Amsterdam remained polyglot even after it became New York. In between these were immigrants from farther north and west, including the Quakers brought by William Penn.

Thus three main dialects built up on the eastern seaboard of the United States: (1) Northern, extending south to a bit beyond New York City; (2) Southern, extending from Maryland south to the Spanish settlement in Florida; and (3) Midland, between them. This gave Midland much the narrowest base on the east coast when the dialects started moving west, but it had the advantage of the central position and fanned out to comprise much of the Middle West and most of the Far West. Population pressures in New England were eased by the growth of factories and shipping. Southern dialects were pretty much occluded by the devastation of war, so that even the speech of the Southwest developed on a Midland base.

Within these dialect areas sub-areas developed. For example, Southern broke rather readily into two. Along the coast, the fat lands encouraged plantations, with mass agriculture, tobacco, and later cotton, carried on as big businesses utilizing slave labor. Poor white immigrants could become artisans in that society, and many did, but they would not have the money to be planters or merchants. Many of the poorer folk moved farther inland, toward the mountains, where the land was thinner and generally poorer, but where they could become small farmers. Thus, these two areas tended to attract people with different social levels, with different speech, and once more the differences were accentuated by a degree of isolation.

4. The Working of Dialects

Dialectal divergence can be encouraged by any sort of isolation, and isolation in space is not the only possible type. Any kind of barrier, social station, wealth, education, occupation, even religion, may spawn dialectal differences. For generations, practitioners in the Church of Jesus Christ of Latter-day Saints had common qualities of speech, which persist in some areas today, so that what is a *farm* among the Gentiles is a *form* among the Mormons and *born in a barn* becomes *barn in a born*. Texas has at least six dialects that can now be distinguished. The plantation dwellers along the south Atlantic seacoast moved west through the Gulf States and influenced eastern Texas; meanwhile, Highland Southern filtered through the mountains into Tennessee and Kentucky, southwest through Arkansas, and altered speech in northern Texas.[5]

Often, the social dialect is the most permeating; George Eliot has one of her characters say:

> They're cur'ous talkers i' this country, sir; the gentry's hard work to hunderstand 'em. I was brought up among the gentry, sir, an' got the turn o' their tongue when I was a bye. Why, what do you think the folks hereabout say for "heven't you?"—the gentry, you know, says "heven't you"—well, the people about here says "hanna yey." It's what they call the "dileck" as is spoke hereabout, sir. That's what I've heard Squire Donnithorne say many's the time; "it's the dileck," says he.

There would have been at least three dialects spoken in the area, none of them distinguished by region—all these people were neighbors. There was the dialect of Squire Donnithorne and his fellows, albeit an accepted one—no doubt he would have been insulted if you had told him he spoke a dialect. Then there was the speech of the cottagers, locally called "the dileck," which they would have recognized was different from what the Squire spoke but, like him, they would not have called their own speech a dialect. Then there was a third use, the talk of the speaker and no doubt of others in the community who thought they had "got the turn o' their tongue," and they had, enough to be "hunderstood" by the gentry, but not enough to save them from being looked down on.

In short, everyone, in addition to his idiolect, speaks a dialect, you and I and Squire Donnithorne along with everybody else, or a blend of several dialects—George Eliot's speaker used a blend of at least two to make a new dialect, a regional dialect of the area, and a social dialect, which we might call an occupational dialect, since it was sustained by the speaker's being a personal employee of the Squire.

5. For a detailed study see E. Bagby Atwood, *The Regional Vocabulary of Texas* (Austin, Tex.: University of Texas Press, 1962).

We are here using the word *dialect* in so many senses that we should pause to distinguish them. To Squire Donnithorne the word *dialect* would refer to some body of speech he disapproved, not spoken by him or his family or their friends, or by important people anywhere. I have not been using the word *dialect* in that sense, and will not. To a student of language, dialects are like souls, at least in this, that they are all equal before the Lord. Each has its utility. Otherwise, it could not exist, because it has grown from older language materials to serve the needs of its users. And all dialects are precious because they preserve language. Thus, to a student of language there is no such thing as a bad dialect; but that all dialects are good does not mean that they are all good for the same ends or that they all serve an equal number of persons or offer a comparable spread of communication. Some are more practical, even much more practical than others; they serve more people for more uses. But the non-prestige dialects serve somebody. Otherwise they could not exist.

Whether we like it or not, the fact is that languages work by dialects. Languages, all languages, change constantly, and these changes always include tendencies to break up and to draw together. There are at once centripetal and centrifugal forces in language. Apparently any medium of communication that exists long enough, that serves as the means of communication for a group of people large enough so that we can call the medium a language, must fragment into dialects. That is the way language works, apparently the way it must work, so that to say a language has no dialects is only to say that it is dead.

Why does language work by dialect? We do not know in any detailed way; often in language study we can describe what happens, without being sure why it happens. Most people want language to remain fixed, and some try to keep it from changing by calling "wrong" anything that seems to be new. Why, then, does language not remain unaltered? Why did Englishmen not go on talking as the Angles and Saxons had? Why do natives of York, Chicago, and Melbourne speak differently? Part of the explanation is surely that language is learned anew by each generation and no learning is complete or accurate.

Of late this subject has been much studied, and to some effect. Most language learning is unconscious, and inevitably an infant will imitate its parents and siblings, especially the mother. That is, the pattern for learning is the speech of the home. But beginning about age five or six, the child acquires a new standard of speech; it tries to imitate its own peer group, the other children or some selection from them. Thus language change acts faster than had once been supposed, and a peer group provides a basis for language standards. Perhaps we can guess that the speakers of a dialect comprise a group large enough or cohesive enough to function as something of a unit. A dialect may represent a good equilibrium between the forces of change and the conservative forces that try to keep the language as it is.[6]

Above we defined a dialect as one of the ways a language works, although we might more accurately call it one of the combinations of ways. Thus we may speak of American English as a dialect or dialects of English, and we can use terms like Australian English, British English, and the like, which are collections of Australian and British dialects. Neither American nor British English is a single thing, so that we can speak of a Yorkshire dialect, a Lowland Scottish dialect, or any of several Texas dialects. We can even speak of the New Orleans dialect, or the dialect of the Lower East Side in New York. And these regional dialects will be combined with other linguistic influences, with the patterns heard on the floor of the Stock Exchange, with the talk associated with prize-fighters, with the technical speech of neural surgeons. Such limited bodies of language are dialectal and may be called dialects, but they are sometimes characterized as *cant* or *jargon*. And the speech of an individual person may be popularly called his dialect—*idiolect* is mainly a technical or learned term—reflecting as it must the influence of one or more dialects, whether regional, social, or occupational.

5. Use and Usage

Most words have several uses, these being what are popularly thought of as the word's *meanings*. They are approximated in dictionaries; the lexicographer may decide that a given word is used in four main ways, and will number these (1) through (4). He may find subdivisions within some of these categories and catalogue them under letters. Each of these senses will have also some social standing, some range and degree of acceptability, a concept that we may call *usage*, in contrast to *use* or *sense*.

Consider the word *cock*. It comes from Latin, presumably echoic, imitative of the sound of a startled chicken. Chaucer reports that when the rooster Chanticleer saw a fox, he "cride anon, Cok! Cok! and up he sterte [leaped]." *Cock* became the name for the male of any gallinaceous bird, was specialized to the male of chickens, and was extended

---

6. For the machinery of language change, see Chapter VII.6 above.

to any human male that strutted like a cock. It developed compounds like *cockerel, cockatrice, cocksure*, and phrases, including *cock of the walk* (a *walk* being a run for chickens, and the *cock of the walk* was the creature that dominated the place). It became a name for a spill or spigot, the latter perhaps because a *stop-cock* was thought to resemble the head and comb of the barnyard male. But now humor enters; the human penis was called a *cock*, possibly from a comparison with the *stop-cock*, possibly suggested by an erect penis pointed up, a meaning seen also in a *cocked hat*. The term started as slang and became vulgar, so that, although it appeared as early as the fifteenth century, most dictionaries have ignored the use. It must have been common: Shakespeare used it in a pun, "Pistol's cock is up," *Pistol* being the name of one of Prince Hal's rowdy friends, and *cock* having become the name for the hammer of a firearm.

Soon the use of the word *cock* as a sexual organ began affecting other uses of the term. In the sense of *stop-cock* it was largely replaced by *tap*, presumably from Old Norse, *faucet* from French, *spigot* probably from Old Italian; and the use of *cock* as the standard term for a male chicken was replaced with *rooster* in a few British dialects and almost universally in American English, although gallinaceous males are no more addicted than females to roosting. *Rooster* has found its way into Australia enough to account for the slang *ruptured rooster*, a cocktail. Neither Webster nor Worcester entered the use of *cock* as penis, and Webster explained rather lamely under *rooster* that the male is "the head of the roost." There has been some tendency to make fun of this American prudery about the word *cock*, replacing it with *rooster* even as part of a firearm; a writer in the *American Mercury* reported that "the local experts with the shotgun do not 'cock' it. Instead, they pull back both roosters." That is, *cock*, like most words, has developed various uses along with compounds, and each enjoys its own degree of respectability, although some uses may influence others, and the usages may change, becoming more or less respectable.

Obviously, usage is a complex problem.[7] And we have not even raised the question of usage as an adjunct of grammar, of the impropriety of *he don't* because it combines a singular subject with a plural verb (*do not* rather than *does not*) or the acceptability of the combination because it has become common. Likewise, what is the state in usage of *Mary and myself*, which most speakers in the United States now feel is appro-

7. For *taboo* as part of usage, see Chapter VI.7 above.

priately modest; they use it on all occasions, whereas for generations all handbooks of usage condemned it as ungrammatical and recommended *Mary and me*, now seldom heard. Rules and authoritative pronouncements will inevitably help, but command of the usage of the language requires wide acquaintance with contemporary practice and sensitivity to language impact.

6. The Patterns of Rectitude

Confusion arises in part because individuals want different sorts of things from language. Some want something new; they delight in slang, and are intolerant of rules and injunctions. Unconventional, even shocking language gives them a means to protest and revolt. Others want no change in language; they are convinced that alteration is corruption. They dislike anything new, and they tend to justify their pronouncements by logic, grammar, taste, or something else that they feel is enduring. They seldom know that what they defend is itself the result of innovation, that all language changes sooner or later, that the conservative uses of today are the radicalisms of yesterday, that grammar is not one thing but has internal contradictions, and that logic always has combined, and doubtless always will, with custom, even illogical, uninformed, and unreasonable custom, to direct the flow of speech.

Thus two distinct trends can be identified in modern usage in the United States, as in many other parts of the world. The traditionally approved view was *prescriptive;* adherents assumed that one locution was right and another wrong, or more frequently that one was right and all others wrong. The theory was that if you are intelligent enough and learned enough you can figure out the correct form by logic and grammar, and if you cannot, you should learn a rule for it and apply the rule rigidly in all instances. For example, *It is I* was said to be correct, *It's me*, incorrect. The reason was asserted to be that *I* is the actual subject of the sentence and should appear in the nominative case, not in the objective case, *me*.

This is logical, but it is not uniquely so. No grammar has ever been discovered that works on only one principle, and in English the principle that case form is determined by whatever has survived the ravages of the OE inflectional system is a minor one. Why should we prefer it to all others in this instance? Why should we not recognize that order is the basic device in NE grammar, and that *me* is the common form in the predicate? Or why should we not recognize that logic did not make language, nor has it ever controlled usage except sporadically, that language must have started as use, and that in language, use—logical or illogical—has determined usage in the past and will again?

Or consider, *Who* (or *whom*) *did you invite?* The prescriptive answer would be that *whom* is correct because *whom* is the objective form, and the word is the object of the verb *invite*. But *who* is now common and growing in use, presumably because *who*, although it is not logically the subject, seems to be occupying the subject position at the beginning of the sentence. Another example appears in *That is the silliest thing I ever heard of.* Prescriptivists formerly (although fewer recently) would have said this sentence should read, *That is the silliest thing of which I have ever heard.* The objection was that *of* is a preposition, that the term preposition means *pre-position*, and that the position at the end of the sentence cannot be *pre-* anything. Similarly, *She is older than me* was condemned on the theory that the sentence is "understood" to be, *She is older than I (am old).* Many dissenters would call this statement nonsense; they would say that *than* would here seem to be a preposition, and that the pattern of English is to follow a preposition with the objective form, in this instance *me*. They would say that the *I (am old)* sequence is not "understood," that the speaker does not think a sentence *She is older than I am old* nor does the hearer imagine such a sentence to grasp the meaning.

Thus the prescriptivist position can easily be shown to be questionable, even ridiculous, particularly when prescriptivists try to defend a construction like *than I.* But much can be said, as well, for the approach. It promotes standard, regular use, and it is the easiest for many people. Many teachers, and especially editors, tend to like prescriptive usage because style can be standardized with a set of rules that can be learned and applied. The most common problems in usage are few anyhow; the easiest solution for many people is to have a set of rules that can be learned, and when the rules have become second nature, can be forgotten.

By contrast, *usagists* deny that because one way of saying something is "right," all others must be "wrong." They assume that all ways must be good for something or they would not exist, and ask what each use is good for. They generally do not, as their adverse critics have sometimes charged, believe that "everything goes," in the sense that every locution is equally fitted to formal use, equally fashionable, or equally expressive. Rather, they avoid concepts like right and wrong, correct and incorrect, as being inapplicable to most of language, which they point out is neither wicked nor immoral of itself. It is bad only if it is badly used. They prefer terms like *appropriate* and *suitable*. They would say that the difference between *She hasn't any* and *She hain't got none* is not that the first is correct and the second incorrect, that the first is grammatical and the second ungrammatical, but that the two sentences have different effects, and that in modern speech there are few situations wherein *She hain't got none* will do the job the speaker wants done. Hence he had better avoid using it. They would point out that various locutions—grammatical constructions, idioms, and vocabulary—have their associated effects. To use the language well one should know it well and choose whatever will promote the desired effects.

7. Language Levels and Usage Labels

This fluid approach to use and usage works smoothly for the experts but not so naturally for those who cannot afford to spend their lives studying language. Usagists defend their approach by saying that it represents the truth. Whether we like it or not, language does work by use and usage, and we are only deceiving ourselves with simplistic generalities if we try to pretend there are rules that are always and forever true. Usagists try to temper the austerity of their recommendations, however, by recognizing what are called **language levels**. On the whole, use of language falls into a few natural situations, and we readily develop habits suited to these levels. Some language is highly formal, the Constitution of the United States, for example. Most of us may be unable to write or speak such language, but we may never need to, and meanwhile we have a sense of what it is and will know when it is appropriate. In sharp contrast would be **nonstandard**, or **vulgate**, the speech of unlettered people, who have inherited the talk of other unlettered people, and who jumble the whole, sometimes carelessly. Literate speakers readily understand such language, but they know better than to use it. On the whole, conversant speakers will recognize language levels like these, and will need only a little guidance in using English that is suitable to the occasions and the purposes and audiences involved. These language levels will become clearer as we consider usage labels.

Both prescriptivists and usagists have encouraged the setting up of usage labels, although on the whole the usagists have opposed very rigid categories and the prescriptivists have tended to want firm, even categorical condemnations. One of the broadest contrasts opposes **standard** to **nonstandard**. Standard would include all the locutions that pass current, wherever English is the native language, without occasioning censure and without being avoided by cultured, discriminating speakers and writers. It includes what is often called **edited English**, that is, the language characteristic of reputable publications of all sorts, plus some additional speech that might be avoided in print but would be used by educated persons in conversation, especially in their most familiar conversation. Nonstandard is everything else, any language that would not be used by well-informed speakers and writers. Such speakers, if they do use such speech, do so aware that the locutions are not generally acceptable.

This distinction between standard and nonstandard is neither objective nor eternal, but it is as near to being both as any criterion we have. Most educated speakers would agree about most locutions, and in general, criteria are now being somewhat relaxed. An example may be informative: *gut(s)* started as standard and most of the uses that have developed have remained so. It comes from an Old English word meaning "to pour out," and was probably a hunting or butchering term. It is paralleled by a British use of *pluck*, now mainly obsolete in the United States, meaning the entrails, what was "plucked out" of the carcass. By c. 1300 *guts* referred, also, to human viscera: the chronicler Robert of Gloucester wrote, "On him smot . . . In about þe fondement . . . & so vp toward [th]e gottes." The verb, meaning "to eviscerate," was apparently standard, as were a number of derived uses: a narrow passage on land or water (the *Gut* of Gibraltar), a prepared intestine *(catgut)*, silk from a silkworm, a few others. Some standard uses continue to develop; in Australia and New Zealand the *guts* is the drive shaft in a power sheep-shearing device.

With the nineteenth century, changes developed. Webster (1828) includes as his first definition an extensive description of the intestinal canal and gives no indication that the term *gut* is offensive in this sense, but his second and third uses are *The Stomach* and *Gluttony*, both of which are branded *Low*. Lexicographers contemporary with Webster, revising the British dictionaries by Ainsworth, Stornmouth, and Walker, found no occasion to condemn the use of *gut*, nor did the American Joseph E. Worcester (1860), but forty years later the *Century* was using Webster's term *low* to stigmatize *guts* as a term for "the whole digestive system," although it did not condemn the verb. At about the same time, the *Supplement* to the OED calls *guts* as "energy, verve, staying power" *colloquial*. The Funk and Wagnalls of 1898 said that *gut*, meaning an intestine, was "not in polite use," and that *guts* used to indicate the stomach was "vulgar," but made no adverse comment on *gut* as "the alimentary canal or any part of it.'' The much-venerated *New International*, second edition (1934), called *guts* "now coarse" in the sense of bowels or entrails, and "slang" in the sense of "belly; stomach; hence gluttony.'' Meanwhile, *gutsy*, which developed as Scottish, seems not to be condemned on either side of the Atlantic.

Suggestions that *gut(s)* is nonstandard are apparently declining, although not consistently. *Webster's New World* says of the sense "bowels or entrails": "Now generally regarded as an indelicate usage.'' It labels the sense "basic, inner or deeper parts" *colloquial*, the figurative uses for "courage" and "impudence" *slang*. The *Random House* and *American Heritage* dictionaries concur in calling the sense meaning "courage" *slang*, but make no comment on the other uses. Bergen and Cornelia Evans say that *"Guts* is now a coarse word, the mildest of the four-letter words, but outside the realm of polite usage.'' They call the American sense of "impudence" *slang*. The *Supplement* to the OED finds *gut*, meaning "basic, fundamental," and "instinctive and emotional rather than rational" as in "There are some gut reactions the pacifist must face,'' current and apparently not in bad taste. The most recent dictionary of usage[8] has the following:

gut reaction / gut feeling / gut issue

Gut reaction is a rather inelegant Slang phrase used instead of "instinctive reaction" in an effort to indicate honesty and forcefulness. A *gut feeling* is a deep feeling . . . . *Gut issues* are basic issues. Some politicians and businessmen consider these phrases suitable for emphasis but we do not.

A considerable number of slangy uses are unquestionably nonstandard: *bust a gut*, "to try hard"; *gutser* (Australian), "a disaster," especially in the air force; *gut-shoot*, "to shoot in the abdomen"; *gutful*, "too much"; *rotgut* or *gut-rot*, "bad liquor"; *gut bucket*, "crude jazz music," "a bass viol," "a pail to collect drainage," "any receptacle for contributions for food and drink,'' and several more.

A somewhat similar distinction is that between **formal English, informal English**, and **vulgate**. Formal English would include official documents, legal and technical descriptions, serious scientific and scholarly writing, standard reference works, and the more conservative discus-

8. *Harper Dictionary of Contemporary Usage* under *gut reaction*, etc.

sions. Informal English would include most writing in magazines, most nonfiction books and fiction insofar as it is not composed of quoted vulgate, relatively literate journalism, the correspondence and the more literate conversation of cultured people. Vulgate would be roughly equivalent to nonstandard, considered above.

Following are other usage labels:

Regional (which may appear only as an indication of the region: U.S., Sc. or Scottish, Anglo-Indian, etc.)   This label carries no usagistic implication; a regional term may be standard, but in a limited area, and hence may need explanation when used outside that area.

Field terms   These terms are professional, technical, specialized, etc.; they are likely to appear as *Boxing, Chem.* for *chemistry*, etc. They may be standard, but may need explaining for a general audience.

Dialectal   This term is somewhat variously used, sometimes as *regional* is used above, indicating use within a dialect, which dialect has a regional spread, but whose locutions are standard within that area. On the other hand, *dialectal* may refer to locutions that are felt to be nonstandard even within the dialect where they are known.

Colloquial   This term is mostly used in one sense as a usage label, but is often misinterpreted. Many persons accept it as meaning what is designated above by *regional* or *dialectal*, because they relate the word to *locus* or *local*. It derives from *loqui*, "to speak," and with informed speakers refers to uses that are appropriate to conversation but might be avoided in writing. The category *colloq.* would include a considerable portion of the terms under *informal* above. They are uses that would come naturally to cultured users of the language, but terms that might be restricted enough so that they would be appropriate with certain audiences, not with others. In conversation, the audience is always known and can be adjusted for. Mostly, colloquialisms would be included within standard.

Slang   This is a somewhat loosely used term. Popularly it may include almost anything disapproved by the speaker, including faulty grammar. As used by lexicographers it refers to locutions that have not yet become established, but may. Slang tends to be spirited, playful, transient. Slang terms may become popular and be so broad as to have almost no meaning, or they may be charming and picturesque but of limited currency. All slang is nonstandard. Usually, uses, not words, are slang. When *ripe tomato* refers to an edible garden vegetable it is standard; when it refers to a gushy or promiscuous female it is slang.

Illiterate   These are the least acceptable of nonstandard or vulgate speech. They include many locutions felt to be grammatically "wrong," such as *done* in *He done it*. Often such uses do not appear in dictionaries. They may be found in the glossaries of faulty uses that appear in handbooks.

Obsolete or **Archaic**   These are terms once standard, and still to be encountered in written form, especially in the older authors, but not likely to be used in current prose.

Poetic   These are terms once excused by what was called *poetic license: e'en* instead of *even, eftsoons*, etc. They are mostly archaic; to call them poetic is misleading; they would not be tolerated in good modern verse.

CHAPTER **XI**

MINDS AND MEANING

The self is surrounded by mirrors of language.
—Hans Hörmann

1. New Thought about Minds and Tongues

Minds make language. As we encounter it, language is a string of uttered sounds or a string of written or printed symbols, but these sounds and symbols are the machinery. Speech itself arises from the needs of minds, and it works through the medium of minds, particularly of minds interacting with one another in society. And language makes minds. Obviously, minds can exist without language and they can work without language, but language is for most purposes so incomparably the best mental tool that it subtly colors the way the minds work. To deal with his subject a specialist needs specialized terms, and the terms encapsulate his thinking.

These two, minds and language, interact with each other, a fundamental fact ignored for many centuries and only now gaining modest recognition. Thus recently two new interdisciplinary sciences have been born, known as **psycholinguistics**[1] and **sociolinguistics**, respectively the areas where language and psychology, and language and sociology, blend into each other. Neither of these areas is as yet well organized; we have no sure body of accepted doctrine for them, nor any agreement as to how research can best be pursued. Most of the research we have has not as yet been distilled into popular applications; thus this chapter will break some new ground.

---

1. For a scholarly survey, see Hans Hörmann, *Psycholinguistics: An Introduction to Research and Theory*, trans. H. H. Stern (New York, Heidelberg, Berlin: Springer-Verlag, 1971). For a more readable treatment see Roger W. Brown, *Words and Things* (Glencoe, Ill.: Free Press, 1958).

2. How Does Meaning Mean?

Speech has many uses. It does something to break through the cloud of loneliness that surrounds each of us—people talk to themselves. It makes people feel better; individuals become reassured and can admire themselves when they talk even though they may be boring everyone else. It eases the tensions of society: "Good morning. How are you?" "Fine, and you?" "Fine, too. Be seeing you." One person may be dying of cancer and the other suffering through a headache, but they both feel a little better because they have exchanged words and sentences, even though this language has little meaning. Language may provide a means of artistic expression, as any lover of poetry, either a writer of it or a reader of it, can testify, but more than anything else, language is intended to mean and does mean.

We know only vaguely how it means. It has no precise, exact, inevitable worth that can be measured objectively. In a very real sense, meaning is not in the language but in the users of speech. A speaker or writer knows—more or less exactly—what he wants to express, and he emits locutions that he believes or assumes embody this wish. The linguistic symbols are heard or read, and the recipient assumes—more or less confidently—that he knows the "meaning" of this body of language. In any precise way, neither of these assumptions is well-founded; no speaker or writer ever puts into a grammatical sequence of terms exactly what he meant to express. Likewise, no two listeners or readers will get quite the same "meaning" from the emitted language, nor will either of them apprehend exactly what the generator of the locutions had in mind. That is, for a speaker or writer, language is a means of allowing him to trust he has said what he meant. For a listener or reader it is a means of allowing the recipient to believe he has grasped what was intended. Any body of speech will trigger meaning, but never precisely the meaning of the begetter.

All this has a practical use that will allow us to simplify our thinking about meaning. Speakers and writers—unconsciously if not consciously —use the language as though it has an exact meaning, as though they know this meaning, and so will all other literate users of the language. Likewise, the listener or reader assumes that any body of speech has relatively objective meaning, a meaning that can be extracted, and normally will be, by any literate user of the linguistic medium. He is likely to believe further that his own interpretation is the right one, the only possible correct one in fact, a meaning so obvious that its rightness need not be questioned. All this is psychologically unsound, but it is a working fact, a fact of the way minds handle language, and as a working fact we can use it to work with.

People assume that words, even grammatical constructions, have meaning. Speakers and writers, listeners and readers, use these linguistic counters as though they have objective, measurable meaning. Consequently, in a practical treatment of language, we can treat them as though they do. Here we shall be doing for meaning what the phoneticians have done for sound when they recognized the phoneme. As we have seen, a phoneme has no measurable, objective existence; it is a learned approximation of what the users of the language accept. Rather, it is a formalization of about what users of the language associate with a symbol or an assemblage of symbols. Similarly, even though a spelling like *and* or *thermonuclear* has no objective, measurable meaning, we can use these words as though they do have a determinable meaning, because the users of the words mean to employ them that way.

3. Use and Meaning: Our Unwritten Social Contract

Even though no grammatical device has a use that can be exactly described, and no word or phrase has a meaning that can be weighed on a semantic scale, we do have a value for all linguistic units, a value that can be stated approximately and is commonly accepted. How did we get such a set of accepted values? Once more, we do not know exactly, but our community of feeling about language must have grown in part from our common means of learning language. Roughly, we all learned in the same way most of what we assume to be the truth about language. All speakers start even, with aptitude for language but no knowledge of it. If they are born into normal households, they hear language from birth and start imitating what they hear, as they start imitating what they see. They imitate badly, but as they gain control of their muscles— including those that contribute to seeing, hearing, and moving—they correct themselves. Most of all this is unconscious. If they are occasionally told to say one thing and not to say another, as they are told to drink their orange juice and not to throw the toothpaste down the toilet, this conscious learning is infinitesimal compared with what they learn without knowing they do so.

As the years go by, they learn the words their parents and playmates use, pronouncing them and assigning values to them that will approximate those of their family and friends. But these friends and relatives have acquired similar vocabularies, which they use in approximately the same ways, coupling them with similar applications of grammar. Thus, everybody grows up agreeing as to about what words mean and how they should be used, and anything else will automatically be assumed to be "wrong." Of course the language will be changing during all this process; none of the learners will ever acquire speech exactly as it is used by parents and friends, but users of the language will be no more aware of these changes than they were aware of the processes they used to learn language. They assume that language was born in them, that the way they use it is the right way, and that this is the way the language has always been and always will be.

Thus, henceforth in this chapter, I shall assume that words have meaning and use, and that these can be rather objectively determined. I shall assume, also, that these meanings and uses are approximated in all good dictionaries—even though the dictionaries differ from one another. And lastly, I shall assume that we can learn more about meaning and use when we have the occasion, since all dictionaries are abridged, including those that call themselves "unabridged."

4. Semantics: Names and References

Semantics, the study of meaning, is a recognized branch of linguistics, but until recently it was more the concern of the philosopher than the scientist.[2] With the fever to make the study of language rigorously scientific, the study of meaning, which is hard to make objective, was neglected, even frowned upon, but happily that day is past.

We have made a start on semantics in previous chapters, partly because words are not one thing and do not all "mean" in the same way. We noticed names; every person, some creatures, and many physical features have names. Such words provide the simplest sort of definition, pointing. If I say, "Will Joan Drackert stand up, please?" I have done essentially the same thing, and probably will produce the same result, as if I had pointed at the girl in question and said, "You. Will you stand up, please?"

That is, a proper name refers. It picks out a particular person or thing,

2. Related terms are *semiotics, semiology, semasiology.* In recent decades we have also had the term **general semantics** for the study of language in society, in propaganda, and the like. For a lively treatment, see S. I. Hayakawa, *Language in Thought and Action* (New York: Harcourt, 1949).

as though someone had pointed. If a child points, and says, "Who's that?" and the mother says, "That's Aunt Agnes," Aunt Agnes the woman is what is called the *referent* of *Aunt Agnes* the name. Similarly, if the child asks, "What's that?" and the mother replies, "That's a kitty," the cat is the referent of the word *kitty*. That is, the word points, and in this context that is about all it does.

In passing we should mention what are sometimes called **aspect names**, terms that become names. In introducing a female, instead of the name *Mary*, a man might use any of the following, depending on his relationships to her: *my wife, my beloved, the guiding spirit of our household, my closest companion and severest critic, my daughter, our youngest, Jane's sister, my son's fiancée, our neighbor, our cleaning woman, the wife of Senator Jones, our best customer*. During the Middle Ages, Mary the wife of Joseph, became not only *The Blessed Virgin* and *Mother of Jesus*, but she acquired hundreds of other aspect names in many languages: *Reine de Paradis* (Queen of Paradise), *Felix Fecundata* (She Who Was Happily Impregnated), *Flour of Alle Thinge* (Flower of Everything), *Parens et Puella* (At Once Mother and Daughter), *Rosa Sine Spina* (The Rose Without Thorns), *The Wellspring of Virtues, Mother of Mercy, Bright Star of the Sea*, and dozens more.

We are now in a position to offer a very simple definition of a proper noun: A *proper noun* is one that, as used, has only one *referent*. In the sentence, "Lacelles Abercrombie wrote *The Sale of St. Thomas*," the first two words refer only to one human being. There probably have not been two writers of verse dramas named *Lacelles Abercrombie*; the sequence has only one referent.[3] In contrast, the word *kitty* is not a proper noun, although it could be so; a girl whose name is Catherine might be nicknamed *Kitty*. But the term *house cat* does have a referent; it is a way of pointing. The word *cat* may do many things. Used by an adult, it may imply that somebody is a *catty* person, but in the sense that the word has a referent, it does relatively little, and does much the same thing for everybody. This is one of the few ways in which a word is the same for all of us. Of itself it may tell us little; it does not reveal whether the creature is mangy or sleek, male or female, but it does tell us that the object is not an automobile, a mayor, or a virus.

3. As a matter of fact the name need not be unique to be a proper name. James Jones wrote *From Here to Eternity*, and there have been thousands of persons named *James Jones*, but the name was a proper noun in each instance, since it referred to only one of these Joneses in any one sentence.

We should note in passing that a word may have as many referents as it has uses. The word *cat* may refer to a domestic feline, but it may also be used in a sentence like, "The lion is one of the great cats," in which *cat* still refers to a quadruped, but to a somewhat different one. *Cat* may also have a piece of machinery as a referent, since it is a slang term for a caterpillar tractor. It may refer to a whip, since *cat* became a shortened form of *cat-o'-nine-tails*. It may refer to a capstan and have that as a referent. Should the word *Cats* become the name of a football team, the word would immediately acquire a new sort of referent, a human being, one of a certain group of athletes.

This concept of the referent helps us to see how some words mean. The impact of a word like *cat* may combine the referent, which will be the same for all of us whether we love cats or suffer from a phobia about them, plus our individual feelings about cats, which will not be the same for any two human beings. But for some words the concept of the referent does not help much. On the whole the notion works best for physically existent objects like cats; it is less useful with more abstract terms. Take *beauty*; what is beautiful for one person will be ugly, homely, fussy, messy, maudlin, or dull for another. And many grammatical terms have no referent at all; what is the referent of *the, of,* or *why*?

As we have seen in Chapter II, closely related to the concept of the referent is that of naming. A baby is called *Mary*, and thereafter the sound /meri/ (in some dialects) and the letters M-a-r-y "mean" a certain small creature, a baby girl, who eventually becomes a larger creature, a woman. This meaning would work for the family, and eventually for some other persons, some neighbors perhaps, and at least in one instance *Mary* came to have meaning for the whole world. Something similar works with many common nouns; presumably the child's name for its maternal parent had something to do with our words *mama* and *mother*, and although these relationships may not be one thing, the giving of the names and the use of words for reference to a class as well as pointing at an individual become involved in what we call meaning.

5. Words in a System

We have seen that the great bulk of English words—and consequently the bulk of meaning—comes by growth from within the IE language family (see especially Chapters III–V) either by direct descent within the English ancestry or through borrowing from other IE languages. We have observed, also, that wherever these linguistic shapes and their uses came from, the speakers of English in the course of using their inheritance of terms, have built them into a system—or a system of systems. Word patterns color what the words can do, and more particularly what they do in any given use. If I call something "a dead soldier," the object may be a human being if we are cleaning up after a military engagement, but it may be an empty bottle if we are cleaning up after a party. If we are in the Australian bush, it may be a defunct red ant or a bird, and if we were trying to pull your car out of the mud, it might refer to a bar of wood or iron that we had buried to provide an anchor. These meanings do not exist because of the environment, but the selection among various uses almost always will hinge upon the circumstances of use.

Even though the formal meaning may not change, the import for both the user of language and its recipient will be altered subtly by a great variety of background that may never be mentioned but will be understood. Assume that I have said, *Bill drinks*.[4] If you and I are planning a party, and we know that Bill comes from a prudish family, I may be reassuring you that you can serve wine without embarrassing either you or Bill. If you are considering hiring Bill for a very delicate assignment I may be warning you that Bill may not be the person you want. If I have just told you that Pam is suing Bill for a divorce, and you have expressed surprise that any woman would want to divorce a man as handsome and wealthy as Bill, I may be offering an explanation. In the following sequence the words would have a fourth use: *He wanders for hours in the desert, and finally stumbles onto a desert well. Bill drinks and drinks.*

In each of the uses it "means" differently than in the others. In the first it means that Bill has no religious, social, or other scruples about consuming alcohol, at least socially. In the second it means that Bill has what is sometimes called "a drinking problem," and that on some occasions he may be untrustworthy. In the third I am in effect accusing Bill of being an alcoholic. In the fourth use *Bill drinks* means only that he is supplying his bodily need for water. The form of the word is the same in all four uses; even the referent, insofar as *drinks* can have a referent, is the same. But the meanings, in the sense of what I mean to say and you probably understand, are quite different. To a greater or lesser degree, differences like these affect every sentence and many of the words in them.

4. I have borrowed the example, somewhat altered, from George A. Miller, "Psychology and Communication," *Communication, Language, and Meaning*, Miller, ed. (New York: Basic Books, 1973), pp. 10–11.

Take the single word POOL. Printed in boldface type at the left margin of a dictionary it has almost no meaning to a user of the book, but if it is the word you want to look up, you know you have come to the right place. Printed on a board or other raised sign it may mean that you are at "the part of the Thames (River) between London Bridge and Cuckold's Point." If the signboard takes the form of an arrow and appears in a resort hotel, it may be directing you to a place to swim. If it is lettered on an American building, particularly a commercial building in a not very reputable area, it may mean that for a fee you can there play billiards. On an open enclosure it may mark the car pool, where an authorized person may be assigned an automobile. In a building it may identify Dr. Pool's office. In Canada the word may indicate a grain operation or a railroad train, although the word is not so likely to appear singly.

Words also appear in grammatical systems, and will be altered in meaning by the grammatical pattern. A vehicle has the following sign: *This Truck Being Driven By a Blind Man.* If *blind* is here an adjective, the sign is frightening. If, however, it is what is called an adjunct, that is, a noun being used to modify, the *blind man* is a man who puts up Venetian blinds, and he will probably not drive his truck into you. Or we might notice the sequence attributed to Chomsky: SHIP SAILS. If *ship* is here a noun, then *sails* must be a verb, and the two of them record the fact that a vessel is putting to sea. On the other hand if *ship* is a verb, as it might well be in a telegram, *sails* is a noun and the sequence becomes an order for a shipment of marine gear. The world and human life fall into patterns, and words follow the patterns—*arctic, temperate zone, tropics; babyhood, childhood, youth, middle age, old age.* Each of these means something as part of a pattern that it would not mean alone.

Furthermore, human beings force their social patterns on the natural ones. Color provides the most famous example. Color results from different wavelengths and the degree of light; these are the same the world over, but probably no two cultures see color in the same way because peoples have segmented the color continuum variously, have given different values to light as against wavelength, and have given these segments names. The names have then altered the way we see color. Many societies have associated *red* with blood, *green* with grass and foliage, *blue* with the sky or with water. Other groups, including many North American Indians, have seen mostly light and dark, and have lumped most of the shades into a term associated with darkness. Gray and other middle sorts of tints constituted a second category, and all the bright colors acquired names suggestive of sunlight or snow. Even closely related societies may not use the same color terms. French has no word comparable to English *brown*, but uses *brun, marron*, and *jaune*, terms for colors that would overlap with colors called *cinnamon, orange, yellow*, and some others in English. *Royal purple*, a color obtained from shellfish, was more nearly what we would call *crimson*, and *pink* is close to what many societies think of as *rose*. Russian has no word for *blue*, but uses two words, one that we would call *light blue*, another *dark blue*. *Red* is such a broad spread of color with speakers of English that we have dozens of terms for it: *cerise, scarlet, crimson, Chinese red, brick red, turkey red, fire engine red, chrome, ruby, garnet, maroon, claret, rust, russet, terra cotta, magenta, damask, coral, solferino, nacarine, hyacinth, rose, morocco, caldron, aniline*, and dozens more, shading into pink, purple, and brown. Aquamarine, the color of sea water, has many equivalents in many languages, most of them with no clear equivalent in English. Homer may have been colorblind; at any rate, he has used such color terms that translators of the *Iliad* and the *Odyssey* have not known what to make of them and have had to obscure their uncertainty under such epithets as *the wine-dark sea*. What color is wine? We do not know, and about all that can be said with certainty is that, like beauty, light and color are in the eye of the beholder, and that the eye of the beholder is in turn tinted or shaded, lightened or darkened by the color terms his language includes.

6. Meaning and Field Theory

Lately the concept of semantic fields has grown—although the fields are not very sharply defined—and these fields have something to do with meaning and the interplay of uses. These fields are in constant flux, shifting with the rise and decline of various terms. Obviously, transportation and communication are now larger fields than they used to be, whereas baptism and sea serpents are smaller. Others have changed almost imperceptibly.

Consider collective names for young people. All societies will include some, and presumably when life expectancy was short, young people would have constituted a large part of society. Our scanty records supply few names for them in OE. They could be *juguth*, our word *youth*; the boys could be *cnappan* and the girls *maegden*. The plowman in Aelfric's *Colloquy* says he has *sume cnappan* (which might be freely translated *a bunch of kids*) to goad the oxen; *maegden*, modern *maiden*, implies virginity. A young servant was a *cnicht*, a student a *leornungcnicht*, "a learning servant." As a group these young people could be called *cildra* (modern *children*), and there were *sons* and *daughters*. If *babe* and *baby* were used, we have no record of them. There were slang terms; a baby could be called, at least in Old Norse, *a milkbeard*. At about the time of Chaucer and a little before, a number of terms came. *Infanse* (*infant*, meaning "not speaking") could be anyone not an adult. A *bachelor*, who could be married or unmarried, was a young man of station, as was a *squire*. There were *prentyses* (apprentices), and *boyes* (mostly servants and young rascals), and *gerles* (girls), who could apparently be either male or female. There were *lads*, male servants or other males of low birth, and in the north of England, *lasses*, "unmarried women" (the word not related to *lad*).

Partly, we have more terms for young people in ME than in OE because we have more records, but partly we probably can assume that more terms are now crowded into the same semantic field, and the old words must have yielded some of their currency to the newcomers. Thus when *prentys* became a common term, the other words for young lower-class males, words like *lad, gerl,* and *cnicht* must have relinquished some of their use to it. And *juguth*, about the only surviving OE term for a young man—except *young man*—was shrunk with the new popularity of *bachelor* and *squire*. This play of new words for young people continued, and in our own time we see the arrival of *teenager, bobbysoxer, dropout, student, kid, youngster, miss, coed, undergraduate, pupil, juvenile, minor, stripling, fledgling, urchin, adolescent, nonadult, young learner, tenth-grader, twelfth-grader, freshman, sophomore*, and many more. There are other terms in Canada, Australia, and the British Isles. Accordingly, a similar semantic field—or a smaller one, since the average age increases every year—must accommodate many more terms, and inevitably each of these occupies, on the whole, less semantic territory than would have been characteristic a few centuries ago.

7. Exponential Analysis

Recently, some scholars have pursued what is called **exponential analysis**. The idea is this: words may imply units of meaning, but they also imply clusters of meaning made up of smaller units. Consider the word *bull*; the word implies *animate* as against *inanimate*; *quadruped* as against other forms of life, for example *reptilian*; *bovine* as against *lupine* or some other classification of quadrupeds, *male* as against female, *virile* as against *castrated*, and the like. Obviously, this approach would work with a number of other words. *Boys* could be distinguished from *girls* by such an approach, *diamonds* could be contrasted to *putty*, *nations* could be distinguished from *hamlets*, and the like. The original hope was that these components, these limited areas of meaning, could be so drawn that they would be universal, and all words could be distinguished from all other words in meaning through a single set of objectively measurable components. Understandably, this ideal has not been attained; all clusters of meaning can be broken into components, but the set required to distinguish chemical elements from one another will not serve as the set to isolate barnyard animals.

Even if this technique can be perfected so that it does infallibly isolate each word from all others, it may have only limited uses. At best, the more nearly complete and objective it becomes, the more cumbersome it will have to be. Nor does it respond very well to the way minds work. It is not likely to suggest the prudery with which the term *bull* has at times been viewed. Neither will it reflect the attitude of the person who dreads being caught in an open field, face to face with a charging bull. It is not likely to parallel the feelings of an *aficionado* who is following the action in the bull ring. It would face handicaps handling what a bull does and what he inspires in a society, like that in parts of India, where bovines are sacred. The approach does not handle well even such a measurable but variable fact as that a bull may or may not have horns.

8. Synonyms, Antonyms, Homonyms, Specific Equivalents

A few tried and true approaches have long been used to investigate meaning. They are still useful, if not very useful. The commonest is *synonymy*, a word made up of *syn-*, "together," and *onyma*, "name," the implication being that this is another name for the same thing, that the two synonyms have the same meaning. A *son* is a boy or a man, and a *boy* is always somebody's son, and thus the two may have the same referent, John Jones; but the two imply somewhat different things about John—they mean differently. If there are exact synonyms they are rare indeed, but the concept of synonymy can be useful. One word can be substituted for another, one phrase can replace another; *recover one's health* is synonymous with *get well, get better, get over an illness*, and the phrases can be used in various sentences having the same intent, even though a discriminating writer would prefer one to another in a given context. Often, in fact, the true quality of a word or phrase will appear only after we have discriminated synonyms, and have endeavored to describe for ourselves the differences among terms like *define, distinguish*, and *discriminate*. In fact, the concept of synonymy has its greatest use in words of this sort, relatively abstract words whose meanings blend into one another. Words that have referents usually do not have many synonyms, or anything approaching an exact synonym. What is the synonym of *eye*, or *football?* Words of this sort are more revealingly dealt with under the concept of *specific equivalents* (see below).

Antonyms are terms that theoretically have opposite meanings, and if exact synonyms are scarce, exact antonyms are not likely to be more frequent. Within limits we can have antonyms; the word *down* can have an almost exact antonym in *up*, in the sense that each is limited to direction. In other senses the words will not be antonyms; *drink it down* is more nearly a synonym of *drink it up* than it is an antonym. But antonyms do help reflect meaning. We have a better understanding of *down* because we also have the word *up*. The book title *Up the Down Staircase* gains impact from the opposites involved as well as the symbols that are suggested.

Homonyms have the same sound. They may have the same spelling, as *bear* can mean either a furry animal or carrying something, or the same sound may be spelled *bare* and mean "without covering." Homonyms may have a common origin; in *A good father can do good with his goods*, all three uses of *good(s)* have a common source, but the *ear* that is corn on a cob is etymologically different from the *ear* that hears. Homonyms are intriguing, and troublesome to bad spellers, but they do little to illuminate meaning or use.

Quite the contrary are terms that I have called *specific equivalents*.[5] Consider the word *horse*. In the sentence, *Sharon bought a horse*, we could substitute the term *colt, mare, gelding, stallion, racer*, or even *Morgan, Arabian, quarter horse, Clydesdale, Percheron*, etc. The meaning would be the same, except that the substitution of a term like *Clydesdale stallion* makes the sentence mean more. This is often the best way to handle concrete terms, to make them more concrete and specific. Only in a limited way can such substitutions be referred to as synonymy; a colt is obviously a young horse, and may be a *yearling*, but most horses are not colts any longer. The meaning of the sentence is thus not essen-

---

5. A more esoteric term is *hyponymy*. For an explanation and defense of its use, see John Lyons, *Introduction to Theoretical Linguistics* (Cambridge: Cambridge University Press, 1968), pp. 453-6.

tially changed, but it is refined. Another term for this handling of meaning is *inclusion*, since the idea of *colt* and *gelding* are both comprised within the concept *horse*.

9. Etymology and Meaning

A good bit—perhaps too much—has been said of etymology in this book. If the idea has never been put baldly and bluntly, that knowing the origin and growth of a term will enhance our sense of its meaning and sharpen our feel for its use, the notion has been implicit in chapter after chapter. Anyone who has worked through the survey of *for/fore* in English and the corresponding terms in Latin—*pre-/pro-/per-*, etc.— must have gained insight into many locutions in both languages. One would even hope that etymology might have social impact; *man* means primarily "a human being," and "the male of the species" is only secondary. One would hope that knowledge of that fact might encourage the more feverish of the feminists to concern themselves with more significant concerns than any sexist overtones that linger in words like *chairman* and *manhole*. If nothing else, etymology can promote interest in words and induce people to think about them. And of all the questionable generalities about language, this one is surely not in doubt: the more one works with words, the more time he spends with them, the better he is likely to use them.

But a caution may be in order: the etymology of a locution can never set the limits of a term, and no one should try to make it do so. At times, members of what we might call "the school of usage and abusage" have attempted such policing. They have, for example, objected to the use of the word *aggravate* to mean "to irritate or make angry," pointing out that the Latin *aggravare* meant "to make heavier." This is sheer pedantry. We may probably safely say that no word exists that has not undergone change. All locutions current in English, or in any other tongue, take their form and meaning from the users of the language, only secondarily from their origin. Whatever the great body of speakers of English want a word to mean, that is what it will mean, wherever it came from and however this use was developed. However dubious the theory may be in morality, in meaning, "Whatever is, is right." To assume anything else is simply to ignore the nature of language. Etymology can offer many helps in studying language and in using it, but there can scarcely be a more idiotic "abusage" than trying to limit a locution to its etymology.

10. Denotation and Connotation

These two terms long comprised much of the thinking about meaning, and they still have their uses. Speaking broadly, the denotation of a word is what is likely to appear as the sum of all its uses in a good dictionary. Connotation implies the emotional impact of a locution. Thus, in theory, the denotation of a word would be roughly the same for all persons who command the term. Connotation would inevitably be individual; *mother* presumably has lively connotations for all sons and daughters but will not be identical for any two of them. Within limits, this distinction—between the formal "meaning" of a word or phrase and the effect it is likely to have on readers and listeners—is valid and revealing. The limitations of the terms are obvious: they are not very precise, and they cut across approaches to meaning that seem to be more nearly measurable. But they work, perhaps especially for relatively inexperienced users of the language. And if they work, one can only say, let them do so.

11. The Future of English Vocabulary

In a broad way we can predict the future of the English word stock with some certainty. Mainly it will grow, and along the lines traceable during the last century or so. Shapes will increase, uses will grow, and meaning will be refined.

First we might notice a few principles of language change and language survival. Language always changes, but unless its users suffer, it survives and grows. Some changes may be rapid, appearing without much warning and vanishing as quickly. Innovations are mainly unpredictable; we cannot know which words will become slang epithets for nubile teenagers, nor how long these exuberant growths will last, but we know there will be such fads and that most of them will not last long. Slang as a phenomenon can be predicted, but the individual slang uses cannot be. Or, to put this more broadly, whatever springs up quickly in language may die as quickly, but once deep-rooted movements become an integral part of a language, they are likely to continue for a long time, and even to decline as slowly as they grew. For thousands of years, English structure has been moving toward reliance on compounding, and especially on phrase-making. That this trend would stop in a few years and that English would suddenly develop elaborate new systems of inflection and conjugation is unthinkable. Likewise, the vocabularies of the languages that have given us NE have been growing for thousands of years. NE vocabulary will not stop growing, and it will continue to produce new terminology in the twenty-first century very much as it has in the twentieth.

Thus, to envision the future English word stock, we have only to review the growth of the present vocabulary. The United Kingdom, the United States, Canada, and Australia/New Zealand—these four at a minimum—are likely to prosper as communities and to grow as forces in the world; therefore, the English language will grow. Political and social directions in China, India, South Africa, most of the Arabic-speaking countries are less predictable, and consequently the future of English is less obvious for these areas; but once more, if our forecast is broad enough we can make reliable generalizations. As a second language, English has grown and it will continue wide and various use.

We can even predict many of the kinds of growth. Terms in technology and science will continue to burgeon, with new fields of knowledge and new terms in the old ones. Recently a new area has been promoted, including such specializations as *cryonics, cryogenics,* and *cryobiology,* collectively the study of the effects of very low temperatures on matter.[6] It includes freeze-drying, quick-freezing, and preservation that is called *suspended death.* It is developing its own vocabulary, and as we could predict, this terminology follows the practices well known in the older sciences. The names are coined from the Classical tongues; *cryo-* comes from the Greek for "frost." Established words are slightly changed; bodies preserved by cold are put in a *dormantory*—a *dormitory* is for the active. There are other terms like *cryocapsule* for a device that preserves a prospective *resuscitee.* Overwhelmingly the new terms are phrases, chains of words or syllables, partly from NE, partly from Classical bits: *cryonic suspension, dead patient, cadaver-patients, freezer-program, freezing and reanimation,* fifty or so terms in a few years.

Perhaps equally numerous, and much more widely used, will be the terms generated by new ways of living and new concepts. Awareness of the cyclical character of an industrialized economy popularizes a sequence like *recessionary period.* Attention to the effects of wonder drugs makes a phrase of *side effects,* and terms like *fallout,* which became a household word with atomic bombs, acquire figurative uses. Anything incidental and disastrous can now be called *fallout,* and these sorts of

6. See W. T. Gordon, "The Vocabulary of Cryonics," *American Speech,* 50 (1975), 132-5.

derived uses will continue. Furthermore, as we have noticed, such terms used by serious commentators dealing with affairs of moment gain immediate acceptance, and are likely to go on doing so. Most people are unaware they have only recent currency; they are taxed with being neither slang nor misuse. Thus the bureaucrat and the board chairman are to a degree replacing the local dialect-speaker as an innovator in vocabulary, and such shifts are likely to continue.

In short, to plot the future of English vocabulary, we need to study what our words have been and what they are. In a broad way, in language, whatever has been will be—with infinite and unpredictable variety in the details.

CHAPTER **XII**

APPENDIX
A Tool Kit for Studying English Words

If you can teach me a word, I'll walk all the way to China to get it.
—Turkish proverb

1. The User of English and His Tools

A good workman needs good tools, and he should know how to use them. We are all workers in words, all of us who try to use our native language well. This chapter will describe the most useful tools.

Surprisingly, most users of English do not know why the common tools are made as they are, and accordingly do not know exactly what to do with them. The schools should teach all young users of English how word-tools should be used, and no doubt one day they will. But that day is not yet, and even when an informed program is well started, many years can be expected to elapse before the information has seeped through society.

2. How Word Books Got That Way

Historical reasons account in part for the state of our ignorance. An early volume was that by Elisha Coles, *An English Dictionary, Explaining Difficult Terms* . . . (London, 1685). Coles and other lexicographers of his day leave us in no doubt as to what they thought they were doing when they created a book. They assumed that they were learned men, that they knew, and that they were addressing ignorant people who did not know—common folk who would not be able to do much more than read simple prose and write enough for record keeping, foreigners, children, and relatively unlettered tradesmen. These presumed users of the books would have been the first to admit they did not know how to speak or write well, even how to use the language without gross blunders. They were glad to be told. The editors of these books frankly admitted that the volumes were not intended for gentlemen and ladies, who would be familiar with all the common words and would know how to use them. As for writers, Shakespeare, Milton, and their contemporaries probably never saw such books; if they did, they would not have used them. The books were intended to help ignorant people with what they would consider "hard words."

Accordingly, Coles included only one meaning for the word *horse*, as follows: "A rope fastened to the foremast shrouds, to keep the spritsail sheats clear of the anchorflookes." He does not mention that horses are also quadrupeds that can be ridden or driven, and that other four-footed objects like *sawhorses* can be used by workmen. If you had tasked him with these omissions he would have pointed out that everybody knew those uses of *horse*, and that he was including only the "hard words" or the rare uses of common words. And in fact when, during the next century, Nathaniel Bailey produced a much better dictionary and included *horse* in the commonest sense, he dismissed it by calling it "a beast well known." He told you nothing about this beast, except that the word could be used for either sex. For anything you can learn from him, it may resemble anything from an aardvark to a zebu.

With the eighteenth century, the idea of a dictionary grew, or more likely was imported. The idea that a dictionary may have entries defined by examples of use, by what are now called *citations*, apparently sprang up in Italy, as did so many ideas, was imported into France, and thence got across the Channel to England. Dr. Samuel Johnson was impressed and contracted to write a great dictionary of the English language. He did not, however, have the notion of a modern dictionary at that time. He must have been aware of the idea that Voltaire wrote into his dictionary, as follows:

All languages being imperfect, it does not follow that one should change them. One must adhere absolutely to the manner in which the good authors have spoken them; and when one has a sufficient number of approved authors, a language is fixed. Thus one can no longer change anything in Italian, Spanish, English, French, without corrupting them; the reason is clear: it is that one would soon render unintelligible the books which provide the instruction and the pleasure of the nations.

By *fix* Voltaire did not mean the commonest American use of that word today; he meant that one could establish a language so firmly that it would never change again. Nobody has ever been able to fix a language in this sense, and presumably nobody ever can, but neither Voltaire nor Johnson knew this; the idea of permanence in speech was widely accepted.

Johnson spent years creating his dictionary, and in the process he educated himself. When he finally published it he included an apology, asserting—and one must believe him—that when he promised to fix the language, he had honestly trusted he could. He had now become convinced that nobody can, and he apologized to those persons whose money he had taken to edit and publish the book. Apparently nobody complained much, probably because few people knew about his confession; most people do not read the introductions to dictionaries. The book became one of the landmarks of English language and literature.

During the next century, when Noah Webster set out to prepare what became *An American Dictionary of the English Language* (1828), he, too, believed he could fix the English language in the New World. Like Johnson, he was a smart man, and he learned better, but few others did, and during the great War of the Dictionaries that enlivened American life toward the middle of the nineteenth century, one of the questions was still, which was the authority, Webster or his younger contemporary Joseph E. Worcester? *Authority*—authority for correctness—that was what users of a dictionary expected of it, what they thought they were paying for when they bought it, and few of them would have imagined that such a volume is an impossibility, or would have had the background to understand why.

Then came the OED. Started in the late 1850s as a project of the Philological Society of England, it was promoted by a number of distinguished scholars, of whom Richard Chevenix Trench, dean of Westminster, was as much as anyone the articulate voice. He asserted firmly that "in the treatment of individual words the historical principle will be uniformly adopted." By this time, what was meant by "the historical principle" was fairly clear. Roughly it was this: each word, and each use of a word, should be traced historically. That is, its first recorded occurrence in the language should be noted, every new use of the word should be recorded and dated, and the word should be traced so long as it continued to be used. Anything worth knowing about a word—its spelling, its meaning, its usage, and its pronunciation, insofar as that could be inferred—should be based upon the appearance of the word in existing records. The purpose of the dictionary would not be that of Elisha Coles' little volume two centuries earlier, to tell ignorant people how to use English. Nor would the dictionary pose as an omniscient judge, determining what is eternally right and what irremediably wrong. The book would be intended to describe the language, as fully and reliably as possible in the space available.

The job was pursued on both sides of the Atlantic and took more than three-quarters of a century to complete. It survived various publishing arrangements, and several editors, and was not finished until 1933 under the aegis of the great lexicographer C. T. Onions. Meanwhile, it had colored two good American dictionaries, the *Century* (which was based on the principles of the OED, but was much briefer), and the *New International*, which resulted from a thorough revision of Noah Webster's old book. Thus, by the twentieth century the new notion of a dictionary was well established for English. Never again would a scholarly dictionary presume to tell people what use they should make of their native tongue. Dictionaries that purport to be comprehensive will attempt to describe the language. Presumably, once a user knows what the language is, he can adapt this awareness to his needs. That is, dictionaries are now *descriptive*, not *prescriptive*.

3. How to Use a Dictionary

Unfortunately, most users of English, including users of dictionaries, have been unaware of these historical changes. They tend still to use great modern dictionaries as though they were Elisha Coles' little textbook on how to speak properly. The users are some three hundred years out of date. The result is that modern dictionaries do not do as much good as they might because many speakers and writers do not know how to use them. Instead of respecting the books as admirable descriptions of the language, as tools to be used in learning to use the language better, they try to treat these dictionaries as "authorities" to be venerated and followed blindly like commands to children. Here we should admit that some dictionary publishers are in part to blame. The editors of the second edition of the *New International* certainly knew what they were doing, but apparently the publisher, or the publisher's promotion department, found they could sell more books if the dictionary was "the authority," and they drilled into the American people the unsound notion that "Webster decides." By *Webster* they meant the second edition of the *New International*, a monument that bore little resemblance to the volumes a New England lawyer–textbook writer had brought out a century earlier.

This principle, that a dictionary should describe the language not prescribe it, appears all through modern volumes. In a desk dictionary, editors will not find space for many citations; a desk dictionary must be cheap enough so that almost anybody can buy one, and abridged enough so that it can be handled easily, but the principle remains. A modern desk dictionary will be founded on the citations collected for the OED plus citations since collected for other dictionaries based on the same approach, such as the *Dictionary of American English* and the *Dictionary of Americanisms*. The better of these publishers also maintain staffs of readers, who supplement the citations already collected by the scholarly dictionaries, and try to digest all this material into readily usable volumes. What such a dictionary looks like and works like will best appear if we examine a small chunk of a dictionary in some detail. Following is the entry for *full*, along with other entries that follow it, as they appear in *Webster's New World Dictionary*, Second College Edition:

full[1] (fool) *adj.* [ME. ⟨ OE., akin to G. *voll*, Goth. *fulls* ⟨ IE. base **pel-*, to fill, whence L. *plenus*, full & *plere*, to fill, Gr. *plethein*, to be full, W. *llawn*, full, & (?) FOLK] **1.** having in it all there is space for; holding or containing as much as possible; filled [a *full* jar] **2.** *a)* having eaten all that one wants *b)* having had more than one can stand (*of*) **3.** using or occupying all of a given space [a *full* load] **4.** having a great deal or number (*of*); crowded [a room *full* of people] **5.** *a)* well supplied, stocked, or provided; rich or abounding (with *of*) [woods *full* of game] *b)* rich in detail [*full* information] **6.** *a)* filling the required number, capacity, measure, etc.; complete [a *full* dozen] *b)* thorough; absolute [to come to a *full* stop] **7.** *a)* having reached the greatest development, size, extent, intensity, etc. [a *full* moon, *full* speed] ☆ *b)* having attained the highest regular rank [a *full* professor] **8.** having the same parents [*full* brothers] **9.** having clearness, volume, and depth [a *full* tone] **10.** plump; round; filled out [a *full* face] **11.** with loose, wide folds; ample; flowing [a *full* skirt] **12.** *a*) greatly affected by emotion, etc. *b*) occupied or engrossed with ideas, thoughts, etc. ☆ **13.** *Baseball a*) designating a count of three balls and two strikes on the batter *b*) with a runner at each of the three bases —*n.* the greatest amount, extent, number, size, etc. [to enjoy life to the *full*] —*adv.* **1.** to the ⟵_____6 greatest degree; completely [a *full*-grown boy] **2.** directly; exactly [to be hit *full* in the face] **3.** very [*full* well] —*vt.* to make (a skirt, etc.) with loose folds; gather —*vi.* to become full: said of the moon —*SYN.* see COMPLETE —**at the full** at the ⟵_____7 state or time of fullness —**in full 1.** to, for, or with the full amount, value, etc. **2.** with all the words or letters; not abbreviated or condensed —**one's full** as much as one wants —**to the full** ⟵_____8 fully; completely; thoroughly

full² (fool) *vt., vi.* [ME. *fullen* ⟨ OFr. *fuler* ⟨ LL. **fullare,* to full ⟨ L. *fullo,* cloth fuller] to shrink and thicken (cloth, esp. of wool) with moisture, ⟵_____9 heat, and pressure

full‧back (-bak′) *n. Football* a member of the offensive backfield, stationed behind the quarterback: ⟵_____10 traditionally the back farthest behind the line, used typically for power plays

☆ **full blood** [from obs. notion that blood is the medium of heredity] **1.** the relationship between offspring of the same parents **2.** unmixed breed ⟵_____11 or race

☆ **full-blood‧ed** (-blud′id) *adj.* **1.** of unmixed breed or race; purebred: also **full′-blood′ 2.** vigorous; lusty **3.** genuine; authentic **4.** rich and full

full-blown (-blōn′) *adj.* **1.** in full bloom; open: said of flowers **2.** fully grown or developed; matured

full-bod‧ied (-bäd′ēd) *adj.* **1.** having a rich flavor and much strength [a *full-bodied* wine] **2.** large or broad in body or substance

full-dress (-dres′) *adj.* **1.** of or requiring full dress; formal [a *full-dress* dinner] **2.** complete and thorough [a *full-dress* inquiry]

full dress formal clothes worn on important or ceremonial occasions; esp., formal evening clothes

full•er[1] (fool′ər) *n.* [ME. ⟨ OE. *fullere* ⟨ L. *fullo*] ◄————12
a person whose work is to full cloth

full•er[2] (-ər) *n.* [⟨ ? obs. *full,* to make full, complete ⟨ FULL[1]] **1.** a tool used by blacksmiths to ◄————13
hammer grooves into iron **2.** a groove so made

Ful•ler (fool′ər) **1.** (Sarah) Margaret, (*Marchioness Ossoli*) 1810-50; U.S. writer, critic, & social ◄————14
reformer **2.** Melville Wes•ton (wes′tən), 1833-1910; U.S. jurist; chief justice of the U.S. (1888-1910)

full•er's earth (fool′ərz) a highly absorbent, opaque clay used to remove grease from woolen cloth in fulling, to clarify fats and oils, etc.

Ful•ler•ton (fool′ər tən) [after G. H. *Fullerton,* a founder] city in SW Calif.: suburb of Los Angeles: pop. 86,000

full-faced (fool′fāst′) *adj.* **1.** having a round face **2.** with the face turned directly toward the spectator or in a specified direction —**full′-face′** *adv.*

full-fash•ioned (-fash′′nd) *adj.* knitted to conform to the contours of the body, as hosiery or sweaters

full-fledged (-flejd′) *adj.* **1.** having a complete set of feathers: said of birds. **2.** completely developed or trained; of full rank or status

☆**full house** *Poker* a hand containing three of a ◄————15
kind and a pair, as three jacks and two fives: it is higher than a flush but lower than four of a kind

full-length (-leŋkth′, -leŋth′) *adj.* **1.** showing or covering the whole length of an object or all of a person's figure: said of a picture or mirror **2.** of the original, unabridged, or standard length; not shortened [a *full-length* novel, a *full-length* sofa]

full moon 1. the phase of the moon when its entire illuminated hemisphere is seen as a full disk **2.** the time of month when such a moon is seen

full-mouthed (-mou*th*d′, -mouth t′) *adj.* **1.** having a full set of teeth: said of cattle, etc. **2.** uttered loudly

full nelson [see NELSON, *n.*] *Wrestling* a hold in which both arms are placed under the opponent's armpits from behind with the hands pressed against the back of his neck

full•ness (-nis) *n.* [ME. *fulnesse*] the quality or state of being full (in various senses)

fullness of time the appointed or allotted time

full-rigged (-rigd′) *adj.* **1.** having the maximum number of masts and sails: said of a ship **2.** fully equipped

full sail 1. the complete number of sails **2.** with every sail set **3.** with maximum speed and energy

full-scale (-skāl′) *adj.* **1.** of or according to the original or standard scale or measure [a *full-scale* drawing] **2.** to the utmost limit, degree, etc.; complete and thorough; all-out [*full-scale* warfare]

full stop a period (punctuation mark)   ⟵————16

full-time (-tīm′) *adj.* designating, of, or engaged in work, study, etc. for specified periods regarded as taking all of one's regular working hours

full time as a full-time employee, student, etc. [to work *full time*]

full•y (-ē) *adv.* [ME. *fulli* ‹ OE. *fullice* ‹ *full*, FULL¹]
1. to the full; completely; entirely; thoroughly ⟵————17 **2.** abundantly; amply **3.** at least [*fully* two hours later]

Reprinted by permission from *Webster's New World Dictionary*, Second College Edition. Copyright © 1980 by Simon & Schuster.

1) This is the entry word, usually as here in boldface type. The raised number *1* means there will be at least one more word entered in this dictionary as *full*, but here treated as a different word. If another spelling is common, that spelling would appear in the appropriate place with a cross-reference.

2) This is the pronunciation; for the value attached to *oo* there will be an explanation somewhere, in this dictionary, as not infrequently, at the bottom of every second page. If more than one pronunciation is common, it would be given here. For *laboratory* the same dictionary gives four pronunciations, two American and two British. For *orange* the dictionary gives two, but that does *not* mean no more are possible and that all others are "incorrect." A half dozen pronunciations of *orange* are in good use, and the fact that only two are given means only that these two are acceptable, and in the judgment of the editors are the most common of the acceptable pronunciations. Others have been omitted for space; of the two given the first is not necessarily preferable to the second. One had to come first in the printing.

3) This is the grammatical designation. Like many words, *full* has several grammatical uses, and this dictionary treats them all under one headword listing, with the senses grouped by grammatical use. Some dictionaries use a separate entry for each grammatical use. Again, the fact that the editors do not include all grammatical classifications does not mean they are saying no others exist or that others are inevitably "wrong." As a matter of fact, *full* formerly had another use as a noun, and may again. In *Beowulf* the hostess passes a *ful*, that is a *full beaker*, to each of the assembled warriors. The editors of the dictionary will have known this, but have omitted the use because they consider it rare or obsolete or both.

4) This is the etymology. The symbol ⟨ means "comes from." Thus the editors are here saying that NE *full* comes from ME, that it descended into ME from OE, and is related to Modern German *voll* and Gothic *fulls*, all of which descend from the IE base **pel-*, which meant "to fill." From the same source came Latin *plenus*, meaning "full," and *plere*, meaning "to fill," and Greek *plethein*, meaning "to be full." The word is seen, also, in Welsh *llawn*, meaning "full," and probably in English *folk*. The printing of the word *folk* in small caps implies a cross-reference, and suggests that if you will look up *folk* you will find more there. As not infrequently, the whole etymology is enclosed within square brackets. Some dictionaries put the etymology at the end of the entry.

5) Here the meanings begin. This dictionary endeavors to isolate eighteen uses of the word as adjective, numbered under thirteen major uses, some of which can be subdivided. These uses must be put in some order. In a book constructed on strictly historical principles, like the OED, the earliest known meanings are likely to come first. In a dictionary devoted to understanding, a central meaning may come first, and in a dictionary intended to be popular, the most common may come first, since editors know that users may never look at more than one use, or may be too lazy or feel they are too busy to work through a long list.

Or the editors may use a practical blending of these. Once more, that the dictionary recognizes eighteen uses does not mean that all others are wrong. The editors mean to say only that these eighteen are now sufficiently distinct and enough in use so that they felt justified in including them. The *New International,* second edition, recognizes twenty-four. The *Century* recognized nearly as many, but numbered them as eight. These are not the only known uses. The OED distinguishes thirty-four uses of *full* as an adjective, with other uses in combinations; and the editors of the *Supplement* to the OED remind us that even that great work was neither complete nor infallible. It missed the meaning "extremely drunk," along with a Kentish noun meaning "the ridge left on the beach by high tide," a verbal use, and so many compounds and phrases—including two uses for *full house*—that these fill some three columns. That is, nobody has ever managed to get all the English words into one set of volumes, and we may safely assume nobody ever will.[1]

This dictionary gives no citations; presumably the editors felt that citations would take too much space. But they do give examples of most uses: "a *full* jar," "a room *full* of people." Usage no. 2 is broken into *a* and *b*. The editors could have made these separate uses, but apparently felt that "having had more than one can stand" is sufficiently close to "having eaten all that one wants" so that each use is made clearer by being associated with the other. On the other hand, they did not include these two uses under their no. 1, presumably because that concerns being physically full, and use 2 involves being full in a figurative sense. Usage 7b is marked with a small star-shaped symbol; it means that this use is an Americanism. Uses 13a and 13b—since the symbol precedes the number and not just the letter—are also Americanisms, restricted to baseball. In special uses the editors have been selective; they have not here included a use in poker, recognized by the *Century* and defined there as meaning "having three of a kind and a pair," but see 15 below in this list. Likewise, they do not include *full* as meaning "filled with liquor; drunk," which the *Century* includes and labels "*colloquial* or *slang.*" Presumably the editors of *Webster's New World* assessed this use as now archaic slang.

6) Here appear other grammatical uses of what this dictionary treats as the same word. The editors could have treated each grammatical use

---

1. The *Middle English Dictionary*, eds. Hans Kurath and others (Ann Arbor, Mich.: University of Michigan Press, 1954—; being printed in fascicles), contains more uses, and if the *Dictionary of Early Modern English* ever sees print, it is likely to add still more.

as a separate word. In a book like this, these abbreviations will be explained somewhere; *vt.*, for example, means "verb, transitive."

7) This is a reference to a paragraph that will discriminate synonyms, including *full*. In this dictionary they appear under the entry *complete*, and the fact that *complete* is printed in small caps is intended as a cross-reference to that entry.

8) Here are phrases using *full*. Presumably, to be entered here, the combination of words must have a use different from that of the individual words considered separately. One of the marks of a good dictionary is the number and selection of phrases it includes.

9) This is the second word spelled *full*, the distinction marked by the raised figure *2*. The editors have elected to consider this a different word, not merely a different use of the same word, probably because it has a different etymology, coming as a loan from the conjectured Latin **fullare*, rather than descending directly from IE into OE. Likewise, it has a different meaning and a different history, having been kept separate from *full¹*, even though they both appeared in ME.

10) Here the compounds begin. One might notice that this use is restricted to football, as another use was restricted to baseball.

11) Here we have a common distinction between a modifier and a noun as evidenced in spelling. *Full-blood* is treated as a single word, hyphenated, when used as a modifier meaning "purebred," but recognized as a noun with its modifier in a sentence like "The Indian was recognized as a *full blood*." The same distinction will be found below between *full time* (she worked *full time*) and the modifier *full-time* (she had a *full-time* job). We might notice that one of the marks of a good dictionary is to be observed in the number of compounds that are included.

12) Here the derived words begin, *fuller* being one who *fulls* in the sense of the second word indicated by that spelling. Once more, two words are recognized and differentiated by numbers, since a *fuller* as a tool has an unknown but presumably different origin.

13) We might notice the entry **fuller²**. The symbols ⟨ ? indicate that the etymology is in part unknown. The abbreviation *obs.* in the etymology tells us that that verbal use is now obsolete. Other usage labels employed in dictionaries include *sl.* or *slang, colloq.* or *colloquial,* etc.

14) American dictionaries include some encyclopedic material on the theory that to a degree a desk dictionary is a general reference work, and users may not distinguish between common and proper nouns. Here are brief biographical statements for two famous Americans whose last name was *Fuller*.

15) The phrase *full house* is worth noting. The open star identifies it as an Americanism; the word *poker* indicates a field use. We might recall that the *Century* treated *full* in this sense as a separate use, but the editors of this dictionary have recognized that the sense is so restricted that it is better treated as part of a phrase.

16) This is an American dictionary. If American English includes a word having an exact synonym in British English, the British word will be entered in the proper alphabetical place with a cross-reference to the American equivalent. In British use, a period (.) in the sense of a sign of punctuation is more commonly called a *full stop*. Accordingly, the phrase is entered here, with "a period" as the definition and, "(punctuation mark)" identifying the sense of *period* involved.

17) This dictionary treats the adverb *fully* as a separate word rather than as a run-on at the entry for *full*¹, presumably because not all of its meanings can be inferred from the meanings for the adjective.

4. Other Word Books

Dictionaries are the most numerous and generally the most useful word books, but speakers of English have at least three other sorts available. One includes usage books, volumes that are intended to expand such entries as *slang* and *colloq.;* see Chapter X. These books somewhat resemble the older dictionaries in that they are intended to tell the user how to police his usage, but even so the better ones tend to make judgments on historical bases or by some relatively objective evidence, something more than the convictions of the author. A glance at Margaret Bryant's *Current American Usage* will be instructive. The entry for *for to* starts with a "Summary," as follows:

> For to, *as in* for to tell, *is chiefly colloquial usage;* to *followed by the infinitive is standard usage in educated and written English.*

This is presumably the editor's statement, but we soon become aware that this is not merely her guess; it is her summary, for the convenience of the user who wants a ready answer, of the evidence she has assembled. This summary is followed by three paragraphs headed *Data.* They provide evidence, some from other printed works, some from reports made by local informants. They reveal what sorts of current speakers use this locution and in what areas. A final paragraph, headed *Other Evidence,* is a bibliography of articles and passages in books that treat this locution.

Not all editors of usage books have labored as has Bryant to be objective and to rely mainly on assembled evidence—she was long chairman of the Current English Usage Committee of the National Council of Teachers of English—but even the most authoritarian now make some gestures toward basing usage on use.[2]

Another sort of book, concerned exclusively with the discrimination of synonyms, has grown naturally from dictionaries. Definition inevitably involves discrimination—etymologically, the word means setting boundaries, from *de finibus* in Latin, "concerning the ends," that is, the borders, first the geographical borders and by extension the borders of meaning. Thus all dictionaries are more or less concerned with discriminating among synonyms. Lawyers have been professionally involved in definition; it is essential in all laws and is involved more or less in all cases in court: what is the difference between manslaughter and murder? what constitutes fatherhood and hence what are the rights of the father in the child? Webster was a lawyer before he became a lexicographer, and his definitions, based on his legal training, remain the solidest part of his dictionary-making. Another lawyer, George Crabb, further enlarged the study of definition; his *Dictionary of English Synonyms* (1816) adorned the desks and sharpened the wits of many a writer, and, revised as vocabulary changed and grew, remained standard for a century and a half. Now we have a dictionary of synonyms structured on historical principles; it allows the user to discriminate among terms having similar uses and to trace the growth of these distinctions, the more because the uses are illustrated through copious citations.

Below is the entry for *full* from *Webster's New Dictionary of Synonyms,* 2nd ed. (Springfield, Mass.: G. & C. Merriam, 1968):

> **full, complete, plenary, replete** are not interchangeable with each other, but the last three are interchangeable with the most comprehensive

2. The most famous of all usage books is that of H. M. Fowler, *A Dictionary of Modern English Usage* (1926). He was as much curmudgeon as compiler, but he had good taste and good sense, and is engaging even when downright, so that his book was used for delighted browsing as well as for reference. It has been revised for British users by Sir Ernest Gowers and for Americans by Margaret Nicholson. I have had occasion above to refer to the *Harper Dictionary of Contemporary Usage,* and to *A Dictionary of Contemporary American Usage* by Bergen and Cornelia Evans. There are many others, some quite prescriptive. A handy practical volume is William W. Watt, *A Short Guide to English Usage* (Cleveland: World Publishing Co., 1967).

term, *full*, in at least one of its senses. **Full** implies the presence or inclusion of everything that is wanted or required by something or that can be held, contained, or attained by it; thus, a *full* year numbers 365 days or, in leap years, 366 days; a *full* basket is one that can hold nothing more; a *full* mind is stocked to the point of overflowing with knowledge or ideas; a *full* moon has reached the height of its illumination by the sun; a *full* stomach is one that can contain no more food with comfort or is completely satisfied; a *full* meal is one lacking in none of the courses or sometimes in none of the elements to make a satisfying or balanced meal; a sponge *full* of water has absorbed all the water it can hold. **Complete** comes into comparison and close synonymity with *full* when the latter implies the entirety that is needed to the perfection, consummation, integrity, or realization of a thing; thus, a fire in which the fuel is quite consumed may be described as involving either *full* or *complete* combustion; a *complete* meal is the same as a *full* meal; a teacher should have *complete,* or *full,* control of his class ⟨if you consider the ritual of the Church during the cycle of the year, you have the *complete* drama represented. The Mass is a small drama, having all the unities; but in the Church year you have represented the full drama of creation—*T. S. Eliot*⟩ ⟨the panorama of today's events is not an accurate or *complete* picture, for history will supply posterity with much evidence which is hidden from the eyes of contemporaries —*Eliot*⟩ **Plenary** comes into comparison with *full* when *full* implies the absence of every qualification or even suggestion of qualification as to a thing's completeness. *Plenary,* however, heightens the force of *full* in this sense and carries a stronger suggestion of absoluteness; thus, to give *plenary* powers is to give full power without the slightest qualification; a *plenary* indulgence implies the remission of the entire temporal punishment due for one's sins ⟨by this word "miracle" I meant to suggest to you a something like *plenary* inspiration in these . . . men; an inspiration at once supernatural and so authoritative that it were sacrilege now to alter their text by one jot or tittle—*Quiller-Couch*⟩ **Replete** (*with*), the more bookish term, as compared with *full* (*of*), heightens the implication of abundant supply or of being filled to the brim with something ⟨he is quick, unaffected, *replete* with anecdote—*Hazlitt*⟩ ⟨an anxious captain, who has suddenly got news, *replete* with importance for him—*Henry James*⟩ Often, however, the term implies fullness to satiety or to the point of being surfeited ⟨right reading makes a full man in a sense even better than Bacon's; not *replete*, but complete rather, to the pattern for which Heaven designed him—*Quiller-Couch*⟩ ⟨*replete* with hard and book-learned words, impressively sonorous—*Southern*⟩

Ana including *or* inclusive, comprehending *or* comprehensive (see corresponding verbs at IN-CLUDE): teeming, abounding (see TEEM): glutted, cloyed, gorged, surfeited, sated (see SATIATE)

Ant empty—*Con* void, vacant, blank (see EMPTY): *bare, barren: stripped, dismantled, divested, denuded (see STRIP)*

*By permission. From *Webster's New Dictionary of Synonyms* © 1978 by G. & C. Merriam Co., Publishers of the Merriam-Webster Dictionaries.

The entry starts by separating those synonyms that are interchangeable from those that are not. Thereafter it defines each and provides citations; for *replete* it provides citations from William Hazlitt, an early nineteenth-century essayist; Henry James, a late nineteenth-century novelist; Sir Arthur Quiller-Couch, one of the most distinguished British educators and critics of this century; and Richard William Southern, a contemporary English educator. The entry also includes several analogous words (under *Ana*) with cross-references, and several antonyms, also with cross-references to points at which the antonyms will be discriminated. Since a volume like this is expensive to edit and print, it probably will have few imitators.

A third sort of word book, known as a thesaurus,[3] is linked to the name of Peter Mark Roget. Being a young intellectual, and finding himself incarcerated for a time—for no fault of his, one should add—he amused himself by trying to distinguish the major ideas and incorporating under these headings all the words related to them. He hoped his list might be useful to philosophers, helping them to refine basic concepts. During a long and busy life as surgeon, professor, and city planner, he occasionally added terms to his list of words, and when he was an old man, semiretired, he offered it to a publisher, who sensed that it would have a market as a handbook for writers.[4] It was an immediate success, was revised by Roget's son, was enlarged and recast with an alphabetical arrangement, and is still popular.

Recently, thesauruses based on a different theory have begun to appear. Most of the revisers of Roget's volume were lexicographers, and they seem to have assumed that a thesaurus is another sort of dictionary. A little thought, however, will suggest that a thesaurus is different from a dictionary, in some ways quite the opposite. When a user consults a dictionary he knows the word he wants to investigate, but he wishes to know more about it, its pronunciation, meaning, etymology, or whatever. It is especially useful to readers who have encountered a strange word. A thesaurus, on the other hand, is useful almost exclusively to writers and speakers, and the person who consults a thesaurus does so because the word he can think of is one he does not want at that time. The purpose of a thesaurus is not to give more information about a known word; it is intended to suggest a word that the user does not know, or has not been able to think of.

This idea has implications that extend throughout the book. The editor of a dictionary classifies words very much as a taxonomic botanist classifies plants, because they exist and should be described. The com-

---

3. From the Greek word for a treasure, it was used by Anglo-Latin writers to mean a "treasure house," but only in the figurative sense of a storehouse of knowledge. The word did not get out of Latin until the nineteenth century.

4. *Thesaurus of English Words and Phrases Classified* (1852). It is only one of many influential books written in jail; *Mein Kampf, Pilgrim's Progress*, Malory's *Morte d'Arthur* are among others that come readily to mind. But it must be unique, or nearly so, as a standard work that filled a purpose never intended by its author. Roget was an accomplished textbook writer; if he had known how his book was to be used he would doubtless have produced a very different volume.

piler of a thesaurus, on the other hand, is not concerned with classifying; he has only to ask himself, "When a user looks up this term, which for whatever reason he does not want to use, what word or phrase would he use if he could think of it?" One of the results is that the word list for a thesaurus differs radically from the word list of a dictionary. The dictionary must enter rare words; those are the sort most likely to be sought out by the user of the book. But rare words never need be included in the word list of a thesaurus; no user looks up *latitant* because that is the first word to pop into his head but he does not know its synonym *hidden*. A thesaurus does not need a long word list, but it must have all the common words in the language, even the colloquial and slang words. A writer may, for example, think of the sentence, "It was a swell party," but realize that *swell* is not the best term. *Swell* in the sense of *lavish, elegant, memorable,* or what not should be in the word list so that the user can look up the word he thought of and let it lead him to the term he wants.

Following is the entry for *full*, and entries following it, in a thesaurus built along these lines:[5]

> **full,** *mod.* **1.** [Filled]—*Syn.* sated, replete, brimful, running over, plethoric, abundant, burdened, depressed, weighted, freighted, borne down, satisfied, saturated, crammed, packed, stuffed, jammed, jam full, glutted, cloyed, gorged, surfeited, abounding, loaded, chock-full, stocked, satiated, crowded; *all* (D): full as a tick, stuffed to the gills, jam-packed, crawling (with), up to the brim, packed like sardines, fit *or* likely to burst *or* bust.—*Ant.* empty*, exhausted, void.
> **2.** [Occupied]—*Syn.* assigned, reserved, in use; see **taken 2.**
> **3.** [Well supplied]—*Syn.* abundant, complete, copious, ample, bounteous, plentiful, plenteous, sufficient, adequate, competent, lavish, extravagant, profuse.—*Ant.* inadequate*, scanty, insufficient.

5. Charlton Laird, *Webster's New World Thesaurus* (Cleveland: Collins-World Publishing Co., 1976), reprint of the 1971 edition. The discussion I have been summarizing appears as an introduction, which is an enlargement of the same author's *Laird's Promptory* (New York: Holt, 1948). A more recent volume, Marie Weir Kay, *Webster's Collegiate Thesaurus* (Springfield, Mass.: G. & C. Merriam Co., 1977), is built on similar principles. See also *The Synonym Finder*, 2nd ed., Laurence Urdang, ed. (Emmaus, Pa.: Rodale Press, 1979).

4. [Not limited]—*Syn.* broad, unlimited, extensive; see **absolute** 1, 2.

5. [Loose]—*Syn.* flapping, baggy, flowing; see **loose** 1.

6. [Mature]—*Syn.* grown, entire, complete; see **mature** 1.

7. [Deep]—*Syn.* resonant, rounded, throaty; see **loud** 1.

in full—*Syn.* for the entire amount *or* value, fully, thoroughly; see **completely.**

to the full—*Syn.* entirely, thoroughly, fully; see **completely.**

fullback, *n.*—*Syn.* backfield man, safety man, blocking back; see **football player.**

full blast (D), *mod.*—*Syn.* wide open, full throttle, to the hilt; see **fast** 1.

full dress, *n.*—*Syn.* livery, formal, finery; see **clothes.**

full-grown, *mod.*—*Syn.* adult, prime, grown-up; see **mature** 1.

fullness, *n.*—*Syn.* abundance, saturation, completion; see **plenty.**

fully, *mod.* **1.** [Completely]—*Syn.* entirely, thoroughly, wholly; see **completely.**

2. [Adequately]—*Syn.* sufficiently, amply, enough; see **adequately** 1.

The editor has recognized seven uses of *full* as being common enough so that he assumes prospective speakers and writers might think of them and want suggestions. Partly this number is obtained by compressing and combining uses that might appear in a dictionary, and partly by omitting rare uses. For the most common use of *full*, under 1, he provides an extensive list of synonyms, including slang and colloquial uses, here identified by (D). We might notice use 3, which contains a number of relatively rare words, which are needed as synonyms but not as entry words. The asterisk after *empty* in use 1 indicates that the word is a main entry in the thesaurus, and that more antonyms can be found by looking up that entry. The remaining uses and most of the phrases and compounds are treated mainly as cross-references, with only the commonest synonyms provided here.

Phonemic Symbols

Roughly speaking, a phoneme is a speech sound (such as the sound of *b* or the sound of *p*) that distinguishes one word from another (as *bat* is distinguished from *pat*). Actually each phoneme is a spread of sounds generally recognized as the same sound although there are slight differences. For example, the sounds of *p* in *pin, spin,* and *tip* are produced in slightly different ways, but they are thought of as one phoneme. Also, different speakers may pronounce a given sound in various ways, typically because of the regions from which the speakers come or because of the varying social or educational backgrounds of the speakers; thus, in northern parts of the United States, the pronoun *I* usually sounds like "ah-ee," whereas many speakers in southern parts use a sound that comes closer to a simple "ah." Similarly, the *ou* sound in a word like *house* may vary considerably from region to region, some speakers using a sound like "ah-oo," while others, for the first part of the sound, may use a vowel like the *a* of *bat* or like the *e* of *bet*.

Such differences in pronunciation occur throughout the sounds of a language. Unless the differences are quite marked, most native speakers of a language barely notice them. For such speakers the sounds remain more or less the same as those they themselves use. The sounds are recognizable and distinctive, often constituting a single phoneme.

A variant sound of a phoneme, such as one of those listed above, is known as an allophone of the phoneme.

Because any one phoneme includes a range of varying sounds, any simple list of symbols representing the phonemes is bound to be arbitrary, valid for one group of speakers but not necessarily valid for another group of speakers. Accordingly, I shall give conventional equivalents, with some suggestions of what I suppose the spread of sounds may be. Symbols representing phonemes will be placed within slant lines: / /; symbols representing allophones will be placed within square brackets: [ ].

A distinction may be said to be phonemic if it involves distinguishing one word from another (such as *pin* from *pen*); otherwise, the distinction may be called an allophonic distinction.

Vowels

In English, all vowels are voiced (uttered with vibration of the vocal cords). Vowels may have other characteristics (rounding, aspiration, etc.), but the phonemic distinction is likely to stem mostly from the way the tongue is used in producing the vowel. Thus, the position of the tongue for the vowel is described as high, mid, or low; the part of the tongue where the vibration mainly seems to take place is described as front, central, or back.

Symbol	Sound	Comment
/ɔ/	low back, as in hawk, maudlin	
/ɑ/	low central, as in got, modern	These sounds may be thought of as a continuum, with sounds in the sequence that may be allophones of other sounds; e.g., god may be heard as [gad] or [gɔd].
/a/	forward from /ɑ/ and higher, as in father	
/æ/	low front, as in at, cat	
/ɛ/	mid front, lax, as in get, letter	
/e/	mid front, tense, as in gray, stray	Mostly front vowels, these interchange less than do the low vowels, but some interchange has occurred or may still occur; thus, death was formerly tense and pronounced /deθ/ and, in some current dialects, [diθ]. The distinction between /ɨ/ and /ɪ/ is not usually phonemic.
/ɨ/	mid central, as in trigger, ding	
/ɪ/	high front, lax as in sit, pin	
/i/	high front, tense, as in heat, meet	
/u/	high, tense, central to front, as in too, dude	
/ʊ/	high central, lax, lower and farther back than /u/, as in book, put	English has no high back vowel. The farthest forward, /u/, is usually tense. Tense /u/ and lax /ʊ/ interchange readily; e.g., room may be [rum] or [rʊm].
/o/	mid, tense, central to back, as in hope, pole	
/ʌ/	mid central, tense, much lower than /ʊ/, as in but, puff	
/ə/	very close to /ʌ/, but lax and unstressed, as in commit, balloon	

Diphthongs

A diphthong is a sound made by combining two simple vowels. The vowel sound in *pine*, for example, is equivalent to /a/ + /i/. The vowel sound in *mouse* is equivalent to /a/ + /ʊ/.

Pure vowels, as contrasted with diphthongs, are vowels that are uttered without any appreciable change in their quality. In English, such vowels are relatively rare. Vowel sounds usually shift at least slightly; they develop an in-glide or an out-glide, the latter especially in open syllables (open syllables are syllables that are not terminated by a consonant or by another syllable). The morpheme *day*, for example, may be pronounced [de] (the vowel quality remaining pure) or [deᴵ] (with the out-glide—an articulation that is added to the [e] without being recognizable as a really full sound—being represented by the raised symbol [ᴵ]). But the two pronunciations do not involve a phonemic distinction. The addition of an in-glide or of an out-glide is generally unnoticed by native speakers and is generally ignored by transcribers. Diphthongization is admittedly involved, but it is negligible insofar as meaning is concerned.

Some diphthongs, however, do involve a phonemic distinction. While the possible diphthongization in *moose* is negligible and nonphonemic, the strong diphthongization involved in *mouse* is semantically distinctive and therefore phonemic.

Only a few combinations of two vowels are recognized as true diphthongs that are phonemically distinctive. These diphthongs include the following:

Symbol	Sound	Comment
/aʊ/	as in h*ou*se, *ou*ch; low, then rising	Most of these diphthongs show some spread. The sound I have written /aʊ/ can begin either higher or lower, [ɑʊ], [æʊ], or [ɛʊ], the latter two usually nasalized in what is popularly called the American "twang." Likewise, [aɪ] may start farther forward or become a pure vowel [ɑ], notably in some Black dialects. In some dialects of the eastern United States [ɔɪ] alternates with [aɪ]; in others [ɪʊ] alternates with [u]. *News* is [nuz] in Chicago, [nɪʊz] in Boston.
/aɪ/	as in *I*, *cry*; starts low, but moves forward as it rises	
/ɔɪ/	as in j*oy*, av*oi*d; starts far back, low or mid; moves rapidly forward and upward	
/ɪʊ/	as in f*ew*, m*u*sic; level stress; starts relatively high, then draws back a little	

Consonants

Consonants are much more stable and regular than vowels are. They are produced by altering or even by completely stopping the breath stream.

Consonants may be either stops or plosives (in which the breath stream is first checked and then released with a somewhat explosive effect) or continuants (in which the breath stream remains unchecked). These sounds are produced in four major locations in the mouth: through the use of both lips (1st location); through the combined use of the teeth, or of the alveolar ridge just back of the upper teeth, with the tongue or with either of the lips (2d location); through placement of the tongue on the roof of the mouth (3d location); through the use of specific parts of the tongue, as the tip, dorsum, or root, or through the use of structures at the back of the mouth (4th location). This last area is not much used in uttering Modern English and can mainly be ignored in distinguishing the phonemes.

While consonants can be distinguished in various ways, the best approach for the phonemic analysis of consonants in Modern English is to indicate how the consonants are produced and whether or not voicing is involved.

The consonant symbols may be distributed as follows:

STOPS

Symbol	Location	Made with	Voicing	Comment
/p/	1st	} both lips	voiceless	As in *pip*; aspiration varies but is not phonemic.
/b/	1st		voiced	Voiced stop corresponding to voiceless /p/, as in *bob*.
/t/	2d	} tongue and teeth or alveolar ridge	voiceless	Made with the tongue on the upper teeth or just back of them, as in *tot*.
/d/	2d		voiced	Voiced stop corresponding to voiceless /t/, as in *dad*; made somewhat farther back.
/k/	3d	} tongue and roof of mouth	voiceless	Moves with adjacent sounds, as in *kick*, *talk*.
/g/	3d		voiced	Voiced stop corresponding to voiceless /k/ as in *gag*.

CONTINUANTS—FRICATIVES

Symbol	Location	Made with	Voicing	Comment
/f/	1st	} teeth and lips	voiceless	Fricative corresponding to stop /p/, as in *fife*.
/v/	1st		voiced	Voiced fricative corresponding to voiceless /f/, as in *vivid*.
/θ/	2d	} tongue and teeth or alveolar ridge	voiceless	Fricative corresponding to stop /t/, as in *thing*.
/ð/	2d		voiced	Voiced fricative corresponding to voiceless /θ/, as in *this*.
/x/	3d	tongue and roof of mouth	voiceless	Heard only in a few dialects, e.g., Lowland Scots.

Symbol	Location	Made with	Voicing	Comment
/s/	2d	tongue and ridge back of teeth	voiceless	Tongue channels narrow stream of air to teeth, as in si*s*ter.
/z/	2d		voiced	Voiced sibilant corresponding to voiceless /s/ as in *z*ip, ha*s*.
/š/	2d	tongue and teeth	voiceless	Tongue channels air in broad stream, as in *sh*e, fi*sh*.
/ž/	2d		voiced	Voiced sound corresponding to voiceless /s/, as in mea*s*ure.

CONTINUANTS – AFFRICATES

Symbol	Position	Made with	Voicing	Comment
/č/	2d	tongue and roof of mouth	voiceless	Presumably begins with stop and moves to affricate, as in *ch*urch, for voiceless sound; as in *j*udge, for corresponding voiced sound. Initial stop may be lacking.
/ǰ/	2d		voiced	

CONTINUANTS – NASAL

Symbol	Position	Made with	Voicing	Comment
/m/	1st	lips	voiced	Glottis closed so that air passes through nose, as in *m*em*b*er; nasal corresponding to /b/.
/n/	2d	tongue on alveolar ridge	voiced	Glottis closed so that air passes through nose, as in *n*an*n*y; nasal corresponding to /d/.
/ŋ/	3d	tongue on roof of mouth	voiced	Glottis closed so that air passes through nose, as in si*ng*ing; nasal corresponding to /g/.

OTHER CONTINUANTS

Symbol	Voicing	Comment
/j/	voiced	Called a glide; starts at back, high or mid, and moves forward as in *y*oung, *y*ou.
/l/	voiced	Called a liquid; tongue withdrawn and spread, splitting the flow of air as in *l*i*l*y.
/r/	voiced	Tongue more or less reflex, not much trilled, as in fai*r*er, *r*eader; in many dialects terminally silent.
/w/	voiced	Lips much rounded, as in *w*ater.
/h/	voiceless	Aspiration, made with tongue raised, but not to roof of mouth, as in *h*ill.

General Index

Latin 47, 49, 51-52, 56, 57,
62, 64-65, 74, 77, 89, 92,
94, 96-97, 98, 109, 111,
112-114, 125-126
confusion with French 74,
88
from Greek 96-97
in compounds 107
through French 97-98
Old Norse 126
Oriental 86-87, 91, 95
Portuguese 87, 88, 92, 104,
106, 109-110
Russian 91, 110
Scandinavian 100-103
Spanish 87, 88, 104, 105, 110
Yiddish 91, 110
calque 129
dates of 81-82 (fn)
from travel and reading 87
patterns of 131, 132
through French 87
loan prefixes 219-221
logic 254-255
logograms 169
Lowell, James Russell, passage
from 200

"m" 178-179
Mackin, R. *see* Cowie and Mackin
Malay *see* loans, Hawaiian, *under*
loans
Marckwardt, Albert 106 (fn),
107 (fn)
Melanesian *see* loans, Hawaiian,
under loans
metaphors 121-123
Micronesian *see* loans, Hawaiian,
under loans
mistakes in words 141-143
Mannyng, Robert 103

ME *see* Middle English
meaning(s) 1-9, 12-16, 18-19, 252,
261-276
altered by environment 267-268
and grammar 1-9, 185-187
and verb phrases 238-239
assumptions about 262-263
by compounding 207
by patterns of words 268-269
etymology and 273
field theory of 269-270
figurative 122-123
general to specific 126-129
not measurable 262-263
pointing and reference in 266
specific to general 126-129
use and 263-264
merged verbs *see* verb sets
Middle English (ME) 55, 77, 80,
103, 108, 110, 138, 142, 175,
204, 209 (fn), 238-239, 270
future tense in 234
Great English Vowel Shift 157-
160
loss of endings in 197
relatives in 198-199
sample of 197
Middle English Dictionary 80,
209 (fn), 286 (fn)
Miller, George A. 267 (fn)
minds 261
mistakes 164: *see also* etymology,
folk *or* false
modification 192-193
modifiers 188
in compounds 229-230
in Old English compounds 204
in Proto-Indo-European 194
Mormon dialect 249-250
morphemes 18
bound and free 211-212

Index of Terms

For Reading and Reference

Dictionaries and Other Word and Usage Books

The American Heritage Dictionary of the English Language, Ed. William
  Morris (New York: American Heritage Publishing Co., Inc., 1969)
  Calvert Watkins' treatment of Indo-European roots is the best
  survey of its sort readily available. Not easy for the uninitiated.

American Speech: A Quarterly of Linguistic Usage, vol. 1—; 1925—.
  Contains "Among the New Words," Ed. I. Willis Russell and
  others, scholarly studies of current usage.

Brewer's Dictionary of Phrase and Fable, Ed. E. Cobham Brewer, rev.
  Ivor H. Evans (New York: Harper and Row, 1970)
  Word list is selective, but many of the entries are both unusual
  and delightful.

The Century Dictionary and Cyclopedia, 10 vols. plus supplements, Eds.
  William Dwight Whitney and others (New York: The Century Co.,
  1889-1897)
  Outdated for many purposes, but still a mine, especially for
  obsolete words and encyclopedic matter. Variously printed and
  bound.

Collins Dictionary of the English Language, Ed. Laurence Urdang and
  others (Glasgow: Collins Publishers 1979)
  A new dictionary of British English, hospitable to Australian.

A Comprehensive Etymological Dictionary of the English Language,
  2 vols., Ed. Ernest Klein (Amsterdam: Elsevir Publishing Co., 1966-
  1967)
  Very good, but generally less useful than the Oxford dictionary
  cited below, except for classical, Oriental, and other Eastern
  loans.

Current American Usage, Ed. Margaret M. Bryant (New York: Funk
  and Wagnall's, 1962)
  Highly selective entry list, but long, scholarly treatments of the
  locutions included.

A Dictionary of American English, 4 vols., Eds. Sir William Craigie and
James R. Hulbert (Chicago: The University of Chicago Press, 1938)
    Similar to Mathews, below, having some citations not included
    there, but no slang.

Dictionary of American Slang, Eds. Harold Wentworth and Stuart Berg
Flexner (New York: Thomas Y. Crowell, 1960)
    Too limited, but the best we have; many dated citations.

A Dictionary of American-English Usage: Based on Fowler's *Modern
English Usage*, Ed. Margaret Nicholson (Oxford: Oxford University
Press, 1957)
    Competent; more conservative and less interesting than the
    modernization by Gowers.

A Dictionary of Americanisms, 2 vols., Ed. Mitford M. Mathews (Chicago: The University of Chicago Press, 1951)
    Excellent, as is Craigie and Hulbert above, with many dated
    citations. *Our Own Words*, Ed. Mary Helen Dohan (New York:
    Alfred A. Knopf, 1974) is easy to use, but limited and not
    always reliable.

A Dictionary of British Surnames, 2nd ed., Ed. P. H. Reaney (London:
Routledge and Kegan Paul, 1976)
    Standard for reference.

A Dictionary of Canadianisms, Ed. Walter S. Avis (produced for W. J.
Gage, Ltd., by Lexicographical Centre for Canadian English, University of Victoria, Victoria, B.C.; Toronto: W. J. Gage, Ltd., 1967)
    For its area, comparable to Mathews, and Craigie and Hulbert.

A Dictionary of Contemporary American Usage, Eds. Bergen and Cornelia Evans (New York: Random House, 1957)
    Probably the best of several dictionaries of American usage;
    extensive, scholarly, readable.

A Dictionary of Modern English Usage, H. W. Fowler (Oxford: Oxford
University Press, 1926)
    Fowler was beloved as an engaging and penetrating curmudg-
    eon; the 2nd ed., Ed. Ernest Gowers (1965), is less charming
    than the original, but generally more useful.

A Dictionary of Slang and Unconventional English, 7th ed., Ed. Eric
Partridge (New York: The Macmillan Co., 1970)
    Probably the best in a field where there are many engaging
    books, but few that are commanding.

Dictionary of Word and Phrase Origins, 3 vols., Eds. William and Mary Morris (New York: Harper and Row, 1962)
> Notable because phrases tend to be neglected, especially their origins. Much evidence not readily available elsewhere is assembled here.

The English Dialect Dictionary, 6 vols., Ed. Joseph Wright (New York: Hacker Art Books, 1963; orig. 1898-1905)
> Treats the British Isles. So good it seems timeless; detailed for reference, engaging for browsing.

An English Pronouncing Dictionary, 11th ed., Ed. Daniel Jones (London: J. M. Dent and Sons, 1956)
> Standard for British Received Pronunciation.

Johnson's Dictionary, Eds. E. L. McAdam, Jr., and George Milne (New York: Pantheon Books, 1963)
> Judicious selections from a monument of lexicography.

Modern American Usage, Ed. W[ilson] Follett (New York: Hill and Wang, 1966)
> Prescriptive, capable; useful notably for edited English.

The New Century Cyclopedia of Names, 3 vols., Eds. Clarence L. Barnhart and W. D. Halsey (New York: Appleton-Century-Crofts, 1954)
> One of many; for a popular work restricted to North America see *Illustrated Dictionary of Place Names: United States and Canada,* Ed. Kelsie B. Harder (New York: Van Nostrand Reinhold, 1976); to be recommended for British English is *The Concise Oxford Dictionary of English Place-Names,* 4th ed., Ed. Eilert Ekwall (Oxford: Oxford University Press, 1960).

The New York Times Everyday Reader's Dictionary of Misunderstood, Misused, Mispronounced Words, Ed. Laurence Urdang (New York: New York Times Books, 1972)
> Less a usage book than a dictionary of words hard to use well.

Origins: A Short Etymological Dictionary of Modern English, 4th ed., Ed. Eric Partridge (London: Routledge and Kegan Paul, 1966)
> Easiest to use of the adequate etymological dictionaries.

Oxford Dictionary of Current Idiomatic English, 2 vols., Eds. A. P. Cowie and R. Mackin (London: Oxford University Press, 1975)
> The best study available; especially strong in verb sets; many, though undated, citations. Damaged by being restricted to British publications.

The Oxford Dictionary of English Etymology, Ed. C. T. Onions (Oxford and New York: Oxford University Press, 1966)
> For investigating a word often the best place for a serious student to start. Gives Indo-European roots and roughly dates common borrowings and new meanings.

The Oxford English Dictionary, 12 vols., Eds. James A. H. Murray, Henry Bradley, W. A. Craigie, and C. T. Onions (Oxford: Oxford University Press, 1933); reissue with revisions of *A New English Dictionary on Historical Principles,* 10 vols. (1884-1928)
> Known as OED and NED respectively. The great monument, without peer in any language; endeavors to record every English term in reputable use from the beginnings to 1900, with each use dated and richly illustrated. For later terms and evidence missed in the earlier issue, see *Supplements,* 1933, 1972, 1976 – .

The Penguin Dictionary of Surnames, Ed. Basil Cottle (Harmondsworth, England: Penguin Books, 1967)
> Especially good for Celtic; available in paperback.

A Pronouncing Dictionary of American English, Eds. John A. Kenyon and Thomas A. Knott (Springfield, Mass.: The G. & C. Merriam Co., 1944)
> Standard, but little attention to dialects.

The Random House Dictionary of the English Language, Eds. Jess Stein and Laurence Urdang (New York: Random House, 1966)
> Called "unabridged" and adequate for most purposes, but not to be compared with the *New International.* Prized by many who value its conservative use of usage labels.

Scottish National Dictionary, 10 vols., Eds. William Grant and others (Edinburgh: National Scottish Dictionary Assn., Ltd., 1931-1976)
> Has been called "superb." Covers from about 1700; for earlier times, the *Dictionary of the Older Scottish Tongue* is in process.

Webster's New World Dictionary of the American Language, Second College Edition, Ed. David B. Guralnik (Cleveland: Simon & Schuster, 1980)
> Generally superior treatment of vocabulary items; strong in phrases; has the best etymologies, based on Indo-European roots. A good place to start.

Webster's New World Thesaurus, Ed. Charlton Laird (New York and Cleveland: World Publishing Co., 1971)

Revision of *Laird's Promptory* (1948), ancestor of a new generation of thesauruses. Long standard were the various revisions of a pioneer work by Peter Mark Roget.

Webster's Third New International Dictionary of the English Language, Ed. Philip Babcock Gove (Springfield, Mass.: G. & C. Merriam Co., 1961)

A remarkable book, notable for its comprehensive treatment of modern English vocabulary and its citations revealing both usage and meaning. Crippled for historical study by neglect of Proto-Indo-European. The 2nd ed., Ed. William Allen Neilson and others (1934), is still useful, containing much material excised for space from the 3rd ed.

Studies of Vocabulary

Allen, Harold B., *Linguistics and English Linguistics* (New York: Appleton-Century-Crofts, 1966)
To its date a good working bibliography.

Arnold, I. V., *The English Word,* 2nd ed. (Moscow: Vishaya Shkola, 1973)
Informed, but intended for Russian courses in lexicography, it is not well suited to most native speakers of English.

Bloomfield, Leonard, *Language* (New York: Henry Holt and Co., 1933)
Long the foundation of American language study, it was never easy and is now somewhat dated.

Bolinger, Dwight, *Aspects of Language* (New York: Harcourt Brace & World, Inc., 1968)
Reliable and readable; between Lyons and West in difficulty.

Brown, Ivor, *A Word in Your Ear* and *Just Another Word* (New York: E. P. Dutton & Co., 1945)
Witty and informed; brief essays about individual words.

Brown, Roger Williams, *Words and Things* (Glencoe, Ill.; The Free Press, 1958)
What psychology can tell us, in readable English, about words and meaning. For a scholarly treatment see Hörmann, below.

Burke, Kenneth, *Language as Symbolic Action* (Berkeley: University of California Press, 1968)
One of several collections by a modern philosopher interested in words and meaning.

Dillard, J. L., *Black English* (New York: Random House, 1972)
An exciting book, which may push too far its thesis about American creoles and pidgins.

Entwistle, William J., *Aspects of Language* (London: Faber & Faber, 1953)
Fine study of language, with much attention to vocabulary.

Foster, Brian, *The Changing English Language* (London, The Macmillan Co., 1968; New York: St. Martin's Press, 1968)
International, though with focus on British English; can be supplemented with Charles Barber, *Linguistic Change in Present-Day English* (Edinburgh: Oliver and Boyd, 1964). Sensible advice on usage, especially British usage. Published in England as *The Complete Plain Words*, the combination of two earlier pamphlets, *The ABC of Plain Words* and *Plain Words*.

Greenough, James Bradstreet, and George Lyman Kittredge, *Words and Their Ways in English Speech* (New York: The Macmillan Co., 1901; many reprints, in various countries)
Words as philology; long standard, and still interesting for Greenough on the classical heritage and Kittredge's far-ranging scholarship.

Geipel, John, *The Viking Legacy* (Newton Abbot, England: David and Charles, 1971)
Scandinavian borrowings, long underestimated, are here given their due.

Hayakawa, S. I., *Language in Thought and Action,* 4th ed. (New York: Harcourt Brace Jovanovich, 1978)
Most widely used adaptation of "general semantics" to modern American English. Earlier editions published as *Language in Action;* later editions in consultation with Basil H. Pillard and others.

Hörmann, Hans, *Psycholinguistics: An Introduction to Research and Theory,* trans. H. H. Stern (New York, Heidelberg, Berlin: Springer Verlag, 1971)
Excellent for advanced students; others may prefer Roger Brown, above.

Hudson, Kenneth, *The Jargon of the Professions* (London: The Macmillan Co., 1978)
An assault, often hilarious, usually lethal, on "that clogged-

up pretentious gibberish used by people who want to sound impressive.''

Jespersen, Otto, *Growth and Structure of the English Language,* 9th ed. (Oxford: Basil Blackwell, 1948)
Long standard; inevitably somewhat dated, but still engaging; available in paperback as Doubleday Anchor Book A 46.

Joos, Martin, *The English Verb* (Madison: University of Wisconsin Press, 1964)
Uses testimony in a murder trial; grammar made both exciting and meaningful.

Kučera, Henry, and W. Nelson Francis, *Computational Analysis of Present-Day American English* (Providence, R.I.: Brown University Press, 1967)
The first of a new generation of word-frequency books; for another, see Dahl Hartvig, *Word Frequencies of Spoken American English* (Essex, Conn.: Verbatim Books, 1980)

Kurath, Hans, and others, *A Word Geography of the Eastern United States* (Ann Arbor: University of Michigan Press, 1949)
Based on the monumental *Linguistic Atlas of New England* 3 vols. in 6 (Providence, R.I.: Brown University Press, 1939-1943), the first of a number of studies calculated to survey American and Canadian English. To date they include E. Bagby Atwood, *The Regional Vocabulary of Texas* (Austin: University of Texas Press, 1962) and Harold B. Allen, *The Linguistic Atlas of the Upper Midwest,* 3 vols. (Minneapolis: University of Minnesota Press, 1973-1976). Linguistic atlases, although highly revealing, are difficult for laymen.

Lehmann, Winfred P., *Historical Linguistics: An Introduction,* 2nd ed. (New York: Holt, Rinehart and Winston, 1973)
Readable and reliable; more detailed treatments are available.

Marckwardt, Albert H., *American English* (New York: Oxford University Press, 1958)
An excellent little volume, mainly concerned with vocabulary. No attempt to be comprehensive.

Mather, J. H., and others, *Linguistic Atlas of Scotland* (London: Croom Helm, vol. 1—, 1975—)
Beginning to appear after 25 years of collecting and editing.

Mencken, H. L., and Raven I. McDavid, Jr., *The American Language* (New York: Alfred A. Knopf, 1963)
  Delightful browsing and a mine of Americanisms; standard. For most purposes supersedes Mencken's pioneer work (orig. 1919) with two supplements (1945, 1948).

Murray, K. M. Elisabeth, *Caught in the Web of Words: J. A. H. Murray and the "Oxford English Dictionary"* (New Haven, Conn.: Yale University Press, 1977)
  A biography; scholarly and delightful.

Nash, Walter, *Our Experience with Language* (New York: St. Martin's Press, 1971)
  Pleasantly conceived and beautifully written, with more than the usual attention to vocabulary.

Orton, Harold, *A Word Geography of England* (New York: Seminar Press, 1975)
  Orton was editor, with Wilfred J. Halliday, of the *Survey of English Dialects* (Leeds, England: E. J. Arnold for the University of Leeds, 1962 –). It is going forward, as is *The Atlas and Survey of Irish Dialects,* Ed. H. Wagner and others, and the *Atlas* for Scotland; see above. These dialect studies require years, and are mainly directed toward scholars.

Pyles, Thomas, *The Origin and Development of the English Language,* 2nd ed. (New York: Harcourt Brace Jovanovich, 1971)
  For many beginners, the best historical survey; contains lists of words.

Pyles, Thomas, *Words and Ways of American English* (New York: Random House, 1952)
  Written from wide knowledge, and with a twinkle in the eye. Much to be recommended, also, is the collection of his shorter pieces on language, *Selected Essays on English Usage,* Ed. John Algeo (Gainesville, Fla.: University Presses of Florida, 1979).

Reaney, P. H., *The Origin of English Surnames* (London: Routledge and Kegan Paul, 1967)
  For reference or reading; loaded with fact. See also his *The Origin of English Place-names* (New York: Hillary House, 1961).

Reed, Carroll E., *Dialects of American English,* 2nd ed. (Amherst: University of Massachusetts Press, 1977)
  Dialects and linguistic geography; succinct and reliable. For

other brief treatments, see Raven I. McDavid, Jr., "The Dialects of American English," in W. Nelson Francis, *The Structure of American English* (New York: Ronald Press, 1958) and Jean Malmstrom and Annabelle Ashley, *Dialects-U.S.A.* (Champlain, Ill.: National Council of Teachers of English, 1963).

Serjeantson, Mary S., *A History of Foreign Words in English* (London: K. Paul, Trench, Trubner & Co., Ltd., 1935)
    A fine, scholarly study of loans into English; directed to specialists but usable by beginners; now somewhat dated.

Sheard, J. A., *The Words We Use* (London: André Deutsch, 1954)
    A general study of the English vocabulary from a philologist's point of view; innocent of recent approaches and somewhat dated, even for etymology.

Sledd, James, and Wilma R. Ebbitt, *Dictionaries and THAT Dictionary* (Chicago: Scott, Foresman & Co., 1962)
    The brouhaha over the *New International,* 3rd ed., turned to a serious study of dictionary-making. Revealing for the ends to which a zeal for purism can drive otherwise sensible persons.

Stewart, George R., *Names on the Land,* 3rd ed. (Boston: Houghton Mifflin Co., 1967)
    Standard for American place names; includes the notes eliminated from the first edition.

Strang, Barbara M. H., *A History of English* (London: Methuen, 1970)
    The best one-volume history, with due attention to vocabulary; strong British bent. Difficult for beginners.

Turner, G. W., *The English Language in Australia and New Zealand* (London: Longmans, Green and Co., Ltd., 1966)
    At once engaging, scholarly, and popular; bibliography of more detailed studies.

West, Fred, *The Way of Language: An Introduction* (New York: Harcourt Brace Jovanovich, 1975)
    Provides a pleasant beginning in language. Comparable is Joseph H. Friend, *An Introduction to English Linguistics* (Cleveland: World Publishing Co., 1967). Still simpler, and with emphasis on vocabulary, is Charlton Laird, *Words, Words, Words* (New York: Harcourt Brace Jovanovich, 1972).

Fun With Words

Espy, Willard R., *An Almanac of Words at Play* (New York: Clarkson
N. Potter, distributed by Crown Publishers, 1975)
  More in the vein of the same author's *The Game of Words.*

Hogben, Lancelot, *The Mother Tongue* (London: Secker & Warburg,
1964)
  Rightly called "an adventure in learning." The work of a
  finely honed and quirky mind at play. Many game books containing word games such as Richard B. Manchester, *The Mammoth Book of Word Games* (New York: A&W Publishing,
  1979) and *The 2nd Mammoth Book of Word Games* (the
  same), do not find their way into bibliographies.

Lipton, James, *An Exaltation of Larks* (New York: Grossman Publishers, 1968)
  Authentic terms from venery—"a pod of whales," "a pride
  of lions"—along with ingenious inventions and engaging
  illustrations.

Rosten, Leo, *The Joys of Yiddish* (New York: McGraw-Hill, 1968)
  "A relaxed lexicon"; one of the world's wits has fun with the
  charm of Yiddish.

Schur, Norman W., *British Self-Taught: With Comments in American*
(New York: The Macmillan Co., 1973)
  A scholarly work, with its learning carried lightly: good fun
  about the difference between British and American English.

Urdang, Laurence, Ed., *Verbatim; The Language Quarterly,* vol. 1–
(Essex, Conn.: 1974–)
  Informed and informative; genial and light in tone; a quarterly
  delight.

About the Author

Charlton Laird says he would rather write than eat. At times, notably when he was working his way through college as a free-lance stringer and the copy was not selling very well, he had literally to write before he could eat, and figuratively he still puts writing first. For much of his life he has been a college teacher, in universities from one coast to the other. He retired in 1968 as Hilliard Distinguished Professor of the Humanities at the University of Nevada, Reno. He was trained at the University of Iowa, Columbia, Stanford, and Yale in Middle English, Anglo-Norman, and Medieval Latin literary relationships, but he became convinced that being a generalist is at least as useful as being a specialist and for him is rather more congenial.

He has written many books, among them The Miracle of Language *and* Language in America, *along with dozens of articles and reviews, perhaps most notably on American English. He was also the compiler of* Webster's New World Thesaurus *and is the author of a number of textbooks, including (with Robert M. Gorrell)* Modern English Handbook, *now in its Seventh Edition.*

When he is not writing or lecturing he likes to garden, travel, read, or listen to classical music. His wife, born Helene Gent, was until her death an editor and an author of books for children. The Lairds have one daughter, Mrs. Nancy Hunt, and three granddaughters.